HARVARD STUDIES IN AMERICAN–EAST ASIAN RELATIONS

The Harvard Studies in American–East Asian Relations are sponsored
and edited by the Committee on American–Far Eastern Policy Studies
of the Department of History at Harvard University.

CONTRIBUTIONS BY

M. SEARLE BATES

ADRIAN A. BENNETT

PAUL A. COHEN

JAMES A. FIELD, JR.

SHIRLEY STONE GARRETT

WILLIAM R. HUTCHISON

KWANG-CHING LIU

STUART CREIGHTON MILLER

CLIFTON J. PHILLIPS

VALENTIN H. RABE

ARTHUR SCHLESINGER, JR.

PAUL A. VARG

PHILIP WEST

THE
MISSIONARY ENTERPRISE
IN CHINA AND AMERICA

Edited and with an Introduction by

JOHN K. FAIRBANK

Harvard University Press, Cambridge, Massachusetts, 1974

Contents

Contents

Illustrations

Tables

THE MISSIONARY ENTERPRISE IN CHINA AND AMERICA

JOHN K. FAIRBANK

Introduction: The Many Faces of Protestant Missions in China and the United States

Americans and Chinese have figured in each other's histories since 1784, but people-to-people contact has occurred during only about one century, mostly under the unequal treaty system from the 1840s to the 1940s. During this time the chief protagonists were Protestant missionaries and their Chinese audience, including a growing number of Chinese Christians. The foreign and Chinese members of the Christian community probably came into closer touch than did the merchants or the officials of the two countries. The first American missionaries had joined the small Anglo-American community at Canton about 1830. By the 1860s, after two British wars and the resulting treaties had opened up the main treaty ports, some of these pioneers, like S. Wells Williams and W.A.P. Martin, wound up in Peking. By the 1920s their successors were scattered across China and totaled some 5000 persons if one includes the missionary wives, who often served as teachers or nurses. Together with a similar number of British and European missionaries, they had built up an impressive establishment of Christian churches, schools, colleges, hospitals, and other institutions, which were inherited in 1949 by the Chinese People's Republic. By that time it had also become evident that few of the Chinese people were likely to become Christians and that the missionaries' long-continued effort, if measured in numbers of converts, had failed.

1

Curiously, however, the Chinese Communist revolution of recent decades has stressed the spread of literacy to ordinary people, the publication of journals and pamphlets in the vernacular, education and equality for women, the abolition of arranged child-marriages, the supremacy of public duty over filial obedience and family obligations, increased agricultural productivity through the sinking of wells and improved tools, crops, and breeds, dike and road building for protection against flood and famine, public health clinics to treat common ailments and prevent disease, discussion groups to foster better conduct, student organizations to promote healthy recreation and moral guidance, and the acquisition and Sinification of Western knowledge for use in remaking Chinese life. Missionaries of the nineteenth century pioneered in all of these activities. Little wonder that the revolutionaries of China since 1949 have resented them in retrospect. The missionaries came as spiritual reformers, soon found that material improvements were equally necessary, and in the end helped to foment the great revolution. Yet as foreigners, they could take no part in it, much less bring it to a finish. Instead, it finished them. But in the Maoist message of today, "serve the people," one can hear an echo of the missionary's wish to serve his fellow man.

THE MISSIONARY INTERLUDE

Outsiders customarily see foreign influences at work in China, of which the people living there seem largely unaware. The missionaries' achievements have consequently been little studied in China. After all, to the Chinese they could only offer examples of new ways which, once adopted, were no longer foreign. The Western impact on China is thus eternally ambivalent—"I taught him English to bring him to salvation," says the missionary; "I learned English so I could help save China," says the convert. Like parent and child, teacher and pupil, they are stuck on opposite sides of the relationship. In the end, Chinese youth find they can save China without English or even Christianity, and the missionary influence on an earlier generation is easily forgotten.

The ambivalence of personal aims between the missionary and his Chinese audience was not their only problem. The missionary himself had an ambivalent status. He had the chance to preach and innovate in China only because he was part of the Western invasion. Gunfire and the unequal treaties initially gave him his privileged status and opportunity. Indeed, extraterritoriality made him a part of the newly added foreign wing of the Chinese-Manchu ruling class. Like the Chinese gentry degree-holders, missionaries legally did not need to kneel before magistrates nor fear a beating with the small or large bamboo. Yet as outlanders, they could be reviled or stoned in the streets, and as teachers of a different social order, they had at once become rivals of the scholar gentry. They extolled the Bible over the Classics and Jesus over the Buddha, Lao-tzu, and even Confucius. They attacked the tyranny of the family over the individual and so undercut the Three Bonds (the idealized obedience of subjects, women, and youth). These views appeared dangerously subversive. Jealous Confucian gentry suspected missionaries from the start and fomented a long series of riots to make them desist and go away. In the Chinese official record of the nineteenth century, missionaries often figured as aggressive or insidious troublemakers.

After 1900 they had their heyday. Missionary institutions, including not only schools and hospitals but also the Young Men's Christian Association and many other activities and publications, began to nurture "Young China," a new generation of patriots and reformers. In so doing, they contributed directly to the rise of China's modern nationalism. Although Christianity was not the only influence inspiring the regeneration of China in the decades after 1900, it was undoubtedly one major element.

Yet in the second quarter of the twentieth century, missionaries sometimes found themselves classed as enemies of the revolution. The fact that before 1911 they had worked to reform the *ancien régime* now became irrelevant. They remained foreigners and gradualist reformers, not revolutionaries. As reformers capable of working only within the increasingly conservative system of the Nationalist government, many missionaries in the 1930s and 1940s seemed to be no longer apostles of China's transformation but more often worried bystanders, who helped to manage and therefore defend established institutions. They assisted valiantly in China's resistance against the Japanese invasion, but when this was followed by civil war and revolution, they became targets of China's revolt against foreign participation in Chinese life. In the end, some missionaries supported Chiang Kai-shek. Under the People's Republic they were at first stigmatized as "cultural imperialists," who had allegedly added their quota of exploitation and humiliation to the long night of "feudal" China before liberation. Their role in China had gone through many phases.

Thus, a clear view of the influence of Christian missions in China is obscured by the complexities of both time and standpoint. Over time their social role underwent many changes, even though the great diversity among the missionaries themselves makes it all but impossible to treat them as a group. These changes reflected the rapid movement of events in modern China as it was wracked by Western aggression, domestic rebellion, reform, and revolution. The complexities of standpoint are equally confusing, for the public's attitudes toward missions and the missionaries' own aims and self-images have also gone through many phases, which, moreover, have differed markedly in America and in China. Each country has been in rapid motion, as has the Christian Church itself.

Even the record of Christian missions in China is imperfectly known. The bare data on who went where, when, and to what end have hardly yet been assembled, despite the zeal of many contemporary recorders in trying to keep track of a highly fragmented and idiosyncratic movement. Hagiographic memoirs abound, but few institutional studies and even fewer historical syntheses are available from foreign sources. On the Chinese side, there has been scant historical research on the schools, hospitals, periodicals, and trends of thought that attended the growth of the Chinese Christian community. The most voluminous single record is probably that of the late Ch'ing government in handling antimissionary cases, from which many volumes of documents may soon be published. But this represents merely the official cognizance of problems created as Christianity interacted with the old China. Modern scholarly studies of Chinese Christian literature are rare. Biographies of eminent Chinese Christians are few. Nor had the church in China reached the point of historical self-examination when disaster struck.

The subject is thus a highly controversial one, full of built-in ambiguities, with an utterly inadequate basis of factual knowledge. Not that facts are in short supply. There are simply too many, and they have been too little gathered, winnowed, and processed by historical researchers.

The problem is unfortunately compounded by another recent factor—the need of Americans to reappraise the American record in

East Asia in light of the Vietnam War. Minds that feel themselves untouched in some fashion by this searing event are probably lacking in self-awareness. Although the impact of the Vietnam episode on American thinking has only begun to be assessed, certain general propositions may be suggested: Vietnam and China are to some extent connected in American minds, though how closely is uncertain; American East Asian policy since 1941 has been in part motivated by an inherited idealism, though precisely how is subject to dispute; and Christian missions abroad have been one expression of this traditional idealism, though its bearing on Vietnam remains a matter of opinion.

This train of thought may conclude that our missionary zeal, so long nurtured in China, helped get us into Vietnam. In very general terms this conclusion may have suggestive value for social historians appraising the American character, yet it must be seriously qualified, for it assumes a degree of causality between earlier and later periods of our East Asian activities that is unwarranted. In the earlier period, long before the nuclear era and mainly before the rise of the United States to world power, American governmental programs in China were few (and nonexistent in Vietnam), and American activity there was almost wholly private. Today it is the reverse: the United States government has been the principal actor in recent years, and most Americans in East Asia have been under its aegis, subject to the concerns of great-power politics and national security. These concerns no doubt derive partly from America's past, but from its whole national past, not just its East Asian past. In the Vietnam episode the entire history of American growth and development is in question, not merely a geographical segment of one particular activity.

To find out how Protestant and Catholic missionaries really contributed to American policy in East Asia, as well as to the rise of modern China, will require historical research of the multi-archival kind, to which neither the Vatican nor Maoist revolutionaries have been noticeably addicted. One fact is plain: mission history in China cannot be separated from the history of the Christian Church there, and together they touch on all aspects of Chinese life over many decades. Because of the vastness of the subject, this volume is limited to Americans and to Protestantism. Europeans and Catholicism deserve a separate treatment as important elements in the Christian approach to China.

5

But missions in China are again only half the story. What did the several generations of Protestant missionary endeavor contribute to American life? What was the role of China missions in the growth of Christianity within the United States? Were foreign missions essential to the health of the church? What images of China were created? What self-images of America's role and duty abroad? This other side of the coin deserves equal attention.

The research conference from which this volume derives tried to bring the American and Chinese nodes of missionary activity into a common view. The conference, held at Cuernavaca in Mexico in January 1972, was orgnized by the Committee on American-East Asian Relations of the American Historical Association and financed by a grant from the Ford Foundation. The conference benefited from papers by Suzanne Barnett, Irwin Hyatt, Jerry Israel, and Robert McClellan, which have been published elsewhere.

During the conference, it became clear that the mission movement was pre-eminently a people-to-people phenomenon. The flow of influence may seem at first glance to have been one way, through Americans going to China. But this eventually induced a flow of Chinese students to the United States, and meanwhile the mission work in China had an impact on the missionaries themselves that was transmitted to the American people. Very soon, from missionary efforts on the two sides of the Pacific, the missionary movement became a part of American life. There are thus three foci of this large subject: the American missionary expansion or outward thrust, the impact of this missionary effort on the Chinese people and society, and the backflow of influences affecting the missionaries' home constituency and the American people in general. Causation among these three aspects goes in all directions, because the missionary experience in China created a backflow of reporting that stimulated new initiatives from the United States. The following papers, partly surveys and partly case studies, explore all three aspects.

PROTESTANT MISSIONS IN AMERICAN EXPANSION

In the course of modern history, industrialism and nationalism have abetted each other, often accompanied by a surge of faith or religion. In the American case, as all three of these forms of national growth appeared together in the early nineteenth century, they were represented abroad by the triumvirate of trader, naval diplomat, and missionary.[1] The early Republic was felt to be a nation growing on a frontier not of men but of nature, free of the feudal class structures of Europe and ready to exalt the individual and his enterprising use of technology. To ensure opportunity for the individual's initiative, his constitutional rights were to be safeguarded, and the powers of the government limited by law and due process. Missionaries, like traders, were supremely private enterprisers.

It is often forgotten that in the early years of the nineteenth century, dynamic American individuals went eastward by sea just as often as they went westward by land. The Atlantic community had more to offer than the Western wilderness. After 1800, American traders, gunboat diplomats, and missionaries became increasingly active in the Mediterranean, the Near East, and even South Asia. Coming from a new nation born of political revolution, these Americans abroad often felt they had a message for mankind. They were apostles of liberty under law, of one-class egalitarianism (except for the anomaly of black slavery), and of the self-determination of peoples. When the Second Great Awakening of religious fervor in the early years of the century sent forth missionaries devoted to spreading the Protestant gospel of individual salvation through faith in Christ, the foreign missions thus launched had many of the features of American life in general: a strong sense of personal responsibility for one's own character and conduct; an optimistic belief in progress toward general betterment, especially through the use of education, invention, and technology; and a conviction of moral and cultural worth, at times even superiority, justified both by the religious teachings of the Holy Bible and by the political principles of the Founding Fathers.

To put China missions in their world context, James A. Field's modestly titled but remarkably comprehensive essay notes the initial expansion of American missions in the Near East and later in the Far East, as well as their general motivations in religious thought and feeling. He then traces statistically the world-wide deployment of missionaries and the growth of their financial support during the nineteenth century. Many anomalies emerge. For example, not until the 1880s did the Far East outstrip the Near East, and even as late as 1890 India remained ahead of China as a target of endeavor. Foreign missions had many byproducts. They led to Anglo-American

7

cooperation abroad. In education, just as the state of American geographical knowledge had influenced their original deployment, so the backflow of missionary writings built up America's image of foreign parts. Missionary offspring also began to make their mark in the States. Thus, Protestants in the Near East, beginning earlier than in China, achieved an earlier maturity in the form of several-generation families whose members branched out into public life. In general, the Turkish Empire before World War I posed missionary problems and inspired solutions that would later seem "typical" of the Chinese Empire. Mr. Field offers a salutary corrective for the natural Sinocentrism of China specialists.

Once deployed in foreign lands, missions became institutionalized as big business, the first large-scale transnational corporations. In the era of the mid-century and the Civil War, Protestant missions suffered a decline, but in the 1870s and 1880s came a renascence, a second great surge of interest and endeavor. In this period the growth of missions to China was far greater than the growth of the American China trade. Valentin H. Rabe notes the influx of lay businessmen as administrators of the large-scale mission boards, in the age of trusts that characterized American industrialization. He depicts the new type of revivalist-organizer, who eventually started the Laymen's Movement to assist in large-scale fund raising after 1907. Drawing on mission boards records, Mr. Rabe characterizes the kinds of persons who typically experienced conversion and received the call to mission work, ordinarily a small-town boy or a young spinster from the rural scene, with some higher education but not much urban sophistication. They sought religious dedication and committed themselves to a lifework in exotic surroundings. Together, the new businessmen-administrators and these devoted field workers built the new transnational mission boards that managed institutions in foreign lands. Their appeal for support at home was often couched in terms of stewardship but also stressed social themes and even national ambitions, until ultimately the promotion of evangelism became less a religious duty than the responsibility of all good people to help others in need. The number of missionary candidates, the institutions to provide for them, and the financial contributions kept on increasing through World War I and into the 1920s.

The use of organization and salesmanship for pious ends was illustrated by one of the most active mission agencies, the Student

Volunteer Movement for Foreign Missions (SVM). Clifton J. Phillips examines its origin and growth as a case study of mission motivation and outlook. The SVM grew out of the millenarian concept of the second coming of Christ and the urgent need to achieve the work of the church before that time. This idea, which lay behind much of the revivalism that appealed to college youth in the decades after the Civil War, was expressed in the agency's grand slogan, "the evangelization of the world in this generation." In particular, the movement was promoted through the student YMCA and YWCA as part of a major evangelical strategy to enlist college graduates for missionary work overseas. Its leaders presided over mammoth conventions held every four years from 1891 to 1919, usually in a Midwestern city. They initiated international efforts like that of the World Student Christian Federation to expand and unify Protestant youth activities. In the end the SVM recruited large numbers of foreign missionaires—over 8000 by 1919—including a great many for China, and thereby made China missions a regular part of American campus life.

Along with this growth in size and organization after the 1880s came a parallel development in theology. Liberalism (or modernism as it was called from about 1910) was the theological response to the new view of man and his world that developed with Darwinism and the rise of sciences such as geology, archaeology, and anthropology. William R. Hutchison studies the effort at the turn of the century to fit foreign missions into this expanding intellectual horizon. The accommodation was to be achieved by reaffirming the absolute necessity of Christian salvation, but freeing this overriding religious imperative from its accumulated connections with Western civilization and culture. The effort was to make Christianity, which in its long course had entered into and been assimilated by so many cultures, more independent of Western industrial civilization. Christianity was felt to have value for all mankind if only it could be brought to the non-Christian peoples in its pure form. This effort had its denouement in the 1932 report of the Laymen's Foreign Missions Inquiry, which urged the universal merit of religion, over and above the irreligious trends in all countries. This view denied that the Christian religion was indissolubly tied to the modern Western culture and could not be supracultural.

But however one defines religion and culture, and thereby deter-

9

mines the relationship between them, the fact remains that all religions entering China have had to accommodate their message to the Chinese scene. Accommodation began in the very act of translation into Chinese written characters, for certain characters and not others, together with their burden of accumulated connotations, had to be chosen to convey the foreigner's ideas. Thus began the interaction between the China missionaries and their far from passive Chinese environment.

CHRISTIANITY AND THE TRANSFORMATION OF CHINA

When the Western package of expansion with its traders, diplomats, and missionaries exploded on China's doorstep in the early nineteenth century, the immediate Chinese reaction was to lock the door, but it proved to be too late. After 1860 the treaty ports gradually expanded to include most of the major centers of Chinese commerce and urban life. Trade operated of its own accord, and Chinese and American merchants cooperated with each other across national lines, while the diplomats had their own channels of contact. But the missionaries posed an irreducible cultural threat because they were rivals of China's elite, the scholar gentry. As educators, even though in foreign ways, and privileged persons, even though under foreign protection, missionaries seemed to be essentially subversive to the traditional Chinese order both in aim and in result. However, as China's old order began to crack, beginning at the top with the emperor's supremacy, there began an interaction between Chinese and foreign individuals, mainly between the missionaries and their Chinese audience. Through this interaction, the Protestant missions began to make their contribution to the Chinese revolutionary process.

M. Searle Bates, writing from a long and intimate background in China, is able to picture the variety and complexity of Protestant missions there in the early twentieth century. Having developed in an era of free enterprise, the missions were now feeling a need for greater cohesion. As their contact with the Chinese people grew in volume and variety, the missionaries found themselves woefully fragmented, representing various sects and constituencies, and sometimes rivaling each other in the field. They reacted by forging bonds of cooperation through a multitude of committees and associations, and also by reaffirming their theology so as to minimize doctrinal mission differences and stress their common church denominator, faith in Christ.

Mr. Bates notes the varying degrees of accommodation or simplification by which American Protestant missionaries adjusted themselves theologically to the Chinese scene and tried to reach their often semiliterate Chinese audiences. He notes also how the tremendous variety of missionary agencies and approaches induced a growing desire for unity within the church. In response to these needs, the Christian message became simplified and strengthened, emphasizing the community of the church, and much of this was summed up at the centenary conference of Protestant missions in China in 1907. The conference's statements to the Chinese brethren and to the Chinese government indicate the missionaries' stress on the "person and work of Christ" as represented in the Bible, and reflected the established posture of American Protestantism in China at its height in the first decades of the century. In the early 1920s, the significance of the church as a community of love and faith gradually supplanted the nineteenth century stress on individual salvation. Greater unity was achieved by the organization in 1922 of the National Christian Council. However, the China Inland Mission, which had worked so long in the rural scene, clung to the fundamentalist theology and in 1926 withdrew from the council. To avoid injurious schism, the missionaries generally left doctrine to the respective churches. The Church of Christ in China, which was organized in 1922 and became fully active in 1927, provided another common bond.

Although the missionary movement has been recorded extensively by its members and studied sporadically from the American side, the vital point of the missionary's contact with his Chinese audience has been little researched. Adrian A. Bennett and Kwang-Ching Liu break a new trail in their analysis of the first church newspaper in China, published after 1868 by a missionary from Georgia, Young J. Allen. They examine the contents of the articles offered in Chinese, especially the letters from Chinese readers that touch upon current topics of Christian teaching and human values. As editor, Allen, like other missionaries, faced the considerable problem of how to convey Christian concepts in Chinese terms without losing their meaning. The Chinese pastors who wrote letters to the journal provided one of the first dialogues between Americans and Chinese. Allen used Chinese examples and classical quotations to explain Christian ideas in Chinese, a tactic followed by all missionaries since the Jesuits. But inevitably, some Chinese Christians went further and used their new faith as a basis for criticism of Chinese social evils and outworn practices. Christianity thus entered the lists as an element in the Chinese reform movement. Allen, meanwhile, was drawn to the good works of both Christian and non-Christian Chinese. He held up examples of philanthropy and public spirit. The revolutionary idea of the equality of women was brought forward in a Chinese attack on foot binding, one of the principal movements for reform in which missionaries would later make their mark. Allen also turned more and more to the demonstration effect of modern science and its usefulness in education. All this led into the broader reform movement of the late nineteenth century, in which Western industries and institutions were advocated as a means of China's national salvation.

Paul A. Cohen studies some of the early members of the Chinese church and seeks to determine whether they embraced Christianity primarily as a religion or more as a part of Western modernity in general. He approaches the problem by setting up a framework of geographical-cultural analysis. China's modernization is seen as a process of interaction between the hinterland, on the one hand, still dominated by traditional orthodoxy and the imperial regime, and on the other hand, the littoral or treaty ports on the coast or main rivers, which in the late nineteenth century were under increasing foreign influence. Within this analytic structure Mr. Cohen looks at the career profiles of eight leading reformers, seven of whom turn out to have been at one time or in part "Christian" through baptism or intensive involvement with missionaries—even though this Christian aspect of their careers was not advertised in the Chinese scene. In the late nineteenth century these were men on the border, who consorted with foreigners and could not make their way into the power structure of the hinterland. Yet they were later used as specialists by power holders like Li Hung-chang. Eventually they became forerunners of rebellion and revolution because their ideas of reform could not be made effective within the old order. Yet the very ideas of reform that they picked up in their contact with the West inspired them also to become Chinese nationalists, eager to save China by modernization or even, as it then seemed, Westernization, using the foreigner's devices to obviate his dominance. At first the Christian teaching seemed to be a key to Western power, as the missionaries implied. No doubt it was. But Chinese patriots found they could make a selection of foreign ways to adopt or emulate. They discovered that no special faith was required to operate steamships.

In the end the Christian influence was probably strongest in education. The missionary schools and colleges, by aiming to spread modern education as well as Christianity, eventually dominated the Christian scene in China. Although it was not until 1925 that the total enrollment of Christian colleges in China reached 3500, the students in the Christian middle schools were several times that number—about 26,000 in the mid-twenties. Many of them had graduated from missionary primary schools, which then enrolled more than a quarter-million pupils. By the mid-thirties, at the height of their influence, the thirteen Christian colleges had a total of 5800 students, and the 255 Christian middle schools had a total of 44,000.[2] The decline in the number of missionaries during that decade did not arrest the growth of these educational institutions, which were increasingly in the hands of Chinese Christian educators. The fact that their few thousand students were so important a part of the educational system in a land of some 400 million people did not diminish their contribution, though it sadly reflected the abysmal degree of China's backwardness at the time.

The Christian colleges and schools were a disruptive as well as a constructive influence—disruptive by virtue of their Western orientation, which in the 1920s aroused antiforeign sentiments among students even in the Christian colleges themselves. These institutions did a solid job of teaching modern subjects, and under the influence of the liberal trend within the Christian community, they increasingly stressed God's kingdom on earth and dedicated service as the ideal of life. Words like "give," "service," "sacrifice," "self-denial," were as much used by teachers in Christian schools as by left-wing novelists. The Christian colleges led in such fields as agriculture, medicine, journalism, and sociology. It was no accident that James Y. C. Yen (Yen Yang-ch'u), in developing the Mass Education Movement, found his earliest recruits among students and graduates of the mission schools and colleges. Christian institutions had pioneered in the education of women. Now they took the lead in agricultural

extension work and joined in experimental projects for rural reconstruction. Yet inevitably, the foreign connection of Christianity in
China made it vulnerable to patriotic attack.

A case study of the conflict between Christianity and nationalism
is offered by Philip West in the history of a Chinese Christian leader,
Wu Lei-ch'uan, who was trained as a Confucian scholar but sought
through Christianity to find the key to China's salvation. Wu was one
of a small, ardent group of American missionaries and Chinese
Christian scholars who made Yenching University a leading Sino-
foreign enterprise in the two decades after 1917. This was the era of
the May Fourth Movement, China's cultural renaissance, the discard-
ing of Confucianism, and the search for modern values. Scholars of
the People's Republic today rightly regard the Chinese Communist
movement as emerging from this background. However, Yenching
University and its leaders must be examined in another context, not
only as a seedbed of the new, but also as a culmination of the
Christian missionary effort of the preceding hundred years. In Yenching, as in several other colleges, foreign missionaries committed to
helping China's spiritual regeneration through education joined hands
with a group of Chinese Christian leaders who were the fruit of
earlier decades of evangelism. For a time, Chinese members of this
leadership saw their way to saving China through Christianity.

In the 1920s, however, the natural limitations of this approach
began to appear, not so much because Christianity still seemed like a
foreign religion, but rather because as a religion it was nonpolitical.
Necessarily it stressed the salvation of the individual within the
accepted political framework. This made Christianity, like any religion, inadequate for mass mobilization in the cause of violent revolution and social change. Christians continued to support schools and
colleges, famine relief, public health, mass education, and rural
reconstruction, which in many cases was pioneer work. But the
Christian movement, which had begun by offering so many stimuli
for China's national salvation, now proved inappropriate for the
political action that the times demanded. Nationalism in the 1920s
began to turn against it, although the Japanese invasion of 1937–
1945 again brought Christianity and patriotism into a natural alliance
for national defense. Unfortunately, in this era of warfare, the
Nationalist government under Chiang Kai-shek mobilized Christian
support from abroad but failed to mobilize the Chinese people for

rapid change at home. In the end, Christianity found itself condemned after 1949 as part of the old order associated with the Kuomintang. The secular faith of communism, in some ways a rival movement, eventually turned the force of nationalism against it.

CHINA MISSION IMAGES AND AMERICAN POLICIES

Part One of this volume suggests the dynamics of the American Protestant expansion, while Part Two shows features of the actual Sino-American contact within Chinese society. Part Three is concerned with American perceptions and policies connected with the missionary movement. Here again the emphasis is on case studies, because the rudimentary state of the field makes generalization foolhardy if not impossible.

Americans, and especially missionaries, drew from their contact with the Chinese state and society a profound impression of China's ethnocentrism. This was a pervasive sentiment more widespread than any religious or doctrinal creed. As a result of this ethnocentrism, the early frustration in China of Christian believers from the United States was to be repeated generations later by the frustration of Communist believers from the Soviet Union. In neither case was their sense of regret much assuaged by the fact that Chinese who condemned them as foreigners still proceeded to use many of their teachings.

Although nationalism arose in China partly in imitation of the Western powers, Chinese nationalism is a considerable variation on the European type, being a good deal more comprehensive and more intent on the unity of the social order, economy, polity, and cultural life in a single Chinese realm—in fact, a civilization. Westerners with a history of crusading against the Philistines, the infidel, and the heathen in so many times and places can hardly cavil at the enthnocentric Chinese tenacity in being Chinese.

To understand the China in which American missionaries were active, one must understand Chinese life as it used to be, before its recent transformation. One must also be past-minded about the missionaries themselves, for they were Americans of an earlier generation who lived in a far different and simpler world than we face today. The present-minded impulse of the historian, to reappraise the past in the light of today's concerns, thus regularly conflicts with the necessity to understand the circumstances, aims, and values of a vanished era. This discrepancy makes definitive history impossible and a reinterpretation on the basis of new knowledge continually necessary. It is therefore impossible for today's researchers in this new field to "do justice" to American Protestant missions in China as a whole. The case studies in this volume are offered only as bits and pieces, as beginnings, not as finished structures. Their findings and insights should be a challenge to further work.

To live in China in the nineteenth century, representing a different civilization, was an experience not easily communicated in words. Treaty-port denizens tried to avoid the experience by creating their own foreign enclaves. Missionaries who took on the burden of changing China from within suffered at first a high mortality, and those who did not die or leave sometimes knew despair, fear, or even rage along with the hope and charity more customary in their calling. They were on a frontier that in time of crisis could seem utterly hostile. Most of them were prepared to suffer and sacrifice, but a good proportion were also activists who believed in defending their cause, at times by force. Particularly in the early days, they sometimes turned to gunboats. Stuart Creighton Miller documents the observation that in the nineteenth century leading missionaries time after time favored the use of violence and coercion to overcome Chinese resistance to Western contact and evangelism. Such leaders in times of crisis were carried away by a spirit of righteous bellicosity and even revenge. Although there were also long periods of peaceful and constructive intercourse, and many missionaries, when threatened, repeatedly turned the other cheek, the vigor of the basic American self-righteousness remained undiminished.

Mr. Miller is concerned less with the facts in China than with the images formed in America. Missionary expansionism easily became a target of American critics in that era of controversy over science and religion, between modernism and fundamentalism. In the Boxer crisis of 1900, humanitarians at a great distance, like Mark Twain, took issue with the bellicose statements emanating from some missionaries in the field. But the point was that they were indeed in the field, on a cultural frontier in a daily struggle with the Chinese resistance to Christian values or at least to the foreign presence. One can easily extract from the records of the East India Company before 1834 a similar refrain that the Chinese would yield only to force and, without it, that the Western system of trade and contact could never be extended to China. This suggests that the degree of cultural gap, the apparent gulf between two civilizations, may be indexed by the demand of one side for the use of violence against evils perceived in the other.

Shirley Stone Garrett deals with a later day, when the use of force to protect Christianity in China had become not only less feasible but also much less easy to sanction. In the 1920s, when all foreigners in China felt to some degree threatened, the basic decisions lay with the mission boards at home, which handled the funds and set the policies. The missionary enterprise had long since become big business. It was peculiarly dependent on public relations, on its image among potential givers in the constituency. Institutional momentum thus seemed to require that, if the church at home was to grow, so also must its work abroad. The decision to send missionaries back into China after their sudden exodus during the Nationalist revolution of 1925–1927 was made partly out of concern for the health of the church as a whole. However, in support of the new and promising Kuomintang government, some board personnel in America began to see communism as a great new enemy in China.

The question arises whether the China missions, as vested interests now on the defensive, were influential in Washington. Paul A. Varg examines the State Department record and the missionary archives to determine how far the missionaries in the 1920s supported the maintenance of treaty privileges. At this time the first patriotic attack was made in China on Christianity as a foreign religion somehow associated with imperialism. Some members of China's new generation were beginning to accept a different faith from abroad, which promised more directly to provide the rationale and mechanism for China's political rebirth. In the face of rising patriotism, the choices presented to the missionaries were merely those of timing— how soon to give in to the demands of the Nationalist cause. In the denouement, as the Nationalist government came into power and faced the almost immediate threat of Japanese aggression, the anti-Christian theme was muted, and for another two decades the foreign missions had the opportunity for service to the Chinese people, albeit in the midst of disorder and warfare. Meantime, in the councils of the American government there was little indication that the missionaries called the tune in developing policy. Divided among themselves, the China missionary interests failed to speak with one voice.

This negative finding does not settle the larger issue of American imperialism—specifically, whether Christian missions should be classed as only a politer, and perhaps for that very reason more insidious, form of Western penetration of non-Western societies. Arthur Schlesinger, Jr., examines the types of imperialism and the place among them of foreign missions. After surveying the general interpretations of imperialism, he looks at the literature dealing with connections between the missionary movement and both capitalism and nationalism. In neither case was there a complete linkage, though the missionary enthusiasm of the 1890s was not out of keeping with the American expansion of that era. Mr. Schlesinger concludes that if the missionary can be related to imperialism at all, it must be as a "cultural imperialist," namely, one who claims that his way of life is superior to that of people abroad, which justifies his effort at evangelism. This claim became perhaps most vigorous in the period of the social gospel, when the good works of modernization were pushed vigorously by missionaries in both medicine and education. Mr. Schlesinger analyzes the resulting "resentment against the missionary for his violation of the integrity of native culture." In the end he sees the "missionary heritage" (though still a vague and protean concept) as one factor encouraging Americans in their ventures at nation building in Japan and Korea, eventually even in Vietnam.

Research topics suggested by these studies are legion. One that stands out is the work of women missionaries. As indicated by both Mr. Bates and Mr. Rabe, women became the major factor in the mission work force in the field (64 percent in 1936), yet because they lacked ordination as preachers and executive positions, they remained in the background, their work largely unrecorded. Men did the preaching and administering in the vocal leadership roles, whereas women did most of the teaching, all of the nursing, and much of the visitation within Chinese homes. Even so, these activities may have given women missionaries a range of experience and opportunity not equally available to them at home.

Other enormous opportunities for analysis lie in the Christian literature in Chinese—the terms used, the adjustment of religious ideas to the Chinese idiom, the values conveyed.[3] Recently, the

China Records Project in the Day Missions Library within the Library of the Yale University Divinity School, New Haven, has emerged as a central repository for missionary papers. This collection of family documents can now take its place along with the other centers, such as the Missionary Research Library in New York. The field is rich in intellectual challenge and rewards.

The papers in this volume demonstrate how new fields of historical inquiry are born. China studies in the United States are almost as old as the Republic itself. It is high time that the *interactions* between China and the United States—the American activities in China, their contributions to Chinese life, and the backflow of aggressive as well as humanitarian attitudes in American policy and folklore—be examined more closely and systematically by scholars. While the British have long scrutinized the record of the British Empire, Americans, though lacking a formal empire of importance in East Asia, have had a similar economic and cultural contact with that area. The exploratory surveys and case studies in this volume suggest the dimensions of the missionary contact and its repercussions, as yet largely unexplored, in China and America.

PART I

Protestant Missions in American Expansion

JAMES A. FIELD, JR.

Near East Notes and Far East Queries

An exercise of some interest, although one requiring a certain temerity, is to attempt (after suppressing all memories of the War with Spain and of the history that followed) a comparison of American relations with the Near East and the Far East in the 1890s.[1] These relations, at first glance, show certain obvious similarities. In the Near East the Ottoman Empire and in the Far East the empire of the Manchus, large traditional societies with long histories, were in serious trouble, owing to the corrosive effects of an expanding Western civilization and the pressures of European powers. With both of these empires the United States carried on some trade, small in the case of China and minimal in that of Turkey. Both of these trades had long histories, and both had given rise to talk of expanding markets for American exports. But both were in fact primarily import trades.

Both empires were the targets of impressive American missionary endeavors, and while the Chinese effort was by now the larger, the work in Turkey had the longer history. In China, as in the Ottoman Empire, this situation raised problems concerning the protection of citizens and property for American diplomats and for the American squadrons stationed in neighboring waters. In both Turkey and China, American influence and American sympathy worked generally, if somewhat contradictorily, on behalf of American ideas of self-determination, upholding the integrity of the empires against external pressures while undermining it by support of religious, linguistic, or ethnic minorities. One can draw some not wholly fanciful parallels between American attitudes and actions as they bore on the questions of Bulgarian and Korean independence or on the crises brought about by Arabi Pasha and by the Boxers.[2]

By the nineties, the nature and history of American involvement in these empires had given each a set of American constituencies, religious, commercial, intellectual, and scientific. How much influence these constituencies possessed and which area appeared the more important to the American government (if either could be said to be important at all) is perhaps impossible to establish, yet some evidence can be adduced. Although disinclined to mediate the Sino-Japanese War, the Cleveland administration gave serious consideration to intervening in Turkey, in cooperation with Great Britain, on behalf of the oppressed Armenians. Although he would later find himself faced with the problem of Asia, Theodore Roosevelt in 1898 merely wanted to help "smash" Spain or Turkey. The views of the bureaucracy can be inferred from the fact that the Constantinople legation was elevated to embassy status in 1906, a distinction for which Peking had to wait until 1935.[3]

The first American contacts with both these civilizations had been commercial, and while the China trade dates from the immediate post-Revolutionary era, that with the Mediterranean had colonial antecedents. Indeed, a case can be made that the Muslim societies of North Africa and the Near East provided the school in which the American approach to the non-Western world was worked out. There the problems of the expansion and protection of commerce early involved the government: the Moroccan treaty of 1787 marked the conclusion of the first of many negotiations with non-European potentates aimed at educating them with regard to the virtues of trade and the norms of international intercourse. The recalcitrance of the rulers of Algiers and Tripoli brought the refounding of the navy, war in support of trade, and the establishment of the first permanent distant cruising squadron. Accompanying these commercial and diplomatic developments was a growing export of American skills, in the first instance by captives in Barbary, and later by a variety of salesmen and soldiers of fortune. By the 1820s the Levant had seen the commencement of an American missionary and philanthropic effort that was to grow to large proportions.

In this Mediterranean history are many precedents for what came later. The trade in Turkey opium led on to China. Efforts to deal with exotic rulers by civilian agents with naval support, as in the negotiations of Tobias Lear, Luther Bradish, and Charles Rhind, were echoed in the missions of Edmund Roberts and Caleb Cushing. The diplomatic negotiations of such naval officers as Stephen Decatur, William Bainbridge, and John Rodgers had their more famous sequels in the voyages of Matthew C. Perry and Robert W. Shufeldt. The theoretical justifications for Perry's errand to Japan were anticipated in the North African context by Timothy Pickering and William Eaton. Following the establishment of diplomatic relations with Turkey in 1830 the treaty-making process was extended eastward, first to Muscat and Siam and subsequently to the Far East. The employment of George B. English in the army of Mehemet Ali had later analogs in the Chinese activities of Frederick Townsend Ward, Henry A. Burgevine, and Philo McGiffin, and in the Japanese service of Henry W. Grinnell. The great expansion of the Near Eastern missionary effort in the 1830s was followed by a considerable, if short-lived, effort in Southeast Asia and by the commencement, if on a small scale, of work in China. As earlier in the Mediterranean, the establishment in 1835 of the East Indies Squadron provided a force, deployed in the interests of commerce, which could be used for the protection of missionaries. The early education of Greek youths in America, mid-century Turkish naval missions to the United States, the Syrian relief effort of 1860, and the founding of overseas schools and colleges all had later Far Eastern counterparts.[4]

The eastward sequence of treaty negotiations, from Mediterranean to Indian Ocean to Far East, and the chronology of the work of missionaries and synarchists raise the question of whether, to what extent, and at what times the Far East was east or west of the United States. Although Bishop Berkeley's views on the westward march of empire were echoed both by Americans of the revolutionary generation and by expansionists and railroad enthusiasts in the mid-nineteenth century, and although it comes naturally to historians to see the Far East as a farther West, luring "a stream of New Englanders across the Pacific," the assumption that the high road to China led only by way of Cape Horn or the Union Pacific needs qualification.[5] The *Empress of China* and some two dozen other American ships had reached Canton by way of the Cape of Good Hope before the *Columbia* arrived from the West Coast. An American naval vessel reached Java by way of the Indian Ocean thirteen years before the first American warship entered the Pacific.[6] Roberts, Cushing, and Perry went out via the Cape of Good Hope, and so did Shufeldt. En route homeward from China, D. W. C. Olyphant died in Egypt and C. W. King died in the Red Sea. The missionary effort was projected from an Atlantic-oriented United States by an East Coast ecclesiastical establishment. Late nineteenth-century customs district figures suggest that those coarse cottons, so presumedly central to "China market" concerns, traveled eastward.[7] Although Dewey went out by Pacific passenger liner, the revenue cutter *McCulloch,* which joined his command with the reporters who were to make his name, reached Hong Kong by way of Suez, the customary route of naval vessels deploying to the Far East. The problem of getting the Great White Fleet through the Straits of Magellan was worrisome to contemporaries.[8] Cable connections with the Orient long ran by way of Europe. There are of course various forms of being west—cartographic, cultural, commercial, and strategic.[9] But it may be tentatively suggested that China, although in some degree west of America while the sea otter and sandalwood held out, and again in the two decades between the discovery of California gold and the opening of the Suez Canal, only became so in serious operational terms with the completion of the cut at Panama. The question has some importance in relation to the expansionists of 1898 and the problem of "insular imperialism." A China reached by way of the Atlantic and Indian Oceans makes the delays in Hawaiian annexation more comprehensible.

Yet however persuasive, this picture of a generally eastward extension of a consistent pattern of overseas activities requires qualification. If one accepts the four-part package of commerce, the commerce-supporting navy, the missionary effort, and the secular evangelism of salesman and synarchist as defining the developed American approach to the non-Western world, there are obvious and striking parallels between Near East and Far East, and the former, in fact, appears to have been the school for the latter. But in other regions the export of Americanism went on piecemeal. Trade with Europe was carried on without naval or missionary accompaniment. The navy was employed against West Indies pirates and on the coasts of South America, regions in which the missionary effort lagged. Missionary work in India and among the Zulus took place in areas conspicuously uninteresting to naval officer, trader, or entrepreneur. In Hawaii, where the missionaries were early in force, the first naval visit of Mad Jack Percival brought little pleasure to either party. The last two decades of the nineteenth century saw an immense expansion of Far Eastern missions, but so far as trade and investment went, the American "New Empire" was located in Canada, Mexico, Cuba, and Brazil.[10]

The point, however obvious, should still perhaps be emphasized: that national manifestations are neither necessarily defined by the activities of government nor necessarily unitary, that cultural manifestations are not necessarily very "national," and that national and cultural interactions are generally not one-sided (or perhaps even two-sided) games.[11] For the Americans, the sequence of activity in Near and Far East was a function of accessibility: one region was in fact much closer than the other. But in both areas the nature of American activity was affected by the persistent British presence, itself varying in commercial, diplomatic, naval, or missionary emphasis. And finally, with regard to the similarities in American activities in these two areas, much derived from the similarities in the areas themselves.

Both Ottoman and Chinese empires were, or at least were often described as being, regions of commercial promise. Both had governments, however exotic, with which one could attempt to negotiate. Both were devoted to various kinds of heathenish practices and, at the same time, desirous of more or less selective types of modernization. Some of these conditions tended to draw the trader and some the navy; some were attractive to missionary enterprise. Where the whole run of conditions existed, as in the Ottoman regions, China, and Japan, the developed American package appeared; elsewhere it did not. So far as the Americans themselves were concerned, there was no very consistent relationship between the various aspects of overseas activity. The nature of the receiving society was as important as that of the sending one for the situation that developed.

MOTIVATION AND DEPLOYMENT

If the characteristics of the great traditional civilizations were responsible for the full development of the American overseas package, they were by no means necessary for the deployment of American missionaries. For while the foreign missionary effort, and the nineteenth-century expansion of Christianity of which it was a part, can be seen as an aspect of the outburst of Western energy that gave rise to the American, French, and Industrial revolutions, and to the increasing dominance of the periphery by the North Atlantic societies, the links between the various manifestations of this phenomenon are complex. The motivations of revolutionary, trader, and missionary were by no means identical.

Of all these motivations, those of the missionary seem the most nonspecific. Although variously classified by various commentators, and deriving in America from a missionary tradition that went back to the Virginia and Massachusetts company charters, the work of John Eliot, the aspirations of Cotton Mather, and the missionary Americanism of the first generation of independence, these motives can perhaps be reduced to three. First and foremost was the theological imperative to follow Christ's Great Commission, to share the blessings of Christianity, and to preach the gospel to every living creature; this imperative, in the early years, was greatly reinforced by the doctrine of disinterested benevolence deriving from the writings of Samuel Hopkins and by the felt imminence of the millennium. Second, and growing in strength as the nineteenth century wore on, was an allied humanitarian compulsion, stemming from the contemporary equation of Christianity and civilization, to bring the blessings of modernity to the backward. Third, although this motive was specifically repudiated by missionary leaders, one can assume the romantic and adventurous attraction, sanctified no doubt but still exciting, of life in distant lands amid exotic civilizations.[12]

These motives, which in their broad outlines were shared with the Protestants of Europe, were sufficiently general to support a missionary effort in any part of the world, however slight the region's political or commercial interest. It is hard to find political or economic motivation in the two Moravian volunteers who left Herrnhut for the West Indies early on an August morning in 1733. Tahiti was evangelized by the British but annexed by the French. In the Near East, a region of prime importance to nineteenth-century British policy, American missionaries were predominant. The first, and long the largest American missionary effort was centered in India and Ceylon, an area of minimal American trade and no American political interest, controlled by the greatest of Protestant powers and the main focus of that power's own missionary enterprise. It may be observed, in this context, that generalizations on the American foreign missionary effort that do not account for India do not account for much.[13]

Since the motivation was applicable to the unconverted anywhere, the fortuitous or "providential" origins of the various American mission fields seem, in the first instance, largely explicable by the state of geographic knowledge. In the years before the commencement of American foreign missions, this knowledge had been rapidly expanded by the voyages of Captain Cook and the travels of such explorers as James Bruce and Mungo Park. By 1810, when the American Board of Commissioners for Foreign Missions came into being, a good deal of the new information had made its way into reference books, which one can perhaps assume were consulted by the members of this organization, the more so since one of the most important of the new publications was the work of the Reverend Jedidiah Morse, a founder of both the Andover seminary and the American Board.

Given the general plagiarizing tendencies of the time, these writings indeed provided a body of common knowledge. The foundation work appears to have been William Guthrie's *Geographical Grammar,* which Morse copied almost *in toto* for his information on the non-American world and which also formed the basis for many of the geographical articles in the third edition of the *Encyclopaedia Brittanica,* a pirated version of which appeared in Philadelphia in 1798. In later editions Morse drew heavily on John Pinkerton's *Modern Geography,* a possibly more accurate but certainly less entertaining book than Guthrie's. These works are of considerable interest in suggesting the generally received view of the outer world and in providing background for the assessment of missionary procedures and goals. The American Board's predilection for sending out none but married missionaries may well have derived from the available descriptions of far places: the inhabitants of Owhyee were the most sensual people in the world; the women of Turkey possessed an "admirable chest" and many were "complete beauties," witty, vivacious, and "exceeding amorous." More important perhaps, these descriptions suggest the great interest attaching to romantic and divinely-favored Asia, the site of both the Creation and the Incarnation and the home of great exotic civilizations, which made that continent so eligible a target of missionary endeavor.[14]

Within the limits of existing knowledge, these works appear to have provided balanced descriptions of both lands and peoples. In no sense can they be described as anti-Asian or anti-Chinese. If Chinese commercial dishonesty is reprobated by the *Encyclopaedia,* so is "the avarice and profligacy of Europeans who resort [to Asia] in search of wealth and dominion"; the reason that the best of Chinese art is never seen in Canton is that the European merchants "delight only in obscene pictures"; China as a whole shows a "decency of public manners, and a total ignorance of scandalous intrigues and gallantry"; the Chinese have manners and customs of the highest civilization.[15] Yet however appreciative these accounts of the extensive and populous countries of Asia, of their mild and delicious climates and fertile lands, and of their progress in the arts and sciences, one overriding fact remained. Their many millions of inhabitants were either pagan idolaters or Mohammedans. Christianity had not reached them.

As stimuli to missionary enterprise, therefore, the descriptions of far places in Guthrie, Morse, and other early works were more than adequate; for the rational planning of a missionary campaign, however, the available information was insufficient. There was, in consequence, a good deal of happenstance in the development of the American Board's effort. The mission to India and Ceylon had originally been intended for Burma, but only the schismatic Baptists got there. The mission to the Sandwich Islands resulted from the chance arrival at Yale College of a young Hawaiian orphan. The effort in the Ottoman Empire derived in part from the suggestions of the brethren in India, in part from the historical importance of the Holy Land and the eschatological importance of the Jews. The Nestorian mission resulted from some chance reading of the Board's corresponding secretary. The commencement of work in China was encouraged by the urgings of pious merchants. The African mission, early proposed by Samuel Hopkins and Ezra Stiles and only tardily undertaken by the Board, combined in its motives a bad conscience about slavery and a desire to check the southward progress of Islam in the Dark Continent. Inevitably, no doubt, given this absence of strategic planning and this reliance on targets of opportunity, the

results were .mixed. Work among the Jews and Greeks proved fruitless and was abandoned. The Indian, Sandwich Islands, and Near
Eastern fields prospered and grew. China and Japan, although destined for great futures, long lay fallow. The working out of the
providential design was a very complex matter.[16]

Viewed from the mid-twentieth century, the situation seemed
clearer. Writing in 1949, at a time when China was much in the
public eye, Kenneth S. Latourette noted that American missionaries
were "particularly prominent" in the Far East.[17] So they were, and
so they had been for some time, but this was a comparatively late
development. The American Board, long the predominant missionary
organization, had focused its efforts first in the Indian subcontinent,
then in the Levant, and only latterly in that farthest of regions, the
Far East. The Baptists long concentrated on Burma; the first Methodist ventures were to Africa and Brazil. The growth of the overseas
missionary effort, and the shifts of emphasis between the various
fields, can be illustrated by statistics on the allocation of funds and
deployment of personnel derived from the reports of the several
missionary boards.

The first mission established by the American Board, that to India
and Ceylon, was also for long the largest in terms of expenditures.
But in 1849 it was permanently passed by the Near East, which since
the early twenties had enjoyed the faster growth rate. The Sandwich
Island mission, founded at the same time as that to the Eastern
Churches but on a larger scale, grew more slowly. Overhauled by the
Levantine effort in 1829, it experienced in the next decade a sudden
burst of growth and then, with the evangelization of the islands
apparently assured, entered a gradual decline (Fig. 1).

The last years of the Jackson administration saw the American
Board in occupation of three major fields—India, the Sandwich
Islands, and the Levant—and of three minor ones—Southeast Asia,
Africa, and China. Although the effort in Southeast Asia was for the
moment enjoying a startlingly rapid expansion, within a decade this
field would disappear. By the middle fifties the deployment encompassed two major fields—the Near East, one-third larger than India
and Ceylon—and three minor ones—the Sandwich Islands, Africa, and
China—whose combined budgets barely equaled half that of the
Levant. This history of the regional allocation of funds over the first
half-century of effort set the pattern for the deployment of mission-

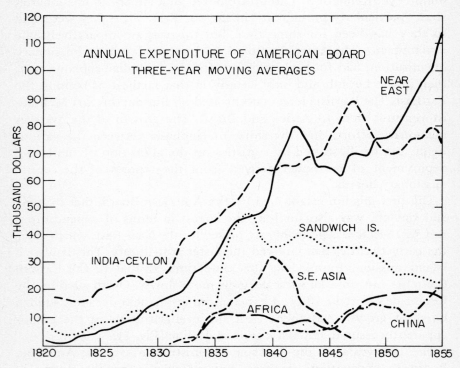

Fig. 1. Annual Expenditure of American Board, Three-Year Moving Averages

Table 1. Deployment of American Board missionaries, 1812–1860.

Field	Ordained missionaries	Physicians & other male ass't missionaries	Wives & female ass't missionaries
Levant	114	12	142
India-Ceylon	91	10	117
Hawaii-Micronesia	54	27	89
East Asia	46	4	49
Africa	37	6	43

Source: Memorial Volume, pp. 414–426.

aries. The total numbers assigned to the various missions by 1860 reflect the early emphasis on India and Hawaii and the remarkable growth of the Near Eastern effort (Table 1).

Great changes followed the Civil War. Increased missionary efforts on the part of the Presbyterian Church (North), the Methodist Episcopal Church (North), and the American Baptist Missionary Union ended the period of predominance of the American Board; by the century's end, these four groups would together dominate the country's foreign missionary enterprise. Withdrawing from the American Board in 1870 and assuming sole responsibility for some previously shared missions, the Presbyterians greatly increased their endeavors, first in the Near East and subsequently in East Asia, while the Board for its part evinced a lively concern with Japan. In the early seventies there developed a great expansion of Methodist missionary activity, with a growing emphasis on China. In the years after 1875 an enlarged Baptist effort, focused on South Asia, brought a notable extension of work in Burma and Assam, and among the Telugus of Madras. Taken together, the Asian expenditures of the four boards suggested a beginning shift of American missionary interest: although the Chinese budget remained generally stable throughout the seventies, the expansion of work in Japan gave the Far East, as a whole, a rate of growth equal to that of the Near East and considerably greater than that of the Indian field (Fig. 2).

This trend was to continue. The decade of the eighties, happily situated between the depressions of 1873 and 1893, saw both a remarkable growth in overall missionary expenditures and a strikingly increased emphasis on East Asia. In 1880 the foreign expenditures of the four major boards were approaching a million and a half

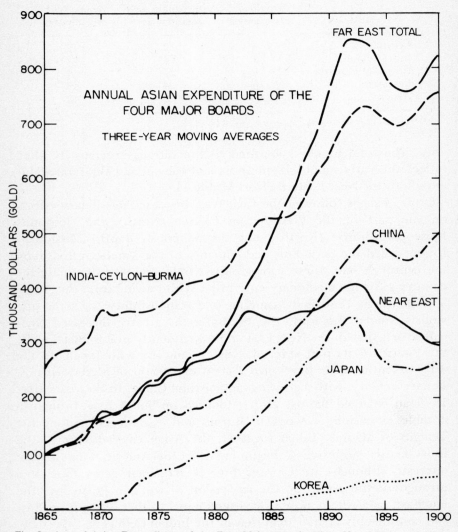

Fig. 2. Annual Asian Expenditure of the Four Major Boards, Three-Year Moving Averages

dollars a year; in 1893, the peak year of the nineteenth century, the figure topped the three million mark. In this period of presumed burgeoning imperialism the moneys assigned the Near East grew by about 50 percent, while those for India (under which rubric the missionaries included Burma and Ceylon) almost doubled. But these developments, remarkable though they were, were overmatched by an explosive expansion in Far Eastern budgets which, nearly tripling, ended up well in the lead.

This startling growth in Far Eastern expenditure was in considerable measure the result of an increased interest in Japan. For while the China budgets more than doubled from 1880 to 1893, surpassing those of the Near East from 1890 on, expenditures in Japan more than tripled, amounting at their peak to about four-fifths of those in the longer-established Chinese field. An even faster growth was shown by newly-opened Korea, which more than doubled (although from a much lower base) between 1885 and 1890. Taken all in all, this sudden upsurge of interest in the Orient in the years between 1880 and 1893 made this a period of crucial importance in the history of Far Eastern missions.

A final noteworthy aspect of the nineteenth-century missionary movement was its pattern of regional specialization by nationality and by denomination. As of 1890, both the largest British effort and—remarkably—the largest American effort as well were in India, with China in both cases the second largest field. For America, however, although not for Britain, the total East Asian deployment of funds and of ordained missionaries exceeded that in India. In China, as in India and Africa, missionaries from the British Isles outnumbered their American colleagues. If, however, the Far East is taken as a unit, the situation was reversed. In the Near East, Latin America, and Japan, the Americans were predominant. The focus of Germany, the third missionary nation, was principally on Africa. Among American denominations, the Methodists and Baptists maintained the largest establishments and the Baptists spent the most money in India; the Presbyterians led in China; and the American Board dominated the Near East and Japan (Tables 2–4). How far these figures correlated with the strategic concerns of governments, or with the economic interests of national or denominational constituencies, is a question not devoid of interest.

Table 2. Deployment of ordained Protestant missionaries by field and nationality, 1890.*

Field	Ordained missionaries	Nationality	Ordained ministers
INDIA	824	PRINCIPAL AMERICAN FIELDS	
Great Britain	408		
United States	262	India	262
Germany	99	China	198
Canada	21	Japan	146
Other	34	Near East	111
		Latin America	108
AFRICA	611	Africa	103
Germany	249		
Great Britain	185		
United States	103	Total Far East:	
Other	74	China+Japan+Korea	350
CHINA	537	PRINCIPAL BRITISH FIELDS	
Great Britain	302		
United States	198	India	408
Germany	29	China	302
Canada	8	Africa	185
		Australia-N.Z.	164
LATIN AMERICA	214	West Indies	51
United States	108	Madagascar	32
Germany	94		
Great Britain	12	Total Far East:	
		China+Japan	322
JAPAN	175		
United States	146		
Great Britain	20		
Canada	9		
NEAR EAST	135		
United States	111		
Great Britain	24		
WEST INDIES	112		
Great Britain	51		
Germany	50		
United States	7		
Canada	4		

Source: Bliss, *Encyclopaedia of Missions*, II, 620–624.

*All Basel Society and Moravian missionaries have been counted as German. All 171 CIM missionaries have been assigned to Great Britain. Some 500 SPG missionaries have been omitted from the tabulation, owing to difficulties in allocating them to specific fields; most, however, appear to have been stationed in India and Africa.

Table 3. Deployment of American Protestant missionaries by major field, 1890.[a]

Field	Ordained missionaries	Wives & other women
INDIA	262	425
Methodist North	77	108
ABMU[b]	73	134
Presbyterian North	37	71
ABCFM[c]	30	46
United Presbyterian	12	23
CHINA	198	314
Presbyterian North	48	68
Methodist North	36	66
ABCFM	33	54
ABMU	18	23
Methodist South	15	26
JAPAN	146	283
ABCFM	26	58
Presbyterian North	21	47
Methodist North	19	50
ABMU	15	26
Episcopal	13	25
NEAR EAST	111	215
ABCFM	58	116
Presbyterian North	28	59
United Presbyterian	14	25
Methodist North	4	6
Reformed Presbyterian	4	8
LATIN AMERICA	108	159
Presbyterian North	31	40
Methodist South	22	35
Methodist North	21	38
Presbyterian South	12	17
Southern Baptist	11	17
ABCFM	7	8
AFRICA	103	124
ABMU	23	16
ABCFM	20	32
United Brethren	18	21
United Presbyterian	14	25
Presbyterian North	9	10

Source: Bliss, *Encyclopaedia of Missions*, II, 620–624.
[a]Totals include minor sects, not itemized separately.
[b]American Baptist Missionary Union.
[c]American Board of Commissioners for Foreign Missions.

Table 4. Deployment of American Protestant missionaries by principal societies, 1890.

Society	Ordained Mission- aries	Wives & Other Women	Society	Ordained Mission- aries	Wives & Other Women
Presbyterian North			**ABMU**		
China	48	68	India-Burma	73	134
India	37	71	Africa	23	16
Latin America	31	40	China	18	23
Near East	28	59	Japan	15	26
Japan	21	47			
Africa	9	10			
Siam	7	11	Denominational totals	915	1491
Laos	6	10	Presbyterian North	190	321
Korea	3	5	ABCFM	183	333
			Methodist North	169	286
ABCFM			ABMU	129	199
Near East	58	116	Methodist South	48	75
China	33	54	Presbyterian South	36	46
India	30	46	Southern Baptist	33	45
Japan	26	58	United Presbyterian	26	48
Africa	20	32	Episcopal	23	47
Latin America	7	8	Dutch Reformed	23	34
Micronesia	5	14	Disciples of Christ	19	16
Hawaiian Islands	2	2	United Brethren	18	21
Europe	2	3	Seventh Day Adventists	18	20
Methodist North					
India	77	108			
China	36	66			
Latin America	21	38			
Japan	19	50			
Malaysia	5	5			
Near East	4	6			
Europe	4	4			
Korea	3	9			

Source: Bliss, *Encyclopaedia of Missions*, II, 606–611, 620–624.

IMPLEMENTATION

The prosecution of the evangelical ends called for the development of specific means, which had not been precisely spelled out during the prayer meeting of 1806 when Samuel Mills and his fellow Williams students, sheltering from a rainstorm in the lee of a hay-stack, first resolved to carry the gospel overseas. To begin the work required only the support of the Congregational elders; to continue it, some rationalization of procedures was necessary. But all this went step by step. With the somewhat impulsive dispatch of the first missionaries to India, and increasingly with the ventures to the Sandwich Islands and the Levant, the American Board found itself, without precedent or conscious planning, responsible for the management of America's first multinational corporation. In this position it was faced with problems—the recruitment of personnel, the need for money, the necessity of defining policy—which had hardly been contemplated in advance and which would require considerable working out.

As the country's first multinational enterprise, the Board confronted tasks previously undertaken only by the government. Of all American institutions, only the State Department during Jefferson's tenure as secretary and the navy during his presidency had grappled with the difficulties of creating, staffing, and supervising a transoceanic structure. In other respects, too, the situations were similar. Like the State and Navy Departments, the Board found itself obliged to issue periodic reports for the edification of its constituency. Like the government, it had to set up a tax system, reaching out in its own case through Sunday school and church collections to the creation of a network of regional agents. Faced, like the State and Navy Departments, with the problem of overseas transfer of funds, it came, after early experiments with the shipment of bullion and with bills on Indian merchants, to the same answer: the use of the international banking facilities of the English firm of Baring Brothers.[18]

These administrative problems, however unanticipated during the original rainstorm or in the course of later study at Andover, appear to have been efficiently handled. By the 1820s the establishment of Sandwich Island and Near Eastern missions and the expansion of work among the American Indians had called for full-time administrative personnel and permanent quarters. In 1838 the Board moved from rented rooms to the occupancy of its own building, an event that can be taken as marking the time by which procedural problems had been solved and an administrative structure created that could cope with the expansion of existing efforts and with the opening of new fields in Africa and the Far East.[19]

As important as the development of supporting structures was the choice of fields for evangelization. Here the translation of the Great Command into specific efforts depended in large degree on the actions of those in the field. Like other pioneering Americans—the Smyrna and Canton merchants, the Astorians, the emigrants to

Texas—the early evangelists were both far ahead and independent of their government. Closed out of Burma, the first missionaries had sought out fields in India and Ceylon on their own. Ten years before the Turkish treaty of 1830, Pliny Fisk and Levi Parsons had toured Egypt and Palestine, and negotiations with the Turks were still in progress when Eli Smith and H. G. O. Dwight commenced the remarkable journey that would take them through Anatolia, Armenia, and northern Persia. While the Greek war for independence still continued, missionaries had entered the Greek islands and the assistant secretary of the American Board had explored the Morea. The mission to the Nestorians preceded the establishment of treaty relations with Persia by twenty-two years and the opening of the Teheran legation by half a century. This adventurous and energetic approach provided suitable precedents for the subsequent investigation of the Dutch East Indies, for the travels of David Abeel, and for the voyage of the *Morrison* to Japan in 1837.

With the need to seek out suitable mission fields went that of developing suitable missionary techniques. Just as the aim of sharing the blessings of a pure Christianity gave little specific guidance as to the choice of targets, so it afforded little by way of concrete procedural instruction. The first missionaries to India were adjured to form themselves into a church and a community and then, presumably, to hope for the best. Those to Western Asia were instructed to consider their mission as "part of an extended and continually extending system of benevolent action for the recovery of the world to God, to virtue, and to happiness;" in furtherance of these ends, they were to ascertain "What good can be done? and By what means?" for the various peoples of the region. The orders to the larger band dispatched to the Sandwich Islands were to aim "at nothing short of covering those islands with fruitful fields and pleasant dwellings."[20] Instructions as general as these reflected not only the generally benevolent attitude of the Americans but also, it would seem, their considerable ignorance of the situation on the far shore.

The procedures that were adopted, then, were not so much dictated by the Board as worked out first between the missionaries and their clients overseas, and later in the interaction between the missionaries and their Boston headquarters. In this three-way interplay between the emissaries of American benevolence, the receiving societies, and the home base, a position of the greatest importance came to be held by the Reverend Rufus Anderson, who as corresponding secretary dominated the work of the Board from 1832 to 1866.[21]

From the general and understandable nineteenth-century tendency to consider Christianity and civilization as opposite sides of the same coin, Anderson was curiously exempt. "The proper test of success in missions," he wrote in 1869, "is not the progress of civilization but the evidence of a religious life." Reflecting on the civilizing intentions evidenced in the original Sandwich Island mission, he observed that the sending of "Christianity and civilization forth together, as cooperating forces . . . [was] found to be inappropriate. A simpler, cheaper, more effectual means of civilizing the savage, was the gospel alone." In this spirit Anderson refused requests from overseas for the dispatch of "pious mechanics" and of philosophical apparatus and worked steadily for an emphasis on preaching and itineration, for education in the vernacular rather than in English, and for the removal of schools from the seductions of cosmopolitan seaports to the Jeffersonian environment of the interior.[22]

Such aims, no doubt, did Anderson credit, but the effort to separate Christianity and civilization ran against the Hopkinsian precepts and involved him in a continuing struggle with both the missionaries in the field and the spirit of the age. The education intended to produce Bible readers and native preachers turned out to have wider uses. The translation of Bible and tract was followed by the translation of textbooks. With such publications as Daniel Temple's Greek *Magazine of Useful Knowledge,* the missionary presses opened new paths. The use of medical missionaries and the work of missionary wives and female assistants for the women of their communities had important secondary implications. Although William Goodell at Constantinople clearly recognized that it was the Gospel and "not the American gospel" that he was appointed to preach, even he found it hard to resist the attractions of teaching modern science. For Cyrus Hamlin, concerned for the development of natural resources and for a modernizing education, these tensions eventuated in separation from the American Board and in the founding of Robert College, " a decided Christian school," but one that was also decidedly independent. On all the missionaries in the field the Westernizing aspirations of their client populations exerted continual pressure. For what Anderson deplored as deracination and what others would applaud as modernization, the missionary effort turned out to be a potent force. In the Near East, by the late nineteenth and early twentieth centuries, its effects would be visible in the brain drain, the depopulation of rural villages, and emigration to America.[23]

In all these practices, doctrines, and tensions there was a sufficiency of precedent available against the time when access could be gained to the traditional civilizations of the Far East. There, too, education began on a small scale and grew apace, evangelization became increasingly identified with social service and modernization, and the notable pioneers followed much the same patterns. Early Near Eastern linguists and translators, such as Jonas King and Eli Smith, had their distinguished successors in S. Wells Williams and Elijah Bridgman. As missionary printers, Williams and Ira Tracy built on the tradition of Homan Hallock, the gifted Beirut printer and designer of types. Peter Parker, who "opened China to the Gospel at the point of his lancet," followed in the path marked out by Asahel Grant, the medical missionary to the Nestorians. Most significant of all the inheritances from the early years, and one that subsumed all specific precedents and practices, was the emphasis on the importance of the individual which the missionary movement brought to every group with which it came in contact through its stress on the conversion experience, on education, on medical care, and on the status of women. The importance of the extension of modern education and modern medicine to the outer world is obvious enough. But it is one of the curiosities of history that all the countries in which women have recently exercised significant political power—Israel, India, Ceylon, and China—were nineteenth-century targets of American missionary endeavor.

Finally, any consideration of the American effort to evangelize the world should take note of its intended duration. This, it must be emphasized, was to be brief. As in the educational system of Joseph Lancaster, whose precepts the missionaries embodied in their schools, the function of the teachers was to plant the mustard seed, to start the leaven working. This concept, dating from the earliest aspirations of Samuel Hopkins for the evangelization of Africa, was the basis of Rufus Anderson's pressure for the speedy establishment of self-governing, self-supporting, and self-propagating native churches. With time, as the imminent millennium receded steadily into the future, the sense of urgency perhaps diminished, but the basic idea was slow to disappear. Asked how long he and his colleagues proposed to sojourn in Turkey, William Goodell replied that they would stay only until there were so many good schools that theirs were no longer attended, and so much good preaching that none came to hear them preach. Firm in their faith, the early missionaries were confident that with God's providence a few conversions in a pagan society or a beginning purification of the Oriental Churches would start a self-perpetuating process.[24] In time the institutionalization of the missionary effort, the slowness of actual progress, and the growing gap between the Western world and the periphery, the result of the trick played on humanity by steam, would combine to change this attitude. Ultimately the missionaries would find it very hard to let go. But in the beginning there was no idea that they had come to stay.

MISSIONS AND THE LARGER COMMUNITY

It has already been noted that the American presence in far places did not always take a standardized form. In the Near and Far East, the extension of missionary effort was paralleled by the outreach of commercial and naval activity; in India and Africa, missionary work went on without these accompaniments. But whether alone or in company overseas, a work of such magnitude and duration could hardly be mounted in isolation from other aspects—intellectual, economic, or political—of American, or indeed Anglo-American, life.

In contributing to the remarkable nineteenth-century growth of Western knowledge of far places and to the development of a cosmopolitan world culture, the missionary movement played an important role. Indeed, an elevated curiosity about the outer world seems to have been a part of the enterprise from the start. In his famous election sermon of 1783, Ezra Stiles had not only expressed hope for the success of American missions and the expansion of American commerce, but had also foreseen, as an important by-product of these activities, the importation, digestion, perfection, and re-exportation of the "wisdom and literature of the east."[25] The American Board's instructions of 1819 to Fisk and Parsons suggested that, in addition to communicating suggestions as to how best to do good, and "facts, descriptions, notices" concerning the peoples of the Levant, they might "send home some books or ancient manuscripts, interesting to the student."[26] From the beginning such "facts, descriptions, notices" were published in the *Missionary Herald,* and this periodical literature was soon supplemented by works in book form. The early deaths of Parsons and Fisk gave rise in the 1820s to memoirs descriptive of lands and labors overseas. The account of the greatest early Near Eastern exploratory venture, Eli Smith's *Researches in Armenia,* remains today an interesting description of a region then very little known. But the real harvest began in 1841 with the publication of Edward Robinson's *Biblical Researches in Palestine,* in which, on the basis of explorations carried out with Smith three years earlier, the author laid the foundation for all subsequent work in Palestinian archeology. In the next year the American Oriental Society was founded, with a large infusion of missionary charter members. In 1848 Williams' *Middle Kingdom* was published, and in the fifties there came major works by American missionaries on the civilizations of India and Africa.[27]

By this time, too, the successors of Parsons and Fisk had gone far beyond the mere transmission of books and manuscripts. Mineralogical samples, archeological artifacts, pagan idols and weapons of war, birds' eggs, snakeskins, and corals decorated the cabinets of Williams, Amherst, and Yale, expanding the undergraduate intellectual horizon and serving as recruiting propaganda.[28] In 1842 some members of the Persian mission brought home for exhibition a live Nestorian bishop.[29] Inevitably, what many had conceived of as an export of religious truth turned out, as Stiles had anticipated, to be an exchange of goods; and while the targets of missionary zeal were being enlightened about the gospel religion and the arts of the West, the sending societies were having their world view broadened. How far one can distinguish the missionary from the intellectual in all this is uncertain, but it is worth remembering to what extent, as late as the mid-twentieth century, American expertise regarding Near and Far Eastern cultures and languages was concentrated in the missionary community. In the Second World War the "BIJs"—individuals born in Japan of whom most were missionary-connected—formed an important part of the intelligence effort. In 1953, when the Korean armistice talks began at Panmunjom, the American interpreters were two grandsons of Horace B. Underwood, who in 1885 had founded the Presbyterian mission to Korea.

With commerce in goods, as opposed to commerce in ideas, the relationship of the missionary enterprise was less clear-cut. Plainly enough the occupation of any overseas mission field depended on the existence of shipping connections, however exiguous. To Edwards and Hopkins, moreover, as to many of their lay contemporaries, commerce was both an obvious part of God's design and a primary means of uniting humanity and bringing about the happy world society. In time, missionary publications would argue that the use of chairs, tables, and Yankee clocks were visible signs of grace, and that the commercial development of the Hawaiian Islands stood as justification for their evangelization. By the end of the nineteenth century some of the claims about the relationship between God and trade had become both sweeping—"Missions promote commerce by correcting heathen dishonesty"—and vulgar—"Races that accept Christianity almost invariably increase their imports."[30] They may also, of course, have been correct.

But these latter-day arguments seem to have been largely contrived in the hope of securing increased support for the greater end of conversion. In fact, the two streams of a growing commerce and an expanding missionary effort appear to have run more often separate or parallel than merged. The traders had preceded the missionaries to the Levant, and while the latter were affably received by the Smyrna merchant community, their prime target was Jerusalem, where there was no trade at all. Commencement of missionary work at Constantinople did coincide with the establishment of diplomatic relations and with hopes for an expanded commerce. But the missionaries by no means limited their efforts to capital or seaport, and the work invested in Greece, and in inland missions in Anatolia, Persia, Egypt, and Bulgaria, was out of all proportion to the commercial attractions of these regions. Although commerce, over the long run, continued to be seen as a civilizing influence, grave doubts were felt about its initial impact—"the first contacts of commerce are for the most part evil"—and the remorse elicited by the Levantine trade in New England rum was the same as that produced in other times and places by Hawaiian prostitution, the Chinese opium traffic, and Pacific Ocean blackbirding.[31]

Whatever their relation with commerce, the missionaries were in one respect similar to the overseas merchants, as indeed to the Western pioneers: they were, in the early years, very much on their own. For these evangelical frontiersmen, bringers of glad tidings that were not always welcomed by the intended recipients, this situation presented occupational hazards. In British-controlled India the problem was minimal, once protection from the East India Company authorities had been gained, and the same was true for areas of British influence in Africa as well as for the Sandwich Islands. But elsewhere the position of the missionaries, subversive actors in regions of doubtful or at least very different systems of law and order, was less secure. Legend to the contrary, few were in fact eaten, but their situation did give rise to two important questions. How far could American missionaries rely for support on their government, which itself, of course, recognized no establishment of religion? Could their wards, as well as they themselves, expect protection against local intolerance and opposition?

Here the relations between missions and government required some working out. Although the missionaries ultimately became a focus of gunboat diplomacy, this was far from the case at the start. Theoretically they were engaged in a nonpolitical effort for the salvation of individual souls—their missions, they insisted, were not to Greece but to the Greeks, not to Palestine but to the Jews—and their early indifference to the secular arm was matched by governmental ignorance of their existence. The first naval visits to the Levant were concerned exclusively with the negotiation of a treaty of commerce with Turkey. In the 1830s a Constantinople missionary urged his colleagues not to compromise themselves by close association with the representatives of the American government, and this attitude was supported by Commodore David Porter, the chargé d'affaires. [32] Curiously enough, naval support for the Near Eastern missionaries, and by implication for those elsewhere, was in large part a consequence of the need to support, on the far side of the globe, the missionaries against the navy.

In Hawaii in 1826, the arrival of the U.S.S. *Dolphin,* Lieutenant John Percival commanding, had led to a struggle with the emissaries of the American Board over whether the amorous proclivities of the local females should be encouraged or restrained. Although Mad Jack and his crew won out, the victory was short-lived. At home the Board took up the challenge, a court of inquiry followed, and in 1829 the U.S.S. *Vincennes* reached the islands with a message from President Adams which commended "letters and . . . the Religion of the

Christian's Bible" as "the best, and the only means, by which the prosperity and happiness of nations can be advanced and continued." Shortly reprinted in Jonathan Elliot's *American Diplomatic Code,* a manual adopted by both the State and Navy Departments, this endorsement appears to have acquired pretty much the force of policy. In time a Mediterranean Squadron commander would write the Beirut missionaries in similarly gratifying terms, emphasizing the interest that the President and the Secretary of the Navy entertained for their enterprise and their well-being.[33]

For the missionaries in the Ottoman Empire the existence of diplomatic relations, the presence of the squadron, and the presidential endorsement of their purpose provided a foundation on which to build. When the Syrian wars brought chaos to the Lebanon, Commodore Porter secured the establishment of consulates at Aleppo, Beirut, and Alexandria and arranged for visits by squadron units to the Syrian coast. But by 1841 Porter's attitude had begun to seem too restrained: at Constantinople the missionaries took the extraordinary step of intercepting and returning one of his dispatches to argue for a change in phraseology, while in America the Board pressed the State Department to provide stronger support. In 1844 missionary concern for the security of the workers among the Nestorians brought about the first move toward a treaty with Persia. Two years later the American minister at Constantinople threatened to break relations if the Turks did not mend their attitude toward the missionaries. In 1852–1853 a dispute over a real estate claim between the Greek government and the solitary and beleaguered representative of the American Board gave rise to the greatest Mediterranean show of naval force since the Neapolitan claims controversy of 1832. Renewed trouble in Syria in 1858 led to another naval demonstration, a tour of the region by the American minister, and his participation with the emissaries of the other Protestant powers in a joint protest to the Porte, for which act he was scolded by the Buchanan government on principled Monroeist grounds.[34]

As the century wore on, matters got worse. In Turkey, as in most other areas, missionary successes had been confined to minorities, discovered or created, and with the progressive decay of the polyglot Turkish Empire this situation brought increasing tension. By the time of the Eastern Crisis of 1876 the problems of protecting missionaries and missionary property were such as to frustrate the desire of the

Navy Department to shift the squadron base to the Atlantic coast of Europe, and to cause the squadron commander to note both "the importance of the interests which American Citizens have . . . created, in Turkey and in Syria" and the "many and influential friends at home" who expected effective protection of these citizens and their interests.[35] By this time, too, the development of Armenian nationalism and Turkish xenophobia had brought the question of the missionaries' clients to the fore. Here the difficult and lasting problems that arose were reflected in increased emigration to America, in repeated naval visits to the East, in the Cleveland administration's tentative agreement to joint intervention with Great Britain, and in a growing twentieth-century commitment that would lead to proposals for an American mandate over most of the former Ottoman Empire.[36]

This discussion of the relationships between the American missionary movement and the intellectual, commercial, and governmental sectors has so far been set in purely national terms. Such an approach is perhaps too narrow, for the nineteenth-century Protestant missionary enterprise, far from being confined within national boundaries, involved the entire Protestant world. The point has been made in a related connection by John K. Fairbank, who noted that American merchants in China can hardly be studied in isolation from their British opposite numbers.[37] What was true of American merchants was also true of American missionaries, whose work intersected with various aspects of British life at almost every turn.

Jonathan Edwards' *Life of Brainerd* had been influential in the early British missionary movement, and especially in its effect on William Carey. Carey's career in India was an inspiration to the Americans. The infant American Board had sought to join the pre-existing British effort. That India became the first American field resulted from the British presence, and free access to that field from pressure exerted in Parliament by British evangelicals. The martyrdom of Henry Martyn called the attention of the Americans to the possibilities of work in Persia. Books such as Smith's *Researches in Armenia* were published in both countries for the edification of the transnational evangelical community. In the early years the emissaries of the American Board benefited from the support of British consuls and the shelter of the British base at Malta. Even after the United States had established diplomatic relations with Turkey, the more forceful attitude of the British had its attractions. Although to American diplomats Stratford Canning seemed the personification of "English egotism," his successes in gaining abolition of the death penalty for apostasy and recognition for the Protestant Armenians made him, to the American missionaries, a person beyond all praise.[38]

As the movement grew, other connections developed. British banking facilities moved the American Board's funds. British philanthropy supported the Turkish Missions Aid Society and contributed to the founding of the Syrian Protestant College. At Constantinople during the Crimean War, Cyrus Hamlin did the British army's laundry and baked its bread. The British and Foreign Bible Society and the American Bible Society cooperated in spreading the Word. By the close of the nineteenth century the ecumenical and cooperative aspects of the enterprise had begun to be institutionalized in regional and world missionary conferences.[39]

One need not, however, postulate an identity of Anglo-American interest. Between the two main parts of the English-speaking world there were obvious differences in social structure, economic development, religious organization, and military and political style. The Americans pursued happiness and looked forward to the millennium; the British acquired an empire.[40] Within each country, moreover, there were functional differences in attitude. On numerous occasions British diplomatic and consular officers gave assistance to American missionaries. Surprisingly, perhaps, despite two wars and a succession of diplomatic crises, the two navies got along well, and the support provided the Mediterranean Squadron by the Gibraltar and Malta dockyards had its later reflection in "Blood is thicker than water." But the merchants were generally competitive and the diplomats still more so: one of the most persistent themes in nineteenth-century correspondence from Mediterranean posts was suspicion of British political aims in Turkey, Persia, and Egypt.[41]

Despite national differences, commercial competition, and political rivalry, one can distinguish here an expansive Protestant culture, spreading from the two sides of the North Atlantic to the uttermost ends of the earth. For the historian this presents the problem of dealing with transnational cultural manifestations and with the permeability, varying by time and function, of national boundaries and national labels. How are we to describe this particular culture, which in any event was not limited to overseas evangelism but extended to railroad building, resource development, and other aspects of modernization? The Protestant missionary movement of the nineteenth and early twentieth centuries was part of a larger development that transcended Anglo-American differences and boundaries and quarrels in much the same was that Islam transcends its own internal divisions. What is the name for this Anglo-Saxon Islam?[42]

THE PROSOPOGRAPHY PROBLEM

Despite the extensive infiltration of the American academic and diplomatic establishments by former missionaries and missionary descendants, the movement and its members have until recently attracted little but pietistic attention. Serious biographies are in short supply. There is no life of James L. Barton, and Rufus Anderson is not noticed in the *Dictionary of American Biography*. More important than the absence of lives of individuals is the lack of any good missionary prosopography or collective biography.

Regrettably, perhaps, the interest in genealogy, so lively during the period of Jukeses and Kallikaks and unrestricted immigration, ebbed noticeably a couple of generations ago. Although there are various fields in which such information would be of great interest, it is hard to find a precise analog to the Carnegie Institution's volume of 1919 on the heredity of naval officers.[43] Yet this work, however inadequate as a guide to breeding a race of heroes, is extremely useful in its demonstration of family links and of who was connected to whom. For the missionaries and for their domestic constituency, such knowledge can be very suggestive.

The early appeal and potential leverage of the missionary idea was evidenced by the composition of the original American Board, with its weighty membership of college presidents, learned divines, and men of affairs. Some of the links between missionaries in the field and other sectors of American society were apparent in the early interplay of American activities at Constantinople. The missionaries at Canton received valuable support from the trading firm of Olyphant and Company. Peter Parker was connected by marriage to Daniel Webster. The virtues of an appropriate ancestry were demonstrated by missionary rejoicing at the appointment as secretary of state of William M. Evarts, whose parents had been married by

Timothy Dwight and whose father had been an early secretary of the American Board.[44] With the passage of time an important new phenomenon developed in the growth of missionary dynasties.

The form such dynasties took was greatly influenced by an aspect of the missionary career that differentiated it, for example, from that of naval officer or diplomat. This was the lack of intertheater transfer. Among the missionaries, tours of duty were not limited, promotion in any systematic form did not exist, and experience gained in one assignment was not generally transferable to a higher level of responsibility in another mission field. For this aspect of personnel policy the linguistic problems inherent in a career devoted to preaching, teaching, and writing in the local vernacular provided a sufficient reason. But the consequences of the policy were both important and presumably unanticipated: a specialization by area of endeavor, which was passed on from father to son and which led to the formation of what can almost be described as regional ruling families.[45]

The family of H. G. O. Dwight, the explorer of Armenia and long a dominant figure at the Constantinople mission, had a lasting connection with Turkey: two of his sons figured importantly in the planning of Robert College; a third became an important missionary writer and editor; a grandson wrote *Stamboul Nights*. From 1857 to 1889 Isaac Bliss, a former missionary at Erzerum, served as Near Eastern agent of the American Bible Society; his son Edwin, a missionary editor, later became an important propagandist for the Armenians. Charles Riggs, son of the great translator Elias Riggs, taught at Robert and Anatolia colleges before becoming, early in the twentieth century, the Near Eastern secretary of the American Board. By this time most of the pioneer Constantinople missionary families had become connected by intermarriage, and in Syria the situation was much the same. There a son of the pioneer Isaac Bird had joined the mission in 1853. One son of the noted doctor and educator Cornelius Van Dyck became a missionary, and another became secretary of the consulate general at Cairo. Howard Bliss, son of the founder of the Syrian Protestant College, succeeded his father in the presidency and was himself followed (like Cyrus Hamlin at Robert College) by his son-in-law.[46]

All this might seem to be of purely antiquarian interest, given the lifetime exile that was the usual missionary lot, save for some important considerations. One was the fact that some missionaries, linked with a particular field by ancestry or experience, returned to the United States to work on mission boards and so to influence policy. In the ancestral category the case of Charles Riggs, already noted, provides an example of the transfer of expertise from the field to the area of central administration. Of the apostolic as opposed to the familial succession, an outstanding example was that of James L. Barton, educated at Middlebury during the presidency of Cyrus Hamlin. After theological study and ordination, Barton became first a missionary at Harput and then president of Euphrates College. In 1892 he was called back to Boston, where as foreign secretary he became the dominant personality of the American Board and a leading figure in the organization of Near East Relief and in the politics of the proposed Armenian mandate.[47]

In addition to the transfer of theater personnel to headquarters duty, the missionaries had other links with home. Missionaries and missionary children went to college, and there acquired friends in an age when higher education was the prerogative of the few. Missionaries, like ordinary people, married and acquired in-laws, and so did missionary sons and daughters. Returned missionaries and missionary descendants entered academic life, and it seems safe to attribute some influence, however hard to measure, to the Gouchers and Gulicks, the Labarees, Latourettes, and Lybyers, the Morses, Millses, and Speers, who infiltrated the colleges of the United States. Since the cause of missions required money and a means of approaching those who had it, these developments were very helpful in providing the movement with useful leverage through its "many and influential friends at home."

By the latter part of the nineteenth century the philanthrophy of the many, expressed in the penny in the plate, had been joined by that of the increasingly prosperous few. The result was a close linkage of the missionary establishment, and perhaps still closer of the overseas colleges, to the newly coalescing financial community at home. The merchant Christopher Robert was instrumental in founding the college that bore his name. The banker Morris K. Jesup was an important supporter of the Syrian Protestant College; his sometime partner John S. Kennedy headed the Robert College board. The industrialist Charles R. Crane was a trustee and supporter of both the Constantinople colleges. Most important of all was the Stokes,

Phelps, and Dodge clan, which for five generations contributed both wealth and devotion to the Near Eastern missionary and educational effort.[48]

In addition to the familial and financial connections, the collegiate links were important. These too varied over time, for the contributions of American institutions of higher education to the cause of foreign missions have been extremely diverse. Yale produced Jonathan Edwards and Samuel Hopkins, Yale-in-China, and Henry Luce. Unitarian Harvard appears to have given little or nothing. The up-country colleges, first of New England and New York and subsequently of the Middle West, provided the bulk of the missionaries. Mary Lyon's "Protestant nunnery" at Mount Holyoke sent forth a steady stream of female workers and replacement missionary wives. In 1881 the "Oberlin band" set forth for China.

By the early twentieth century a leading place in the American involvement with the Near East had been assumed by graduates of Presbyterian Princeton. After teaching in Turkey, Charles Riggs became a secretary of the American Board. In the Persian revolution of 1909 Howard Baskerville, a teacher at a missionary school, was killed while leading a charge on a royalist position. Through the catastrophic period of the First World War the missionary physician Edward M. Dodd stood by his Nestorian clients, isolated but not forgotten. A. H. Lybyer, who had taught at Robert College, at Oberlin, and at the University of Illinois, played an ambitious part in Colonel House's Inquiry, at the Paris peace conference, and with the postwar King-Crane Commission. Allen W. Dulles, related on one side to two secretaries of state and descended on the other from a line of Presbyterian missionaries and clergymen, served as assistant to Admiral Bristol at Constantinople and later in the State Department as chief of the Division of Near Eastern Affairs. Since a number of Princeton graduates were also working for the Peking YMCA, the connection was clearly not limited to the Near East. But in any case, the record of Old Nassau in the export of disinterested benevolence during the Progressive period was impressive.[49]

The most striking example of this web of interconnected influence, at least in the Near Eastern context, appears in the history of the Dodge family and in the person of Cleveland H. Dodge, a Princeton graduate of the class of 1879. His great-grandfather, Anson G. Phelps, had given generously to the American Bible Society and the

American Board. His grandfather, the "Christian merchant" William E. Dodge, had been a vice-president of the Board and a contributor to the Syrian Protestant College. His father had been a trustee of that institution; an uncle taught at the college, contributed to its funds, and served as president of the board of trustees; a sister was an important supporter of the American College for Girls at Constantinople. Among Cleveland Dodge's own philanthropic interests the Near Eastern field came first, as he carried on the family tradition as president of the Robert College board and as an organizer of Near East Relief, as well as through the lives of his children. One of these married a Robert College professor; another married a daughter of Howard Bliss and in time succeeded to the presidency of the American University of Beirut; a third became the first president of the Near East Foundation. Most important of all, the individual at the center of this generational web of Near Eastern philanthropic interest was a college classmate and lifelong friend of Woodrow Wilson, whose professorial salary he had supplemented, whose educational reforms he had supported in his capacity of Princeton trustee, whose gubernatorial and presidential campaigns he had helped finance, and on whom at the crucial moment he brought pressure to keep the United States from going to war with Turkey and Bulgaria.[50]

Yet however central the role of the Dodges and of the Princeton connection, these by no means exhausted the avenues of influence available to the missionary interest. In this period of new wealth the railroads, joining cities and seashore, had nationalized the upper class; everyone who mattered lived within train ride and walking distance of everyone else, and links between the missionary, financial, and political communities abounded. Theodore Roosevelt had known Cleveland Dodge most of his life and had been a boyhood friend of Howard Bliss. John Hay was a cousin of George Washburn, the second president of Robert College. Summering at Magnolia, Massachusetts, Colonel House found himself near neighbor to George Washburn, Jr. Close by in Ipswich lived Charles R. Crane, chairman of the board of Constantinople Woman's College, trustee of Robert College, and future member of the King-Crane Commission, whose only son in May 1915 became personal secretary to Robert Lansing.[51]

So extensively and comfortably ensconced within the structure of the eastern American establishment, the Near Eastern Presbyterians found themselves in an enviable position. Some of their influence clearly derived from the moral and intellectual currents of the Progressive Era, and some from the geographical and social location of the Presbyterian community. It would be interesting to have comparable if similarly impressionistic information on the Baptists or Methodists, or on those Presbyterians for whom East Asia was the primary concern. Yet in addition to all the domestic variables—sectarian, geographic, economic, and social—some importance would appear to attach to the history of the particular mission field. The picture here sketched of the expansion and solidification of the Near Eastern interest suggests the importance of maturity, and of a half-century or more of continued work as a prerequisite for establishmentarian status. If, at the time of the First World War, the Chinese missionary effort lacked a comparable degree of influence in high place and gained such influence only in the 1930s, the fact may reflect the prosopographical differences between an endeavor that blossomed before the Civil War and one whose great period of expansion came only in the 1880s and 1890s.[52]

VALENTIN H. RABE

Evangelical Logistics:
Mission Support and Resources to 1920

When the eight young Americans who are numbered as their country's first foreign missionaries set sail one cold February morning in 1812, perhaps one-tenth of their homeland's population were actually members of the young nation's Protestant churches. Many of their countrymen were at best half-hearted Christians, and thousands of Indians had never heard the gospel preached. The inexperienced American Board of Commissioners for Foreign Missions, which these young men had prodded into existence with their petition to a Congregational ministers' meeting two years earlier, provided them with no guarantee of permanent support or guidance. Yet they were dedicated to "*foreign* missions and *missions for life*."[1] They initiated an outflow of thousands of American Christians no less patriotic, ambitious, or aware of the imperfect evangelization of their homeland than the millions who stayed behind, but equally convinced that their duty lay with the unfortunate peoples who had never had the opportunity to choose the only religion which promised salvation.

During the decades after independence, foreign missions were an aberrant cause, for unlike the galaxy of evangelical reform groups organized to deal with specific political and social issues, the missionary societies addressed no immediate national objectives or problems. Their proponents could not even count on purely religious and evangelical motives for support from other Protestants, because the absence of a clear theology of missions, and authoritative objections to overseas evangelization dating back to the Reformation, provided comfortable rationalizations for continued disinterest.[2]

Since there was neither an orthodox incentive nor prohibition, however, the insignificant minority of foreign mission advocates who became active after the spread of the Second Great Awakening through New England at the turn of the century were free to select and emphasize the texts or interpretations that supported their own convictions. They drew support from two themes in Protestant thought that also contributed to other expressions of the early nineteenth-century missionary spirit, such as the founding of numerous home mission societies and organizations dedicated to a variety of domestic moral reforms.

The most relevant incentive to missions lay in Samuel Hopkins' stubborn defense of a waning Puritanism. Jonathan Edwards' most influential disciple had admitted in his apologetics that a sovereign God could undoubtedly change the heart of the most depraved and ignorant heathen as easily as that of the most enlightened American sinner. But if He exercised His power unilaterally, the regeneration achieved would be incomplete, while Christians would be deprived of the benefits of "right and proper exercises of Christian virtue and holiness."[3] Hopkins developed this theme into a doctrine of "disinterested benevolence." The elect, he argued, had the duty to serve the greater glory of God by engaging in pursuits that would add to the sum total of happiness—of "being in general." This was to be done without expecting any reward either in this world or in the future.[4] Hopkins, having insisted on a disinterested love of God's glory, would not tolerate the liberal theological drift that promised eternal happiness in return for devotion to the common good.[5] In so doing, he made certain that the men and women who responded by offering themselves to service overseas would be a selfless, supremely self-confident group.

The varied religious influences and imperatives that motivated the missionary pioneers eventually focused on a traditional Christian objective. The kingdom of God, references to which abound in both the Old and New Testaments, and which H. Richard Niebuhr identified as the dominant concept in American Christianity,[6] provided a flexible intellectual framework to serve as a synthetic theology of missions. During the revivals that produced the American missionary movement at the beginning of the nineteenth century, the Puritan notion of an invisible kingdom composed of the regenerate changed its emphasis to the realization of Christ's kingdom in and through individuals. Since God's grace would inevitably be reflected in the lives of individual Christians, the realization of the kingdom came to be expected in visible form on earth. Still later, the kingdom of God came to mean almost exclusively the "Kingdom on earth," an interpretation that lent itself most effectively to the revitalized foreign mission activity at the end of the nineteenth century.[7]

The mission of the American evangelical churches to the world, then, was undertaken by a distinct minority, led by a few outstanding, heroic figures. Similar conditions prevailed in Europe. During most of the nineteenth century it was the Careys, Judsons, Morrisons, and Livingstones who characterized the movement and achieved successes against overwhelming odds. Their achievements were the fruit not of a militant missionary church but of a handful of stubborn pioneers, which the board and other agencies of the Protestant churches later in the century sought to preserve and institutionalize. The motives of the early missionaries were largely the personalized imperatives of their religious convictions, because the churches and theologians paid them only passing attention.

DECLINE AND RENAISSANCE IN THE AGE OF TRUSTS

The early missionary spirit usually took institutional form in the creation of denominational mission boards and societies, although the pioneer American Board remained a nondenominational agency until the Civil War. Flourishing as part of an evangelical crusade of temperance, Bible, abolitionist, and other voluntary reform associations, the foreign mission societies were aided by a growing public awareness of the rest of the world. As naval expeditions and increasing American participation in world commerce provided both fuller geographical knowledge and easier access to Asia, several societies rapidly developed sizable overseas commitments.

By 1854, for example, the Presbyterian Board of Foreign Missions had an income of $140,502, used to support 48 ordained missionaries and an equal number of lay teachers and other Americans abroad, while the American Baptist Missionary Union maintained 115 missionaries and female assistants outside the United States.[8]

Less than thirty years after the first American Board evangelist had left Massachusetts, there were 384 such missionaries laboring abroad.[9] By 1850, American Board missionaries were active in India, Ceylon, China, Siam, Micronesia, Hawaii, South and West Africa, Syria, Persia, and Turkey, having surrendered in previous decades a number of other foreign stations as well as terminating work among the American Indians.[10] Although during its first decade the board had supported this work with an average annual income of only $20,000, it received well over $250,000 yearly throughout the 1840s, and collected $429,799 in 1860 despite the loss of several supporting denominations and the distraction of the impending war.[11]

Despite these promising advances, the decades after the middle of the nineteenth century were marked by a general decline of public support, which required decades to repair. During only one year between the end of the war and 1880 did the American Board's receipts reach even the 1865 level.[12] Its high point of 395 missionaries in the field in 1850 had decreased by 80 at the end of the Civil War and did not creep back to the prewar level for another decade. [13]

Although the decline in funds and volunteers was not disastrous, there was disappointment that the release of energies and resources that had been absorbed by the war did not automatically result in at least the rate of steady expansion which had attended the 14.5-fold increase of communicants in the evangelical churches between 1800 and 1860.[14] An American Board secretary complained in 1865 that "the earnest supporters of modern missions are almost as few as ever," while the participants in the annual meeting preceeding the depression year of 1873 were told that mission societies on both sides of the Atlantic were faced with "an increasing reluctance to engage in this service."[15] Despite the depression's end and a magnificent $1,000,000 bequest in 1879, the members at the American Board's 1881 meeting were warned that "with all our enlarged opportunities, with all our growth in numbers and in power as churches of Christ in this country, it is a painful fact that distinctively missionary effort has not kept pace with other religious activities."[16]

A comparison of the evidence of ebbing missionary interest among American Protestants at the beginning of the 1880s, with the energy that was directed toward such new concerns as the application of social Christianity to the problems of an urban industrial society, could lead to the conclusion that the foreign mission movement was a waning relic of the enthusiasm and theology of past generations. Like the temperance, sabbatarian, and home mission societies born in the same period and environment, some of the foreign mission agencies might be expected to survive with dwindling support from a faithful minority, but their days of influence apparently lay in the past. Even Protestant members of the post-Civil War generation showed interest in more profitable crusades. As if to verify this general impression, Arthur Pierson, a Presbyterian minister, published the emotional *Crisis of Missions* in 1886 to publicize "the great fact that we have reached the most critical point in mission history."[17]

The crisis identified by Pierson consisted primarily of the apathy that met calls to seize the unprecedented opportunities available to the mission movement. Imperialism was opening up countries previously closed to the missionary. Innovations in communications and transportation were making these fields accessible. Industrialization and population increases were making the United States wealthy and powerful as never before. Yet despite the Moody revivals, numerical increases in church membership, and the propaganda provided by organizations such as the Evangelical Alliance, the foreign mission effort lagged.

Pierson's analysis of the mission movement's weaknesses led him to make proposals for reform and innovation, which by World War I would come to characterize the revitalized movement. To solve the problem of insufficient missionary candidates, he counseled a return to harnessing the youthful enthusiasm of students.[18] He called for vigor and innovation in planning mission work, and for expenditures of energy and resources at least comparable to those being used for contemporary business ventures. Although he did not foresee the type of organized survey conducted for the Edinburgh Conference in 1910 or the application of business methods to the organization and financing of the movement conducted by such agencies as the Laymen's Missionary Movement, he at least pointed the way. He also saw the need for international cooperation and coordination of world evangelization and was one of the first to suggest the creation of a World Missionary Council, although it would take over forty years to realize that goal.[19]

At the end of the Civil War, a list of the existing sending agencies would have provided an inclusive chart of the whole American foreign mission movement. Four decades later, these agencies formed only part of the movement and were relegated to a largely functional role, while expanded interest and enthusiasm for the cause was expressed by other groups. The Student Volunteers enlisted thousands, while the Missionary Education Movement spread the message to additional thousands who could not go. The Laymen's Missionary Movement agitated for the necessary funds, and the Foreign Missions Conference of North America provided a unified voice for the dozens of sending agencies. A Continuation Committee of the unprecedented World Missionary Conference in 1910 developed into the World Missionary Council and became an international sounding board for the movement.

The multimillion-dollar budgets and complex interrelationships of this world-wide conglomerate were the characteristics less of a spontaneous movement than of a giant service industry. The organization was the product of English-speaking Protestants whom President Samuel Capen of the American Board had asked pointedly in 1902 "to combine in something larger than a billion-dollar steel trust." It developed so rapidly that in 1910 Capen could recall his own prescription and then assert that "through the Laymen's Missionary Movement that world-wide trust has been formed."[20]

The formation of the mission trust was accompanied by escalating demands for resources. Neither mite society financing nor a patient wait for volunteers could fuel the machinery being constructed by a generation intent on the evangelization of the world within their lifetimes. Functional specialization in new auxiliary organizations and intensive promotionalism eventually produced far more funds and personnel than the movement previously had available, although never enough to support the ambitious plans proposed.

Meanwhile a perpetual debate over priorities pervaded both the mission conference reports and promotional literature. Dozens of citations could be produced in which earnest and experienced board executives averred that they had more applications from qualified mission candidates than funds to send them. At least an equal number of dire warnings could be quoted proclaiming the spiritual decay of a Christian nation whose prosperous churches had no applicants to send as reinforcements to existing mission stations.

One source of this persistent difference of opinion was the organizational fragmentation of the mission movement as well as the diverse personnel standards and business practices of the denominational agencies. Another derived from the vagaries of the American economy at the end of the nineteenth century and the related problem of adjusting the fiscal policies of organizations totally dependent on donations to the fluctuating supply of candidates graduated by the seminaries. Other reasons for the conflicting assessments of the primary requirements of the movement were the fact that both men and money were chronically inadequate as measured by the standards set by its leaders, and the chimerical nature of many schemes for the Christian occupation of the world that appeared in promotional literature. Despite these factors, the inability of the directors of the mission enterprise to agree is puzzling, and it makes an evaluation of the movement's strength more difficult.

Even tracing the declarations of a single board over the period of a century reveals little consistency in evaluating relative financial and personnel needs, but the 1842 report of the American Board shows that its officers had discovered a principle which gives a decidedly utilitarian cast to later jeremiads. The officers revealed that thirty years of experience had shown a constant interaction between pecuniary resources and the number of missionary candidates: "When there has been a supply of missionaries ready to go, that has called forth the funds to send them; and when ample funds have been furnished by the churches, that has multiplied the number of missionaries offering themselves to be sent."[21] A prudent secretary applying this experience would thus make it his business to keep his constituency aware of current deficiencies in one area or the other. Built into this promotional technique was thus a constant escalation of requirements, which would prevent an adequate supply of either men or money being reached before the millennium.

THE MISSION MOVEMENT LEADERSHIP

In 1916 a small executive committee elected by the twenty-eight member Board of Managers of the American Baptist Foreign Mission Society arranged the distribution of $1,364,268 to the 127 mission stations and dozens of related schools and hospitals maintained by the society. The travels, supplies, and salaries of 712 missionaries in every part of the world had to be supervised, and indirect administration exercised over 6054 native laborers and 2841 churches in the field. A similar committee, aided by a small staff, paid the 1276 missionaries and 5863 native workers of the Northern Presbyterian Church their share of the board's $2,262,061 income and allocated the remainder to some 163 principal stations, 1678 outstations, and their attached medical and educational facilities. The twelve-member Prudential Committee of the American Board disposed of $1,207,126 to 664 missionaries and 4877 natives assigned to 106 stations and 1461 outstations.[22] In addition to their stewardship of funds, the boards, committees, and secretaries of about thirty American foreign mission agencies were concerned with planning for the future, maintaining general support, and raising over $19,000,000 for the next year's work.

Clearly, therefore, by World War I missions had become a unique form of big business. The administration and supervision of such large-scale philanthropic enterprises on an international basis could no longer be trusted to clerks and retired clergymen. While the secretariats of individual societies continued to consist largely of such men, they were joined by educational, business, and promotional specialists and drew a larger number of laymen from business and professional circles to serve on their agencies' governing boards. Such committees and boards also became less inclined to take a passive attitude in the making of budgetary and other policy decisions. The traditional mission board functionary also tended to be excluded from the new interdenominational and international service organizations and auxiliaries of the movement, and to be replaced in the public eye by dynamic missionary statesmen acting as spokesmen for the entire movement.

As traditional personnel sources proved inadequate to the staffing of the movement's expanding hierarchy, far greater attention had to be given to the recruitment of laymen. Since foreign missions remained the preoccupation of a minority of even Protestant church members, the laymen willing to serve these specialized voluntary agencies were a select group with peculiar characteristics. Whether professionals who eschewed potentially more prestigious opportunities in denominational affairs or unpaid board trustees who made an equally conscious decision to ignore opera funds and fresh-air camps to concentrate their spare time and money on foreign missions, they opted out of the normal patterns of their peers.

The emerging lay leadership in the movement had grown up as

members of another confident and self-conscious minority: the approximately one-third of the American population in 1900 who were formally affiliated with the Protestant churches. While the non-Christian and unchurched majority might outnumber them, they were confident, as a popular mission lecturer asserted in 1912, that their "thirty-three millions, most of them women and children, control the sentiment of the United States and make it a Christian country."[23] Being identified as a member of this Protestant minority scarcely distinguished the reformer from the conservative, or the businessman from the mission board or YMCA secretary. It did, however, identify a group of men who, regardless of their profession, organizational affiliation, or special interest, confidently applied moral and evangelical standards to public life and social issues in a manner that would strike the current generation as both quaint and impolitic.

As foreign mission organizations sought to solve the personnel problems caused by expansion and bureaucratic specialization by drafting these energetic Christian gentlemen into service, they found themselves competing with agencies serving both the traditional evangelical and philanthropic ends of the churches and the new emphasis on social Christianity. Under the circumstances, it became necessary to waive customary practices by allowing laymen to fill positions that had traditionally been the preserve of the clergy, and also to create a different type of hero in the missionary propaganda intended for the American audience.

Unlike the nineteenth century literature in which the pioneer or martyred missionary had held the spotlight, the movement's propaganda gave central position to a handful of home board administrators, promoters, and organizers. Missionary statesmen such as John R. Mott and Arthur J. Brown, who had at best made brief tours of the field, were decorated by foreign governments and accepted by the public as spokesmen for entire denominations or for newly created interdenominational national organizations. This shift of attention and prestige explains both the attraction of a domestic mission career and the failure of the boards to meet their personnel problems by drawing more heavily on women. Women eventually found greater opportunities as missionaries and continued to bear much of the burden of local fund raising and propaganda. But except for the auxiliaries and subordinate women's boards, they were not acceptable for higher office in the regular branches of the mission movement.

Instead, a vigorous campaign was launched to dispel the traditional prejudice that foreign missions were the special concern of ladies' clubs and idealistic youths. The Laymen's Missionary Movement was organized in 1907 with the specific purpose of enrolling experienced and practical businessmen in the crusade. Individual denominations made their own efforts to enlist professional and businessmen on their boards. In addition to the expertise that such men could bring to the work, they were valued as potential contributors and recruiters of additional funds. What caused some concern among the veteran bureaucrats, however, was the impatient tendency of practical laymen to replace traditional principles and measures with standards prevalent in contemporary business. The result was an ambiguous combination of conservative and liberal influences on the existing evangelical movements.

The practical laymen who entered into mission policy making were antitraditionalists both in the changes they effected and in their impatience with theological issues that threatened to interfere with the job at hand. At the same time they were generally conservative in politics, of which they gave oblique evidence by affiliating themselves with traditional evangelical endeavors, such as missions, rather than by joining other equally moralistic Christian gentlemen in the progressive movement.

The laymen who entered the service of their churches after 1900 were similar in background and outlook to the average progressive, but an individualistic view of salvation, rather than political or social solutions, was central to their activism. They remained closer to the evangelical tradition and were more apt to seek change through existing church agencies. Beyond this difference, there was no clear-cut distinction between conservative, liberal, and radical among the men expressing either the domestic or foreign concern of the American Protestant churches. Neither party allegiance nor mere reactionary dissent distinguished these men, but their individual interpretations of the duties prescribed by the need to apply a common gospel to the secular world.

The much-heralded laymen's awakening in American Protestantism, like the progressive movement, was characterized in part by an unprecedented influx of interested and well-meaning amateurs into areas previously monopolized by professionals. In some areas the awakening effected a virtual revolution, as laymen disposed of long-established procedures and shouldered aside venerable placemen. Declining clerical influence and the layman's practical experience combined to make him a far more influential figure, of which he became increasingly aware. His sense of importance was also increased because he was wooed by Bible leagues and Sunday school, home, and foreign mission groups, the YMCA, Epworth League, Missionary Education Movement, Christian Endeavor Society, and a host of others. In responding to these calls, the volunteers tended to pay little attention to denominational lines.

Not only did Protestant church members remain a minority of the population, but able laymen willing to serve constituted a tiny portion of that body of Americans. With dozens of opportunities available to each member of this elite to exercise his sense of duty, it was never possible for foreign missions to receive what was considered an adequate force of laymen to supply existing agencies. There was competition for volunteers not only with secular agencies or between denominational and independent groups, but also within the churches. Thus, despite the persistent theme that home and foreign missions were all part of the same grand work, the advocates of overseas work had to fashion a specialized appeal.

It was an appeal based not so much on the traditional evangelical or humanitarian considerations as on secular attractions. A nonmilitary form of patriotic service and the ability to influence world history and policy making were offered to the small-town businessman willing to serve on mission committees. Just as Richard Hofstadter found the expansionist leaders of the 1890s disillusioned with reform and eager to discover a larger, more statesmanlike, less restraining theater of action than domestic politics,[24] so the mission leaders offered an opportunity to magnify influence on a broader horizon. While the temperance, ecumenical, and peace movements all touched intimately on world affairs, Christian missions provided the broadest avenue of influence. To take part in the recreation of one catholic church, to help shape the emerging nations of the Orient, was the way to help make history as part of the world forces of organized Christianity.

The movement for more vigorous participation by laymen in the work of the churches drew volunteers from all classes and was national in scope. The headquarters of most mission societies and auxiliaries, however, were in the Eastern cities, in which the nation's wealth and population were concentrated. Efforts to tap these resources thus produced an apparent Eastern establishment, which had no relation whatever to the superior piety or dedication to philanthropy of the region. A number of boards recognized this tradition as a handicap to enlarging their Western and Southern constituency. Their reaction, however, consisted largely of the judicious selection of a few Western leaders to their governing boards or the recruitment of promising young men into the New York or Boston office.

As a group, Protestant laymen were more representative of the native-born, socially conservative *nouveaux riches* than of any social or political aristocracy that had inherited a common tradition of trusteeship. The single common factor which united a Seattle lawyer with a British-born Chicago banker was the primary role that religion played in their lives. Whether Calvinist, catholic, or liturgical in background, banker, lawyer, or railroad treasurer by profession, they felt a common drive to express religious commitment actively in the work of their churches or of broader interdenominational bodies. Whatever means or motive brought a particular individual to feel most strongly a sense of Christian duty, that incentive was also the most important determinant of a special commitment to foreign missions.[25]

Except for the occasional retired businessman, the layman's service remained an avocation. He was a part-time functionary, and his influence was channeled by the equally modern and able professional secretaries and organizers who both functioned in a liaison capacity and after the turn of the century began to replace the clergy in the executive and administrative positions of religious societies. The pensioned missionaries or ministers seeking an alternative to a life in the pulpit who in the nineteenth century had filled secretarial positions were either joined or replaced by dedicated Protestants who were also specialists in some secular field, such as accounting, fund raising, or public relations. The personnel qualifications for a Laymen's Movement secretary, for example, included such criteria as good education and health, attractive personality, and ability as a salesman, administrator, promoter, executive, and public speaker.[26] With the exception of the requirement for "missionary vision and commitment," the identical description might have been made for an executive position by the personnel department of any contemporary business firm. That the men in the field felt estranged from these administrative specialists is obvious from criticism raised in 1932 during the Laymen's Foreign Missions Inquiry and from the frequent suggestion that preference in staffing home board positions be given to returned or retired missionaries.[27]

Men with similar education and background were filling the expanding business and government bureaucracies at the turn of the century. What distinguished the religious bureaucrats was a stronger commitment to service while pursuing a non-ministerial career. The same motive which eventually brought other laymen into avocational association with mission societies and similar religious agencies, usually had been felt earlier and more strongly by the board or Student Volunteer secretary facing a career decision.

The potential religious bureaucrat felt duty-bound to serve the Protestant churches in some way, whether he received the impetus from home training, a summer camp experience, or religious influence in college. If the pressure became too intense, he might rebel, like John R. Mott, who moved to Cornell from Upper Iowa University because that "college became too religious for me." He might also object to the dull restrictions of the parish ministry, like Sherwood Eddy, who refused ordination after completing his theological training because he "wanted to work as a layman in the broad Christian movements that brought me in contact with men of all religions rather than to be confined to a particular denomination." [28]

Most of these men went through a period of restlessness, during which they discovered that they were equally unsuited to a routine money-making job and to the withdrawal from the mainstream of society that seemed to be demanded of the missionary or rural minister. At some point during this stage of uncertainty, they usually accepted a secretaryship in one of the less tradition-bound national organizations, such as the Young Men's Christian Associations, Student Volunteer Movement, or Laymen's Missionary Movement. Once embarked on such a career, they switched and multiplied their organizational affiliations with ease and frequency as part of the new fraternity of liberated if not always liberal religious bureaucrats.

Distinctions inevitably developed between the anonymous professionals who conducted the prosaic administrative functions of the expanded movement in the United States and the missionary statesmen known to the public and routinely associating with heads and ministers of state. In such successful career mission leaders as John R. Mott, Robert Speer, and Sherwood Eddy, the line between layman and clergyman tended to become a technicality. Their concept of missions was a catholic one, which was all but synonymous with the church's work on earth. They saw themselves as Christian statesmen who could rise above political, sectarian, or even national ties. In technique and theology they displayed the same disregard for divisions and categories. While critics labeled them as liberals or religious eclectics and relativists, they were most concerned with accomplishments and with awakening in American churches the same broad concern for mankind that their consciences had created in them.

The men who rose to the top positions in the established mission organizations often possessed exceptional intellectual curiosity, but they restrained their interest when it came to embracing a particular doctrinal point of view. Following a career in an area where only moral turpitude or theological unsoundness constituted an insurmountable handicap, they were quick to adjust and keep abreast of change because they were preoccupied with their work, not with dogma. Combined with these assets was a driving ambition, tempered but not eliminated by a Christian conscience. As long as the stamp of Christian service could be used to sanctify ambition's proddings to achieve great things and to act on a world-wide scale, these men tended to be blind to ambition's existence. They were disturbed when they caught occasional glimpses of this drive and periodically, almost ritually, refused offers of advancement in other fields. Both Mott and Bishop James Bashford, for example, rejected White House offers of ambassadorships, as well as prestigious college presidencies and high denominational offices. This self-denial does not prove, as many of their contemporary admirers maintained, that they were devoid of ambitious feelings. Rather, it helps to define the peculiar nature of their ambition.

MISSION PERSONNEL

In dedication to Christian service, zeal for world evangelization, and social background, there was little to distinguish the men who administered the home base of foreign missions from the volunteer who went into the field. They were all tangible products of Horace Bushnell's prescription of Christian nurture, and thus part of an idealistic and dedicated minority in American life who chose mission work as the means of expressing their religious convictions. But while many board officers became almost interchangeable with their counterparts in business and government bureaucracies, the missionary remained a totally different type, who posed unique personnel problems. Unlike most other professionals, the missionary expected to retire at the rank and in the position to which he had been initially appointed. The men and women whom board secretaries sought to send to a lifetime in a foreign country were impelled to go there for reasons quite independent of loyalty to the society that provided the means for the journey, or of the normal career incentives. As a result, to assure an adequate supply of new recruits for the field posed personnel problems faced by no comparable organization in American life.

The missionary was basically a minister or churchworker who surrendered home, family, friends, and professional advancement for the sake of spending a lifetime preaching to or working with apathetic aliens. Unlike his home colleagues, he was not invited to serve a congregation which had freely chosen him. Furthermore, he accepted from his mission board a tighter discipline in all areas of work and life than any American pastor had to endure. Added to these requirements were the not inconsiderable sacrifices demanded of a ministerial candidate. The chronic shortage of qualified missionary volunteers described in the promotional literature of many Protestant sending agencies thus seems to have been inevitable.

If one looks past the calculated pessimism of public appeals for volunteers, however, the picture that emerges from mission agency reports in the early decades of this century is one of qualified sufficiency in candidates. There were generally enough candidates for available positions, but they did not always have the advanced training in education, medicine, and other developing specialties that the administrators would like to have insisted on. The high point in the availability of candidates was reached immediately after World War I. "We look for a large increase of missionary forces as a result of the war," a missionary journal predicted in 1918. Men who had fought in that crusade by serving in Red Cross or YMCA contingents overseas would not be content to return to pedestrian civilian jobs, maintained the editor, and their training and spirit should be employed. "These new-found recruits should not be demobilized," he proposed. "They should simply be re-distributed."[29]

To a considerable degree this hope seems to have been realized. The American Board sent more new missionaries to the field in 1919 than in any other year between 1900 and the depression.[30] Most of the major sending agencies reached a peak in the number of missionaries in the field during the early 1920s which was not approached again until after World War II. The high point for Student Volunteer enlistment, as well as for total number of new American missionaries sailing for the field during the first four decades of the movement's existence, was 1920. The largest number of Volunteers sailing during the same period left in 1921.[31]

With a few exceptions in the pioneer days at the beginning of the century, the ideal nineteenth-century missionary was an ordained minister expected to function with equal facility in all phases of his station's work. Methodist Bishop W. F. Oldham rationalized this practice for delegates at the 1914 Foreign Missions Conference, pointing out "that an ordained man costs no more than a layman and that until you come to specialization the ordained man can easily do all that the layman does, and do some things by reason of his ordination that the layman can not do."[32] By the time he spoke, the growing complexity of the mission establishment in China had already forced the major boards to accept various degrees of specialization. To set an ordained minister to teaching elementary school was a waste of talent, as was making him the principal of a mission school or a science instructor in a college. Similarly, medical work in China had gone beyond the point where ministers with a haphazardly collected knowledge of first aid could run a station infirmary. Yet qualified applicants for medical positions would have been discouraged if the administrators had continued to insist on postgraduate Bible school courses or even theological training. Many of the younger men also came to the field strongly influenced by social Christianity and refused to consider street preaching or tract distribution as their primary ministerial function.

Such objections and the economies of using lay specialists for technical and educational tasks led to their increasing employment. While the missionary services of printers, teachers, mechanics, and doctors had been acceptable only under special circumstances in the nineteenth century, their appointment became commonplace in the twentieth. In 1916 the American Board added the designation "Business Agents" to distinguish accountants, architects, and business managers sent to foreign stations from the traditional missionaries. [33] A number of boards adopted short-term enlistment programs to attract young college graduates, much as the Peace Corps or VISTA were to do for another generation. While this was a convenient way to staff educational facilities, it was also criticized as a wasteful experiment producing inadequate returns for the investment in the transportation, outfitting, and training of the young laymen. Such criticism must have seemed valid, for only 76 short-term workers were listed among the 7663 foreign staff members of all Protestant mission societies active in China in 1925. [34]

Another underdeveloped source of recruits was the single women who, because of a combination of Victorian prudery, the public's overestimation of the hazards of foreign duty, and their inability to receive ordination, were only reluctantly commissioned by the regular sending agencies during the nineteenth century. By 1900, American women had been accepted in areas of public life and employment previously closed to them and had gained easier access to higher education. Since the dangers in foreign service had also markedly decreased, the regular sending agencies found it easy to give in to the urgings of the women's boards to employ more of their sex. The single woman missionary, however, remained for decades a second-class citizen of the mission station. [35] She served, often in combination with missionary wives, as teacher, nurse, or tract distributor, but lacking the opportunity of ordination, she could not administer sacraments or fulfill the ministerial functions of most of her male counterparts. Other reasons for board prejudice against spinsters were the opportunity for rumor and criticism that their presence at a station provided to the Chinese community, and their disturbing willingness to marry eligible males or widowers regardless of denominational affiliation and the consequent loss to the society that had borne the expense of sending them.

Potentially the most satisfactory method of meeting the personnel requirements of the sending agencies was to place greater reliance on the nationals of the mission fields. There was a marked increase after 1900 in the number of native helpers used for tract distribution and other auxiliary purposes. [36] In 1902, for example, 1037 missionaries of all types, including wives, were outnumbered by 2906 native workers attached to the thirty-three American Protestant mission societies active in China.[37] The development of a native ministry, however, was disappointingly slow. This was owing partly to the lack of men willing or qualified to undertake the long course of study required for ordination, and to a lesser degree to the reluctance of some missionaries to surrender responsibility to native pastors, particularly if the churches they served were not financially self-reliant.

The personnel requirements of the expanded mission movement at the turn of the century thus forced administrators to re-examine traditional policies and prejudices, to lower standards, and to experiment with specialization. Single women and laymen were employed in far greater numbers, but the ideal and mainstay of the mission forces remained the ordained male missionary.[38] The effort to reach and recruit these men took on an unprecedented degree of organization on a nation-wide basis and was pursued largely outside of denominational channels.

Decades before psychological testing and rationalized employment standards were introduced by educational, business, and other large-scale employers of college graduates, mission board administrators applied rudimentary versions of these techniques to select a peculiar American elite. Unlike both their secular counterparts and the exclusively college-oriented Student Volunteer Movement, the same administrators were also concerned with the social origin and early training of eventual candidates. The foreign mission boards thus had to translate experience in the field into personnel standards, then interpret these into a program of propaganda and training applicable to all levels of American Protestantism. The integration of such a program with the help of interdenominational agencies like the Missionary Education Movement characterized the period at the turn of the century. A similar trend was the allocation of special responsibilities for particular age groups to such organizations as the Student Volunteer Movement or the Young People's Missionary Movement.

Information about educational and physical qualifications could be circulated through such groups, which had already applied initial standards regarding religious dedication and character in the selection of their own membership. The boards set high standards in these areas, because it was virtually impossible to devise an economical probationary system or test of the candidate's adaptability to work in a foreign land. Hence, the safest policy was to demand a somewhat better educational record, stronger physical constitution, virtually flawless character, and higher dedication than considered necessary for the minister of a local church, or the nurse, or schoolteacher, who could be easily replaced if proven incompetent.

Not only established mission boards but also several new non-denominational religious organizations concerned themselves with the personnel needs of the growing mission movement at the end of the nineteenth century. Most publicized and productive was the student-organized and administered Student Volunteer Movement for Foreign Missions, which for more than fifty years remained a means of channeling the enthusiasm of youth to the existing agencies, while never itself sending a missionary or establishing a station. John R. Mott, one of the founders and a long-time director, estimated in 1920 that "for some time" 75 percent of the male and 70 percent of the unmarried women missionaries of North America had been students who had signed the Volunteer pledge: "It is my purpose, if God permit, to become a foreign missionary."[39] While Mott's estimate is unquestionably inflated, and many of the volunteers would probably have become candidates without the existence of the Student Volunteer Movement, it did arouse unprecedented interest and develop the basis for support of the existing sending agencies among American collegians.

The selection, outfitting, and commissioning of new missionaries continued, however, to be the monopoly of the major foreign mission boards, who also never considered the Student Volunteer Movement and similar groups as more than helpful auxiliaries. Most mission society promotion and recruitment efforts were focused on various Protestant institutions of higher learning, for both before and during the heyday of the Student Volunteer Movement the typical ordained missionary was the product of a small denominational college. The American Board reported in 1880 that of its 139 college-educated men in the field, only fifteen from Yale, seven from Dartmouth, one from Harvard, and a handful of state college graduates were not products of small church-related institutions.[40] A survey of all American Protestant agencies in 1932 produced a unanimous declaration of dependence on church-supported colleges by the board secretaries. Estimates of the number of missionaries initially trained at such institutions ranged from 87 to 95 percent.[41] Such figures, or the fact that well over 90 percent of all theology students in the United States at the turn of the century were products of Christian colleges, merely indicate that the objectives of church-supported higher education were being realized.[42] They do not prove that foreign missions were receiving an adequate or proportionate share of the graduates.

For this reason the mission boards consistently attempted to direct attention toward their special interests by placing returned missionaries on college faculties, cultivating other sympathetic teachers, and providing speakers. Such promotional efforts were directed in particular toward the newer Western colleges, which had themselves been founded as part of a missionary thrust. The American Board, for example, consistently received far more candidates from Beloit, Grinnell, and Oberlin than from any of the Ivy League or large state universities.[43]

The typical twentieth-century Protestant missionary was neither a religious fanatic nor an otherworldly social misfit. He was distinguished from the stay-at-home of his generation largely by a more imperative sense of religious duty. Even here, accidental or chance personal experience often determined whose sense of duty would be exercised at home and whose brought to bear in the foreign field. "The psychological type most likely in the early days to feel the call to mission work," concluded a 1932 survey, "was selfconfident, temperamentally certain, and occasionally self-assertive." The outstanding figures were "men of native force who would probably have made their mark in any calling."[44] And well they might have, if a college education was any criterion, for at a time when white male college graduates in the United States had never approximated as much as one percent of the white male population who had passed college age, and when less than thirty percent of the Congressmen and only 60 percent of the Presidents had earned degrees, the vast majority of ordained missionaries belonged to this educated elite.[45]

The geographical origin of mission applicants followed a predictable pattern. Before the Civil War, the majority of candidates came from the small towns and villages of central and western New England and upstate New York. Not only were there few volunteers from the cities and coastal towns, but the American Board, at least, seems to have been suspicious of city-bred candidates as a matter of policy.[46] As late as 1880, only 19 percent of the American Board's missionaries had been recruited from the interior states.[47]

By the end of the century, however, the home mission effort of earlier generations began to produce results. Not only was the bulk of the Northern Presbyterian Board's force drawn from the trans-Allegheny West by 1888, but some of the largest financial contributors were Westerners as well.[48] And the Student Volunteer Movement reported in 1894 that little progress had been made in establishing the movement on the Pacific Coast or in the Southern states, and that the majority of their volunteers came from colleges in the easternmost part of the Middle West.[49]

A survey of the candidate papers of men and women sent to the field by the American Board during the two decades at the turn of the century reveals no basic change in their backgrounds. An overwhelming number were native-born Americans, most of the foreign-born being children of American missionaries. The Middle West seemed to be replacing New England as the birthplace of the majority of applicants. Fewer missionaries came from farm backgrounds than expected in view of the still predominantly rural nature of the population in 1900. A substantial majority came from small-town or village homes. Surprisingly, there were as many candidates who had been born in the larger Eastern cities, however, as had originated in the far West. Southern candidates rarely applied to the American Board, being recruited instead by the regional branches of the larger denominations.[50] Scattered evidence, however, indicates that the same pattern of largely small-town origins applied also to the missionaries of Southern denominations.

Despite the prevalent assumption that missionaries were largely the children of the poor,[51] the American Board personnel files reveal a predominantly middle class origin. The sons and daughters of Civil War widows, farmers suffering from the agricultural depression, or low-salaried clerics and home missionaries did appear, but in the society of their time they certainly could claim some share of middle class respectability. Educational requirements also tended to bar the children of the poor. Relatively few candidates, however, came from families in "comfortable circumstances," and the rare wealthy applicant was cause for much jubilation and publicity.[52] In the eyes of the sending agencies there was also some reason for mistrust of the financially independent missionary, for he was potentially the source of discontent among his fellows and possessed the opportunity to evade board discipline in policy matters dependent on funds.[53]

While there was considerable variation in the background of male missionaries, the young woman offering her services as an unmarried career worker was a far more consistent, predictable type. As she emerges from the American Board's candidate files, she came usually from a large rural family and had passed the age at which it was reasonable to expect a marriage proposal. Often she had worked her way through normal school or college by intermittent teaching. Once released from obligations to an ailing mother or younger siblings, she determined to teach or nurse in the foreign field. To a greater extent than the ordained male missionary, who was normally accompanied by his wife, she cut herself off from a familiar way of life and surrendered herself to spinsterhood in an environment where eligible males were rare. Her commitment was more difficult to revoke than her male counterpart's, and took on aspects of entering a Catholic order. This spirit was reflected in the answer given by one candidate for China to the question as to why she wished to become a missionary: "The desire to live a holy life and to help others to do the same," read her plaintive reply, "and the fact that what once were pleasures and joys to me in the world are not so now."[54] To such a woman, the work she could accomplish with hundreds of Chinese youngsters seemed more significant than teaching in a one-room country school.

THE MISSIONARY CALLING

Much more difficult than describing missionary candidate backgrounds is to analyze their personal motivation for foreign service and their willingness to abandon all that was familiar except their religion. The only indisputable fact is that a personally experienced spiritual dedication to Christianity was primary among the motivational forces. The appeal of a dramatic career in contrast to mundane small-town life and the inspirational effect of publicized missionary heroes also help explain the attraction of this calling. But the boards' winnowing and testing, and the sacrifices demanded as a matter of course, made sincere religious conviction more important than any psychological or material considerations. Complete submission to

God's will was the catalyst that made possible the surrender of ambitions, homeland, and a normal way of life. If a desire for these things reasserted itself after the first flush of spiritual dedication had passed, the missionary was nevertheless embarked on a career far from home and difficult to abandon with an easy conscience. The overriding religious dedication and certitude of the typical missionary candidate coincided with the emphasis and procedures of the sending agencies. The uniformly accepted *sine qua non* among board secretaries screening applications were spirituality and the experience of a divine calling.[55]

If spiritual dedication and certitude were both expected and characteristic of the average missionary candidate, the only other uniformly applicable generalization is that this condition was never arrived at suddenly. The choice of a missionary career was neither rationally calculated nor the result of some Pauline vision. It was a trip down a progressively narrowing highway, on which the exits became fewer and from which the byways led basically in the same direction as the main road. The first step on the highway was an overwhelming, personal experience of conversion.

The candidate papers of the period are filled with references to this experience, most of them dated as precisely as an army discharge or a wedding in today's personnel records. Mention of the experience of conversion often seemed intended as a self-explanatory reason for the applicant's decision to serve. It was proof of election to an elite, admission to a company bound for service in areas inaccessible to ordinary men. A medical student wrote to the American Board in 1892, for example, that he had no intention of practicing medicine except in connection with evangelical work: "I regard my life as a failure just as *I* am known and loved *instead* of my God—if a knowledge of me does not imply a knowledge of my God, I live in vain."[56] Although not made by a seminarian, the selfless dedication expressed in this statement typified the distinctive missionary spirit at its best.

Whether by means of careful preparation in the home or as a result of the overpowering personality of a revivalist, a personal experience of conversion was only the first step in the missionary's career. The next involved the expression of a keenly felt sense of duty in some meaningful way. Compared with the convert who chose a successful career as a Christian businessman or professional, the potential missionary was a religious activist. Even revivalism or preaching in an established church did not provide sufficient scope for his need to spread the gospel. Bishop James Bashford, for example, who heard Dwight L. Moody early in his career, was quick to recognize the revivalist's limitations but felt drawn to follow him into similar evangelical work. Then slowly the conviction grew on Bashford that "it is not sufficient for one to interpret himself from the pulpit, that the great problem is in the relation of one's ideals and life and that the great work of the Master consisted in personal life and in helpfulness to others."[57] Bashford felt that he could not adequately emulate these qualities as a pastor, bishop, or college president in the United States, but that he could approach them while spending the twilight of his career as a missionary bishop in China.

In most cases it was only after beginning a career of Christian service that missionaries became separated from ministers and board or YMCA secretaries. During the progression from conversion to the call for a life of Christian service, there was little to distinguish the participants. Only rarely was the desire to serve abroad held consistently from youth or early college until departure for the field. Even when such dedication was fixed early by family ties or obligations, virtually every candidate accepted by the American Board at the turn of the century had first spent several years as a home missionary, YMCA secretary, or denominational functionary. Many of them initially considered staying with this work for the rest of their careers, often at the request of their superiors, and seemed to end up overseas almost by chance.

The single most important factor that transformed the Christian worker into a foreign missionary was his conviction that there was a greater need for his services abroad. It is possible that some were disenchanted with unrewarding slum work or dirty Indians and sought a broader, more brightly lit stage for themselves. Without conscious dissimulation, even such feelings were expressed in terms of the heathen's needs. "I want to be a foreign missionary," wrote a California kindergarten teacher, "because God has given me so much that I want to place my life where it can be of most service to Him." Another candidate attributed his decision to numerous factors, "but chief of them all was a growing unescapable conviction that it was God's will that my life be invested where, so far as I could see, the need was the greatest and the forces meeting that need the least adequate." A 1932 inquiry into missionary motives, which was answered by 704 men and women who had left the field, found that 48 percent had chosen their career because of the "greater foreign need," followed by only 21 percent who had acted in response to a "divine command."[58]

It is difficult to explain why the challenge of social service at home made so little impression on the candidates for similar work overseas. Sherwood Eddy, for example, wrote with excitement of his postgraduate year's work with the YMCA in New York, where he "for the first time came in touch with life in the raw." The experience revolutionized his life plans. "I had intended to go into the lumber business and make money—plenty of it, for I believed that money was power," he recalled. But this introduction to urban problems forced him to confront two questions: "Where in the world was the greatest spiritual need? Where was the greatest opportunity for service?" The answer was the foreign field, "the needier half of the world."[59]

Eventually, improved methods of communication and transportation helped to make tenable a more casual view of the differences between home and foreign mission careers. The nineteenth century volunteer had made a more permanent breach with past experience when he set sail. A raising gangplank was virtually the equivalent to a closing monastery door. "To the Missionary, perhaps, exclusively, is the separation from friends like the farewell of death," wrote David Abeel on his departure for China in 1829. "To him the next meeting is generally beyond the grave."[60] The steamship, telegraph, and regular sabbaticals changed all this. It may be true of the Hawaiian missionaries that their abnegation of the common joys of life was ascetic and that their outlook on life resembled that of the monastic orders who had long carried the burden of Roman Catholic missions.[61] However, the typical missionary pioneer was accompanied by his wife and some material comforts of life, and he was paid a salary that allowed him to live well above the standards of the poor he came to convert.

Although a monastic view of mission work characterized the early years, by the end of the nineteenth century it had been replaced by a simile of the frontier. Rather than psychologically severing all ties to his homeland as he boarded ship, the missionary saw himself in the vanguard of the Christian civilization, which the United States represented. Home ties might be stretched, but they remained. The same dedication that placed his classmate in a churchless mining town in Montana brought him to Shensi. And he visualized China not as "something of a monastery where he could attain more fully his religious aspiration to be Christ-like," but as the most challenging and potentially rewarding field of activity.[62] The key to missionary motivation was activism, not contemplation. If initially there was a withdrawal from the secular pursuits of his generation, it was followed by a conscious decision to pursue the most active and challenging religious vocation, a ministry to which only the ablest and most adventurous were called.

Technological progress narrowed the difference between giving service abroad or at home, while the intensity of the theological imperative to save damned souls was waning. These changes explain the efforts to discover other inducements and to harness a variety of marginal motives to the mission movement. They also made necessary a less leisurely process of recruiting volunteers. By the turn of the century the organized revivalism of the youth movement, the complex and businesslike ministrations of the mission boards to their agents, and the new respectability of the mission movement combined to serve the purposes that a grim and rigorous theology had formerly sufficed to meet.

PROMOTIONAL THEMES IN FUND RAISING

Mission literature reflects an ironic conflict between exhortations to American Protestants to build a spiritual kingdom from which materialism and narrow money-grubbing are excluded, and ringing appeals to the constituency for the financial lifeblood without which there could be no movement. It was lack of money that forced the first volunteers for foreign service to stay in the United States for two years after they had offered themselves to the Massachusetts General Association. Financial stringencies accounted for later reverses, particularly the abandonment of certain fields and the reductions of missionary salaries and replenishment during the last decades of the nineteenth century. Despite the unquestioned sincerity of those who dedicated the movement to antimaterialistic and spiritual goals, a predominant portion of the time and energy of mission society staffs was dedicated to cultivating their financial constituency.

The same generalization made about the overall interest in Protestant missions applies to the financial supporters of the movement; they were a minority even among the national minority of loyal Protestant church members. The primary goal of the movement's leaders during the decades at the turn of the century was to make the body of its supporters at least coextensive with church membership. This became the watchword of the Laymen's Missionary Movement during the pre-World War I decade: "The whole church enlisted in behalf of the whole world."[63]

But the whole church remained reluctant to enlist. The American Board's president charged in 1909 that less than one-fourth of the Christians in America contributed an offering to foreign missions worthy of the name.[64] The Laymen's Movement, with its penchant for figures and dramatic illustration, summarized the situation as seen by mission leaders:

> About two out of three in the United States and Canada are outside the membership of all Christian churches. Two out of three people in the world live in non-Christian nations. Two out of three people in these non-Christian nations are beyond the reach of the present combined missionary agencies of Christendom. And, in spite of these appalling needs, about two out of three of the church members of North America are contributing nothing toward the aggressive missionary work of the church at home and abroad.
>
> Manifestly our first business is the enlistment of the other two-thirds of the members of the church as intelligent, systematic missionary supporters and workers.[65]

The descending order of fractions did not extend beyond the one-third or one-quarter of loyal givers. The bulk of the movement's income always came from the moderate contributions of the regular giver. The tiny group from which occasionally came the spectacular gift of a hundred thousand or a million was carefully cultivated but did not match the steady offerings of quarters and dollars by the less wealthy. Experts at the Edinburgh Conference had estimated that nine-tenths of mission money came from one-tenth of the Protestant communicants. And they were not those most able to give, wrote the

American Board's president, for "people in average circumstances are proportionably the greatest givers."[66]

The foreign mission constituency among American Protestants consisted predominantly of native-born Caucasians, with women more active in their support than men. Over 40 percent of the American Board's income in 1899, for example, came directly from the Congregational women's boards, and more might be credited to female members if their share of the regular church contributions could be distinguished.[67] In the small Free Methodist Church of North America, the ten-year-old Women's Society collected more money in the single four-year period before 1914 than the male-dominated General Missionary Board had received during its entire 32-year existence.[68] A more significant indication of the importance of women's activities is the fact that American women's societies contributed more than twice as much as their British counterparts as early as 1891, although combined foreign-mission contributions in Great Britain normally exceeded the total raised in the United States until shortly before World War I.[69]

Liturgical churches, such as the Lutheran and Orthodox bodies, probably made a proportionately negligible contribution to foreign missions because a majority of their members were recent immigrants.[70] Like the Roman Catholic Church at the turn of the century, they were preoccupied with reorienting the new arrivals and establishing their churches. Extension of their activities into foreign missions was the work of succeeding generations, which were no longer foreign to the United States themselves and had risen above the economic level of the unskilled worker.

Similarly, Afro-Americans made no contribution to foreign missions commensurate with their numbers, largely because their economic level barely allowed them to support their own churches and extension work in this country. In the eyes of some mission leaders, however, black support was considered underexploited. In 1917 the Laymen's Movement hired a special Secretary for Colored Laymen and began to cultivate this group "naturally endowed with capacity for strong religious feeling."[71]

Although the constituency of foreign missions had certain general characteristics, its precise delineation is difficult because of geographical and social variations and the idiosyncrasies of individual donors. The appeals for funds reflected this diversity and provided additional insight into the nature of the mission movement's base. As they were addressed to loyal church members, they incorporated such traditional Protestant doctrines as stewardship and tithing.

Both the focus of the campaign and the theoretical basis of mission fund raising was the principle of stewardship. Although stewardship had no special relationship to the foreign mission cause, its acceptance had to be promoted to loosen the purse strings prior to making a special effort to promote the interests of the foreign boards.

The idea that man is only a lifetime trustee or steward for a portion of God's property is expressed in both the Old and New Testaments and was reflected in the primitive communism of several early Christian communities. It received renewed emphasis and a broader interpretation, however, during the period of missionary expansion. "All life is a stewardship," wrote David McConaughy in a widely used church school study book. "Vital energy in whatever form—whether physical or spiritual—is a trust from God."[72] Not only was the biblical concept of stewardship at the heart of the Christian experience, but it was an absolute and all-encompassing obligation, which could be used to solicit money, missionary candidates, or service by laymen.

Indeed, some students of religious history have attempted to describe the spectacular increase in benevolent giving and enterprises during the past 150 years purely in terms of the development of a general stewardship movement within Protestantism.[73] But there is far more evidence to support John Lankford's conclusion that despite increased emphasis on stewardship by American writers and clergymen in the early decades of this century, the traditional principle was only one facet of a much broader Protestant "theology of giving." He found that stewardship lent itself to so many interpretations, was so difficult to put into practice, and appeared so radically contrary to fundamental American values and the principle of private property that it was neither an effective promotional theme nor accepted by more than a handful of American Protestants.[74]

These qualifications do not mean that stewardship and an emphasis on the primacy of spiritual motives was not the ideal of the men responsible for the promotion of missions. It merely indicates that the ideal was too demanding for the rank-and-file supporter, and that the naturalization of stewardship in American Protestantism was too ambitious an objective.

In the translation of these ideals into fund-raising techniques a fundamental distortion occurred. Those developing the stewardship theology looked toward the coming kingdom, sought a national religious revival, or preached of sustaining individual character. But the promoters talked of pledges, every member canvass teams, duplex envelopes, and quotas oversubscribed. Posters, rallies, and mass campaigns were invariably discussed as means of stewardship education, but the emphasis lay elsewhere, and the results were counted in dollars. To mission leaders closer to the true meaning of stewardship, money was only an incidental by-product of dedication to the ideal. "Stewardship is not a mere method of raising money," warned McConaughy, "it is one of God's schools for raising men . . . In this process, giving is made an acid test of character."[75]

The bridge between character building and fund raising rested on a peculiar definition of money. To the inner-directed man, wrote David Riesman, property is merely an extension of the individual self; a kind of exoskeleton.[76] "Money not only measures the things exchanged but in a very real sense it affords a measure, likewise, of those who exchange them," wrote McConaughy as if in corroboration. "It is coined personality."[77] This identification of character with currency made it relatively easy to profess stewardship while practicing promotion. If money measured the man, then the amount he contributed indicated the depth of his Christian character. The most blatant type of high-pressure promotionalism in fund raising could thus be explained as being in accord with a traditional Protestant doctrine. Giving to missions could become an equivalent to buying indulgences, for it served the function of making a subtle distinction between wealth that spelled materialism and wealth that betokened character. In practice, the tendency was to use stewardship rather than to define it.

In this sense the Laymen's Missionary Movement made stewardship its principal watchword. One of its first activities was the formation of a Stewardship Commission, which drew on leading laymen from every denomination to seek their guidance in formulating a policy that would win wider support for missions from American business. Its promotional methods were viewed as an educational campaign to impress the duty of regularly supporting missions on the average church member. The Laymen's Movement, its denominational imitators, and such successors as the Interchurch World Movement preached stewardship, but practiced modern promotional advertising. Had mere stewardship education been effective, it would have obviated the need for the professional fund raiser and for other sophisticated methods to separate men from their money, and the spiritual meaning and satisfaction the movement provided to many of its adherents would have been more than an occasional by-product.

The acceptance of the stewardship principle alone, however, still would not have solved the basic problem of the mission agencies. Since the "acid test" could be passed as readily by contributing to organ funds as to the evangelization of Hunan, further means had to be found to entice the practicing steward into considering distant natives most worthy of his benefices. The employment of other appeals for mission contributions reveals a similar ambivalence between spiritual ends and secular means. "Nothing that is not instinct with the life and motives of the gospel," maintained the American Board's Judson Smith, "can either fully comprehend the work of missions or effectively promote it."[78] But each generation has its own instinct regarding the motives of the gospel, and the mission advocate has traditionally been forced to hitch his cause to other enterprises.

The first American missionary to China went at a merchant's invitation and in his vessel. Others did not disdain a ride on an opium clipper as long as it provided the only opportunity to distribute tracts along the coast of the closed empire. In the decades before World War I, the mission movement rode the bandwagon of expansionism, professed at times to be a means for expanding commerce, offered itself as the mechanism for Christianizing international relations and preserving world peace, and after a patriotic military interlude, sought to provide the avenue for reconstruction and for guaranteeing a peaceful world society. Missions had to be justified in secular terms because support simply for the evangelization of non-Christians was not forthcoming. The fluctuation and variety of these secular justifications of the cause, the ease with which one attribute or slogan was dropped for another, all indicate the lasting and primary concern of converting the neglected non-Christian.

In 1852, at the end of forty years of activity, the American Board had examined the consequences of trying to enlist sympathy for its work by dwelling on the physical and social wretchedness of the heathen. While the initial effect on contributions had been prodigious, the report concluded that a decline in support seemed to indicate "that undue reliance has been placed on motives of a secondary and subordinate character." Yet a half-century later, when the magnitude of the enterprise and the expense of new techniques and facilities made money an even more imperative need, this lesson had been forgotten. Then frustration with Protestant niggardliness in the face of unprecedented need and opportunity drove mission leaders to rely again on motives of a secondary and subordinate character. Many a sermon criticized Americans living in the Gilded Age for their materialism, but it was precisely the money they were accumulating which the mission boards became preoccupied with trying to tap. "We have the money in the pocketbooks of the churches," wrote American Board President Samuel Capen to premier mission fund raiser John R. Mott, "how shall we reach it?"[79]

It was reached by appealing to the layman's interest in the exotic and in participating personally in great enterprises and leaving his mark on history, and also on strictly humanitarian grounds. It was extracted by efficient new business methods and by promising economic benefits. It was promoted by translating the urgency of seizing unprecedented opportunities abroad into an atmosphere of crisis. With the influx of laymen into the mission agencies, a trend toward worldly emphasis was in any event likely, if not inevitable. The exploitation of these motives in fund raising propaganda, however, should not be confused with the basic forces behind foreign missions. The object of this literature was to raise money, not to justify a traditional Christian duty. It also did not reflect a wholehearted commitment to any of these secular goals. To meet the perpetual and harrowing lack of funds, the mission forces might countenance selling kisses in the church bazaar, but they did not resort to prostitution.

FUND-RAISING RESULTS

To the mission leaders whose initiative and ingenuity were applied with unprecedented energy to the financial needs of the movement during the first two decades of this century, the results of sophisticated promotional techniques and nation-wide fund drives were both heartening and disappointing. The total receipts from living donors of the foreign mission agencies of fifteen major denominations soared from $5,300,100 in 1901 to $14,752,854 in 1917. American entry into the war produced a sharp increase to $21,288,749 in 1919, while several major fund drives and the activities of the Interchurch World Movement produced a jump to $29,671,076 in the next year.[80] Already by the end of the first decade, the United States had replaced Great Britain as the largest single source of foreign mission funds and also as leader of the English-speaking nations, who were said to have contributed about 85 percent of the total given for spreading the Protestant gospel in the non-Christian world.[81] Even the proportion of support given by American Protestants before 1920 increased markedly. Between 1904 and 1914, communicant church membership in the United States had grown by 25.3 percent, while total contributions for all local church expenses had risen 39.7 percent, for missionary and benevolent work in the United States 62.8 percent, and for foreign mission work a startling 87.5 percent.[82]

The only objective never realized was the transformation of American Protestantism into militant missionary churches in which foreign missions would be the central concern. Even if this objective had not been unrealistic in human terms, the low initial share of contributions available to foreign mission societies mitigated against its realization before 1920. A survey of twelve representative denominations in 1902 revealed expenditures of $45,700,000 for congregational or parish expenses, $5,138,000 for home missions, and only $2,442,000 for foreign missions.[83] A later study of the share of gifts from living donors to the benevolent work of eleven denominations showed foreign mission boards receiving 31.6 percent of the total in 1913, then dropping to 28.9 percent in 1920, which was the peak year for total benevolences before the depression.[84] The expected continuation of the upward trend in per capita giving to foreign missions failed to materialize during later decades, and the prevalent ratio of contributions in the major Protestant churches during the first three decades of this century averaged approximately four dollars for congregational expenses to one dollar for all benevolences.[85]

With exceptions in individual denominations, a high point in giving to foreign missions was thus recorded at the beginning of the third decade of this century, followed by a relative decline. In relationship to both ideals and gross-income figures, the upsurge of support in the decade before 1920 did not perpetuate itself. Both later studies and the observations of several mission leaders confirm the impression that only the use of unprecedented energy and innovations in fund raising saved foreign missions from losing support during the decades before World War I. The prevalent interpretation of the development of the colossal denominational fund drives and of the efforts of such organizations as the Laymen's Movement which produced the increased financial support was that they constituted a missionary awakening in the Christian public. Whether a rising missionary spirit produced the new methods, or promotionalism created the awakening would be fruitless to argue. In a period of increasing rivalry for funds with other benevolent agencies, organization and business methods were seen to work wonders in the commercial world. The leaders of the mission movement apparently learned this lesson and put more effort into efficient and flexible promotion than into a campaign to effect a general spiritual revival in America.

The foreign mission movement combined a confusing mixture of youthful enthusiasm and ecclesiastical conservatism, traditionalism, and free innovation. An otherworldly spiritualism coexisted with calculated pragmatism, as did parochialism with an idealistic vision of the brotherhood of man in a coming kingdom lacking internal boundaries. Characteristics that during the prewar years had been strongly developed became the targets of scorn in the aftermath of a world war that had marked the end of an era. Before 1920 the terminology of missions had reflected a concept of Christian expansion by conquest, but the world war between Christian states forced a reappraisal of optimistic prophecies concerning the achievements of that generation. Both the fact that Christian nations could engage in the mutual butchery of the greatest war the world had ever seen and the self-conscious growth of national churches in mission lands forced a reconsideration of the assumption that the American Protestant model was indeed a firmly rooted world religion, which merely faced the conquest of a few remaining non-Christian areas. Similarly, the movement's agencies were pressed by hostility and a sober reappraisal of their resources to cooperate more extensively than in the past, when they had proclaimed ecumenical objectives but practiced denominational competition.

The organizational changes that occurred in the mission movement in the decades before World War I were less a response to theory or theology than a pragmatic reaction to necessity. There was no new theological imperative pressing toward an ecumenical ideal and the lowering of denominational barriers to cooperation. But the exigencies of raising sufficient support dictated such cooperation as well as the increasing employment of inter- or nondenominational agencies. The Laymen's Movement, Student Volunteers, Foreign Missions Conference, and World Missionary Council reflect pragmatism more than an ideal, although in some cases both dream and pedestrian necessity coexisted. The proliferation of agencies and auxiliaries, coordinated by both formal and informal means, had created a stronger, more effectively organized Protestant mission movement during the decades before 1920 than during any previous period in the movement's history.

There were indications, however, that in the process of organizing a movement, one former element of strength had been lost. Youth had played a crucial role at the beginning, both through the young volunteers who challenged the New England churches to send them to foreign lands, and through the Brethren, a secret fraternity dedicated to promoting the foreign mission cause among disinterested college and seminary classmates.[86] The dynamism of a spontaneous movement based on religious conviction and compassion for non-Christians eternally damned had by the last quarter of the nineteenth century become interred in denominational agencies paying perfunctory obeisance to the old spirit. Stirred by the idealism and enthusiasm of youth enrolling as Student Volunteers, an effort was made during subsequent decades to transcend the bureaucratic and creedal restraints and to relaunch a true movement. Instead, the existing agencies absorbed the new dynamism in their drive to become bigger and more powerful, while an interdenominational superstructure developed, which became equally bureaucratized and antithetical to the unrestrained and uncalculating enthusiasm that characterizes a true movement. When promotionalism no longer sufficed and the nation's worst economic depression again forced a retrenchment, the young people who were needed to work another renaissance were too busy with other causes.

CLIFTON J. PHILLIPS

*The Student Volunteer Movement
and Its Role in China Missions, 1886—1920*

Student movements have played a prominent part in awakening a missionary spirit in American Protestant churches. In the first wave of evangelical enthusiasm for foreign missions that swept across the Atlantic from England at the beginning of the nineteenth century, a handful of undergraduates at Williams College in 1808 founded the Brethren, a secret fellowship sworn to "effect in the person of its members a mission or missions to the heathen." Transferred to Andover Theological Seminary two years later, the Brethren provided much of the initial impetus leading to the formation of the American Board of Commissioners for Foreign Missions in Boston in 1810. From this society's ranks came not only the five ordained members of the American Board's first missionary band, which sailed for India in 1812, but in succeeding years a continuing stream of foreign missionaries stationed in various parts of the non-Christian world. Although the Andover Brethren developed branches for a time in three or four other theological seminaries, it remained a relatively small, secret body until its dissolution around 1870 and seems to have had little influence on student life in most American institutions of higher education. Its offshoot, the Society of Inquiry, was a nonsecret campus religious association which actively promoted missionary education in a number of colleges and seminaries in the East for several decades but never functioned as a recruiting agency for foreign missions and failed to achieve any degree of national organization beyond a desultory correspondence between some of its branches and the founding group at Andover.[1]

A more enduring and better organized student movement came into existence in the eighties during a similar period of heightened missionary concern within the Anglo-American evangelical community. It originated with the formation of the "Mount Hermon Hundred," a group of young men, mostly undergraduates, who publicly pledged themselves to become foreign missionaries, under the inspiration of a few emotion-packed sessions of the first student summer Bible conference held in America. The conference had been convoked in July 1886 by the popular evangelist Dwight L. Moody on the commodious, unfinished campus of his newly established school for boys in Mount Hermon, Massachusetts.[2] By 1888, a tremendously successful recruiting tour of nearly two hundred colleges and theological seminaries by one of the chief leaders of the Mount Hermon Hundred, Robert P. Wilder, and his Princeton classmate and future fellow missionary in India, John N. Forman, had swollen the number of pledged students to over 2200. In December of that year the Student Volunteer Movement for Foreign Missions (SVM) was formally organized on a national basis under the auspices of the intercollegiate Young Men's Christian Association. Within a dozen years the SVM had spread to hundreds of college campuses and was enlisting thousands of college youth in a veritable religious crusade, whose ambitious slogan was "The Evangelization of the World in This Generation." Under the aggressive direction of an executive committee headed by a young Cornell graduate, John R. Mott, this organization soon became the largest and probably the most influential student movement in North America. It received the enthusiastic endorsement and cooperation of Protestant foreign mission societies of virtually all denominations, and in the persons of its leaders and spokesman—men like Mott himself, Robert P. Wilder, Robert E. Speer, and G. Sherwood Eddy—it produced some of the outstanding missionary statesmen of the era. The SVM maintained a continuous existence as an autonomous body through the sixth decade of the twentieth century, loosely affiliated at first with the YMCA and later with the National Student Christian Federation and the National Council of Churches. Both its formative and its most vigorous years, however, were encompassed in a single generation, the first thirty-three years of the movement.[3]

What conditions and forces made possible the sudden emergence of the SVM in the 1880s? What factors promoted its rapid growth among college and university students as well as its expanding influence on American Protestant missionary statesmanship during the course of the following three decades? What role did it play in the world-wide strategy of evangelical foreign missions? Especially, how much did it affect both the strategy and the tactics of the missionary enterprise in China, which not only attracted by far the largest single contingent of Student Volunteers in this period but finally emerged as the world's leading mission field, based on the number of Protestant foreign missionaries and the amount of financial resources deployed there?[4]

THE MILLENARIAN BACKGROUND

An important element in the renewed missionary concern of the last quarter of the nineteenth century was the revival of millenarianism in evangelical thought. The earlier tide of millenarian speculation, represented in the writings of the prominent American theologians Jonathan Edwards and Samuel Hopkins, had considerably influenced the first foreign missionary awakening. But this tide had ebbed by mid-century, partly at least because of the unpopular extremes to which the Millerites and other Adventist groups had carried such views.[5] By the 1870s, however, a fresh current of millenarian thought, emanating chiefly from the Plymouth Brethren and related religious circles in England, began to have a wide impact on Anglo-American Protestantism. Of particular influence was its "premillennialist" version, according to which the signs pointed to the imminent second advent of Jesus Christ, preliminary to the inauguration of His thousand-year reign as the Prince of Peace in fulfillment of biblical prophecies. Promulgated in the United States by such popular American preachers as Adoniram Judson Gordon of Boston, Arthur T. Pierson of Philadelphia, and Dwight L. Moody himself, premillennialism became a force to be reckoned with in the evangelical churches. It re-emphasized the practice of the "concert of prayer," reinvigorated the study of the Bible, and in various parts of the country called into being great Chautauqua-like summer Bible conferences convened by premillennialist pastors and associations.[6]

Premillennialists argued, in accordance with their interpretation of scriptural prophecies, that the gospel must be preached to all the world before Christ's appearance on earth for a second time. This conclusion clearly made the foreign mission enterprise one of the most urgent, if not the foremost, duty of the churches. They cited the rise of such predominantly Protestant powers as Great Britain, the United States, and Prussia, with the concomitant opening of non-Christian countries in Asia and Africa to Anglo-Saxon pressures and influences, as providential indications of the coming evangelization of the globe. In a similar vein millenarian prophets of the late eighteenth and early nineteenth centuries had interpreted the upheavals of the French Revolution and the Napoleonic Wars as harbingers of the close of the earthly dispensation. The evangelization of the world in turn heralded the advent of Christ and the ultimate inauguration of His Kingdom. This "historicist" argument was a main theme of Arthur T. Pierson's popular book *The Crisis of Missions,* in which that indefatigable champion of foreign missions employed the characteristic rhetoric of high millennial urgency to plead for a revitalized Protestant missionary crusade. "The fulness of time has come, and the end seems at hand, which is also the beginning of the last and greatest age," he announced. Therefore, no delay could be brooked in pushing on with a revived campaign for foreign missions: "Now or never! Tomorrow may be too late for work that must be done today."[7] In this volume, published in 1886, the author proposed that an interdenominational world council be called to draw up a master plan for the efficient deployment of all Protestant forces in a concerted effort to occupy the entire non-Christian world in the shortest possible time. Seven years earlier he had presented this idea in simpler form in Royal G. Wilder's *Missionary Review.* Wilder was an independent-minded former missionary of the American Board in India, who had founded this monthly in 1877 in Princeton, New Jersey, in order to air new methods and concepts of foreign missions. He now gave strong editorial support to Pierson's bold prognosis that the premillennialist goal of preaching the gospel to all the world could be achieved within twenty years, if conducted on business principles by the united action of all the evangelical churches.[8] Although this grandiose scheme came to little, after Wilder's death in 1887 Pierson assumed the editorship of the journal, which he retitled the *Missionary Review of the World.* He made of it a vehicle for his militant views of foreign missions as well as the chief nondenominational organ of the Protestant missionary movement.

Pierson was one of the main speakers at the Mount Hermon summer Bible conference. Along with William G. Ashmore, a missionary on furlough from China, he played a large part in arousing the enthusiasm for foreign missions that led to the organization of the SVM. He was a conspicuous figure at subsequent student assemblies at Northfield, where Moody's summer conferences were transferred from 1888 onward, as well as at the first international conventions of the SVM. He was also the author of the movement's striking watchword, "The Evangelization of the World in This Generation," a phrase that succinctly embodied the prevailing millenarian outlook. In an address before the SVM convention in 1894 he attempted to clarify the meaning of the slogan by explaining that evangelization of the world did not mean Christianization but referred only to the proclamation of the gospel to all men.[9] Under attack in some quarters as reflecting a particular premillennialist theory, the watchword was stubbornly defended by SVM spokesmen as making a general and urgent appeal to *each generation* of Christian students to take upon themselves personal responsibility for the uplift of the non-Christian portions of humanity through presentation of the evangelical message, whether by the medium of evangelism, medicine, or education.[10] Hence, though the premillennialist revival helped to launch the SVM, the movement quickly took on a life of its own. It single-mindedly stressed an absolute but nondogmatic commitment to the cause of foreign missions while hewing to a centrist evangelical position, which could embrace both the premillennialist hope of hastening the advent of Christ by saving souls and the postmillennialist vision of the long-range regeneration of non-Christian society by implanting Christian institutions.[11]

THE INFLUENCE OF REVIVALISM

In both its origins and its early development the SVM owed a great deal to the religious revivalism that flourished within evangelical Protestantism during those years. Many of its first promoters and student volunteers had come under the profound influence of the lay evangelist Dwight L. Moody. Though himself a man of little education, Moody had conducted successful revivals at Yale and Princeton and had made a remarkable impression on British university youth during his two tours of Great Britain. Two Cambridge University athletes converted in his campaign of 1883, Charles T. Studd and Stanley P. Smith, made a stir in student circles on both sides of the Atlantic when with five others they volunteered for service in the China Inland Mission. Shortly before their departure for China, these men, dubbed the Cambridge Seven, toured British universities on behalf of foreign missions, which set a precedent for the many SVM deputations to American colleges in later years. Studd's brother, J. E. K. Studd, who had been captain of the Cambridge cricket team and chairman of Moody's evangelistic meetings there, came to Northfield in the summer of 1885 at the urging of Moody and later that year began a speaking tour of American colleges and universities, which helped prepare the ground for the student movement about to come to birth in the United States.[12]

Paradoxically, Moody himself never revealed a compelling interest in foreign missions, much preferring to invest his time and energy in training lay workers for city evangelism in America. This was one of the chief purposes for the establishment of his girls' school at Northfield and a similar institution for boys at Mount Hermon, as well as the Moody Bible Institute in Chicago. Yet Moody's dynamic personality and commanding presence at the Mount Hermon and Northfield summer conferences combined with his prestige and stature in the Anglo-American evangelical world to bring a potent influence to bear upon the student missionary movement. Moody-inspired revivalistic and Bible-study methods, together with his characteristic emphasis on the consecration and surrender of the redeemed individual's will to God and Christ, were central to the program and procedures of the SVM. Campus study meetings, regional and national summer conferences, and even the great quadrennial international conventions of the SVM had much of the atmosphere and general character of a Moody religious revival, with emotion-charged preaching and prayer sessions focused on the theme of dedication to a life of sacrifice and moral heroism in the foreign mission field. The "conversion experience" induced under such revival-like conditions in college men and women, most of whom were presumably the products of lifelong Christian nurture in evangelical homes and educational institutions, could only mean the reconsecration of lives already at least nominally committed to Christ. For such persons, the often agonizing career decision presented by the SVM pledge offered a seemingly unique opportunity to reconsecrate and rededicate themselves to the highest religious ideal.[13]

A perhaps direct borrowing from the revivalistic techniques of the time was the use of pledge cards, which student volunteers were urged to sign as an earnest of their commitment to the foreign mission service, just as Moody and other evangelists asked their converts to fill out "decision cards."[14] The first SVM pledge, "I am willing and desirous, God permitting, to become a foreign missionary," was taken from the covenant signed by members of the Princeton Foreign Missionary Society, organized by Robert P. Wilder in 1884. Although this pledge was changed in 1892 to the somewhat simpler declaration, "It is my purpose, if God permits, to become a foreign missionary," the movement continued to place great weight on the seriousness and irrevocability of the personal commitment involved.[15] Nevertheless, the number of those who signed pledge or declaration cards was always far larger than those who persevered to the point of actually sailing to a foreign mission field.[16] In order to maintain the momentum and enthusiasm of those who had signed the pledge or declaration, they were encouraged to form "Volunteer Bands" on their home campuses and to organize suitable programs of missionary education, often in cooperation with the college YMCA and YWCA. Each year the executive committee of the SVM dispatched traveling secretaries—usually college or seminary graduates who had already been accepted for missionary service and were soon to go abroad—to college and university campuses to arouse and sustain interest in foreign missions and to help recruit new volunteers. An educational secretary was put in charge of the preparation and distribution of books and pamphlets dealing with various aspects of foreign missions, including the all-important decision to become a missionary. The corresponding secretary kept a voluminous file of pledge and declaration cards, miscellaneous letters to and from volunteers, and thousands of questionnaires containing information about their preparation and plans for entering the mission field.[17]

Not only did the SVM provide a convenient outlet for some of the intense religious idealism generated by the revivals of the time, but it also tended to institutionalize revivalism—normally a largely anti-institutional force within evangelicalism—by channeling the revival impulse, in part at least, into the foreign mission enterprise. Unwilling to rely on the spontaneous emergence of a missionary spirit among students, the SVM created an extensive organizational network completely unknown to the earlier Brethren and Society of Inquiry. State associations of campus Volunteer Bands were formed, and in some cities SVM unions or leagues appeared, chiefly in an attempt to maintain contact with volunteers who had left college or seminary but had not yet gone to a mission field. A major means of promoting the cause of foreign missions remained the summer Bible conferences, which by the nineties had become a securely established institution in the student movement. Besides the Northfield conference, which continued to convene yearly, a second annual summer session was instituted at Lake Geneva, Wisconsin, in 1890, and a third in Knoxville, Tennessee, in 1892, to accommodate an increasing number of students from the Middle West and South. Undoubtedly the largest and most colorful student gatherings of all were the great quadrennial international conventions of the SVM, which in this period met successively in Cleveland, Detroit, Toronto, Nashville, Rochester, Kansas City, and Des Moines. From the modest total of 680 delegates who gathered in Cleveland in 1891, the number attending the nearly week-long sessions—held in late February or early March until 1910, whereafter the meeting time was shifted to the year-end holidays—rose to 2221 in 1898, 4235 in 1906, and 5031 in 1914.[18] Although early student-missionary interest was centered in New England and the East, most of the SVM conventions were held in Midwestern cities. Moreover, while colleges such as Yale and Princeton, where the revivalistic spirit was particularly flourishing, continued to furnish a relatively large quota, by the nineties most volunteers came from the newer denominational colleges of the Midwest, a region that had become the evangelical, as well as the geographical, heartland of the continent.[19]

RELATIONS WITH THE YMCA AND OTHER STUDENT MOVEMENTS

In many ways the real matrix of the SVM was the YMCA, the lay-oriented evangelical youth organization that had been founded in London in 1844 and transplanted to North American cities by mid-century. Originally directed primarily toward young urban workers, by the 1870s the YMCA had thriving branches on a number of college campuses, some of them derived from the older Societies of Inquiry and similar groups. In 1877 the Louisville convention of the YMCA authorized the creation of a college department and named Luther D. Wishard its first secretary. Wishard, who had been introduced to YMCA work at Hanover College in Indiana before transferring to Princeton, set out energetically to found scores of college associations in the East and Middle West. In what the international committee of the YMCA considered to be excessive zeal, he admitted women to many of the campus chapters, a practice that helped to bring about the eventual entrance of the YWCA to the college field.[20]

Wishard, who was chiefly responsible for persuading the somewhat reluctant Moody to call the summer Bible conference at Mount Hermon in 1886, entertained a vision of global evangelization by means of a world-wide fellowship of college and university students dedicated to the expansion of evangelical Christianity. Motivated by this idea, he visited student Christian leaders in England and the Continent in 1888 and spent the next three years on a grand tour of mission fields in Asia. He held evangelistic meetings in China, Japan, India, and Ceylon, where he laid the foundations for the eventual large-scale extension of YMCA activities to students and others in those countries. One of Wishard's closest colleagues in the college secretaryship, C. K. Ober, drew up the plans for the national organization of the SVM in 1888, and another college secretary, John R. Mott, became its first chairman. Throughout most of its existence the SVM was closely associated with the YMCA and the YWCA, and the majority of its volunteers were the products of college and university associations.[21]

A growing interest in foreign missions among theological students led to the organization of the Interseminary Missionary Alliance as early as 1880, largely through the efforts of Robert Mateer, Wishard's Princeton roommate and member of a prominent missionary family in China. For several years, hundreds of students from thirty or more seminaries, as well as returned missionaries and representatives of denominational mission boards, attended its annual conferences, which were the largest meetings of that nature until the quadrennial conventions of the SVM. When the SVM was formally organized in 1888, the Alliance was represented on its executive committee, but ten years later it ended its independent existence to become the theological section of the intercollegiate YMCA. Inspired by the interseminary movement, Wishard called the first Medical Students' Missionary Conference in Lake Forest, Illinois, in 1883, the forerunner of a series of similar meetings in Chicago, New York, Philadelphia, St. Louis, Baltimore, and elsewhere. Although no permanent organization resulted from these conferences, delegates from medical schools regularly attended the SVM conventions, and a medical representative sat on its executive committee from 1898 onward. Another student missionary group antedating the SVM was the Intercollegiate Missionary Alliance of Canada, founded in 1885 but later absorbed into the larger movement.[22]

From its beginnings the SVM was more than a purely national organization, for like its parent body, the international committee of the YMCA, it embraced Canada along with the United States in its purview and always had a good representation of Canadian institutions in its constituency. Its leaders attempted to establish close ties with the transatlantic student Christian movement as well. Delegates from Great Britain attended the first two summer Bible conferences at Northfield, and John N. Forman, a member of the first SVM deputation to American colleges in 1887, made a return visit to universities in that country on his way to take up a missionary post in India in 1888. Three years later Robert P. Wilder, who had been appointed the first official traveling secretary of the SVM, made a second tour of British universities. This tour directly inspired the organization of the Student Volunteer Missionary Union of Great Britain and Ireland, which maintained friendly ties with its American counterpart and for many years sent fraternal delegates to the quadrennial conventions. Similar but smaller, shorter-lived groups also sprang up in Europe, Australia, and New Zealand.[23]

The most enduring monument to the American vision of a truly international organization of evangelical youth was the World Student Christian Federation, founded at Vadstena, Sweden, in 1895. The partial fulfillment of Wishard's dream of a world-wide Christian youth movement, it had as its chief architects Wishard and Mott, who on a European tour that summer persuaded British, German, and Scandinavian Protestant leaders to federate their respective student movements with the intercollegiate YMCA in North America. The missionary outlook of the World Student Christian Federation, with which the SVM was affiliated through the YMCA, was clearly enunciated in the last of the stated purposes drawn up by the Vadstena delegates, "to enlist students in the work of extending the Kingdom of Christ throughout the world." Mott, who was chosen the federation's first general secretary, immediately set out on a two-year world tour, which reached from Paris to Tokyo and added to its membership emergent student Christian movements in Europe, Asia, and Australasia.[24]

THE PROTESTANT MISSIONARY STRATEGY

The SVM made a significant impact on the evangelical missionary enterprise, as shown by the fact that its volunteers for a foreign field—8140 had set forth by 1919—probably composed well over half of the total number of foreign missionaries sent abroad under North American Protestant auspices in this period.[25] As the missionary arm of the intercollegiate YMCA and YWCA, it represented the largest, most active student Christian movement on the continent, mobilizing youth for the foreign service of the church militant in a way that conventional ecclesiastical organizations could not match. For these and other reasons the SVM enjoyed close, harmonious relations with all the major Protestant mission boards. Their secretaries regularly attended and frequently addressed its quadrennial conventions, which became an important forum for the discussion and propagation of current foreign-mission policy. Moreover, as a widely representative and interdenominational body, the SVM lent its influence to the growing movement for interfaith missionary cooperation, manifested in the convening of the Foreign Missions Conference of North America in 1893, the Ecumenical Missionary Conference in New York in 1900, and the World Missionary Conference in Edinburgh in 1910. This last chose the SVM's chief executive, Mott, for its presiding officer and chairman of its continuation committee.[26]

The student movement's militant posture and its spokesmen's tendency to employ a rhetoric abounding in military figures of speech may well have influenced the whole evangelical missionary outlook, which seems also to have been colored by the general thrust of the imperialist expansion of the time. William G. Ashmore, the returned missionary who helped to inspire the gathering of the original Mount Hermon Hundred, set the tone for this new mood of militancy in appealing to his student audience in 1886 to "look no longer upon missions as a mere wrecking expedition, but as a war of conquest."[27] The theme of the second international convention of the SVM in 1894 was "The World's Conquest for Christ," and at the next such meeting in February 1898, when men's minds were beginning to turn toward the possibility of American military action against Spain, Mott closed the convention, which on opening night had been termed a "council of war," with a fighting speech full of the metaphors of the battlefield.[28] At Toronto in 1902, Mott unself-consciously expressed his frank acceptance of an Anglo-American missionary imperialism in describing to the assembly of delegates from Canada and the United States "the wonderful destiny before the great British Empire and the Republic of America," because they stand for "introducing into the unevangelized nations and setting at work among the depressed and neglected races those influences which alone can ameliorate the conditions of mankind, build up a lasting civilization and make possible the evangelization of the world."[29] Although the rather strident tone of the turn of the century was moderated in later years, SVM leaders continued for some time to discuss foreign mission strategy in terms of military victory and territorial conquest and to confuse the Christianization of the world with the expansion of American or Western civilization.

The SVM required no theological tests whatever but emphasized a warm, vital, practical piety and refused to become involved in doctrinal controversies. For the most part it avoided the liberal-conservative cleavage that was beginning to appear in American Protestantism. Faithful to the prevailing evangelical stance and temper, the SVM based its missionary appeal on the solid conviction of the universality of human sin and the resulting need of all mankind for salvation through Jesus Christ. Thus, the primary task of the missionary was assumed to be evangelistic, that is, to preach the gospel of Christ and serve as a personal witness to its saving efficacy. Yet from the outset evangelism was never conceived in narrow terms, and the claims of auxiliary undertakings, particularly medicine and education, were consistently placed before would-be volunteers no less urgently than was preaching. Indeed, the main trend of speeches printed in the quadrennial convention reports was clearly away from the older emphasis on saving individual souls to a "social gospel" for the mission field. In 1898, for example, President Charles Cuthbert Hall of Union Theological Seminary explained to the convention that the "latest thought on missions" was that "the gospel for heathen lands is not alone a gospel of deliverance for a life to come, but a gospel of social renewal for the life that now is—a gospel that patiently and thoroughly renovates heathen life in its personal, domestic, civic, tribal, national practices and tendencies—aiming to make the heathen commonwealth, as well as the heathen individual, a new creation in Christ Jesus." To accomplish such purposes required the dedicated leadership of the student class, "men and women who have prepared themselves by years of academic discipline to grasp and apply the sociological functions of Christianity."[30]

Implicit in the very nature of an appeal directed almost exclusively to students in institutions of higher education was an emphasis on the specialized function of highly trained men and women in the missionary enterprise. Although the SVM enlisted a number of volunteers from such noncollegiate institutions as the Moody Bible Institute in Chicago and the Gordon Bible and Missionary Training School in Boston, its explicitly stated preference was for students who planned to complete a full four-year college course, plus, for ordained clergymen and physicians, the additional years of professional training normally required in the United States for these callings.[31] Mott reiterated the demand for quality rather than quantity in his report to the 1906 convention in Nashville, Tennessee: "The ultimate success of the missionary enterprise does not depend primarily upon vast numbers of missionaries, so much as upon thoroughly furnished missionaries. For the reason that our Watchword requires haste, we, above all others, should insist on the most thorough preparation and training of workers, knowing full well that this will save time in the long run and enormously increase the fruitage."[32] As a result of this policy of forming an elite corps of Christian crusaders, increasing numbers of volunteers in the mission field were able enthusiastically to turn to more specialized tasks than simple street evangelism.[33] Another possible factor in encouraging greater functional specialization in foreign missions in these years was the rapid growth in the number of women student volunteers. Disqualified for clerical ordination in most cases, they took up missionary careers in female education, public health, and YWCA work.[34]

Closely related to the SVM demand for well-educated missionary volunteers was the thesis, beginning to be widely developed in the 1890s, that the evangelization of the world in one generation, or indeed in any finite length of time, could be accomplished only by raising up a body of indigenous Christian workers who would themselves be responsible for bringing the gospel to the millions of their unevangelized countrymen. The chief task, then, of the foreign missionary was conceived as primarily the training of native cadres, which called for leadership and administrative skills as much as evangelistic zeal. In 1894, Judson Smith of the American Board of Commissioners for Foreign Missions told an SVM convention that volunteers must be prepared to become generals, selecting and training the captains and privates from the ranks of native converts for the final assault on heathendom.[35] This view of foreign missions was in close accord with the scheme of Wishard to extend the student Christian movement to Asia and other parts of the unevangelized world. In reporting to the SVM convention of 1894 after his return from a protracted tour of the mission fields of Asia, Wishard argued that YMCAs planted there among college youth by American student emissaries would eventually flower in an indigenous student-volunteer movement, which could then furnish native evangelists to preach the gospel to their own countrymen.[36]

The idea that the key to success in the self-imposed task of world evangelization lay in reaching educated youth in non-Christian countries was a plausible, attractive notion, especially to North American college and university students, and was many times repeated in SVM meetings. Emphasizing that "the day for evangelistic missions alone has gone by," Ernest D. Burton of the University of Chicago Divinity School observed at the 1914 convention of the SVM that in Asia in particular, "the great task which lies before Christian missions is the preparation of men and women to be field-leaders in Christian communities, as well as leaders of nations." For such an important work, he asked, who should be sent but the "brightest and best of our countrymen, the product of the richest culture, trained in the best schools, with hearts filled with enthusiasm and desire to use their best efforts to meet the bright students before them?"[37]

What was taking shape as the student movement gained momentum and influence in the Protestant missionary enterprise was nothing less than a major shift in the grand strategy of foreign missions. It was a shift away from the traditional evangelical policy of proclaiming the gospel among the unevangelized masses toward a broader endeavor to Christianize heathen society essentially from the top down by concentrating on winning an educated elite. This was more than simply a switch in missionary methods, for mission schools and hospitals had been utilized from the first as auxiliary instruments, and personal evangelism remained a popular technique throughout this period. The big change was not so much in tactics as in overall strategy. The student movement made a significant contribution to this strategy with its dream of joining hands with a world-wide body of educated Christian youth for the extension of Christ's kingdom. The goal of blanketing the unevangelized world with a host of foreign missionaries held personally responsible for conveying the message of salvation to the unoccupied regions was being replaced by the objective of creating an indigenous Christian leadership to nurture the developing nations by means of the gradual infusion of Christianity. As W. M. Forrest, a returned missionary from India, told the student convention of 1906, "No Church can succeed anywhere in any land simply by contenting itself with reaching the lowest classes." Conceding that no country had ever been Christianized from the top downward, he argued that "in order to make a whole land Christian, if it begins at the bottom it must take of the ablest of that lower stratum and develop from them a thinking class, a class of leaders."[38]

THE CHINA MISSIONS

The empire, and later the republic, of China offered a tempting arena for the testing of this developing missionary strategy, and SVM statistics reveal a decided bias toward the China mission field. In the first breakdown by geographical location of the recorded figures for all "sailed volunteers," it was reported in 1906 that, out of a total of 2953 volunteers who had sailed to all points up to that date, 826, or around 29 percent, had gone to China, in comparison with 624, or 21 percent, who had gone to India (including Burma and Ceylon), the second largest category. The next decade and a half greatly augmented the predominance of the China field. In 1920 the SVM executive committee reported that, for the entire period 1886–1919, 2524 out of 8140 "sailed volunteers" were bound for China, increasing that contingent's proportion to 31 percent.[39] The roster of student volunteers who labored in China for a shorter or longer time during this period is filled with the names of founders, administrators, and teachers of institutions of higher education, YMCA and YWCA secretaries, whose work was primarily with educated Chinese youth, and other "missionary literati," who wrote and translated textbooks, biblical commentaries, and miscellaneous pamphlets, edited and published newspapers and journals, and in general concerned themselves with the more intellectual aspects of the missionary enterprise. An extraordinarily large number were also inspired to undertake serious study and research concerning the history and culture of the ancient civilization in which they served. On the whole, they produced a remarkable literary output in Sinology and modern Chinese affairs, and in many cases they returned eventually to university posts in the field of Chinese studies in the United States and elsewhere.[40]

With its centuries-long tradition of political, social, and intellectual leadership by a responsible intellectual elite, China undoubtedly constituted a particularly appealing mission field to college and university students in North America, who composed at that time only a small fraction of the total populations of their countries and whose education was intended to prepare them for entrance into the learned professions and other leadership roles in American society. In the SVM convention of 1894 Gilbert Reid, a Presbyterian missionary in Peking who had just initiated a "Mission among the Higher Classes in China," elucidated his conviction that it was possible "to convert these men of influence in China, and turn their influence unto the evangelization of their fellow-countrymen." A missionary colleague from North China, Henry Kingman, endorsed the same strategy in an address on "The Need of Men and Women of Literary Tastes in China." He pleaded for volunteers equipped with the high educational and intellectual qualifications necessary to meet the Chinese literati on their own ground by composing literary tracts that would refute their errors and bring them to Christ.[41]

The same convention that heard these proposals for the conversion of the scholar gentry also listened to missionary educator A. P. Happer argue the case for mission-sponsored education in China as a means of breaking the grip of the old intelligentsia. "Now, if Christianity ever takes the citadel of China," he said, "it will be done by undermining, by our schools and colleges and a Christian education, the system of education and institutions of China, and taking it by the fall of the walls of their own education." This view was strengthened by the growing interest in modern, Western-style education displayed by Chinese reformers and even by some government officials after China's humiliating defeat at the hands of Japan in 1895. Moreover, the abolition of the Confucian classics-based civil service examination system in 1905, while signaling the approaching close of the literati domination of Chinese culture, gave a strong impetus to the emergence of a new class of students beginning to throng the halls of modern educational institutions. Commenting on these changes at the 1906 student convention, Robert R. Gailey of the Peking YMCA continued to express the forlorn hope that the remaining body of traditional scholars might yet produce an Augustine, an Erasmus, or a Jonathan Edwards to help lead China to Christ. But he placed his main emphasis on the need to evangelize the new student class, which like the old would eventually sway the destinies of the country. Just as England bore a responsibility for the students of India, Americans had a special obligation to those of China. "Men and women," he concluded, "the responsibility is upon us to reach these millions of students in China and the new literati that are to come. Who are ready?"[42]

The student Christian movement in America was deeply impressed by the apparent success of the evangelistic tour of China and other parts of Asia conducted by Mott and Sherwood Eddy in the winter of 1912–1913. Tens of thousands of students, scholars, and government officials, including Yüan Shih-k'ai and other national leaders of the newly established republic of China, came out to meet and listen to the American religious leaders. Their enthusiastic reports to the SVM convention in 1914 helped raise high hopes for the Christianization of the new nation emerging from revolution in China through working with its educated classes.[43]

As early as 1910 the SVM leadership began to recognize the missionary potential of the rapidly growing body of Chinese students enrolled in American institutions of higher education.[44] In an address before the student convention of that year held in Rochester, New York, C. T. Wang, a student at Yale University who later became the first Chinese general secretary of the Chinese YMCA, urged that Chinese be given the primary responsibility for evangelizing China and be trained for this by several years of study abroad, preferably in the United States. Striking a new note of equality between foreign missionaries and native Christian leaders, he added, "With sincere and hearty cooperation as our watchword, let us Orientals and you Occidental students join hand in hand to advance God's Kingdom in China and the Far East."[45] Four years later Chinese students in America held their first national conference in conjunction with the seventh international convention of the SVM. Approximately 150 Chinese studying in American universities attended the special sessions in Kansas City, which were chiefly devoted to discussions of their role in the Christianization and national salvation of China. Mott, taking time from his duties as convention chairman to address the assembled Chinese students, conceded that "the evangelization and Christianization of China is not an American or a European enterprise, but a Chinese enterprise." This and similar sentiments expressed by Chinese and other speakers did not mean that the SVM—and certainly not Mott himself—was ready to abandon the role of the foreign missionary in China. But it did indicate that the shift from direct evangelization to the creation of an educated native leadership responsible for Christianizing the broad masses required some modification of the unilateral character of the movement as originally conceived. An American missionary on leave from his post in China, Abram E. Cory, furnished the convention with an amended version of the SVM watchword that took cognizance of the changing mood of missions: "This generation of students, foreign and Chinese, will be largely responsible for the evangelization of China."[46]

World War I brought temporary disruption to the foreign mission enterprise in many places but hardly slowed the flow of American volunteers abroad. A large increase in the number of women among the "sailed volunteers" for 1918 almost made up for the reduction in the number of men in that year. When the eighth international convention of the SVM was finally held after a two-year delay on the last day of December 1919 in Des Moines, Iowa, its leaders faced the largest such gathering ever assembled—6890 delegates from 949 institutions, including 5086 North American and 342 foreign students. Chairman Mott, who had presided over every convention since 1891 but was to resign from his post after this one, opened the proceedings with a fresh challenge to the student movement in the midst of the bewilderment and change of the postwar world: "We stand on the threshold of the greatest opportunity which North American students have ever confronted."[47]

So it must have appeared to many delegates at the Midwestern parley. In the immediate aftermath of the war and the peacemaking, the American student Christian movement seemed to reach new peaks of enthusiasm and faith in its ability to make the world over in the image of Christ. In 1920 and 1921 the SVM recorded the largest number of "sailed volunteers" in its history. But the next few years witnessed the beginning of a gradual decline in the movement's appeal to students. This was related perhaps to a general disillusionment with the idealistic internationalism of the Wilsonian war and peace aims, with which much of the missionary movement had tended to identify. Other factors in the decline of the SVM included the growing fundamentalist-modernist split, which broke up the evangelical united front on which the student Christian movement was firmly based; the Great Depression of the 1930s, which undercut the financial support of foreign missions; the rising secularism in American higher education, as reflected, for example, in the relative growth of public universities vis-à-vis denominational institutions; the spread of the social gospel, which turned men's minds to the need for Christianizing America first; and perhaps most important of all, a developing crisis in missionary thinking, which in the 1920s and later shifted even farther from evangelization of the non-Christian world by Americans and Europeans in the direction of partnership and cooperation among the older and younger churches in the building of a Christian world order.[48]

WILLIAM R. HUTCHISON

*Modernism and Missions: The Liberal Search
for an Exportable Christianity, 1875—1935*

Robert E. Speer, the great mission-board administrator of the early twentieth century, once remarked that there had always been "far more speculation on the future fate of the heathen among stay-at-homes than among missionaries."[1] The "heathen" themselves, one might add, probably cared less about technical theological questions than did either stay-at-homes or missionaries. But one should not conclude from these rather patent observations that domestic theological rivalries had no bearing on the practical missionary enterprise. In missions, as in foreign policy, the aspiration to leave ideological differences at the water's edge was never more than partially fulfilled.

Certainly the missionaries found it unfitting in numerous practical situations to stress intra-Christian doctrinal discussions or even to pay heed to them. Yet in other ways that were less direct but more far-reaching, domestic theological change powerfully affected the shape and success of missions. The conservatism or liberality of the proffered faith, which did not always matter to the recipient, did matter to many, perhaps even most, of those at home who were considering giving to missions or becoming missionaries. It also determined to a marked extent what kinds of schools, hospitals, city missions, agricultural stations, and other service institutions the missionaries would establish in the field, or even whether they would establish such institutions at all. The nature of the theology preached helped, moreover, to determine which audience the missionary would reach—what segments or social strata in the recipient society would be most heavily influenced by this particular form of Westernization. And finally, such theological issues as the moral value of non-Christian religions bore upon the larger cultural attitudes that missionaries carried with them into the field—their working assumptions about the degree of respect due to the civilizations within which they sought to operate.

In the decades after 1875, the theological issues that above all others could not be left at the water's edge were those involving the "finality" of the Christian religion and its traditional claims to a right of world conquest. Since liberals or modernists were, almost by definition, especially sensitive to the cultural etiology of particular religious ideas, the application of liberal theology to missions produced serious discomfiture. It also encouraged fairly sustained efforts to disentangle the universal qualities and appeal of Christianity from those elements or expressions of the faith that connoted Western political and cultural expansionism. While the resulting theory of missions usually set itself in opposition to secular forms of imperialism, it did not forego—saw no need to forego—the "fine spiritual imperialism" involved in preaching a world-conquering Christ.[2]

Theological liberalism appeared prominently in the larger American Protestant denominations, particularly those of the North and West, beginning about a decade after the Civil War. The liberals, like other evangelical Christians, professed strong commitments to theism and to a special, indispensable revelation of God in Christ. Their major departures from a more conservative evangelicalism consisted in stressing the immanence or indwelling of God, in presupposing a universal religious sentiment as the common source of particular religious forms, and in determinedly probing the historical and cultural forces that have shaped those forms. In affirmative theology the central point was God's incarnation in man through Christ; on that foundation liberals built anthropologies which in varying degrees asserted the innate goodness of man and the bright prospects for human society. Whether or not a particular liberal essayed the next step to the "social gospel," a step that to many seemed logical and necessary, liberals characteristically considered profession less vital than performance, and thought of either individual or social salvation as largely a function of good works.[3]

Until about 1910, the terms new theology and Protestant liberalism were commonly used to denote this configuration of ideas. Afterward, the first designation dropped away and the term modernism, borrowed from the adaptive movement within Roman Catholicism, came into prominence. This is one instance in which a religious designation was chosen freely by those to whom it was meant to apply, not fixed on them against their will. Liberals called themselves modernists in admiration and support of such Catholic intellectuals as the Abbé Loisy, and in the conviction that, despite faults in the "modern," the adjustment of religion to the contemporary culture was both an admirable and an inevitable process. Critics, especially after 1920, spoke of modernism as synonymous with liberal extremism—specifically with a position that allegedly assimilated Christianity completely to the received categories of contemporary science and secular thought. Liberals themselves, however, tended to use the terms interchangeably, or even to speak of modernism, with its specific concern for the refurbishing of ancient doctrines, as a traditionalist turn in liberal development.[4]

THE CRISIS IN MISSIONS

Both theological liberalism and the social gospel associated with it have frequently been interpreted in the terminology not only of challenge and response but also of shock and adjustment. Sydney E. Ahlstrom, in a study produced in the early 1960s, so interpreted the liberalization of mission theology in the late nineteenth century. He pictured the preceding stages of the American missionary movement as having been conceived and carried forward in a dark Egyptian night of provincialism and ignorance regarding the "heathen," their moral condition, cultures, and religions. The evangelical Protestant mainstream, he wrote, had been "estranging itself from the revolutionary intellectual and scientific developments of the 19th century." Concomitantly, American books purporting to offer information on so-called heathen cultures had been worse than useless: "they simply reflected Protestant prejudices or bolstered them by creating the illusion of factual knowledge." Such a background, Ahlstrom maintained, intensified the conflict that arose when a significant proportion of American Protestants eventually did acquire a reliable knowledge of exotic cultures and religions. Missionary ideology at the end of the century experienced trauma rather than just an invigorating challenge.[5]

Ahlstrom's depiction of nineteenth century ignorance may be overdrawn, with respect to both the contrast between degrees of sophistication in Europe and the United States, and the worthlessness of descriptive works available to the American public before the 1870s.[6] But he was surely right that religious progressives at the end of the century attributed many of the difficulties in the missionary enterprise to an earlier ignorance and overenthusiasm, and issued calls for new self-understanding as well as for more cordial appreciation of exotic cultures.

The criticism from these quarters was rarely unfeeling; on the contrary, it was sympathetic, pastoral, and sometimes poignant. Edward Caldwell Moore of Providence, Rhode Island, later of the Harvard Divinity School, in October 1900 faced the unenviable task of preaching the "annual sermon" to an American Board stunned by the recent loss of literally indeterminate numbers of its personnel in the Boxer uprising. Twice in the three-day meeting the delegates sang:

Let every kindred, every tribe, on this terrestrial ball,
To thee all majesty ascribe . . .

But Moore's sense of his audience as conveyed in the annual sermon makes it difficult to imagine that anyone sang these words with emotions other than anguish or perhaps defiance.

Moore had known since the onset of the events in China that he would have to eschew the usual message of inspiration or financial pleading; and he avoided equally the more common clichés of comfort to the bereaved. Instead, he preached from the passage in First Kings in which the angel of the Lord tells the weary, heartsick Elijah to "arise and eat, for the journey is too great for thee." In expounding this text, Moore was recommending not a giving-up so much as a letting-go, a relaxing of the anxiousness and idealism of modern Elijahs who had asked too much of themselves and expected too much from the enterprise to which they were committed.

Elijah, Moore said, is the very picture of the man "whose zeal for the good is wearing him out before his time." Having been over-confident of himself, the prophet responded to adversity by almost despairing of God. In the same way, "the giant of the humane and Christly spirit of the age seems to me to lie prone today, waiting the touch of the angel. Precisely because of the responsibilities which we have assumed, of the work we plan to do, of the journey for the blessing of our fellows that we mean to take—the more do we need to hear God's voice saying to us, 'but the journey is too great for thee.' "[7]

It seems clear that Moore wished to advise the whole missionary army, not just the troubled people sitting before him, to relax the expectations formed in a romantic age of world-conquering enthusiasm. In this he was not alone; other sympathetic counselors were demanding the same kind of reconsideration. William Newton Clarke of the Colgate Theological Seminary in Hamilton, New York, spoke out on the matter in his *Study of Christian Missions,* which also appeared in 1900. Having produced, six years before, the most influential, and almost the only, full-scale work in systematic theology that was to come out of the liberal movement, Clarke now turned his attention to "the present crisis in missions." Although many other theological writers found the turn of the century an excellent occasion for celebrating the achievements of Western man,[8] this leading liberal had his doubts and expressed them.

With characteristic bluntness, Clarke made short work of current notions that the turn of the century heralded a great new age of human brotherhood. In fact, Clarke feared, humanity had entered upon an age of passion, unrest, racial antagonism, and national ambition. At the same time, the missionary movement, instead of overflowing with enthusiasm, was beset with underfunding, criticism, and uncertainty. "Something has happened," he mused, "to chill the ardor."[9]

To a great extent this "condition of pause" was, Clarke thought, an inevitable relapse from the fine careless raptures of early missionary self-confidence. The expectations of a quick, relatively easy triumph had been romantic, uninformed, and unintelligent. "It was really expected," Clarke wrote somewhat incredulously, "that vast masses of organized humanity would slide easily and without resistance into the kingdom of God, so that a nation would be born in a day, and born into satisfactory Christian life." Rhetorical talk about "planting shining crosses on every hilltop" had been taken too seriously. A warm enthusiasm had been relied on, "not only to do its own indispensable work, but to do a great deal of work besides." Such a period of romantic feeling had had to come, but it also must pass away. The missionary movement would need to live in the real world or not live at all. "The rush is over," he warned, "and the steady pull begins."[10]

Clarke documented at length the point later made by Ahlstrom, that a new sophistication was producing troubled awareness of other cultures among Westerners previously enveloped in "the darkness of ignorance colored only by a glamour of strangeness." But he reversed the coin by remarking that modern knowledge, commerce, and communications had also deprived the heathen of their salutary ignorance of Western civilization. "The defects of Christendom," he wrote, had now "freely and unsparingly advertised themselves in foreign parts. The governments of the so-called Christian nations have appeared exactly as they were." Although the impressions thus created had sometimes been favorable to the reputation of Christianity, too often they had offered only "a most unhelpful commentary on the character of the religion that missionaries were seeking to commend." Worst of all was "the hypocrisy with which nations allege Christian motives in justification of their land-grabbing, oppression, and unrighteous wars."[11]

Clarke believed that the new evolutionary thinking had brought Christians to their senses about the potentialities and limitations of missionary efforts. He rejected as both unconvincing and impermanent those deterministic inferences from Darwinism that made it seem futile to aid suffering people or raise backward races. But he thought that the effect of the Darwinian theory had been almost wholly beneficial in teaching "the length of processes." Nearly all thinking persons, he wrote, even those who believed themselves to be violent opponents of Darwinism, had been made aware of the venerability of some of the civilizations that American Christians were presuming to set right. Francis Peabody, the Harvard social ethicist, once described a mission school in Egypt whose wall charts asserted that the world began in 4004 B.C., whereas visible from the front door were authentic monuments of a civilization ripe well before that date. Clarke's variation on the same theme stressed the difficulties in the way of any attempt to displace ancient religious systems. "The established condition of life in China," he pointed out, "is the result, at a very moderate estimate, of twenty thousand years of continuous resident life in that country." It would be "a far greater undertaking than our fathers thought" to displace the religions so deeply embedded in non-Western cultures.[12]

Neither Clarke, nor Peabody, nor most other liberals proposed to abandon the missionary movement. The enterprise, if it was to recover, needed a quickened and simpler faith. It needed more realism, more scientific knowledge, and far more patience. Above all, the idea of spreading the faith by either war or commerce showed "incredible effrontery" and should be foresworn. Yet the obligation laid upon Christians to preach the uniqueness, finality, and necessity of Christianity for all of humanity was not open to question. Possibly Clarke's opening chapter, in which the finality of Christianity is asserted, sounds somewhat unconvincing and unconvinced, but clearly the author had no conscious reservations about desiring and predicting world conquest for the Christian faith. "Christianity," he wrote, "deserves possession of the world. It has the right to offer itself boldly to all men, and to displace all other religions, for no other religion offers what it brings. It is the best that the world contains."[13]

THE LIBERAL PROGRAM

A reviewer of Clarke's book for the *Biblical World* remarked that the author's way of defending missions would shock more traditional apologists.[14] Yet his stance was broadly representative of a liberal approach to missions that remained consistent and swelled in influence over the long years of controversy from the 1870s to the 1930s. The crux of the liberal theory lay in its attempt to preserve, and at the same time considerably revise, the Christian claims to finality and indispensability. Leading elements in the theory were its conversion of the idea of Christian finality into an almost purely ethical concept, its search for a quintessential Christianity suitable for export, a professed devotion to the ideal of establishing native churches free of Western control, a questioning of the right of Western Christendom to lecture the rest of the world, and a steady assertion that it was the old theology, not the new, that threatened to "cut the nerve of missions."[15]

The redefinition of Christian finality, or absoluteness, appeared most explicitly in the "future probation" debate that wracked official Congregationalism in the 1880s and early 1890s. That controversy followed naturally from the settlement of a previous, even longer-lived confict throughout the Reformed bodies over freedom of the will. Under an older Calvinist dispensation, a Bostonian had, in theory at least, as much chance of arbitrary reprobation as a Maori. But theological theory, launched on the seas of voluntarism, had left the unfortunate heathen marooned. Presumably the Maoris, who had not heard of Christianity, were also oblivious to this latest revision in New England theology and felt no deprivation, but the liberals began to feel such deprivation on their behalf. If God leaves men free to make decisions that will determine their eternal fate, how can he condemn those who have had no chance to decide? A future probation for the heathen, it was argued, must be entertained as a probability.[16]

The controversy suggested the way in which terms like "absolute" were being redirected. Gradually absoluteness ceased to mean that there is no other way to salvation and came to denote, first of all, the ethical absoluteness of the gospel. Just as the Transcendentalists of an earlier generation had argued for ethical instead of miracle-based proofs for Christianity, these later liberals committed themselves to proving an ethical rather than a forensic necessity for world evangelization. Second, in a manner derived directly from the thought of the English theologian F. D. Maurice, absoluteness became a synonym for the universality of divine intentions. God, liberals explained, is the Lord of the whole universe; he does not play favorites among the races and conditions of mankind, nor does he share his lordship with a devil and the forces of darkness. God is in all men, and human sinfulness therefore involves not a succumbing to the natural man but, on the contrary, a betrayal of what is most natural in man. Absoluteness conceived horizontally, conceived as universality, did not quite mean that all of humanity would be saved, but it insisted that all would have the chance to be saved, in either this life or the hereafter.[17]

There is some evidence that the combatants in the future probation dispute failed to make the deeper issues clear to the public and that Americans were as bemused as Maoris. George A. Gordon, the Boston liberal, quoted the complaint of a citizen outside the meeting hall during the furious American Board debate of 1887: "These religious people have jewed us out of our fun on Sunday, they have jewed us out of our liquor, and I'm blamed if this American Board ain't talking about Prohibition after death." But participants knew what was at stake. "The question of the salvation of the heathen," Egbert Smyth of Andover wrote, "is simply one aspect of the fundamental religious question of our time: the claim of Christianity to be the one perfect and final religion for mankind." Whether Christianity is in fact perfect and final was not at issue. The question was the true basis of this supremacy.[18]

Because Andover Seminary, the liberal headquarters during the controversy, had become so thoroughly identified with the probation question, it fell to Gordon, Clarke, and others to flesh out a more positive theology of missions. Gordon was the most productive serious theologian at the turn of the century (Lyman Abbott being the most productive nonserious one). Though his half-dozen books from this period all preached the universality of the work of Christ, his most direct contributions to the theory of missions came in an American Board sermon of 1895, *The Gospel for Humanity*.

In this sermon Gordon sought to define an essential Christ who might be offered to the world without either dogmatic or cultural accouterments. His text was Paul's statement to the people of Corinth that he had "determined not to know anything among you save Jesus Christ and Him crucified." For the revivalist or fundamentalist this text implied biblical literalism, no-nonsense decisions for Christ, and quite frequently anti-intellectualism; but for Gordon it meant that the missionary must try to "preach Christ" rather than preach doctrines about Christ or preach the gospel of a particular sect. David Swing, the liberal preacher and sometime Presbyterian of Chicago, had pictured Christians in alien settings as necessarily suppressing the "dividing dogmas" they had learned at home. "Approaching foreigners not fully drilled in the sectarian method," Swing said, "we fear their smile of unbelief or derision." Gordon similarly assured the American Board that "we are not under obligation to export our entire body of belief." The quintessential Christian message, which must be shown as much as taught, is "the pure idea of self-sacrifice embodied with transcendent fidelity in the career of Jesus Christ." Beyond that, there is no particular call, he suggested, "for our church polity, our special theology, or the traditions of our Christian life. These are not wanted; if sent, they would prove unsuitable." The exportation of these trappings as "the Gospel" is not only impolitic; it is inaccurate. We should prize our ideas of the gospel, Gordon warned, "but we must never make the mistake of supposing that our ideas are the gospel."[19]

Historicism and cultural relativism about one's own religious forms suggested some degree of syncretism in dealing with the religious forms evolved by non-Christian peoples; and they further implied a determination that Christian churches, once established abroad, must be left to themselves. From a later liberal perspective, Gordon's representations on both these points seem flawed: his attitude toward ethnic religions remained condescending, and his assurances to the American Board about the natural "assimilative" powers of a stripped-down Christianity now sound frightening. But he was addressing a body whose neural system, if not destroyed as the conservatives thought, was undergoing a major rearrangement. In view of that situation, the concessions to cultural relativism are impressive. "God," Gordon contended, "has not left any of these people without witness of Himself." No heathen having in them "a spark of original genius" will tolerate the imposition of someone else's theology. Nor is this resistance merely prideful; any extensive transfer of specific cultural forms is clearly unfeasible. "Contrasted previous civilizations and the total diverse character of inheritance and environment will forever make impossible the domination of one division of the race by the rigidly formulated mind of another." A civilization in its immature state, he thought, may accept that kind of tutelage; barbarian Europe, after all, was happiest when in bondage to Plato and Aristotle. But growth to maturity entails intellectual variation. "The nations that are good for anything, and to whom Providence has assigned any considerable task in the advance and enrichment of the kingdom of God . . . simply must go their own way." To force formulations and personnel on them permanently would result "in a measureless sacrifice of power. The nations are to be left to the control of the Holy Spirit."[20]

The idea of cutting umbilical cords between mission boards and native Christian churches was destined to become widely accepted well before the Laymen's Report urged it in 1932. The idea prospered partly because autonomy was a noble, republican-sounding ideal that could cover great divergences in actual practice. The theory often failed to clarify just what degree of elevation of native personnel, of financial independence, and of freedom from American advisers constituted autonomy. There was room for weaseling.

But again the departure from long-standing assumptions was appreciable. Rufus Anderson, secretary of the American Board earlier in the nineteenth century, had advocated "self-government, self-support, and self-propagation" as the three watchwords for native churches, but Anderson's advice had been largely forgotten since the 1850s.[21] Premillennialism, which in theory was compatible with quick missionary withdrawal, was tending in practice by the late nineteenth century to keep the Western missionary indefinitely at his post. Premillennialism, as Clarke explained, makes the missionary the herald of an imminent consummation, the personal evangelist who must pluck a few brands from the burning. But when the millennium is delayed, the missionary stays. Against such a tendency, Gordon and other liberals pitted the concept of the missionary as a "planter," whose duty is to set the receiving society on the long road to salvation and then to get out. The missionary's task, in effect, is to make himself superfluous. "Foreign influence may introduce Christianity," Clarke wrote, "but if it were continued too long it would inevitably deprive the native Christian church of its rights of self-direction and development, and reduce it to a position of permanent tutelage and inferiority. Each people is entitled to be itself."[22]

This diffidence about foreign operations usually entailed some degree of explicit doubt about the superiority, moral and otherwise, of Western Christian culture. Though many shadings of opinion in this matter were evident among the liberals, relatively few voiced the national and racial self-assurance so often quoted from the writings of Josiah Strong. Those who did use the language of an ideal Anglo-Saxon supremacy, moreover, were likely to employ equally strong language about the moral flaws in the existing home culture.[23] Conservative evangelicals, to many of whom the same observations apply, complained principally about such things as drinking, materialism, and vice, as Americans practiced them at home and carried them abroad. Liberals agreed, but were inclined to add observations about structural flaws in American society. Because of their theological relativism, liberals were also more likely to use terms like "presumptuousness" and "effrontery" to characterize the missionizing pretensions of an unsaved society.

The liberal, in his dual role as spiritual expansionist and social critic, relied heavily on distinctions between ideal and reality, between Western civilization as a process or destiny and that civilization in its present state of imperfection. Hence, a common formula would have run somewhat as follows: "Christ and Christian ideals must and will conquer the world. The West, especially America, historically has embodied those ideals most fully. But the evils in our own society provoke severe doubts about the future. To the extent that these evils are allowed to continue, Western and Christian credibility will suffer. Yet we must persist in missions, both because Christianity is true and because it would be disastrous to allow Western commercialism and power to run over the world untempered by Christian influences."

Almost without exception, liberals would have acquiesced in such a statement. Some were reluctant to develop its negative aspect, its critique of American society. Gordon, for example, a Scottish crofter who had literally found an earthly salvation through the educational and other opportunities of the New World, could never bring himself seriously to cloud the picture of a kingdom coming in and through America. But others, like Walter Rauschenbusch and Henry Churchill King, combined a mighty nationalism and Westernism with excoriations of Western society that clearly implied doubts about its missionary pretensions.

Rauschenbusch's opposition to World War I has led some to assume that he could never at heart have been a militant nationalist or expansionist. That is scarcely the case; the social gospel leader considered the Spanish-American War "one of the mountain ranges in the geography of times" and was willing to sit on the speakers' platform at the Republican Convention of 1900, a bit embarrassed by the domestic program of the party, but not questioning the rightness and necessity of American expansionism. Yet Rauschenbusch surely was anything but complacent either about American society or about the effects of domestic injustices on the missionary enterprise. "The social wrongs which we permit," he wrote in 1907, "contradict our gospel abroad and debilitate our missionary enthusiasm at home." The non-Christian peoples, either directly or indirectly, see "our poverty and our vice, our wealth and our heartlessness, and they like their own forms of misery rather better."[24]

Henry Churchill King, the personalist theologian and president of Oberlin College, exhibited the same pattern more sharply. Unlike

Rauschenbusch, whose physical mobility was hampered by deafness, King traveled extensively and observed the morally ambiguous expressions of Western civilization directly in their foreign settings. King also typifies rather clearly the kind of liberal who took Western expansion as a given and then went on to ask how it could be tempered and civilized.

Economic and religious expansion were not the same thing, King asserted gratefully, but they inevitably interacted. While the relationship had been advantageous to economic expansionism, it had usually worked to the disadvantage of religion. And the whole process had been less than fortunate for the peoples of the non-Western world. With table-pounding italics, King reminded his readers that "Western civilization was *introduced* into the Orient . . . *for commercial reasons,* and in almost all cases practically by force." This Western "exploitation of the less advanced peoples" had been "at obvious variance with the underlying principles of the civilization so introduced."[25]

When King nevertheless referred to the spread of Western civilization as somehow good as well as inevitable, he testified to the power of a fervent cosmic idealism to dissolve contradictions. The West, he suggested, is neither great nor noble nor indispensable; yet the West is the chosen instrument of ideals or underlying principles that have all of those qualities. The East would need to "Westernize" in any case, for without Western science, technology, and education the nations of the East could not compete in the world and would not survive. They had a still better reason to Westernize, which was that the underlying principles of Western civilization are necessary and eternally right, for them and everyone else, even though the West itself fails miserably to live up to them. "The Orient," King wrote, "must take on generally, and in its inner spirit, the great fundamental moral and religious convictions and ideals of Western civilization, if it is steadily to reap its fruits." The conditional clause in this statement might be taken as signaling that King's advice was purely pragmatic, but he made clear that the principles he was talking about would be right even if American and Western civilization should cease entirely to embody them.[26]

The heart of the matter, as King's subtitle emphasized, was "reverence for personality." The West would be privileged to lead the world only insofar as it reformed its current practices and became genuinely a champion of this personalistic form of piety. King's passionate denunciation of imperialism, though it left his optimism about such a consummation intact, left it in a precarious balance. At best, Western civilization would have to "pay, sooner or later, the full penalty for its deeds of oppression." But the triumph of a great idea was not in doubt. Regardless of whether the task of leadership was to be given to Americans, "or to the English-speaking peoples as a whole, or to the still broader Teutonic races, or to some other people or groups of peoples," reverence for personality was destined to continue as the guiding principle of all human progress. If American and Western peoples chose not to ride this wave of the future, then they, as surely as anyone else, would be overwhelmed by it.[27]

Here, in spades, was Gordon's determination to deculturize the message of Christ for the purpose of exporting it. The difficulties, as always, had more to do with the feasibility than with the desirability of the operation. Conservatives dissented even from the aspiration to distill a "pure" message of Christ if the result was to be something so ethereal as King's personalism. But others, knowing of unsuccessful attempts throughout Christian history to capture the basic message of Christ without doctrinal or cultural ornamentation, questioned whether the thing could be done. One man's "simple teaching of Christ" had too regularly been another's dividing dogma. The difficulties of disentangling cultural elements were vivified, though not intentionally, by King's own argument that the nations of the East must not try to adopt Western technical civilization without Western religious principles. There was great danger, King remarked, that the Eastern nations would "fail to realize how unified a thing, after all, Western civilization is; and how impossible, therefore, it becomes permanently to reap its fruits and reject its roots."[28] The warning, which in itself was redolent of cultural preconceptions that would later be sharply questioned, suggested again that what the liberals were proposing might be impossibly difficult.

The liberals' answer to such objections, besides stressing the sheer obligation to preach an ethically supreme religion and the necessity of taming a dangerous imperialism, was a pragmatic one: that the new theology in actual fact converted more persons to Christianity than the old. The stripped-down Christian idealism, like the bumblebee with its inadequate wing span, could not fly but did fly. The Andover men in the 1880s had argued ebulliently that ridding the

123

gospel of a bad eschatology would ensure "progress in its extension beyond anything as yet realized," and liberal writers over the next forty years reported regularly that liberalism, far from cutting the nerve of missions, had made possible the unparalleled missionary expansion of that period.[29]

CONSERVATIVE OBJECTIONS

No amount of historical quantification, probably, will yield fully satisfying judgments about the validity of that claim. The distinguishing attitudes of the liberal theology did spread widely among the missionaries and mission boards of the main-line Protestant denominations after the turn of the century, and were transmitted through such undenominational agencies as the SVM and the YMCA. But from a truly conservative point of view, expansion under such auspices offered no refutation at all of the standard charge that liberalism had cut the nerve of missions. By 1920, the hard-line objection to liberalism in the mission field was not "Is it effective?" but "Is it Christianity?" The typical fundamentalist or conservative tract on the subject, after that date, offered extensive, often nearly interminable, testimony to the success of an evangelistic, educational, and medical enterprise that the writer considered disastrous.[30]

Though this form of argumentation, which bypassed questions of intercultural comity, was especially characteristic of the 1920s, a certain damn-the-torpedoes attitude had always colored conservative attitudes about missions. When David Swing of Chicago stood trial for heresy in 1874, his prosecutor was Francis Patton, the scholarly, respectable, and thoroughly rigid future president of Princeton University. At one of several points when Patton lost his temper (he was losing the trial), he shouted to his wayward colleagues in the Chicago Presbytery: "I cannot help it if [eternal punishment] is a doctrine which is unpleasant to the feelings. It is in the Confession of Faith."[31] The possible damage done by necessary doctrines to feelings, or to missionary credibility or international relations, was not a negligible matter to conservatives of this stripe; they simply felt that such considerations must not be controlling.

Few conservatives conceded, however, that the old theology was either ineffective in making converts or especially implicated in an untoward cultural expansionism. Cyrus Hamlin, who had founded Robert College in Istanbul and had recently retired from the presidency of Middlebury College, in 1886 offered a modest proposal to those who wished to preach a milder eschatology to the heathen. More than half seriously he suggested that advocates of the new departure form their own mission board and secure a mission field all to themselves, preferably in the heart of Africa. The organization, he stated, could be called the Dissenters' Board of Missions for the Congo, and "those who should prefer it to the American Board could send in their contributions accordingly." Such a plan would enable enthusiastic young men to go into Africa and "tell the heathen how happy have been their ancestors in knowing nothing of Christ, for their trial has been in far more favorable circumstances, and before this they are probably all in heaven." The natives could be told that though it is a misfortune to a heathen people to have the gospel presented to them in this life, they must make the best of it.[32]

If, in response to this message, "Ethiopia shall soon stretch out her hands unto God" and conversions abound everywhere, the liberals will have proved their point. But Hamlin and men like him remained confident that nothing of the kind would happen. The Rev. Charles Bowen in *The Fundamentals* insisted that the doctrine of the atonement, in its strict substitutionary form, not only does not offend prospective converts, but is the only thing that wins them. Bowen, like George Gordon, wished to preach solely "Jesus Christ and Him crucified," but to Bowen this meant preaching about a God who, in the form of the Christ, died for the sake of men and in legal expiation of their guilt. Nothing less, he maintained, impresses the heathen as superior to their own religions.[33]

Conservative theorists sometimes expressed an across-the-board disdain for foreign cultures. A. A. Hodge in 1885 asked readers of the *Presbyterian Review* to compare the cultures associated respectively with Western Christianity and with the "pantheism" of the East and Eastern Christianity. "Let the fruits of the two systems," he wrote, "in the contrasted life and thought of Eastern and Western Christianity for fourteen centuries bear testimony. Western thought dominates the world, and in this era of missionary activity, we are not likely to accept our theology from the Dormitories of the East. The old dreams will again be found out of place in this working world."[34]

At least as common in conservative arguments, however, was a determination to separate Christ and culture. W. H. Griffith Thomas, at the end of a lengthy catalogue of the depredations of modernism in China, mentioned an *Atlantic Monthly* article which contended that missionaries had gone to China to vindicate Western civilization. "This is interesting," Thomas wrote, "but it is not true. Our sound missionaries have gone to China to proclaim the everlasting Gospel . . . and not to vindicate any civilization. There is much in Western civilization which, because it is not Christian, is not worth vindication."[35]

The *hauteur* or condescension of conservatives, in other words, was likely to appear only by indirection, in the form of a particularly dogged disregard of cultural angularities in the theology they insisted was necessary. The Rev. Albert H. Plumb, reviewing George Gordon's writings of the 1890s, found the crucial error of liberalism to be that it allowed to non-Christian systems some degree of efficacy in the work of salvation. This was a misunderstanding of Christianity, Plumb asserted. Regeneration cannot be a matter of degrees; hence, "in respect to the greatest, the most difficult, the *primal* function of a religion, there is only one true religion, all others are false." Plumb insisted that an unyielding view on that point was perfectly compatible with the kind of respect for non-Christian religions or cultures that the liberals were advocating.[36] A reasonably consistent conservative was nonetheless prevented by such convictions from making cultural concessions that the liberals' theology prompted them to offer.

THE LIBERAL ORTHODOXY OF THE BOARDS

Whatever the culpabilities of the conservatives, the liberal formula of the 1890s had spread so widely by 1930 that liberalism must in great measure be held responsible for the missionary attitudes predominating by that time. The missions of Pentecostals, Adventists, Russellites, and Mormons were also significant and growing; and fundamentalism remained a force, particularly in the field, within the "main-line" denominations. Yet in missions, as elsewhere, liberalism had become a powerful orthodoxy by the 1920s. It had gained the power to organize and, as some complained, the power to exclude that such a status confers. In that sense, at least, the liberal synthesis deserves to be regarded as the official foreign policy of American Protestantism at the time of the Laymen's Report.

That report, compiled under the direction of William Ernest Hocking of Harvard and published in summary form in 1932, might well have gone the obscure way of similar commission reports had it not offered one momentous departure from the liberal orthodoxy of the mission boards.[37] In nearly all major respects the report reiterated the program of Gordon and Clarke, spelling out the implications of that program in the conditions of 1930. Its one departure lay in its preference for a philosophically idealistic world religion, and its consequent failure clearly to assert the finality or indispensability of Christianity.

The Laymen's Report, thanks to the personal force of Hocking and to the commission's independence from the various denominations, struck most sympathetic readers as one of the more eloquent, internally consistent committee documents ever produced on so delicate a subject. The integrating vision was that of Christianity's active participation in an emerging world religion. The "unique contributions" of Christianity were stated with some certainty as just that, "contributions." The world the missionary encountered was no longer seen as binary in the old sense of Christian and heathen, but as divided into the forces of religion and the forces of gross secularism. Whether in the battle against materialism and secularism on the outside, or in the struggle against idolatry and superstition within each faith and sect, Christians were to make their contribution as collaborators, not as competitors, with the truly religious adherents of other faiths.[38]

Responses to the report, because of their abundance and specificity, proved illuminating as indicators of the lines of division in American Protestantism. Denominational and mission board officials had been willing to give a general blessing in advance to a project already so generously blessed by the Rockefellers, and they now found themselves obliged to be uncommonly clear about what they approved in the report and what they disapproved.

Archibald Baker of the University of Chicago, assessing reactions ten months after the report's appearance, discerned three principal positions. A small minority within the churches had responded with general approval of both the report's theology and its recommendations. At the opposite extreme, a larger minority thought the entire book a dangerous document. The majority, centrist position, led and articulated by the mission boards of the main-line denominations, varied from cordial to enthusiastic about the investigatory work and the practical recommendations of the commission, but unanimously rejected the Hocking theology.

Baker reviewed the stands of the major boards. Most emphatic in support of the commission was the American Board, but even that body wished to state much more unequivocally than the report had done its "conviction of the uniqueness of the revelation of God in Christ." The other boards expressed the same reservation with greater emphasis. Concurrently, a number of them repudiated the wholly condemnatory reactions of the fundamentalist right. Though lay people in the great denominations probably were more seriously divided than were their leaders, middle-class American Protestantism in this episode defined its position on missions with remarkable unanimity.[39]

The most broadly representative American theory of missions by the 1930s was neither the syncretism of Hocking nor the fundamentalism of Princeton's J. Gresham Machen, but rather the mediating thought and activism of Robert E. Speer. The tendency of Speer, John R. Mott, Sherwood Eddy, Robert Wilder, and the other great missionary recruiters of the era was to walk the tightrope of the theological center.[40] Speer's personal history epitomizes the whole hazardous process by which Protestantism was brought within one giant step of accepting as a working principle the parity among human religious expressions.

Speer, like Mott, Eddy, and Wilder, was a layman. He first worked for the SVM, then served from 1891 to 1937 as executive secretary of the Presbyterian Board of Foreign Missions. Eddy justifiably identified both Mott and Speer as conservatives, and Speer's involvement in helping to write the last volume of *The Fundamentals* confirms that neither he nor the conservatives found such a classification inappropriate. Once Speer's contribution to *The Fundamentals* reached the editors, however, they may well have felt that they had overdone the effort to include authors who were not hard-line fundamentalists. They juxtaposed Speer's enthusiastic but centrist plea for missions to a premillennialist article whose tendency, and very possibly whose purpose, was to make one forget all that Speer had written.[41] The editors, rather than the author, were also probably responsible for the strange and awkward omission of attributions when Speer quoted passages from the liberal William Newton Clarke.[42]

Speer's eclecticism in this article was not new. He had consistently belittled conservative fears that liberalism endangered the missionary enterprise. Evolutionary thought, he had argued, in no way imperiled missions because it in no way disproved humanity's need for the infusion of the divine life. Speer's statement that "stay-at-homes" worried more about theological details than did missionaries expressed succinctly the combination of activism and theological moderation that informed his entire career. When Presbyterian fundamentalists in the twenties, led by Machen, attacked Speer's Board of Foreign Missions for consorting unduly with modernists, the secretary's preferred reaction was silence. Machen's attacks after the Laymen's Report, however, provoked Speer to a vigorous defense, which was instrumental in the train of events leading to Machen's conviction as a schismatic and his separation from the Presbyterian ministry.[43]

The centrist or "old liberal" attitude toward missions that was thus carried solidly into the world of the thirties by men like Speer experienced relatively little discomfiture from the theological stiffening introduced by neo-orthodoxy in the middle thirties. Neither fundamentalism nor the Hocking world religion posture comported well with neo-orthodoxy. So far as fundamentalists could see, the Niebuhrians were just so many more Greeks bearing dangerous and unacceptable gifts; their allegedly countercultural God and their laudable concern for biblical and Reformation traditions were more than vitiated by their social radicalism and disbelief in biblical literalism. Nor was neo-orthodoxy compatible with Hocking's religious humanism; the new realists of the thirties rejected the world religion outlook of the theological left even more firmly than had Speer's generation.

But neo-orthodoxy and the Speer position were well within the same universe of discourse. The European and American realistic theologies, many of which dealt proudly in paradox, confirmed and greatly intensified the paradoxical elements in the predominating centrist theory of missions. On the one hand, these new theologies involved a heightened sense of the finiteness of one's own cultural and religious institutions; on the other, they rejected any form of theological accommodationism that tended to assimilate Christianity to world religions or to some highest common denominator of human religiosity. The neo-orthodox movement represented the crowning expression or last paroxysm, according to one's bias, of the long effort to strengthen the idea of Christian finality by purging it of its overtones of cultural finality, to find ways to proclaim the supremacy of "our God" without proclaiming the supremacy of "us."[44]

Both the church's theologies and its perceptions of American world obligations underwent mind-wrenching experiences, some heartening and some mortifying, after this convergence in the 1930s between the old liberalism and the new orthodoxy. In particular, clerical and religious opposition to American foreign ventures in the 1960s raised new questions about a rhetoric of missions that seemed, despite intentions to the contrary, to embody assumptions of Western and American cultural superiority. Though official statements of missionary purposes seemed to change very little, it was no shock by the early 1970s to hear a former director of evangelism for the Methodist Church question whether either the United States or its religious institutions should be trying to evangelize the world.[45]

Whether the churches can be persuaded or will be forced by events clearly to repudiate a rhetoric of Christian world conquest remains highly problematic. The almost singular insistence of Christianity on its obligation to displace other religious systems will presumably be harder to modify than were the beliefs and misapprehensions overturned by the study of comparative cultures in the late nineteenth century.

But it is also true that a collaborative, sacrificial, and serving attitude—in effect, a nonproselytizing attitude—has never been uncommon among those involved in the practical work of missions. In some organizations, such as the American Friends Service Committee, service and example were from the first the accepted modes of Christian outreach; and in a number of countries Western missionaries have been required by law to operate in that manner.[46]

The twentieth century's "new knowledge" may well in the end prove more compelling than that which made innovators of the mission theorists of 1900. At the very least, the study of human behavior and human symbol systems has seemed to confirm what those earlier observers only dimly understood about the persistent interpenetration of religious with other cultural values.[47] And historical experience, not just in the 1960s but in two world wars, has confirmed what some of them feared about the spiritual self-righteousness and potential destructiveness of Christian cultures.

A poem from the heyday of mission activity encouraged pious effort by pleading that Christ "has no hands but our hands." To many of the heirs of the older liberalism, in the later twentieth century, the same plea implies doubt whether any rhetoric of Christian world conquest can be purged of the taint of cultural assertiveness.

PART II

Christianity and the Transformation of China

M. SEARLE BATES

The Theology of American Missionaries in China, 1900—1950

Was the theology of American missionaries to China formed essentially by the society and culture of the United States; or was it quasiuniversal, common to Christianity, at least to Protestant tradition in many lands? How was it modified by propagation in China? How was it influenced by Chinese Christians as they played a growing role in the total mission effort? To answer these questions, one must look first at the context and then at certain processes that influenced the theological outcome. American Catholic missionaries need not be considered, because they were few in ratio to the Protestants. Most of them arrived after 1920, and they held a subordinate position in the total Catholic effort, which was firmly European in content, structure, and control.

THE AMERICAN COMPONENT AMONG CHINA MISSIONARIES

Among Protestant missionaries in China, Americans seem never to have been a majority, despite the considerable prominence of China in the full spectrum of American foreign missions. This minority position was of great importance, since the American missionaries had to relate in manifold ways to superior numbers from other lands, some of whom had been long prominent, even dominant, in certain regions or functions. Indeed, the Protestant missions were so grouped that it is almost impossible to determine the exact numbers from the United States. For example, one important channel of information was the Foreign Missions Conference of North America (1893–1950), which comprised the mission boards and societies of both the United States and Canada. Canadians were not rare among the missionaries representing several United States organizations, but they were seldom reported as such. Through much of the period, appointees of Canadian organizations amounted to some 9 percent of the North American total.

Even more difficult is the problem posed by the China Inland Mission, which is further complicated by its smaller Associated Missions. The China Inland Mission had a strong British element of leadership and personnel, yet it was international and had a significant secondary center in North America. Its principle and practice were to organize itself as China-centered and thus not ordinarily to publish figures or name lists, which would have revealed differences of national origin. In 1900 possibly 8 to 12 percent of the missionaries in the China Inland Mission were American, out of a total of 779, which constituted 28 percent of all Protestants. In 1935–1936 the mission's total was 1325, or 23 percent. This mission was by far the largest body in China, almost equaling in 1900 the total of the societies reporting themselves as "British," and approaching four-fifths of the "North American" total. Any estimate of its distribution by nationality, therefore, affects noticeably the reckoning of American missionaries and of their British or European counterparts.

My own best estimate is that the last figures before the dislodgment of the Boxer period, for January 1900, show American missionaries to have been 35 percent of all Protestants, and British 54 percent. The 1910 reports run 43 and 44 percent, respectively. Probably in 1912 the Americans equaled the British. Possibly American missionaries were one-half the Protestant total in 1917, under wartime conditions. In 1935–1936 the Americans were 47 percent and the British 35 percent of the total.

The level of education and theological training of American missionaries can be roughly sketched. The "North American" societies reported in 1900 and again in 1910 that some 29 percent, or less than three in ten, were ordained men. Then and rather consistently through 1936, 60 percent were women. In 1935-1936 the percentage of ordained men had dropped to 23. This evidently reflected the growth of specialized services, the strong tendency to turn over pastoral functions to the Chinese, and perhaps higher standards for ordination among certain missions. The remainder, or about 11–17 percent, were laymen.

It is often assumed that the ordained men had received theological training and that the laymen and women, whether wives or single, had not. In fact, some of the ordained men, especially in the early decades, had not undergone the now familiar three-year graduate course for the B.D. degree. Rather, they had attended a church-related college, in which they received moderately good instruction in the Bible and perhaps a simple introduction to theology, with one or two further subjects, such as philosophy, church history, or comparative religion. Alternatively, and chiefly among the more conservative groups, they had a year or two in "Bible schools," which were set up under a variety of names and built on varying bases of secondary, collegiate, technical, or commercial training. As for the women and laymen, many of them had also attended church-related colleges, where they received some religious instruction, usually as a minor or in odd electives, occasionally as a major. A considerable number of women and some men had studied religious education. Over all, scarcely more than a quarter of the American missionaries had preappointment training to prepare them formally for significant theological understanding or thinking. Nor did all of that fraction have the will and the diligence, amid many competing claims, to develop and use significantly such training as they had received.

This is not the complete story. Some missionaries did advance in China through dedicated theological study, and a good number deepened their knowledge at seminaries and in other graduate schools while on furlough. At times they sought to meet newly felt needs, such as the comprehension of non-Christian religions. Some had special opportunities, such as pursuing Asian studies in American institutions, and many had supplementary training that accompanied language study in their first year or two in China. But the essential picture remains. By far the greater part of the American missionaries had only a general, biblical knowledge of the Christian religion, with experience of Christian homes, churches, and instruction, rather than theological competence. They were workers and teachers rather than theological scholars or thinkers. Often among the German and sometimes among the British missionaries, Americans were deprecated as activists.[1]

Usual understandings of the term "theology" are of little value for the consideration of missionary thought. At one end of the spectrum, theology is strict and systematic thinking on the essentials of the Christian religion; at the opposite extreme, it is a loose and popular set of Christian beliefs, ideas, and related practices, considerably intertwined with the ethos of the American culture from which the missionaries came and in which the sending churches were formed. The theology of the missionaries fell between these two possibilities, being somewhat less austere than the first, but with more character than a generalized Americanism. For one reason, practicing churchmen were a minority of the public, while the mission boards and their active supporters were still more select. Missionaries were further distinguished by their original seriousness of purpose, by the considerable care exercised in their selection and training, and by the gradual growth of their experience in China. As American Protestant Christians, they shared in some of the best as well as some of the most commonplace within that comprehensive heritage. They valued the Declaration of Independence and Lincoln's Inaugural Address, which many understood as expressing a culture considerably affected by Judeo-Christian truth. But missionaries did not confuse these documents with the Bible or teach men so. It was not a missionary but a senator of the United States who, on a visit to the Far East in 1940, declared, "With God's help we will lift Shanghai up and up till it's just like Kansas City."

An undue confidence in American culture and an excessive deprecation of Chinese society for differing from the known and assumed good of the States had been more frequent in the nineteenth century. After World War I, such attitudes were commonly restrained or transformed. Most missionaries continually challenged their own pride by the person of Jesus and by the prayers and literature of Christian humility; they tried to set before themselves and the Chinese as the norm of society not the American Union but the kingdom of God. I remember my dismay, for example, at seeing a missionary shed what she felt to be a Christian tear at the death of

President Harding. But she had the quality and devotion that were eventually to make her a highly effective teacher of Christianity, with special insights for its expression in Chinese aesthetic forms. For thousands of missionaries there were effective restraints on an ebullient, unthinking Americanism, which came partly from the religious discipline and spirit, and partly from the persistent effort of missionaries to understand Chinese life and sentiment, to meet the Chinese helpfully and work with them for good ends. Crude foreignism could hardly survive in this setting.

One important determinant of missionary theology was the confessional and creedal factor in the church. This was generally more explicit for Lutherans, Episcopalians, and Presbyterians than for Congregationalists, Baptists, and Methodists. Yet in China the Presbyterian and Reformed dedication to cooperation and union tempered Calvinist severity, and Episcopalians could tolerate a good deal of liberal thought and social awareness within a firm ecclesiasticism. By contrast, Baptists and Methodists boasted some types of freedom but maintained a potent continuity through particular teachings and practices. The Methodists were especially proficient in spanning continents and oceans with elaborate organization.

Yet the mission scene in China was impressive for its mutual accommodations, which furthered a common, basic Protestant Christianity with substantial yearnings toward organizational unity. The variety of ecclesiastical and national traditions was ample, even bewildering. There were scores of organizations. Among the Lutherans alone, some twenty groups came from Germany, Switzerland, each of the Scandinavian countries, and each major immigrant group in the United States, including separatist bodies from those areas. American Congregationalists, Methodists, Presbyterians, Baptists, and Episcopalians found counterpart bodies in China from Britain and Canada, as well as from Scotland and Australia. They were the ecclesiastical brethren of the Americans—in some cases even the living ancestors or cousins. Yet separation by environment and by history had been reinforced by the inadequate communications of the nineteenth century. In China the ties of kinship did not readily join those whom oceans and generations had long divided. Notably, American Methodists were not able to unite with British Methodists, nor Baptists to forget the Atlantic.

Nevertheless, Protestants combined and generally worked congenially in many nondenominational or interdenominational organizations. These included the major monthly magazine the *Chinese Recorder;* the Bible Societies (British & Foreign, National of Scotland, American), which gradually, through constant consultation, merged their China operations; the Christian Literature Society and the Religious Tract Society; the China Christian Educational Association and its publications; the China Medical Missionary Association and its later form within the China Medical Association; the China Sunday School Union; and the all-China conferences of 1877, 1890, and 1907, which were succeeded by the more Chinese gathering of 1922 and the resultant National Christian Council. Moreover, participation by China missionaries and by the executives of their home offices in the World Missionary Conference at Edinburgh in 1910 increased the cooperative spirit and the sense of a common Christian cause crossing denominational lines. The Jerusalem Conference of 1926 and Madras/Tambaram Conference of 1938 were less decisively cooperative for missionaries, but they moved that goal forward through the greatly increased participation of "younger church" representatives, among whom the Chinese were outstanding. The YMCA was nonconfessional but actively evangelistic, especially from 1900 to 1925, when various missions relied on it as a means of reaching students. They also assigned ordained or other missionaries to its service and valued many of its publications.

The missions early learned to respect each other's commitments and to confer with one another regarding entry into new territories. Such comity was considerable, even though not completely effective. It aimed both to restrain competition or duplication of effort, and to put resources where they were needed to serve the vision of reaching all the Chinese people. It was based on the presumption, whether ready or reluctant, that a Southern Baptist could recognize the validity of conversion and instruction by an Episcopalian, or a Lutheran accept the evangelization achieved by the nonconfessional, nonecclesiastical China Inland Mission. Indeed, interchange of members was widely practiced. There were instances where groups of congregations were transferred to other denominations, in readjustments of territory to make way for a new or expanding mission. Transfers of individual missionaries across denominational lines were also familiar, not merely in the ever-recurring happenstance of marriage but for other personal reasons or because of policy changes.

There were some actual unions of Chinese churches, for which missionaries were largely responsible even though the Chinese joined in the effort and finally took charge of the results. The gradual assembling of a great part of the Presbyterian and Reformed bodies, with elements of the Congregationalists, Baptists, and former Methodists (the latter from British and Canadian churches rather than from American backgrounds), resulted in the formation in 1927 of the Church of Christ in China, which by 1950 comprised one-third of all Chinese Protestants, far exceeding any other body. Meanwhile, missions representing the Episcopal Church and the Church of England had joined in establishing in 1912 the Chung Hua Sheng Kung Hui (Holy Catholic Church in China), while unions in China of various Lutherans, and of the American Methodist bodies in 1939, were largely reflective of unions in the United States.[2]

The China picture, then, was one of many denominational structures within which particularism was taken for granted. But denominational theologies were often qualified and softened in cooperative relationships and sometimes in actual unions. All the way from the China Inland Mission to the YMCA, there were bodies that combined in one organization the missionaries of various church backgrounds. A considerable number of union educational institutions, even including union theological seminaries and Bible training schools, drew into one generalized Protestant effort missionaries of different theological traditions. Problems remained, but the cooperation was largely effective.

In China itself were many factors modifying the theologies from abroad. In Chinese society, unfamiliar with Christianity and largely unlettered, the need and the will to simplify were strong. In that setting, the Bible was exceedingly difficult to use. The remoteness or irrelevance to the Chinese of medieval, Reformation, and Anglo-American particularities, as represented in confessional terms and documents, was grave and occasionally even ludicrous. Merely to distinguish the Hebrew and Greek perspectives was problem enough. There was a persistent need to temper confusion and the apparent conflict of denominational beliefs, in the face of a negative public and of puzzled converts. Through decades of experience there developed a positive will to cooperate, in order to gather fellowship and strength from otherwise scattered weaknesses, and to accomplish tasks that could not be effectively done in isolation, such as translation and publication. The yearning to unite, to share experiences of despair and count more and more on Christian hope, gave increasing value to the work and witness of diverse persons and missions. An impatience with dispute, as hindering sacred and urgent work, generally restrained contentious persons. The understanding across national and ecclesiastical lines advanced irregularly but substantially, through facing common problems, experiences, and sufferings.

Perhaps most important in this whole series of modifying factors were the vision and experience of a Chinese church in the society, culture, and nation of China. Only the Chinese could evangelize China. Only they could develop a Christian community and permeate the enormous mass of people. They would have to form their own spiritual, moral, and conceptual relationship to God in Christ, develop their own sense of how the old life could be changed into the new. They would have to state their own faith in language and deeds meaningful to their neighbors. While the missionaries were convinced that the Christian faith is revealed by God and that its essence is truth eternal, many came to see that the function of the missions from abroad must be introductory, then auxiliary. From an early period, some bodies emphasized the importance of the Chinese church; others had to learn from the experience of foreign inadequacy that their converts needed Chinese fellowship and more congenial leadership.

All of the preceding factors were restraints on missionaries in their natural tendency to import Western theologies under established labels. To preach, teach, and print the central simplicities, always for Chinese eyes and ears, and for Chinese responders, were the essential guidelines. Let the Chinese develop their own statements and applications. Many of the Western confessions, and even the ancient creeds themselves, came to express the faith in the midst of controversy over contemporary cultural issues. Of course, these general guidelines did not answer all questions for the missionaries in China. They still must determine just what was "essential," and who—past, present, or future—was to decide. Within the intended openness of spirit there remained for not a few the absolute assurance of the Anglican Quadrilateral or the Westminster Confession.

Perhaps the height of accommodation was achieved by the China Inland Mission and other proclamationists, who considered presentation of the faith as the missionary's prime duty. They earnestly and always sought to convert individuals, deferring the development of churches. Accordingly, the mission was relatively indifferent to the type of church that was growing in a particular area, leaving it to the missionaries of the Anglican tradition here, or the Baptist tradition there, so long as there was reasonable continuity and freedom from confusion. Up to 1950 it was hard to discover just what was meant by "Nei ti hui" (Inland Mission churches). Missionaries of the China Inland Mission believed that it was right to leave their converts to God's guidance, without attempting to fit them to a church pattern. As neighbors saw it, the choice of an organization and practices was determined basically by the founding missionaries in each area, while a strong core of conservative doctrine was all along prescribed by definite teaching and by controls of property and appointments.

THE CENTENARY CONFERENCE OF 1907

The last major collective expression of their theology by Protestant missionaries in China came in 1907. There was never a significant expression by American missionaries as such, drawn from a considerable denominational and geographical range, yet separate from the non-American majority. However, American missionaries participated heartily in the Conference of 1907, and no significant dissent from its resolutions was uttered. The theological thinking they expressed was in later decades adapted and developed rather than radically revised.

In general, these resolutions reveal a sensitivity to the problem of combining differences in teaching with the will to affirm one faith, of fulfilling the desire for harmony and unity in the Chinese church, while guaranteeing liberty for that church to serve truth according to its own conscience. It is resolved, for example, that instruction of Chinese ministers should include other religions and ethical teachings and should be in the vernacular, so they can speak to Chinese persons. Repentance and salvation are related to common sins. Christians are exhorted toward Christian growth, loyalty, and righteousness. Christian influence is to be extended by the diffusion of good persons in manifold relationships. Special concern is shown for family life, including the development of girls and women, and the fostering of actual rather than conventional filial piety. Patriotism is enjoined, as well as Christian relations across national or cultural

143

lines. For the sake of the church's character and good name, and to ensure tolerance by the officials, care is urged in dealing with unworthy persons who sought the church for wrong motives.

The Centenary Conference Resolutions on the Chinese Church deal with the first subject area considered, the most thoroughly prepared and discussed:

II. RESOLVED . . . That this conference unanimously holds the Scripture of the Old and New Testaments as the supreme standard of faith and practice, and holds firmly the primitive apostolic faith. Further . . . the Conference does not adopt any Creed as a basis of Church unity . . . yet . . . we gladly recognize ourselves as already . . . one in regard to the great body of doctrine of the Christian faith . . . the love of God the Father, God the Son, and God the Holy Ghost; in our testimony as to sin and salvation, and our homage to the Divine and Holy Redeemer of men. . .

We frankly recognize that we differ as to methods of administration and Church government. But we unite in holding that these differences do not invalidate the assertion of our real unity in our common witness to the Gospel of the grace of God.

III. That in planting the Church of Christ on Chinese soil, we desire only to plant one Church under the sole control of the Lord Jesus Christ. . . While freely communicating to this Church the knowledge of Truth, and the rich historical experience to which older churches have attained, we fully recognize the liberty of Christ of the churches in China planted by means of the Missions and Churches which we represent, in so far as these churches are, by maturity of Christian character and experience, fitted to exercise it; and we desire to commit them in faith and hope to the continued safe keeping of their Lord, when the time shall arrive, which we eagerly anticipate, when they shall pass beyond our guidance and control.

These affirmations are followed by recommendations to the sending churches that they sanction the right of the mission-planted churches in China "to organize themselves in accordance with their own views of truth and duty," allowing for representation of missionaries on their governing bodies "until these churches shall be in a position to assume the full responsibilities of self-support and self-government." Any claim to "permanent . . . spiritual or administrative control" is precluded.[3]

Following closely on concern for the Chinese church comes concern for the Chinese ministry:

VI. RESOLVED: (a) That theological teaching, while it should be rooted in the Bible as the Word of God, centered in the person and work of Christ, and culminating in the abiding presence of the Holy Spirit as the power who is to transform the world, should be broad and comprehensive in its scope, should include the study of other religions, of other forms of ethical thought, and should open up to students new avenues of study as to human relationships and responsibilities.

(b) That under usual conditions theological teaching should be conducted in the vernacular of the people among whom students are expected to labour, so that their education may be towards and not away from those for whom they are preparing to labour.[4]

The majority of American missionaries thought along the same lines as the "Letter to the Chinese Church" that was adopted by the Conference.[5] In this letter, the argument for Christian living is presented in universal terms, but the sins condemned are common in Chinese life: harsh quarreling, drunkenness, opium; greed, fraud, oppression; polygamy; suicide; purchase and sale of wives and daughters; neglect, even destruction, of children, especially daughters; futile and wasteful idolatry. The Christian message is declared to be not primarily judgment and punishment, but repentance and salvation through turning one's heart and life to God. Not mere assent of words is required of Christians, but righteous living as effective witness.

Christians are urged to understand the teachings of Christ by reading the Bible, by prayer in the family, and by attendance at church worship and instruction. Every Christian should stand up bravely and righteously for his belief. The hope is that Christianity will permeate Chinese society, increasingly affecting public opinion, shaming people for their evil conduct, and honoring them for good behavior. Poverty is no disgrace; but continual borrowing brings loss and harm, not remedy; and debt for display, as for extravagant weddings, is a serious evil. To use others' money "in order to give one's parents a grand funeral, is not really to honour one's parents but to dishonour them, and to act the part of an unfilial son."

The Christian will devote special concern to his family. He will not apprentice his sons to masters who are not good men, nor allow his daughters to grow up in ignorance. Already the Christian community in China is showing far more concern for the education of girls than is being shown elsewhere. In days to come everyone will see the difference between families whère the wife is an intelligent, educated Christian and families where she is not. Christian parents betroth a daughter only when they can judge the character of the young man. Footbinding is rebuked, with the reminder that the Empress Dowager and the Empress did not bind their feet.

The letter then turns to acute problems in the public repute of the church. All Christians should assist pastors in guarding against the entry of persons into the church who seek to use it for advantage in quarrels and litigation. Seditious persons, notably those active in secret societies fomenting rebellion, should also not be allowed to gain concealment or protection from the church. Christian teaching recognizes the authority of government as necessary under God for order and justice, in order that people may live in peace.

Indeed, the few Christians needed encouragement through every possible lessening of tensions, through every possible realization of fellowship within the nation and in the church universal:

> The missionaries themselves belong to different countries and to different societies . . . but this is no reason why the Chinese Church should, in days to come, perpetuate a number of different societies. In the course of time, the Church in China will be independent of foreign supervision and then, no doubt, those who are now worshipping in separate buildings and with different arrangements, will, in many cases, think it best to unite. . . . Remember that even now, you are part of a very large Church, composed of great numbers of people out of all nations under heaven. Remember, too, that those people all belong with you to the one family of God. Every Christian should love his country, but he should also, for Christ's sake, love his fellow-Christians in other lands. It is God's will that Chinese and foreigners should live on terms of good-will the one with the other.

Missionary theology and a few of its applications are set forth in the conference's two memorials to the Chinese government, copies of which were sent to a large number of officials. The first document[6] of nine pages seeks to give officials a general understanding of Christianity and of the missionary effort, in a blend of information and apologetic. A concise introduction on the origin and spread of Christianity leads the reader to China and to translations of the Bible as the carrier of truth. The memorial then takes up the central issues of teaching the nature of God and man, with explicit reference to China:

A belief in unseen spiritual beings is common to all mankind, but whereas most nations have a religious cult of their own and worship many spiritual beings each with a dominion of its own, as gods of the hills and gods of the rivers, gods of agriculture, gods of wealth and gods of healing, as well as national heroes of antiquity who have been deified, Christians worship only one God, Who is All-sovereign and Whom Christ taught us men to speak of as "Our Father in Heaven." Christians are forbidden to offer sacrifices, incense, prayers or adoration to any other, as being an infringement of the honour due God alone.

Jesus Christ is described in the standard terms of divinity-humanity. He showed to men, in a perfect human life, the glory of God, Who is the source of all perfection in man.

Chinese who read Christian books or listen to Christian preaching often say that our teaching has much in common with the teaching of the sages of China. We gladly recognize such correspondences where they exist, but we are bound also to notice the differences ... [which] gather around the question of God in His relation to man, and of man in his duty to God. Faith in God and knowledge of God make all the affairs of the world, all human duties and all the history of men to look different... Where men honour God truly, filial piety will flourish abundantly in each home; and so with all other human virtues... "All under Heaven are one family" is a truly profound saying. Christians use it as meaning that all nations and languages are in truth one. But every family has its head, and in this family of all under Heaven, God is the Head and claims all as His children. Another Scripture says, "God is no respecter of persons, but in every nation he that feareth Him and worketh righteousness is acceptable to Him "

But further, the teaching of Scripture about God's creation of man shews the true dignity of man. The Scriptures say that in the beginning God created man in His own image and gave him dominion over all creatures. It is this that makes man different from every other living creature, and that encourages us to look for our pattern of virtue and of orderly government among men, to God, and to a Kingdom in Heaven over which God rules. . . Man alone of all creatures can worship and pray and give thanks. Man alone feels that he has sinned against Heaven, and the thought makes his mind ill at ease. Man alone believes in a law of Heaven, and in decrees of Heaven, and knows they ought to be respected.

The memorial proceeds to set forth the impetus of missions and their results, in order to explain the character and methods of their work in China, their nonpolitical and law-abiding nature, and their respect for the Chinese government and nation. First, missions are described as obeying the "last command of Christ spoken to His disciples, 'Go ye therefore and make disciples of all the nations.' " Therefore, the first disciples went throughout Judea and to Rome and Greece. Their descendants preached "one universal gospel of salvation for all men in all lands without distinction of race or colour." Despite opposition, which often led to imprisonment or even death, Christianity eventually won toleration and acceptance in many lands.

The memorial then explains the special character of the missionary societies:

> There is nothing in all China, or in Chinese customs, at all like them. Christian missions from Europe and America are altogether supported by the voluntary offerings of people who believe in Jesus Christ and desire to see the whole world Christian. From our Governments we receive nothing at all. . . Some of the money spent on missions is contributed in large sums by wealthy Christians, but the great part of it comes from those who are not rich, and from even the very poor. These people pray God daily for China, Japan, India and every other country not yet Christian, that God would bless the rulers and the people of these countries and make them good and prosperous. Into all this no political or similar motive enters. . . Devotion to Jesus Christ, a desire to see all the world worshipping the God of Heaven and to see evil practices everywhere done away, is the sole motive for the support of missions. Chinese Christians also give a great deal of money for the support of their teachers, their schools, the building of churches and for helping the poor.

Next, the point is stressed that the church in China has been very careful in admitting people to membership. "There are very many . . . who have not been received because their motive in coming was questionable; and further, of those who have been received, some have been subsequently expelled from the Church, either because they fell into opium-smoking, or gambling, or dishonesty, or showed themselves in other ways to be bad people. The missionary's object is not to get large numbers to join the Church, but only men and women who repent of sin and wish to lead good lives."

Missionary methods are succinctly described: "Our methods of teaching are by public preaching, distributing books, and establishing schools. But our Saviour besides preaching, went about doing good, therefore missions establish hospitals for men and for women and in some places we have asylums for lepers, the blind, the insane, the deaf and the dumb. We open these and similar institutions not to accumulate merit, but in obedience to Christ's command, that for His sake we should love men and be kind to them and show them in this way how much more God loves them . . . Confucius said, 'Heaven produced the virtue that is in me.' We believe that from God all virtue comes."

Finally, this memorial asserts the nonpolitical character of Christianity:

> Some Christian countries have been absolute monarchies like Russia, some have been limited monarchies like Great Britain and Germany, some have been republics like America and France. . . The Scriptures say, 'The powers that be, are ordained of God.' We are bidden to pray for kings and all in authority. In all Chinese churches prayer is regularly offered for the rulers of China. We ourselves constantly exhort Chinese Christians to be loyal subjects, to honour the ruler of their land, to love their country and to pay their taxes regularly. We entirely discourage among them all connection with political and secret societies. Our great desire for China is that it may prosper and take a leading place among the nations of the earth.

The second memorial,[7] entitled "A Petition to the Government Asking for Complete Religious Liberty for All Classes of Chinese Christians," relates the ethical argument for religious liberty to the well-being and good name of China, to good citizenship, and to the example of other countries, including India and Japan. Intense Christian concern is translated into terms that appeal to the non-Christian state. Religious liberty does not merely further the interest of Christians but promotes peace, good will, loyalty, and patriotism throughout the empire. Other states formerly feared that failure to require one type of belief would foster harmful division among the people. But the granting of religious liberty has in fact enabled men to discern more clearly what is true and valuable from what is formal or trivial, while relief from compulsion has induced popular sincerity and contentment. In Western countries good citizens have gone to prison rather than conform against their consciences, and others have gone into exile, which seriously harmed the oppressing society. "We desire for China . . . that she may be saved from the sorrows that our own countries have suffered through religious intolerance."

DIVERGENCES AND AGREEMENTS

Despite the spiritual unity and common purpose manifested at the Centenary Conference of 1907, elements of theological divergence had already appeared. For example, certain teachers and physicians now saw their work as more than a mere preface to preaching. They viewed education and medicine as aids to the development of the Christian community and the larger society. Strict evangelists could approve of such services, especially where it was hard otherwise to get a hearing; and frequently the teachers and doctors were themselves evangelists. But a real theological conflict over the nature of mission work would increasingly mark off those groups who put most effort into educational, medical, and subsequently social work from those who did little or none.

In addition, missionaries who sought to reach the literati and to reform the whole society viewed science and secular culture as parts of the purpose of God. In this respect Americans like Young J. Allen, W. A. P. Martin, and Gilbert Reid seemed radical to the more conservative missionaries. At the same time school men like Sheffield, Pott, and Mateer, who were more obviously churchmen as well, were gaining followers. Both of these groups argued that as technical progress and scientific rationalism were coming to China relentlessly from Japan as well as from the West, it was important that some of the introduction should be under Christian auspices. Moreover, as the old empire confronted change and reform, the need for new men of character and the opportunities for educational influence appeared to be multiplying. When the republic was at last proclaimed by Sun Yat-sen, a professed Christian, along with proclamations of religious liberty, the issue over priorities in the missionary purpose and program was sharpened.

Differences as to authority in religion were also increasing, though not always openly. As the Confucian resistance to Christianity weakened, missionaries became more appreciative of values in the Confucian tradition. No American went so far as Richard or Soothill in adjudging the Buddhist religion to be Christian in character, even in origin. But many Americans were moderating their earlier disdain. Half-consciously the idea was growing that God allowed, perhaps planted, truth and goodness outside the Judeo-Christian line. Meanwhile, the American home constituency, which provided Christian scholarship, training, and recruits, was more given to historical criticism of the Bible and to acceptance of evolution as the way God has worked in creation and in nature, even though this produced rising anxiety among those committed to older views. The widely circulated series of twelve small volumes called *The Fundamentals* (1909–1915) and the *Scofield Reference Bible* (1909 and later editions), with its apparatus of support for infallibility, literalism, and dispensationalism, were signals of conflict. A careful summary of statements by China missionaries gathered in 1909 reported: "Among the missionaries themselves the attitude towards the Higher Criticism differs much. The older men are mostly untouched by it, and fear its effects on the Chinese Church. Some of them also complain of the 'superior' attitude of some of the younger men, many of whom are more or less under its influence."[8]

In the succeeding decade, doctrinal differences among China missionaries were muted by their preoccupation with China's faltering abandonment of the empire, the European war, and Japanese aggressiveness. Public expression of the increasing missionary differences was delayed until the visits in 1920 of the prominent fundamentalists W. H. Griffith Thomas and H. Clay Trumbull. An unusually large influx of new missionaries in 1920–1921 precipitated action. The Bible Union of China originated in the summer of 1920, and in succeeding months it developed an organization and Statement. Its numerical strength is not easy to measure. Within a year or two, fully 2000 members were reported. They seem to have included many tolerant conservatives, who were not overly rigorous in defining their concepts, along with the anxious, the stalwarts, and a few aggressive extremists. The zealots had little success in their efforts to dislodge or weaken certain modernists, but the whole movement undoubtedly aided the conservative forces that over the next several years strove to influence American mission boards. It affected some decisions on appointments within Christian organs in China and some choices of missionary candidates in America.

The Bible Union's Statement followed the familiar evangelical essentials, with a particular thrust at social service:

Being convinced that the state of both the Christian and non-Christian world demands unity of purpose and steadfastness of effort in preaching and teaching the fundamental and saving truths revealed in the Bible, especially those now being assailed, such as, the Deity of our Lord and Saviour Jesus Christ, the Virgin Birth, His Atoning Sacrifice for Sin, and His Bodily Resurrection from the Dead; the Miracles both of the Old and New Testaments; the Personality and Work of the Holy Spirit; the New Birth of the individual and the necessity of this as an essential pre-requisite to Christian Social Service:

We reaffirm our faith in the whole Bible as the inspired Word of God and the ultimate source of authority for Christian faith and practice;

And unitedly signify our purpose "to contend earnestly for the faith once for all delivered unto the saints."[9]

Despite the common ground between this Statement and earlier missionary thought as expressed in the Centenary Resolutions, each of the two sides in 1920 and just afterward felt that the other had broken a needed fellowship. The first overt act of "division" was the Bible Union, whose leaders charged that the modernists or liberals had departed from the established faith, while remaining within the enterprise and subverting it. Although the allegations were usually made against "isms" rather than against colleagues, the animus was serious.

The Bible Union waxed as an expression of concern over the progressive potentialities in the National Christian Conference of 1922 and the resultant National Christian Council, both of which tended to move control away from the known mission bodies to the less predictable Chinese churches. It waned when some of the feared tendencies began in experience to seem less radical, and when the rising tides of Chinese nationalism and the anti-Christian movement beat alike upon fundamentalists and modernists, who were in the same distress and had the same pressing problems. After the first excitement had passed, many in each of these loosely classified groups felt the need to work together, while many others persisted in separation but not in hostility. After years of weakness, the journal of the Bible Union and its moribund organization disappeared in the chaos of war in 1937.

Behind the Bible Union stood that prior and continuing element of organized theological conservatism peculiar to the China scene, the China Inland Mission. After an early blooming of general American and British leadership and personnel, the Union consisted mainly of China Inland Mission members. The Union's organ remarked that only this body frequently reminded its missionaries of the Bible Union's existence. In later years the *Bulletin* was likely to be full of general articles and news on missionary subjects, often from the China Inland Mission work or even reproduced from its publications.

The doctrinal basis of the China Inland Mission, in the early formulation by J. Hudson Taylor, appeared insistently and often in its publications. His last official act for the mission in 1905 was to reiterate this statement. It was slightly condensed in the following articles of faith, as issued in 1928 and through 1950:

(1) The Divine inspiration and authority of the Old and New Testaments.

(2) The Trinity in Unity of the One God, the Creator and Upholder of heaven and earth and all things; the Three Persons being the Father, the Son and the Holy Spirit.

(3) The fall of man and his consequent moral depravity and need of regeneration.

(4) The Atonement of our Lord Jesus Christ, Who died on the Cross for the sins of man, offering Himself as a Sacrifice to God on account of those sins.

(5) The forgiveness and justification of sinners by faith in the Crucified and Risen Lord Jesus Christ.

(6) The bodily resurrection of all men, both the just and the unjust.

(7) The eternal life of the saved, and the eternal punishment of the lost.[10]

In the voluminous literature of the mission appears only one indication of doctrinal challenge, owing to a determined man of prominence who was not named. Before and after his dismissal, he tried for twenty years, apparently with little support, to appeal in the name of a loving God against the literal and extreme interpretation of "eternal punishment of the lost." The question was administratively at issue from 1899 to 1904, and the complainant struggled at least through 1919. Anxious consultations brought to Shanghai and to London the director of the Council for North America, to confer with the aged Taylor and with the directors in those two cities. None of the participants thought it right or possible to soften the doctrine, though there was some concern to avoid absolute condemnation and dismissal of the complainant; while the director for North America, then and repeatedly, insisted on "eternally conscious suffering." Taylor's successor D. E. Hoste, the director in China, declared in Shanghai in 1915: "Throughout the Old and New Testaments we find that appeals to the motive of fear, and warning as to consequences of persistence in evil, form a prominent part of the Divine message to man, and any system of thought and teaching which omits to bring this motive to bear on the consciences of men is radically defective and unsound."[11]

The China Inland Mission was important for the theology of American missionaries, despite the fact that most of the leadership and perhaps 85 percent of its personnel were British. The influence of this large body as specialists in evangelism, as well as the prominence of some remarkable mission pioneers all along to 1950 and the wide circulation of its impressive books, affected missionaries of all bodies. Several associate missions were close satellites. The Christian and Missionary Alliance (American) was frankly imitative, as were some smaller gorups. As with the Bible Union, the China Inland Mission members tended to associate with conservative individuals among other missions, perhaps most often in the Chinese interior and western regions. They were part of the cooperating mechanism, if not central to it, from the conferences of 1907 and 1910 through the China Continuation Committee of 1913–1922, the National Christian Conference of 1922, and the National Christian Council until 1926, when the Mission withdrew without publishing its reasons.

It seems clear, however, that the increased power given to churches in the National Christian Council, added to the now notorious divergence in general theology, was the precipitating cause of this withdrawal. In 1928 the China Inland Mission's Statement of Policy provided strict doctrinal contracts for transfers of property and authority by the Mission to its own churches. The results were apparently calming. At any rate, in 1943 the China Council of the China Inland Mission met for a thorough consideration of "the centrality of the Church in the purposes of God." As the authorized history explains: "It was finally agreed that the Mission would offer its services as an auxiliary agency to the Church; its members would serve within the local churches in a cooperative capacity and under the local church leadership. This decision was a significant step forward in the relation of church and mission."[12] The language, if not the mood and actual practice, had finally come to be almost identical with that of many other missions in this important sector of applied theology.

In the general scene in China, the period 1922–1950 saw a wide measure of cooperation, achieved by leaving doctrine to the respective churches and missions, the latter being agencies of *churches* abroad. The National Christian Conference of 1922, after some strain, voted this resolution:

> A proposal has been made to the Conference that a doctrinal statement expressing fundamental Christian beliefs should be embodied in the resolution appointing a National Christian Council.
> We the members of the Conference joyfully confess our faith in, and renew our allegiance to, God the Father Almighty, Jesus Christ, His Son, our Lord and Saviour, Who loved us and gave Himself for our sins, and the Holy Spirit, the Lord and Giver of life; and acknowledge our loyalty to the Holy Scriptures as the supreme guide of faith and conduct, and to the fundamental Christian beliefs held by the churches to which we severally belong. The Conference however is not constituted as a church council with authority to pass upon questions of doctrine and of church polity or to draw up a credal or doctrinal statement of any kind. While the Conference believes it to be a matter of vital importance that the Church of Christ in China should be established on a basis of true faith and sound doctrine, it recognizes that the authority to determine what are the essential affirmations of the Christian faith lies with the several churches of which those attending this Conference are members.[13]

The Church of Christ in China as an actual body should not be confused with the all-inclusive vision named in this National Christian Conference resolution, since it did not come into existence until afterward. As finally constituted, the Church of Christ in China was the most important church body organized there. It was developed largely by American missionaries with the cooperation of Chinese and British colleagues. Soon the Chinese members were effectively as well as numerically predominant. A very high percentage of the American missionaries in the uniting bodies heartily concurred in the agreed theological position, which provided an adequate minimum for the constituencies of the previously separate churches, while leaving the united church free for future elaboration if desired. The Provisional General Assembly of 1922 adopted a prefatory Bond of Union, consisting:

(1) In our faith in Jesus Christ as our Redeemer and Lord on whom the Christian Church is founded; and in an earnest desire for the establishment of His Kingdom throughout the whole earth.

(2) In our acceptance of the Holy Scriptures of the Old and New Testaments as the divinely inspired word of God, and the supreme authority in matters of faith and duty.

(3) In our own acknowledgment of the Apostles' Creed as expressing the fundamental doctrines of our common evangelical faith.

This affirmation was followed by the constitution, operative in 1926, in which Article II reads: "Our object is to bind the Church of Christ in China with united strength to plan and promote the spirit of self-support, self-governance and self-propagation and to unite the Christian Believers to practice Christ's way of Life, extend His principles and spread the Kingdom of God throughout the world." [14]

These statements are probably the best collective representations of the working theology of the middle-of-the-road majority of American missionaries, even though they were not formulated by a comprehensive American body acting as such. They were, moreover, ratified by some sixteen churches developed or actively aided by American missions, and were sanctioned by the home boards of those missions. In general, the major missionary journals and books depict the American missionary theology in China, especially after 1910, as giving central emphasis to four factors: Jesus Christ as the effectual revelation of God, the Lord and exemplar of human life; the kingdom of God as the ideal of human relationships, inspiring an effort for good in all aspects of society; salvation from human and social ills, as well as from spiritual sin and its natural consequences;

and commitment to furtherance of the church as the community of the faithful and the agency for its extension and nurture.[15]

THEOLOGY IN CHINESE SOCIETY AND CULTURE

Earlier missionaries had gone to China in the firm conviction of having divine authority for a definite, unique, and exclusive faith. God, Christ, the Bible, conversion, and salvation were all understood on this basis. The conspicuous contrast of Chinese miscellaneous beliefs and religious practices, many of them blatantly idolatrous and superstitious, reinforced the missionaries' firmness of stance. Likewise the solidarity and authority of the Chinese family limited its members' freedom to hear and respond to the gospel or to emerge from the web of Chinese life into a strange, barbarian pattern. These factors reinforced the missionary's opposition to "the worship of ancestors," that nurture of filial piety which served paternal, senior, and masculine control. The Chinese convert's renunciation of idolatrous or near-idolatrous beliefs and devotions, in order to believe in the one true God, was a critical test of his commitment. This was the heart of the theological issue, which arose in many related and minor matters of culture.

While the cultural issue was inevitable, it was less sharp as missionaries became more involved in the Chinese scene. Continually there arose comparisons of God with "Heaven"; Moses, the prophets, and Jesus with Confucius and other Chinese sages; the Bible with the Chinese Classics; the Christian complex of sin-conversion-salvation with the Chinese concepts of human nature, self-cultivation, and moral standards. The missionaries' efforts to present Christianity led to a gradual multiplication and deepening of their associations with Chinese as neighbors, fellow-believers, and fellow-workers, who not only continued to live within the Chinese society and culture but also brought into the nascent Christian churches the equipment of their own prior values and ideas. All this increasingly modified the Sino-foreign confrontation. The religious and moral teachings of the Bible could be made meaningful to Chinese only through terms already familiar to them in religious and moral matters. A best term had to be found that represented "God" and carried with it the least objectionable or complicating associations, among such expressions as "heaven," "sovereign-on-high," "the spirit," "lord," or "lord-of-heaven." This process continued through practically every element and virtue in the Christian perspective. Missionary studies of Chinese classical and religious literature were purposive, but also appreciative. As a result, their understanding of the good and the best in Chinese thought and life increased.

The crucial problem was one of competing values and allegiances. In China, there was a tradition of eclecticism and a common tendency to form loose amalgams of disparate beliefs, along with much indifference to religion generally. In the large, Confuciansim had been only marginally religious. Its rationalism combined with bureaucratic attitudes to produce considerable hostility to superstitions, to Buddhism, and to sects. In modern times there was a decline in the older beliefs and institutions, which became more and more marked around the turn of the century, and almost catastrophically so after 1911. Over all, China moved away from Confucianism, and there were vehement denunciations of it and the Buddhist traditions. In the twentieth century, missionaries, Chinese Christians, and other thoughtful persons increasingly deplored the confusion and loss of moral standards in China.

Against this background the missionaries' theological thought and related practices in regard to Chinese culture in the twentieth century went far beyond the nineteenth in recognizing that the good, the true, and the beautiful were of God—in China as in America and the rest of the world. Most missionaries were still convinced that God had made himself known most fully in Jesus Christ, and that the evident response of the human heart and mind to Christ, in China as elsewhere, substantiated that faith. Increasingly they trusted Chinese Christians to make their own decisions as to matters of accommodation, fulfillment, and substitution. Perhaps the chief anxiety among missionaries was over Chinese ethnocentrism or cultural nationalism. At times this seemed to set Chineseness as the first criterion of value, to a degree that encroached on the truth of God in Jesus Christ. But the problem was usually met theologically by devotion to the church, trusting the Chinese community to create its own relationship to Christ.[16]

ADRIAN A. BENNETT and KWANG-CHING LIU

Christianity in the Chinese Idiom: Young J. Allen and the Early Chiao-hui hsin-pao, *1868—1870*

Historians assessing the record of American missionaries in China need to look first at their American origins. Since missionary work involves the confrontation between two cultures, however, it is even more essential to inquire into the receiving end in China—to determine how the Christian message was transmitted and to measure the impact of the missionaries on Chinese people. In missionary work, two cultures either collide or reinforce each other. The Christian message was translated into the Chinese idiom, and Chinese responded to the missionaries either directly or indirectly, in words and in actions.

Inquiries should be made into the many-sided mission undertakings—the hospitals, schools, and colleges; the introduction of science and technology; individual contacts; service and philanthropy of various kinds. The breadth and limitations of the missionary's message can only be gauged from the many concrete encounters he had with Chinese life. Yet to a historian there is special value in approaching the subject on the plane of ideas. Although words are often mere rhetoric (and formalized rhetoric at that), they may also reflect values. The writings of missionaries and their converts, particularly when they were meant for Chinese readers, reveal a great deal of the conflict as well as the compatibility between Christianity and the Chinese value system it sought to transform.

159

One repository of such writings especially during its initial years of publication was the weekly magazine *Chiao-hui hsin-pao* ("Church News"), founded in 1868 by the American missionary Young J. Allen of the Methodist Church, South. British and American missionaries in China had been producing small Chinese-language magazines containing religious and secular information since the 1830s.[1] The *Chiao-hui hsin-pao,* however, was the first periodical of this nature to have a sustained publication history, eventually developing into the famous *Wan-kuo kung-pao* ("Globe magazine" or "Review of the times," 1875–1883 and 1889–1907). Although designed as a vehicle for "church news," the *Chiao-hui hsin-pao* published a great variety of factual reports and essays of opinion. The magazine included scientific and technical material as well as secular news, both domestic and foreign. But, especially in its first two years, it invited its readers to discuss the comparative merits of Christianity and China's ideological heritage, especially Confucianism. In the very first issue of the *Chiao-hui hsin-pao,* Allen expressed the hope that it would be read by non-Christians as well as converts. In 1875, when its name was changed to *Wan-kuo kung-pao,* it openly appealed to a general readership.

The tone of the magazine was set by its editor, Young J. Allen. His outlook had been formed by his religious and cultural upbringing in the United States, as well as his new experiences in Shanghai in a sector of Chinese society exposed to the influences of the West. Allen himself wrote articles and unobtrusive editorial notes that defined the magazine's principal concerns. However, during the *Chiao-hui hsin-pao*'s early years, the largest number of contributors, as Allen had intended, were Chinese preachers and teachers associated with the major Protestant missions. The magazine thus reflected the concerns of the first generation of Christian converts after the opening of the treaty ports. Such concerns were not merely those of the missionaries. The ideas of Chinese Christians, although inspired by their acquired faith, were conditioned as well by China's cultural and social environment. Allen, like other missionaries, wanted to instruct the Chinese, but he was also able to learn from his Chinese contributors. The broadened Christian message that he came to formulate, therefore, was not just a product of his own background. Rather, it was the result of an interaction between his own definite ideas and the cultural and social views of the Chinese Christians.

An orphan from a plantation-owning family of Starsville, Georgia, Young J. Allen (1836–1907) was a product of what may be described as the best religious and cultural influences of the Old South. Under the care of an aunt, he was exposed at an early age to fervent Methodism. At fifteen, as he later recalled, he had "jumped out of a church window" in ecstasy after hearing a sermon. But the young man seems to have calmed down, for three years later as a freshman at Emory College, he pursued his studies with success, while becoming secretly engaged to Mary Houston, who was to graduate from Georgia's Wesleyan Female College. Allen took full advantage of the balanced curriculum that was offered at Emory, learning mathematics and sciences as well as Greek, Latin, and philosophy. During his junior year, his religious enthusiasm returned. Inspired by reading James Caughey's *Methodism in Earnest,* which describes that evangelist's revival meetings in Canada, England, and Ireland, Allen began to attend revival meetings. After one of them, he wrote in a prayer of repentance, "henceforth [I] unreservedly give myself to God in prayer and Holy Living in full confidence that the Lord will fulfill that which He has promised."[2]

While Allen's Christianity was undoubtedly of the prevailing evangelical mode, he was rational enough to think deeply on such theological issues as the reason for the existence of evil and the reconciliation of eternal punishments with a belief in God's goodness. In one essay Allen concluded that the "power to do wrong" or to disobey God was what made of man a moral agent. The human inclination toward sin could thus be explained, since this capacity could not be removed "without the utter extinction of all intelligence and accountability, and reducing man to a mere machine."[3]

Despite his capacity for reasoning, Allen's faith was characterized by enthusiasm, for the propagation of the faith as well as for service. His journal of 1857 spoke of love and virtue as necessarily flowing from the Christian spiritual experience. One of his essays of the period dwelt on "the desire of God for the salvation of all men."

161

Allen held· prayer meetings in his room for schoolmates, and after graduating in June 1858, he conducted revival meetings for several weeks from an old log near the Emory campus. Allen later recalled that, as early as 1856, he had felt a compulsion "to be a missionary to the regions beyond." A month after graduation, Allen married Mary Houston, and in November they both attended the Georgia Conference of the Methodist Church, South. Bishop George F. Pierce made an appeal for foreign missions. Allen rose to say that he was ready for a summons. Pierce, still at the podium, asked, "What think you of China?" to which Allen answered in the affirmative, although this was probably the first time that it occurred to him to go to China.[4] He spent the following year soliciting donations for his missionary undertaking. Receiving few donations, he decided to sell a large part of his property to finance the trip. In December 1859 he and his wife sailed from New York, and during the exceptionally long voyage they read Abbé Evariste Huc's *Travels,* probably the first book on China that Allen had ever perused. In the company of another missionary couple of the same church, the Marquis L. Woods from North Carolina, they arrived in Shanghai in July 1860.

Allen's experience in the unusual new environment of Shanghai contributed to his eventual decision to become the publisher-editor of a Chinese magazine as well as a missionary educator. Although the Southern Methodist mission had had only three American members before Allen's arrival, it was originally planned to send him to Hangchow, in Chekiang province, there to begin the mission. But Hangchow had been occupied by the Taipings in March 1860, and although the rebels soon evacuated the city, it continued to be unsettled. Allen made a trip to Hangchow in December 1860, greatly distressed by the devastation and human suffering en route, and a month later, along with another missionary and an interpreter, he visited Nanking, the Taiping capital. Allen considered the Taipings "a dedicated movement . . . *decidedly rebel [sic]* notwithstanding all their errors and cruelties." Returning to Shanghai, he expressed enthusiasm about the prospects of proselytizing among the Taipings, believing that "the longer we shun them, the worse it will be for the cause of God."[5] But as Allen was still struggling with the rudiments of the Chinese language, he himself was not ready for the ambitious undertaking. Moreover, expansion of his mission's work was made impossible by the outbreak of the Civil War in America, which deprived both the mission and Allen personally of financial support from the American South. The three senior members of the mission departed for home. Allen and Marquis L. Wood, who remained, were able to maintain themselves only by renting real estate owned by the mission, which was in great demand because of the influx of refugees to Shanghai. For the next two years Allen settled down to learning Chinese, and by the summer of 1863 he was preaching in that language at least once a day in a small chapel in the Chinese city that adjoined the foreign settlement.[6]

Although confined to this burgeoning port of traders and refugees, among whom were the poor as well as the rich, Allen's thoughts often turned to the hinterland. The war had spread to Shanghai's immediate environs in early 1862, but by summer of the next year, following the victories of the imperial forces, large areas of southeastern Kiangsu had returned to order. Allen often went out of the city to preach in the villages and small towns nearby. In September, with money raised from the foreign community in Shanghai, he established an "itinerant system" for two major towns within a thirty-mile radius of the port, Nan-hsiang and Chia-ting. A house was rented in each place to be used as a chapel under the charge of native assistants. Allen believed that itinerancy enabled his mission to "identify ourselves with the people, have a sort of home among them," and he himself preached in both Nan-hsiang and Chia-ting at least once a month.

But the experiences that Allen was now to have in Shanghai itself soon led him to the belief that the emphasis of missionary work should lie elsewhere. Like other missionaries, Allen was anxious for "more extensive and abundant harvests of souls." During the four years 1864–1868, he became convinced that preaching and itinerancy were not the only avenues of missionary work. He continued to believe that it was the love of God that had "directed me through the Holy Spirit to this Heathen land and by that alone and through the Spirit shall I be able to sustain the work of the Lord or do successfully those things that are pleasing to him."[7] But he now saw that science as well as Western contacts with China were part of God's revelation, and he thus arrived at a broader view of missionary work.

Allen's new views were stimulated partly by the secular employment he had to undertake. The winter of 1863–1864 found the mission in serious financial straits, for the rental from mission property had plummeted as the refugees of the Soochow area, now recovered by the Ch'ing forces, returned to their homes. Unable to maintain his family, Allen accepted a halftime appointment teaching English at the Shanghai T'ung-wen kuan or Interpreters' College, the first school established by the Ch'ing government in Shanghai that aimed at providing training in foreign languages, mathematics, and sciences.[8] Even before accepting this employment, Allen had become interested in knowing more of the Chinese intellectual heritage. He was depressed by his own lack of success in preaching as well as by the obtuseness of the men who came to hear him, mostly loafers in the street where his chapel was situated. Allen found that he could arouse interest only when he embellished his talks with Chinese proverbs and apothegms. "If the gospel be presented and illustrated altogether from the Bible they seem listless and indifferent hearers, but if their own familiar sayings be introduced they seem pleased and listen with great attention." In January 1864, Allen reread the *Three-Character Classic* and found that this simple primer contained "more learning and system in its compilation than I had previously given credit for." Allen's subsequent association with the Shanghai Interpreters' College made him more curious about the intellectual makeup of the literati. "A great deal of valuable experience and observation," he wrote in April 1864, is "obtainable by being thrown in direct contact with the higher classes of Chinese polite and literary society."[9] Allen now began to read the Chinese classics and dynastic histories in earnest, and his proficiency in the language vastly improved over the next two or three years.

As time passed, Allen found his attention being diverted from the Chinese works to renewing his knowledge of the sciences, to which he had been introduced at Emory. At the Shanghai Interpreters' College Allen discovered that his students and colleagues were more often interested in science than in the English language. Since scientific instruction at the college had not yet started, questions on chemistry and electricity were sometimes put to him. Although Allen's first contract with the government school was only for six months, he found himself, even after his service had ended, conducting chemical experiments at home for the benefit of his Chinese friends.[10] Until his reappointment to the college in January 1867, Allen, still without remittances from America, eked out a living by means of part-time employment in Shanghai; he acted as a broker for

164

a commercial firm at one time, and at another, as interpreter for the Shanghai Municipal Council.[11] All the time, however, he pondered the question of how the salvation of the Chinese could be facilitated by an intellectual approach, that is, by attacking the Chinese mind through a combination of science and the biblical message. By late 1866 he was ready to present his board at home with a new proposal regarding missionary work.

Allen became convinced that old-fashioned preaching could not win any large number of Chinese. "At present we simply discuss the doctrine of salvation, and though we may be able to overwhelm them with argument, they remain unchanged and unbelieving." The prospects for successful conversions were "dull indeed unless some changes are made." Since 1860, for example, Allen had baptized only seven Chinese, and the southern Methodist mission in 1866 had a total of twenty Chinese members in good standing, the others having been "excluded from the church on account of evil conduct, adultery, smoking opium, and persistently breaking the sabbath." Allen was encouraged, however, by "a willingness and a readiness on the part of many of the upper and better classes to avail themselves of foreign teachings provided they were not exclusively Christian . . . but also embraced as well, the useful arts and sciences." Allen felt that, for the sake of both training a "native agency" of high quality and approaching the Chinese at large, the mission should embark on an ambitious scheme of education, including the publishing of reading materials. "We must have schools, teachers, native agents, books, tracts, and allowances made for publishing any useful books that your missionaries may be able to translate for the benefit of schools or otherwise ere we can make an impression on this people to take root among them." The schools must teach the sciences. Allen's study of the Chinese classics convinced him that the Chinese, not only the Buddhists and Taoists but also the Confucians, were "ignorant beyond measure of the simplest laws of natural philosophy, chemistry, and astronomy, as their vague notions, senseless superstitions, and ceremonies and rites . . . fully attest." Instruction in science was particularly valuable for "uprooting and destroying faith in their own theories of the world and nature." The "day of miracles has passed," Allen wrote, "but the sciences skillfully illustrated in China, would be almost as invincible and wonderful."[12]

Since the Methodist Church, South, was long unable to devote many resources to foreign missions, Allen's "comprehensive and effective" scheme was a mere vision—although seventeen years later, after Allen had become the superintendent of his mission in China, he succeeded in founding a system of schools and a college. [13] Meanwhile, in January 1867 he accepted reappointment as an English teacher at the Shanghai Interpreters' College, in the belief that he was "entering an interesting and profitable sphere of influence for the missionaries." In March of that year, the mission received its first postbellum remittance from America, a sum of £ 297. Much of this had to be used to pay the mission's debts. With the remainder, Allen and his colleague J. W. Lambuth, who had returned to Shanghai to replace Marquis Wood after the latter's departure for home in late 1866, managed to establish two small "day schools," each with a Chinese assistant teaching ten pupils.[14]

Allen continued his Chinese studies. In the summer of 1867, he was able to produce a short scholarly article on the history of cotton farming in China, based on material gleaned from the dynastic histories.[15] Meanwhile he immersed himself in the study of chemistry and electricity. The small laboratory at his home now included an electromagnetic machine with a galvanic battery. Allen delighted in showing his friends and students how scientific apparatus worked. "I would explain the phenomena thus illustrated and endeavor to show therein the folly and falsehood of many of their superstitious beliefs . . . and thereby broaden the way of access, if possible, for the approach of truth to their minds." Allen's method was to expound the principles first and then try to demonstrate them. At the start, it was "necessary to deal with the fundamental principles of things in order to produce a clear and intelligent conviction of their truth among the Chinese." This exposition must, however, be followed by evidence: "mere assertion without proof will not suffice." When Allen took his students to the French gasworks that produced light for the Shanghai evenings, he found them "almost paralyzed in thought, when they see such exhibitions of progress far beyond the reach of their deepest and widest conceptions." While preaching, which Allen continued to do in the afternoons, he drew from his scientific knowledge to support Christian teachings. After a short lecture on astronomy in April 1867, for example, Allen pointed out "the folly of their [the Chinese] demonstration on occasion of an eclipse of the moon and then went on to speak of the Universe, etc., and . . . the greatness of their author, God." The audience was not impressed, however, as indicated by Allen's native assistant after the talk, who remarked, "it was pity that they could not comprehend such things, for if they could they would certainly believe the Doctrine and become Christians." On another occasion, similarly talking above his listeners' heads, Allen expounded a view on Confucianism that he had been formulating. He argued that Christianity was the word of God, "adapted by an omniscience comprehensive to the object and the results for which it was designed." Confucianism, in contrast, was developed by man. Since "man cannot comprehend himself, how can his doctrine reach the mainspring of his life and make him new?"[16]

Allen continued to be depressed by the ineffectiveness of missionary work. In Shanghai, he saw "wealth and poverty, robes and rags, beauty and deformity, decency and indecency, the modest and obscene and every possible opposite and variety—these mingled and united in offering common worship to the horrid idols." Returning to his idea of an educational approach, he saw its greatest advantage as lying in the personal influence that missionaries and teachers could exert through youth and their families. Allen was often dismayed by the slowness with which missionary work reached Chinese women. "They [the women] would cherish the truth far more tenderly, faithfully and earnestly than the men, for they [the men] hear but to forget, are callous and hardened. The women alone are the depositories of the good-feeling and kindly sympathies that yet remain toward the truth in China and in its absence they cling to superstition."[17]

Missionary work among women was to be one of the principal focuses of Allen's later career. Meanwhile, from his vantage point as a teacher at the Shanghai Interpreters' College he concentrated on approaching the literati. Although often discouraged, Allen also found hope in the interest shown in science and technology by Chinese scholars, at least those in the Shanghai area. In March 1867, he was elated by news of a major reform sponsored by Prince Kung at court, to the effect that holders of high literary degrees, including members of the Hanlin Academy, should be encouraged to enroll in a department of "astronomy and mathematics" to be created at the Peking Interpreters' College. Allen asked his students to study the edicts and memorials regarding the proposal and to treat them as "signs for better days for China." Although Prince Kung's plans met with strenuous opposition from the scholar officials at court, Allen was encouraged, toward the end of the year, by the fact that the Ch'ing government had decided to send Anson Burlingame, the retiring American minister, as its envoy to visit the Western nations. Allen saw Burlingame's embassy as China's "first step toward a recognition of the brotherhood of nations," and he hoped that this recognition would lead not only to the expansion of trade but also to a greater knowledge of the world on the part of the Ch'ing government. "Knowledge is power," he wrote, "and in a quiet way it will ultimately change the mind of the King."[18]

The Burlingame mission, as well as the discussion in the Shanghai press of the forthcoming Sino-British treaty revision, stimulated Allen to think about the West's relations with China in general. Since going to Shanghai, he had often been distressed by the unedifying behavior of many Western traders and adventurers. He regretted the harmful effects such behavior had on missionary work: "What the vilest do attaches to all alike, and detracts most seriously from our influences and character." Allen hoped that the Sino-Western treaties could be modified so that the rights and privileges of the missionaries would not be associated in the Chinese mind with those of the traders—that the history of evangelism and "that of commerce may be allowed to separate." But he also realized that missionary work in China had been made possible by the treaties won by Western nations chiefly for the sake of trade, and that commerce itself was beneficial to the Chinese, since it "strengthens and increases the material resources of those countries who engage in it and refreshes, quickens, and enlightens the mind of the people."[19] Given such attitudes, Allen accepted, in May 1868, additional secular employment as editor of the *Shanghai hsin-pao,* the thrice-weekly Chinese version of the principal paper of the port's foreign community, the *North-China Daily News.* Allen's colleague Marquis Wood had been the *Shanghai hsin-pao*'s first editor. When Wood's successor, John Fryer, resigned in May 1868 to become a translator at the Kiangnan Arsenal, Allen agreed to succeed him in consideration of the additional income needed by his growing family.[20] Reducing his preaching schedule during the week to alternate days only, Allen spent three afternoons a week on the paper, which had a circulation of a mere 350, chiefly among local Chinese merchants. With the help of

Chinese amanuenses, Allen produced brief items of foreign and domestic news as well as occasional editorials, which he later characterized as "utterly impartial, never siding with the Westerners or disdainful of Chinese friends."[21]

THE FOUNDING OF THE *CHIAO-HUI HSIN-PAO*

Four months after beginning work for the commercially sponsored paper, Allen founded a magazine of his own, the *Chiao-hui hsin-pao,* although he did not give up his post at the *Shanghai hsin-pao* until January 1871. He later recalled that sometime in 1867, at a meeting of missionaries in Shanghai where several Protestant societies were represented, he had discussed the idea of a magazine of religious character which might be read by Chinese "beyond the reach of our ordinary influences."[22] Inspired by his new experience as editor of the *Shanghai hsin-pao,* Allen pursued the idea, and the first issue of the weekly *Chiao-hui hsin-pao* appeared on September 5, 1868, printed with movable type at the American Presbyterian Mission Press. Allen received encouragement from other mission societies regarding the venture, and missionaries of the major denominations in several cities helped to solicit articles and subscriptions. But from the beginning, Allen alone was responsible for the magazine's editing and management. It was published under the imprint of the Lin-hua Academy, a scholarly coinage, located at Allen's address. Allen, who signed himself Lin Yao-chih (also pronounced Lo-chih), employed two Chinese assistants to help with the work. He himself underwrote the magazine's finances. By the end of the magazine's first year, when circulation had risen from the initial 200 to 700, the revenue from the subscriptions (at Mex. $1.00 per year) was still insufficient to cover editorial and production costs.[23]

Since Allen wanted the magazine to be read by the literati at large as well as by Christian converts, he faced the problem of how to approach the scholarly Chinese mind. In his sermons to the illiterate and semiliterate he often cited Chinese proverbs; now he wanted to present Christianity to his readers from a more sophisticated Chinese point of reference.

Allen's plan for the *Chiao-hui hsin-pao* reflected his own conviction that science and Western contacts would help to advance Christianity in China. He sought to arouse the reader's curiosity with illustrations of interesting objects, such as the scorpion, the alligator, and the flying fish, each followed by allusions to Chinese literature and often by simple scientific descriptions.[24] The magazine published articles on scientific apparatus, including the telegraph, the microscope, and the telescope, as well as on astronomy and geography. Beginning in the fourth issue, W. A. P. Martin's textbook on chemisty, which had been published in 1867 in Peking, was reprinted in installments. The *Chiao-hui hsin-pao* presented occasional reports on the activities of the principal Protestant missions in China.[25] The major cases of antimissionary disturbance were reported by missionaries and converts on the scene. Official Chinese pronouncements concerning the missionaries were often fully reproduced. From the beginning, moreover, the magazine regularly published secular news, foreign as well as domestic. Special attention was given to developments in China's foreign relations and to technological progress in the West and in China. The reception of the Burlingame mission in America and Europe was followed closely. Reports of Western technical achievements were frequent, some of the topics covered being railroad mileage in the United States, the Suez Canal, and the telegraph cables connecting Europe with America, Africa, and India. Signs of innovation in China were praised, such as the Kiangnan Arsenal's success in building a steamship or the according of official rank to graduates of the Shanghai Interpreters' College by the Tsungli Yamen.

Allen undoubtedly believed that such information, by stimulating the Chinese to think about the world of nature as well as China's place in the world of nations, would produce stirrings in the Chinese mind and make it more amenable to Christian teachings. But he also realized that these teachings themselves needed to be presented in a form that the literati reader could assimilate. For this task, Allen relied largely on Chinese preachers and teachers associated with the major Protestant missions. In the late 1860s there were more than three hundred such Chinese preachers and teachers, counting only sixteen Chinese ports and cities as well as Hong Kong.[26] In the very first issue of the *Chiao-hui hsin-pao*, Allen invited the Chinese Christians to use its pages to exchange views on the interpretation of the Scriptures and also to answer questions raised by non-Christians, for "light must not be hidden under a bushel."[27] In fact, less than a dozen missionaries contributed religious articles to the weekly during its first two years, from September 1868 to August 1870, and none did so frequently, except for Allen and W. A. P. Martin, whose series of allegorical stories on love, gratitude, and other virtues was republished in the *Chiao-hui hsin-pao* beginning in April 1870. The bulk of the magazine's essays on Christianity, at least during its first two years, were by Chinese Christians who responded to Allen's call for articles and comments on other articles.

The materials contributed by the Chinese Christians included personal accounts of religious experiences, devotional poems written in standard Chinese styles, biographies of recently deceased Chinese Christians, and eulogies of Western missionaries who had died or departed for home. But Allen's policy was to encourage essays that discussed Christian ideas in a language that went beyond biblical phraseology and made use of Chinese philosophical concepts. The early *Chiao-hui hsin-pao* published comparatively little theoretical discussion of Buddhism and Taoism, although the magazine frequently included news stories on the misdeeds of Buddhist or Taoist clergy and the folly of superstition, as when certain villagers near Ningpo plotted to arrange a "miracle" in a temple, but their trick came to light when a member of the gang was murdered by his associates.[28] Allen seems to have been particularly concerned, however, with the more rationally inclined literati, and he guided his contributors toward a discussion of the contrast as well as the compatibility between Christianity and Confucianism.

CHRISTIANITY AND CONFUCIANISM

Even before he had founded the magazine, Allen, working with one or two of his converts who were highly literate, had been trying to select Chinese phraseology that would convey the Christian message.[29] The sixth issue of the magazine published an essay by Hsu Wei-ts'an, a convert of the southern Methodist mission, who wrote that he had learned from Allen and Lambuth two basic ideas—*wu-yin* (concealing nothing) and *kuang-ai* (loving broadly).[30] Under these two concepts could be subsumed the essential biblical teachings: salvation through repentance and through knowledge of Christ and the Holy Spirit, and the resulting transformation of man's "selfish indulgence" into love for God and man. In order to make his point effectively, Hsu referred to the Confucian concepts of *jen* (benevolence or human-heartedness) and *i* (righteousness or sense of duty).

"To love broadly is the principle of *jen*," he wrote, "and to conceal nothing is the principle of *i*. Selfishness and the lack of openness are the beginning of sin, while those who conceal nothing and love broadly rejoice in the truth." Although it is not known whether Allen himself played any part in the formulation of such ideas, he undoubtedly encouraged Hsu Wei-ts'an to write in this vein.

In the next issue of the *Chiao-hui hsin-pao,* Chou Kuo-kuang, a pastor in Ningpo, mentioned in a brief article that "although Confucianism is correct [*cheng*], the way of Jesus is even better."[31] Noting this statement, Allen took advantage of a long letter he had received from a non-Christian Chinese to initiate a general discussion on the subject. Published in the ninth issue, the letter was not entirely hostile to Christianity. The author, who was identified by a pseudonym, "Chieh-yü tzu, of the Soochow prefecture," stated that his chance perusal of Christian literature had led him to believe that the Western faith deserved better treatment from the Chinese. He saw Christianity as complementing Confuciansim at points, but he believed that on the whole there was nothing of importance in Christianity that could not be found in Confucianism. "The principal points [of Christianity] do not go beyond the two characters *jen* and *i*." The writer objected, moreover, that certain Christian practices either violated Confucian precepts or fell below Confucian standards. He criticized the Christian neglect of filial piety: converts were forbidden to participate in ancestor worship, and some Christians had even joined the church against the wishes of their parents. Chieh-yü tzu also found the Chinese Christians lacking in refinement: "When one happens to mention to them an ancient allusion, they are embarrassed and at a loss." The writer would have liked to see the Christian schools employ *sheng-yuan* scholars (or holders of the first literary degree under the government examination system) for teaching the Confucian classics and training pupils in the composition of the eight-legged essay; he suggested that perhaps the Bible need be taught only on Sundays. To these interesting ideas, Allen added an editorial note inviting Christians to reply.[32]

Of the nine replies to Chieh-yü tzu published over the next seven months, only one was written by a missionary, Matthew T. Yates of the southern Baptist convention in Shanghai. Yates' reply, in two installments, began appearing only two weeks after the letter from the non-Christian critic. The missionary pointed to the basic difference between the two doctrines: while Confucianism relies entirely on "human effort" (*jen-li*) for achieving virtue, the Christian, with his concern for everlasting life, derives his moral sentiments from the "transforming influence of the spirit" (*ling-ch'i i kan-hua*). Virtue flows naturally from the Christian experience, but this is the result of God's grace as well as of man's faith—Christ's self-sacrifice and the continued intercession of the Holy Spirit in response to prayer. Confucianism, in contrast, regards virtue as an imperative to be followed by man unaided. Man is exhorted to cultivate his nature, but his nature does not quite naturally incline to *jen* and *i*. "The Confucian teaches man to accord with his nature (*shuai hsing*), but this nature is difficult to attain accord with. Confucianism teaches man to illustrate virtue (*ming te*), but virtue is difficult to illustrate." Since the time of Confucius, innumerable people had learned his teachings, but "very few indeed," the writer asserted, had "really cultivated their virtue and practiced righteousness."[33]

In the eight other published replies to Chieh-yü tzu, the Chinese authors assumed a position similar to that of Yates. Two writers, Chu Hsing-chou of Nanking and Chu Shih-t'ang of Hankow, employed the phrase "heaven's way" (*t'ien-tao*) to describe Christianity, as opposed to the "human way" (*jen-tao*) of Confucianism. Wang Kuang-ch'i, a scholarly convert living in Tientsin, argued that the existence of a spiritual being had been suggested in a passage in the Confucian classic *The Great Learning*: "Things have their roots and their branches." It had been Chu Hsi, the Sung neo-Confucianist, who had mistakenly identified the "roots" (*pen*) with man's own efforts to "illustrate virtue"—that is, to understand and develop his own nature.[34] The other Chinese who replied to Chieh-yü tzu were less philosophical and more concerned with his concrete criticisms of the Christians. Although their views were not necessarily profound, these writers nevertheless took a firm Christian position against what they regarded as the sterile formalism of the Confucian morality and culture.

All the Chinese writers who replied to Chieh-yü tzu argued that, with the Christians, obedience to God is the paramount consideration, certainly taking precedence over "mere form" (*hsü-wen*). Although the writers defended the Christian proscription against ancestor worship, they explained that Christianity was not opposed to filial devotion (*hsiao*) itself; "Honor thy father and thy mother" is after all a biblical commandment.[35] They insisted, however, that true filial feeling must be expressed during the lifetime of the parents; offering sacrifices to the dead (*chi-ssu*) is not only idolatrous but also hypocritical. "In Ningpo alone," wrote Chou Kuo-kuang, "there are millions of people offering sacrifices to their ancestors; yet how many of them are really filial offspring (*hsiao-tzu*)? If offering sacrifices is genuine filial devotion, then every Chinese must be a filial child. How sad it is that I have not come across a single such person!"[36] Chieh-yü tzu had argued that ancestor worship stemmed from man's nature, namely, his natural inclination "to repay the kindness of his roots [*pao-pen*]." Wang Kuang-ch'i, the learned convert, presented philological evidence to show that in the ancient Chou dynasty, as in biblical times, sacrifices were offered, never to the dead, but to the deity, though sometimes through a living person.[37] Wang exhorted his readers that it is in the daily attention to living parents that real and worthwhile sacrifice lies.

Parents were not, moreover, the final claimants to one's loyalty. The writers who replied to Chieh-yü tzu agreed that would-be Christians should discuss their plans with their parents before joining the church. But in the admittedly difficult situation of parental consent being withheld, the dictates of the faith must be followed. Chu Hsing-chou, a preacher in Nanking, argued from the analogy that the command of the emperor takes precedence over the wishes of the parents, an ordering of priorities that was generally accepted in late imperial China. Chu took the position that even the monarch's wishes must defer to those of God.[38] Chou Kuo-kuang, the Ningpo pastor, stated, "It behooves us to serve [God] single-mindedly all our lives; here on this earth we should also be filial to our parents while loving all men [*fan ai-chung*]." But he emphasized the order of priority: "It is proper of course to obey one's father and mother, but how much more should one obey the great Father of heaven and earth—the one and only God?" An anonymous convert who lived in Hankow cited the injunction: "He that loveth father and mother more than me is not worthy of me" (Matt. 10:27). Ch'en Sung-lu, of the English Presbyterian mission in Peking, warned of peril if one should follow the wishes of either father or elder brother and "disobey the great Father of soul (*ling-hun ta-fu*)."[39]

If filial obligations must yield to greater considerations, so must literary culture, which was either ornamental or merely the means to an earthly goal. All writers who replied to Chieh-yü tzu were resentful of his suggestion that Christians were uncultivated and crude. "Within our faith, what is considered elegant is the superiority of substance over appearance—not empty words," wrote Chu Shih-t'ang of Hankow. "Salvation of the soul is the important matter, and it depends not on learning but on earnestness and on divine power," added Ch'en Sung-lu. Two writers, Chou Kuo-kuang and Chang Ting (a pastor in Foochow), saw an advantage in Christians being versed in Chinese literature, provided they were firm in their own faith. "The elegant and the uncultured," wrote Chou, "should both be transformed by the influence of the Spirit." All writers rejected the suggestion that the mission schools should teach the Bible on Sundays only. Chou Kuo-kuang observed that, along with the Scriptures, some mission schools were actually offering instruction in the Confucian classics, as well as in astronomy, mathematics, geography, and natural history. Neither he nor Chang Ting objected to the schools being taught by *sheng-yuan* scholars or the students preparing for the civil service examinations. Others disagreed. "Poetry, calligraphy, and the literary art are only means employed in the quest for earthly fame; they are of little actual importance," commented the anonymous convert in Hankow. Chu Shih-t'ang was not opposed to the Christian schools teaching the Confucian classics, but he insisted that this should be done only to help the people learn how to read and write, not to aim at "the achievement of rank and honor."[40]

CHRISTIAN ETHICS VERSUS CHINESE CULTURE

While the views of the Chinese Christians regarding Chieh-yü tzu's criticisms must have been gratifying to Allen, his search for a more effective way to convey the Christian message continued. During its second six months of publication the *Chiao-hui hsin-pao* continued to publish simple articles of scientific interest as well as news that emphasized technological progress and China's relations with the West, but another emphasis became apparent in the selection of material. Even during its first six months, the *Chiao-hui hsin-pao* had published news and comments that reflected the evangelical social concern. The brothels and gambling dens of Shanghai were attacked as vehemently as was the idolatrous display of the Buddhist and Taoist festivals. Chinese officials were praised for their occasional philanthropy, such as donations given for the relief of the aged by Ying Pao-shih, the Shanghai taotai.[41] The evils of opium smoking were described and prescriptions of herbal medicines for ridding oneself of addiction were offered. Beginning in April 1869, however, the number of articles on humanitarian causes markedly increased. Although descriptions of hospitals had appeared earlier, accounts were now offered of the numerous benevolent institutions under mission sponsorship, such as the antiopium society, the asylum for the blind, and the "charitable schools" (*i-hsueh*). Appeals were made in the name of the *Chiao-hui hsin-pao* itself for the rehabilitation of beggars and for poor relief.[42] Such materials multiplied during succeeding months, at the same time that further discussion of the relative merits of Christianity and Confucianism were carried on in the magazine.

This discussion represented a continuation of the replies to Chieh-yü tzu, with the focus now shifted to the shortcomings of Confucianism itself. In commenting on Chieh-yü tzu's letter, the Chinese Christians had asserted the prior claim of God over men's loyalty, but they did not pursue the implied attack on Confucian loyalties. In fact, several of the writers now urged their readers to observe faithfully the obligations prescribed under the "five relationships" (*wu-lun*), especially the filial obligations.[43] The contributors to the *Chiao-hui hsin-pao* persisted, however, in assailing the formalism and hypocrisy in Confucian behavior. Two causes were seen for the Confucians' failure to live up to their professed standards. The literary culture that had come to be associated with Confucianism was viewed as stultifying and harmful, while the metaphysical system of the neo-Confucian orthodoxy was regarded as spiritually corrupting.

Although not a few of the *Chiao-hui hsin-pao*'s contributors themselves wrote archaic prose and florid poetry, most of it probably produced by the teachers at the mission schools, others revolted against the culture that encouraged such literary forms. Chang Ting, the pastor in Foochow, had no objection to Christians studying Chinese classics and literature, but it was his view that the excessive literary training required by the civil service examinations had a deleterious effect on the scholar's character: "Extracting chapters and verses [from the classics in order to compose the eight-legged essay] benefits neither the body nor the mind." Moreover, the rote memorization practiced by every scholar from youth had the effect of maiming one's faculties like "an ax falling upon the young shoot." Chang Ting saw a definite link between literary training and the arrogance and hypocrisy of Confucian scholars. "Taking pride in their learning, they attempt to suppress other people's capacities; they boast of their achievement and attack the seeming inadequacy of others." The most cultivated, moreover, were often the cruelest. "Though their countenance is kind, their words are artful and boastful. And their inner sentiments are often wrathful and merciless; they love to do injury to others and to intrigue. They talk every day of acting the part of son and brother and of loyalty and faithfulness, but have they ever acted accordingly?" A Chinese Christian writing under the name of Ch'üan-shan tzu agreed with Chang Ting's views. He observed further that ever since the sayings of Confucius and Mencius had been made a standard topic for examination papers, the classics had become tools for the scholars in their quest for personal aggrandizement. "Learning and education are aimed exclusively at the attainment of rank and honor. All this knowledge of the ancient times and of the present age is but a means to achieve profit and success."[44]

While Chang Ting and Ch'üan-shan tzu attacked the elite culture supported by the examination system, other writers offered a simple Christian critique of the neo-Confucian metaphysical doctrine—not carefully thought out, but nevertheless representing a sentiment. The concepts of *li* and *ch'i* ("principle" and "matter"), as expounded by the Sung philosophers Ch'eng I and Chu Hsi, were viewed as lending aid to the superstitions that had, in the writers' opinion, corrupted the Chinese mind and behavior. "Ah!" exclaimed Pien-cheng tzu (a pseudonym) of Hankow, "I had not realized that the doctrine of *li* and *ch'i* had harmful effects to this extreme extent!" He blamed the doctrine for the suffocation of people's minds as well as the misconduct of the literati officials, which in turn brought widespread suffering among the people. "Sad is the blinded and imprisoned condition [of people's minds] and sad is their extreme plight and agony." The cause had to be traced, however, to a man-centered and therefore self-centered philosophy. "All that is said of acting the parts of subject, brother and friend and of cultivating oneself, regulating the family, governing the kingdom, and ordering the world are but empty words." Cheng Yü-jen, a Baptist at Chefoo, explained that to Chu Hsi, *li* and *ch'i* were linked with the cosmic forces *yin* and *yang.* The venerated sage had declared, "The ghost is the spirit of *yin,* while the deity is the spirit of *yang.*" The writer saw a "contradiction" in the statement, for "if the cosmic forces *yin* and *yang* are determined to be identical in spirit with ghost and deity, then *yin* and *yang* are but the variant names of ghost and deity, and ghost and deity are actually the substance [*pen-t'i*] of *yin* and *yang.*"[45] Neo-Confucian concepts thus lent support to a false cosmology and deprived man of his true spiritual resource.

This spiritual resource, the Chinese Christians asserted, lay in the Christian teachings, particularly in the idea of love (*ai,* "charity" in the King James version). For just as Confucian thought and culture in effect encourage self-seeking, Christian ethics are based on an unmistakable spiritual urge to transcend the self. Between February and November 1869, the *Chiao-hui hsin-pao* published seven articles with Christian love as their principal topic, four of them by Allen's convert, Hsu Wei-ts'an. A definition of *ai* was offered, using scriptural language as well as Chinese idioms.

In an early issue of the magazine Hsu Wei-ts'an had employed the concepts *wu-yin* (concealing nothing) and *kuang-ai* (loving broadly) to sum up Christian teachings.[46] In two essays published in February 1869, Hsü explained the sources and the workings of *ai* (love). "Man's mind (*jen-hsin*) originally is ignorant of righteousness and is weak, but God fills it with love." By the crucifixion of Christ God's love is transmitted. "On the cross the myriad sins [of men] have been redeemed." Therefore, those who repent must "invite the Holy Spirit to remove our evil thought . . . to follow the commandments, to promote peace, to humble ourselves, and to love broadly." Love is to infuse one's words and deeds. "Once man is filled with love, he understands the Spirit, he expresses himself in speech, he abides by the faith, and he extends himself in action."[47]

In terms of Confucian culture, Christian love was to remove the selfish ambition that characterized the literati's career goals, for Christian love carries a broadened concern for humanity—primarily for man's soul but also for his general well-being. Lin Ch'ing-shan, a Presbyterian at Tengchow, believed that every redeemed man had the responsibility for other men. "All who love the Lord must love the Lord's people [*chu chih jen*]. The Lord has taken my sin as His own responsibility; to whom shall I assign the responsibility regarding the

Lord's truth? My sinful person has been redeemed by the Lord. To whom does my person belong? Since it belongs to the Lord, who shall make use of it?" Self is therefore subordinate to the Lord, yet the Lord's command is to serve other men, as well as to serve Him. A Chefoo Christian, writing under the name of Chih-tsui tzu, elaborated on the injunction "Love thy neighbor as thyself." The writer explained, "He who loves the Lord must first love man [*pi hsien ai jen*]."[48] Rejoining the discussion, Hsu Wei-ts'an added that love for man is a kind of repayment for God's love, given in gladness. "To love man is something one cannot help but do"; the sentiment comes "truly from the heart." Hsu explained that Christian love does not preclude "love of self" (*ai-chi*), for the only issue here is the self regenerated, such a self as Jesus regained at resurrection. Christianity does not teach the extinction of self in nirvana, as does Buddhism; nor is the Christian view of sacrifice identical with the "self-denial" (*wu-wo*) that Hsu ascribed to the ancient philosopher Mo Tzu. Without denying self, the Christian seeks its rebirth, and a broadened love naturally issues from the rebirth. Adopting the Confucian phraseology, Hsu characterized Christian love as *kung* (regard for the common good), as opposed to *ssu* (selfishness).[49]

SOCIAL IDEAS

During the period in which discussions on Christian ethics appeared in the *Chiao-hui hsin-pao,* the news reports paid greater attention than before to questions of social concern: gambling, prostitution, and opium smoking; poverty and the lack of educational opportunities. In the same period the magazine also published articles contributed by Chinese converts on these subjects. Despite their criticism of Confucianism, the Chinese Christians pointed out literature produced by the Chinese literati that would support the magazine's benevolent causes. But on certain social issues, notably the condition of women, Christian converts went further than the most philanthropic of their Confucian contemporaries.

For many Chinese writers in the *Chiao-hui hsin-pao,* the social application of the Christian message was restricted. A kind of myopia characterized many Chinese Christians, owing as much to their own heritage as to the nature of evangelical Christianity. The welfare of only the immediate community was emphasized. For example, having stressed the importance of the injunction to "love thy neighbor," Lin Ch'ing-shan, the Tengchow Christian, merely proposed a "local public association" (*pen-ti kung hui*). Although Lin urged the Christians of his area to pool their "intelligence, physical activity, money, and labor," what he wanted was no more than a guild-like club for mutual aid within the Christian community. In his final essay on Christian love, Hsu Wei-ts'an stated, "Love issues from the heart but is demonstrated in practical affairs (*shih-shih*)." The practical affairs he visualized, however, included primarily matters of interpersonal relations—dealings with friends, colleagues, and enemies. "I shall repay with kindness those who are kind to me and I shall converse in a generous spirit with those who transgress against me . . . I shall use gentle words in the hope of influencing those who are tricky and have designs against me; I shall be conciliatory to those who hold grudges against me." One had to be forthright as well as forgiving, for merely to allow for a friend's weakness was not to render him service: "When I see the faults of another, how can I not tell him about it?" To such exhortations regarding the conduct of personal relations, Hsu added a humanitarian note almost as an afterthought: "Seeing suffering, one commiserates; seeing extremity, one offers aid and relief."[50]

While this compassionate concern could be broadened, the myopia of the Chinese Christians was strengthened by their general views of society and personal careers. Despite their resentment against China's bureaucrat-dominated society, the permanence of the sociopolitical order was assumed. Thus, Chih-tsui tzu of Chefoo wrote, "The master of the family is the elder (*chang*); the master of the state is the monarch; and the master of heaven, earth and the myriad things is God." While God requires no assistance, "in governing the family, the elder depends on the assistance of sons, young brothers, and servants; in governing the state, the monarch depends on the officials in the numerous posts that have been established." The Chinese Christians often sought the intervention of missionaries in lawsuits or other dealings with officials—a fact that Allen regretted but which his Chinese contributors seldom cared to discuss. Nonetheless, the Chinese Christian writers did not question the authority of the imperial officials or the importance of the family system. Despite his scathing attack on the hypocrisy of scholar officials, Pien-cheng tzu of Hankow described Christians as men who "do their utmost to fulfill their duties under the three bonds (*kang*), the five constant virtues (*ch'ang*), and the principle of the five relationships (*lun-li*)."[51]

Nor could the Chinese contributors to the *Chiao-hui hsin-pao* be entirely free of the Chinese elite's views regarding temporal success. Since most of them resided in the treaty ports or other large cities, they came to esteem commercial pursuits as much as government service. They used the characters *fu* (wealth) and *kuei* (honor resulting from high official rank) interchangeably, as was the practice of many Chinese. In a series of articles entitled "Why Are the Good Poor and the Wicked Rich?" (inspired by an essay by Allen on a related inquiry,[52]) the writers agreed that wealth and honor were of no consequence when compared with eternal life. Yet they did not regard earthly acquisitions as evil in themselves—the camel and the needle's eye notwithstanding. A convert who signed himself Tun-wu tzu asked rhetorically: "If the rich should be constantly inclined toward righteousness, what harm would there be in being exceedingly rich? If the poor would not abide by their lot, what benefit would there be in being poor?" Like the contemporary evangelical Christians in the United States or England, the *Chiao-hui hsin-pao* writers, despite their preoccupation with spirituality, praised the virtues of industry and frugality, as well as the intelligence that helped to advance the individual's career. Hsu Wei-ts'an regretted the fact that many had attained success in civil service examinations or in business through unfair advantages. But he nevertheless believed that it was possible to achieve such success "entirely through one's own effort."[53]

Despite these common assumptions, a number of Chinese contributors to the *Chiao-hui hsin-pao* did not equate Christian love with the encouragement of efforts at self-improvement. Their concern with problems of their immediate communities came to be extended to the society at large, at least on certain issues. The Chinese Christians, to be sure, were men of small means who could hope to gain large influence only through the missionaries or literati officials. Their articles in the *Chiao-hui hsin-pao* nevertheless contain proposals that not only reflected Christian values but were also extremely pertinent to China's problems.

Although the *Chiao-hui hsin-pao* published many didactic stories warning of the evils of gambling and licentiousness, comparatively few Chinese Christians contributed essays on these subjects. Such essays as there were seemed to indicate that the writers did not simply abhor these vices out of puritanical zeal; what was emphasized were the harmful effects to the health, character, and career of the individual concerned.[54] The same may be said of the articles contributed by the Chinese Christians on the evil of opium smoking, which appeared much more frequently, at least once a month in 1869. Several authors were themselves reformed addicts and felt a personal need to spread the word of their own regeneration. Some writers identified opium smoking as sin and Christ's love as the guarantee for cure. But all writers dwelt on the drug's effects on life itself: "the abandon with which the body submits to poison," and "the gradual and willing destruction of life." Some also stressed the consequences of the habit for the family and the country: "the sighing of the parents and the grief of wife and children," and then "the weakening and withering away of the Chinese people."[55]

The Chinese Christians sought through personal contacts as well as the writing of essays and poems to persuade their countrymen to abandon the opium evil. The hospitals and dispensaries of the missions provided medicines to help terminate the habit, but Ch'ien Lien-ch'i, a scholarly convert, confessed that he had cured himself with herbal prescriptions furnished by a pharmacy in Shanghai founded by a former official and specializing in medicine for opium addiction.[56] The *Chiao-hui hsin-pao* collected a variety of herbal prescriptions and eventually published them, but at least one or two Chinese Christian writers turned their attention to the larger question of how to stem the widespread habit on a country-wide scale. In an article published in April 1869, Huang Mei, a Baptist in Kwangtung, proposed that all opium smokers should be regarded as "degraded menial workers" (*chien-i*) and deprived of the opportunity of becoming officials or serving in guilds, academies, and neighborhood or clan councils. He condemned opium as "harmful to the state, the people, and the race," as well as to "wealth, honor, and soul." In August 1869, a convert who styled himself Tun-hsing tzu contributed an article supporting Huang's proposal. Tun-hsing tzu blamed the growing use of the drug on the legalization of its importation; he would have liked to see the prohibition of opium smoking strictly enforced among all civil and military officials as well as all candidates for the examination. Tun-hsing tzu suggested that the provincial governors-general and governors should memorialize the throne to request that such a statute be decreed.[57]

Although the Chinese Christians felt strongly about the opium evil, they were less agitated about a more basic problem—the poverty and the precariousness of life in a land of teeming population frequently visited by disasters. Chinese Christians were of course aware of the problem of poverty. Despite his respect for the wealthy members of the church, Tun-wu tzu lamented the plight of the indigent Christians: "They are unemployed and without proper lodging; they lack clothing and food. They are indeed reverent and righteous and their souls will enjoy the bliss of everlasting life. But how are they to live on this earth?"[58] The solution Tun-wu tzu recommended was philanthropy (*ching-hsu*). He proposed that wealthy Christians affiliated with the foreign firms should contribute a percentage of their salaries regularly to a contingency fund for the welfare of the Christian community. He said that despite his own limited means, he had been giving occasional assistance to colleagues who could not make ends meet. Preoccupied with his own immediate circle, Tun-wu tzu gave little thought to the problems of the society at large.

Other Chinese Christians had directed their attention to those problems, however. The floods in the Yangtze Valley in the fall of 1869, which rendered thousands homeless in six provinces, stirred the consciences of many. In Hankow in October some 120,000 refugees had to be fed. Although the government established congee stations (*chou-ch'ang*), missionary doctors tended to the sick while Chinese Christians preached to the dejected crowds.[59] Refugees flowed into Shanghai itself, aggravating the city's problem of street paupers. Huang Yun-sun, a teacher at an Episcopal mission school, took up as a personal cause the establishment of an asylum for the poor. In an elegantly composed appeal published in the *Chiao-hui hsin-pao* in November, Huang requested the Chinese and foreign "officials, gentry, literati and merchants" to contribute a home for refugees and paupers. Huang wrote of the winter cold waiting to take its toll of human life and of children starving in the streets of a prosperous and luxurious city. He praised a missionary recently gone home, the Episcopalian Elliot H. Thomson, who had in two previous winters established asylums for paupers. "He [Thomson], aware of the Creator's fondness for all that lives, rested his thoughts on the love of men and of the [myriad] things [*jen-jen ai-wu*]." Huang urged the Chinese and foreigners in Shanghai to "extend their benevolence to help those in dire circumstances, to succor the afflicted, and to show pity to their neighbor."[60]

While at least a few Chinese Christians became involved in philanthropic plans, leadership in this matter plainly belonged to others. Huang Yun-sun's appeal in Shanghai was rendered insignificant by the action taken by local officials, merchants, and missionaries. At the initiative of the new Shanghai taotai, T'u Tsung-ying, straw huts were erected south of the city to house the refugees, who were given one congee meal a day. The area north of the city was allocated to the principal non-Christian benevolent institution in Shanghai, the P'u-yü t'ang (Hall of Extended Welfare), which had been established in 1867 with approval of the Shanghai taotai and with funds provided by the Chinese tea and silk guilds.[61] As of 1869, this institution was regularly housing 300 paupers, while giving alms to the families of 300 infants. It now established congee kitchens to meet the needs of the inflowing refugees.[62] Huang Yun-sun, who reported on the relief activities for the *Chiao-hui hsin-pao,* was particularly impressed by the work of Yü Chih, a scholar in his sixties who had since 1867 been in charge of the P'u-yü t'ang's activities. Worried about the widespread infanticide in the areas affected by the flood, Yü Chih was known to have been organizing a campaign with the governor-general at Nanking to get all the villages and towns within his jurisdiction to collect funds for the benefit of pregnant women and their infants.[63]

The Chinese Christians were so impressed by Yü Chih that they brought his writings to Allen's attention. Yü Chih, the *Chiao-hui hsin-pao*'s readers were told, was a *sheng-yuan* scholar from Chinkuei hsien in Kiangsu. A lifelong philanthropist, he was particularly noted for his work during the flood famine of 1848. He had mounted the same campaign against infanticide then and was reported to have saved at least seven hundred infants. Earlier, in September 1869, the *Chiao-hui hsin-pao* had published some documents of the P'u-yü t'ang authored by Yü—material that was brought to Allen's attention by Sung Shu-ch'ing, a Chinese Christian working for the American Presbyterian Mission Press.[64] Sung and Huang Yun-sun now recommended to Allen a book edited by Yü, which included documents and practical guides regarding relief and other

184

philanthropic work.[65] Yü's writings employed a simple argument to exhort the reader to philanthropic action, namely, the importance of saving life. "There is nothing under heaven that is more important than man's life," he wrote in a petition to a high official, "therefore there is no greater benevolent undertaking than to save lives." In appealing for donations, Yü invoked such Buddhist-Taoist concepts as "accumulating virtue" (*chi te*) or "accumulating blessings" (*chi fu*)—a rationale that was acceptable to the Confucians of the day. The title of Yü's book, *Te-i lu,* was derived from a passage in *The Doctrine of the Mean,* where Confucius was supposed to have said of his favorite disciple, Yen Hui: "Whenever he [Yen Hui] got hold of what was good [*shan*], he clasped it firmly, as if wearing it on his breast, and did not lose it."[66] The two Christians, Huang and Sung, as well as Allen, must have found in Yü Chih a man of admirable intentions.

Although a common ground existed between them on the matter of philanthropy, the Christian and the Confucian were in conflict over other questions. From such issues as the nature of the civil service system to the status of women and the system of elementary education, Chinese Christians were either openly or potentially opposed to the literati. As early as August 1869, Ch'üan-shan tzu wrote an article ascribing the suffering of the people—quite apart from natural disasters—to the corruption of the officials that resulted from the existing system of official preferment. The examination system was harmful, the writer argued, for it encouraged scholars to treat learning as a means to financial success; but even worse was the selling of offices, an expedient to which the Ch'ing government had long resorted but which had become worse since the early years of the Hsien-feng period (1851–1861). The practice, Ch'üan-shan tzu lamented, enabled "the descendants of the established families as well as country gentry (*hsiang-shen*)" to gain office by virtue of wealth alone. Men who bought their way into office could "have no regard for the interests of the people and aim merely at profit from the bribes they have dealt out."[67] Complaints of this nature were eventually to move the Chinese Christian writers of the *Chiao-hui hsin-pao* to propose drastic reforms of the system for official preferment and of the examination system itself. As of 1869–1870, however, none of the writers had gone that far. In addition to the proposal regarding the prohibition of opium, the principal reform proposals of the *Chiao-hui hsin-pao* were related to the Chinese institutions regarding women, particularly the custom of footbinding that prevailed especially in urban China.

Although the *Chiao-hui hsin-pao* had long been publishing news reports referring to women, not until September 1869 did Chinese Christians begin writing on the subject. A Ningpo convert named Lu Ts'ung-chou, having read Leviticus 12, wondered why it was that the Lord regarded women who bear children as particularly in need of purifying. "Is woman especially unclean because she disobeyed God first?" Replying to this inquiry, Huang P'in-san, a Baptist pastor in Shanghai, expressed a thought that had long been troubling him—that "in ancient times as well as today," women were regarded as inferior to men (*nü ch'ing yü nan*). In China especially, although no one would condemn a man for frequenting brothels, a woman who experienced illicit love was considered "unclean all her years." For the man who had lost his wife, only a year's mourning was required, but the woman who had lost her husband was expected to wear "complete mourning dress" for the remainder of her life. Huang was at a loss to explain this inequality, although he acknowledged that the Bible did not say that man was created for woman but "the woman for the man" (I Cor. 11:9).[68]

Huang P'in-san reminded the *Chiao-hui hsin-pao* readers of another situation relating to the Chinese woman—the system of polygamy that favored men. Huang reported in April 1870 that a prayer meeting of the Shanghai Baptists had considered a thorny problem: should a man who had a concubine be permitted to join the church? And should his concubine be allowed to do so? Huang reported that the Baptists in Shanghai were of two minds on the question. Although polygamy was not expressly prohibited by the Scriptures, it nevertheless was licentiousness institutionalized; neither the husband nor the concubine could escape the responsibility for adultery. It was true, however, that many women had been driven by "cold and hunger" into concubinage. A concubine would have nothing to do for a living if she should be disowned by a man wishing to conform to the standards of the church.[69]

The clash between Christian ethics and Confucian values was underscored in the comments on Huang P'in-san's article. The Cantonese Baptist Huang Mei scathingly attacked the institution of concubinage. Despite the usual male pretext that concubines were for the sake of bringing children to the family, men's motives were primarily "sexual" (*hao-se*). If it was permissible for a man to take a concubine because his wife had not given him children, why was it that the wife was never allowed to take a "second husband" (*shu-fu*), whose children could bear the name of her first husband if desired? Huang recommended that any man who had ever had a concubine should not be admitted to baptism, although he should be encouraged to attend church service and to make the best terms he could with the Lord. Yet neither the wife nor the concubine should be barred from the church, since the polygamous state was not really their responsibility. Ch'ih-p'ing shou, of Allen's own southern Methodist mission in Shanghai, agreed that the concubine should in no way be penalized. The husband, however, should be allowed baptism, or be restored to good standing with the church, if he would abstain from further physical relations with the concubine. It would be unfair, however, to expel the concubine from the house, particularly if she was "good and had borne children." She could perhaps live in a "separate room" in the man's house and assist in bringing up the children.[70]

Whatever the practical value of these suggestions, the attitude toward concubinage shown in the articles nonetheless represented an affirmation of the equal claims of men and women, regarding the body as well as the soul. A more concrete proposal now emerged regarding footbinding. In the first of a series of three articles on the subject published in May 1870, Dr. John Dudgeon of the London Missionary Society in Peking dwelt on the medical effects of bound feet. The decreased physical activity dictated by the "lotus gait" often caused such symptoms as slowed-down circulation, loss of appetite, and menstrual disorders that might prevent conception. The doctor also stressed the psychological damage: "All her life her mind will never be at ease; she will dread every step she takes."[71]

Two Chinese Christians brought up further considerations and discussed the measures necessary to get rid of the evil custom. Lin Shou-pao, a Baptist at Chefoo, noted that footbinding was an artificial way of enhancing female attractiveness and that women with bound feet were prevented from realizing their full potential. Furthermore, since a large number of women, disabled by footbinding, played no part at all in economic life, the country's production was affected, resulting in "the poverty of the state and people." Lin implied that women should indeed work. Ts'ao Tzu-yü, a native of Chekiang affiliated with the Presbyterian mission in Peking, added that parents who forced footbinding on their daughters were plainly acting against Christian love as well as violating Confucian teachings if the latter were properly understood.[72]

Just as the Christian writers had appealed to the government to prohibit opium smoking, Lin and Ts'ao both hoped that the Ch'ing court would by decree forbid footbinding for all girls below the age of ten.[73] Not all the *Chiao-hui hsin-pao*'s readers, however, shared the views of Lin and Ts'ao. A Shantung Christian named Wang Yü-shan complained that the magazine was descending to "the trivial and the picayune" in taking up the matter. A non-Christian reader who called himself K'ang-shuang tzu doubted the wisdom of pro-scribing the custom since such a proscription could raise other questions about social customs, dress, and hair styles.[74]

In proposing the ban on bound feet, Chinese Christians thus confronted values that may have been consistent with Confucian ethics yet which supported plainly undesirable institutions. A further issue involving potential conflict with Confucian theory and practice began to emerge in the magazine's pages in 1870, namely, the need for expanding and improving educational facilities for the young. To an article on charitable schools in Shanghai by a Chinese Christian, published in October 1869, Allen had appended a note soliciting information on such schools elsewhere in China.[75] Not until the late spring of 1870 was the magazine able to print documents concerning a few such schools in Anhwei and Kwangtung, thanks to the avail-ability of this material in Yü Chih's *Te-i lu*. Meanwhile, Huang Yun-sun, the teacher in Shanghai who had been involved in relief work the previous winter, raised the question of teaching methods at the charitable schools. He confessed that his own teaching in a mission school in Shanghai had been ineffective and that he was afraid of "doing injustice to other people's sons and brothers." His inquiry marked the beginning of extensive discussion on the subject of education in the *Chiao-hui hsin-pao*.

TOWARD AN EXPANDED CHRISTIAN MESSAGE

The modest magazine that Young J. Allen had founded in Septem-ber 1868 turned out to be a major forum of Protestant converts in

China. The comparative sophistication of the articles reflects the literacy of the Chinese pastors and teachers of the treaty ports and other large cities, but many of the grievances expressed were those of Chinese society at large. The missionaries had not only inculcated Christian doctrine but also stimulated thinking on cultural and social issues. At the same time it seems plain that the converts had already been prepared for a revolt against certain indigenous conditions before they became Christians.

These essays also speak well of the wide range of the editor's own concerns, the diversity of opinion he encouraged, and the respect he showed for the Chinese literary milieu. All these contributed to the *Chiao-hui hsin-pao*'s success, which was later maintained by the *Wan-kuo kung-pao*. By the early 1880s, Allen was to emerge as a full-fledged spokesman for a broad Christianity, one which, as he put it, "develops the whole man . . . [and] *comprehends (embraces and understands) his entire being and relations.*"[76] He was to become one of the two or three earliest promoters of Christian higher education in China and, through the *Wan-kuo kung-pao,* was to be an influential exponent of China's need for institutional reform. Certain tendencies of this later development were already apparent in Allen's own articles of 1868–1870.

Allen was more confident than were his Chinese contributors about the way providence was working in China. Although he often despaired of China's seeming imperviousness to change, he also firmly believed that science as well as international relations would prepare China for Christ. As early as January 1868 he wrote to the editor of the *Southern Christian Advocate:* "Confucius and the 'art of composition,' the last boast of the Chinese, will soon yield the practical supremacy to foreign science and new modes of thought, new books, new arts, new laws and universal inquiry will soon change the aspect of China." Allen followed closely the progress of the Burlingame mission and of the negotiations toward the unratified Alcock Convention. In December 1869 he wrote to the *Southern Christian Advocate* that China could see "from some of the 'apples' now falling under her philosophic eye . . . her proper relations to the outside world, amid which she claims to be the *central* sun, and which only does not move." Although critical of both missionaries and merchants who, in flouting Chinese laws, abused their privileges under the treaties, Allen nonetheless urged respect for the treaties on the part of the Chinese as well as the Westerners. He came to the view that foreign trade was beneficial to China as a conveyor of both knowledge and goods. The treaties, he asserted, served to "strengthen the moral force that is brought to bear, and every revision [of the treaties] deepens the impression already made."[77]

Allen did not have to learn from his Chinese contributors about Christianity itself. He was eager to have his faith discussed in reference to Confucianism, but he also felt that Christianity should be presented in what he regarded as the language of science. On specific religious issues, Allen relied on the Bible, and he believed in a future life as well as the immediate spiritual reward of conversion. One of his most important essays, published in January 1869, dealt with the question of why, during the earthquake in the Sandwich Islands the previous year, the good and the wicked had both perished. He cited Romans 2 to show that God's reward was to be given on Judgment Day "to them who by patient continuance in well doing seek for glory and honor and immortality, eternal life."[78] Yet Allen wanted also to present the doctrine of salvation in the context of a cosmology that was scientifically demonstrable. In two essays published in October 1869 and July 1870, he set forth for the *Chiao-hui hsin-pao* readers analogies that must have been very real to him: one essay compared Jesus to the sun; the other, Christian love to the force of gravity.

Allen presented scientific evidence to show that it is to the sun, the source of light and heat, that man and all creatures owe their lives. The sun is "impartial to all and never discriminates" (*ta-kung wu-ssu*). It shines on "the honored and the mean, the good and the stupid, the old and the young, the male and the female." The sun is utterly "pure" (*chieh*) and "constant" (*heng*). Yet the sun is not the final reality; it acts according to God's will. In the spiritual world of the same God, Jesus is the sun. Just as the sun's rays are in three primary colors, Jesus has three manifestations—prophet, redeemer, and king. As the sun radiates light, Jesus imparts "truth" (*chen-tao*); as light carries heat, in His truth lies the Holy Spirit. Just as all creatures in darkness yearn for light, man in his sinfulness seeks Jesus' truth. Christ is utterly pure, constant, and impartial. He purifies man, and man in turn helps to purify others. The truth of Jesus does not belong to any particular country or group; it is accessible to "the honored and the mean, the good and the stupid, the old and the young, the male and the female."[79]

In his second essay on the solar system Allen further asserted that Christian love is like the gravity that originates with the sun and wondrously holds together the heavenly bodies. Without Christ's love, man falls into the abyss like a fallen star. Allen described the movement of the planets and explained that gravity—of both the sun and the planets—keeps each of them in orbit, connected by invisible cords. Just as each individual is saved by Christ's love, each person derives love from Christ, which he naturally directs to others of his kind. This is the binding force in a Christian society. "The mutual love—each person valuing others as much as himself—is like gravity that attracts the planets to the sun yet also to other planets." Having compared the planets to individuals, Allen then compared them with the nations of the world. "All the countries, mindful of the Lord's love, would love each other and maintain peace among themselves."[80] Such was Allen's faith that it brought together in harmony science, evangelical Christianity, and the Victorian view of international order.

As editor of the *Chiao-hui hsin-pao,* Allen considered it his responsibility to ameliorate, if possible, the Chinese literati's antagonism toward the missionaries and their converts. In the fall of 1869, a series of anti-Christian riots occurred in the Yangtze valley, some of which were known to have been instigated by scholars, as was the case at Anking in early November. In order to placate readers who might be hostile and to provide discussion material for church members, Allen wrote an article comparing "Christian morality with the moral code of Confucius," which began to be serialized in December.[81] Allen identified three sets of Confucian precepts: those dealing with the obligations involved in the "five relationships" (*wu-lun*), that is, obligations of subject to monarch, child to parent, wife to husband, brother to brother, and friend to friend; those concerning the so-called "three stages of self-control" (*san-chieh*), that is, control of lust in youth, of combativeness in middle age, and of acquisitiveness in old age; and those inculcating the "five constant virtues" (*wu-ch'ang*), that is, "benevolence," "righteousness," "propriety of demeanor," "wisdom," and "good faith" (*jen, i, li, chih,* and *hsin*). In order to demonstrate that Christianity was not "immoral and uncivilized," as it was accused of being, Allen ransacked the Bible for passages that might be interpreted as supporting some Confucian precept. In support of loyalty to the monarch for example, Allen came up with "Curse not the king" (Eccles. 10:20), or "I exhort therefore that, first of all, supplications, prayers . . . be made for all men; for kings and for all that are in authority" (1 Tim. 2:1-2). For filial devotion, Allen produced: "Hearken unto thy father that begat thee, and despise not thy mother when she is old" (Prov. 23:22), or "Children, obey your parents in the Lord; for this is right" (Eph. 6:1). With some exceptions, Allen was able to cite at least five or six scriptural passages on each Confucian concept.

It was not difficult to show, Allen commented, that the Christian Scriptures were against acquisitiveness, as in "Lay not up for yourselves treasures upon the earth, where moth and rust doth corrupt, and where thieves break through and steal" and "You cannot serve God and mammon" (Matt. 6:19, 24). It was easy, moreover, to demonstrate that Christians cherish *jen,* for there is no greater benevolence than love: "For all the law is fulfilled in one word, even in this; Thou shalt love thy neighbor as thyself" (Gal. 5:14). Allen could find only the most tenuous injunctions to support the concept of *li* (propriety in demeanor or social usage): "Be kindly affectioned one to another with brotherly love; in honor preferring one another" (Rom. 12:10) and "Honor all men. Love the brotherhood. Fear God. Honor the King" (1 Pet. 2:17). Allen pleaded that "Jesus has the heart of Confucius and Mencius."

Despite his eagerness to conciliate the Confucians, Allen felt obliged in the spring of 1870 to write a series of articles on the differences as well as the similarities between Christianity and Confucianism.[82] The series, which eventually included more than a dozen pieces, published at irregular intervals and extending into vol. III, represented Allen's personal conclusions arising from the discussion of the subject in the *Chiao-hui hsin-pao.* From the outset, Allen commented on two basic Confucian teachings: the idea of "self-cultivation" (*hsiu-shen*) according to *The Great Learning,* and altruism as expressed in a passage from the *Doctrine of the Mean:* "What you do not like when done to yourself, do not do to others." Confucian self-cultivation, Allen declared, erred in its reliance on the "strength of the self" (*i-chi chih li*). Neo-Confucians might spend all day sitting facing the bare wall, "seeking mental purity" (*hsin-chai*). Yet few actually would arrive at the "sincere thought" and "rectified mind" that are prerequisites of moral attainment: "One wishes to rectify the mind but seldom is the mind rectified; one wishes to make the thoughts sincere, but it is difficult to do so." With Christianity, however, the power of the Trinity makes man new: yearning for everlasting life begins a chain of spiritual experiences that leads to the presence of the Holy Spirit. "The mind will then be rectified despite itself; the thought will become sincere despite itself."[83]

Just as self-cultivation is often deceptive, the altruism taught by Confucianism is inadequate, for the rule laid down in the *Doctrine of the Mean* is based not so much on benevolence as on "aversion" (*heng-ni*). Man's sensitivity is relied on for not doing unto others "what you do not like when done to you." Such sensitivity may not help, however, when there is a clash of concrete interests. Even if a friend is sick, I might not want to be deprived of my well-being by attending to his needs; the rule laid down by the *Doctrine of the Mean* is hardly enough in this situation. What is lacking is the fatherhood of God. "Reared under the same sky, none of us is not a child of God . . . If I want others to give me their clothes, I should give them mine. If I want others to share their meals with me, I should share mine with them."[84] The cure for Confucian selfishness is the golden rule: "all things whatsoever ye would that men should do to you, do ye even so to them" (Matt. 7:12).

Although this emphasis on Christian ethics was similar to that of the Chinese writers, it is impossible to say whether Allen had been "influenced" by his Chinese contributors in this regard, except that he had learned to discuss Christian love in juxtaposition with Confucian moral precepts. There is evidence, however, that Allen had received inspiration from the Chinese writers on how Christian ethics should be applied to the Chinese environment. While Allen's spiritual and rational qualities remained unchanged, he became more concerned with the issues of benevolence and reform, along with the narrower issues of religion and science. Allen's experiences with the Chinese edition of the *North-China Daily News* undoubtedly contributed to his interest in secular news. But the social grievances so concretely discussed by the *Chiao-hui hsin-pao*'s Chinese writers must have prompted his decision in 1869–1870 to devote greater attention in his magazine to reports on social conditions as well as relevant government policies, to the chagrin of the more narrow-minded among the magazine's readers.

Allen, it must be emphasized, had adjusted to Chinese life in the peculiar environment of Shanghai. His social milieu was the informal British Empire of that treaty port. His work for the *North-China*

Daily News must have made him appreciate more the value of commerce as well as technology. From its beginning, the *Chiao-hui hsin-pao* published notes on such innovations as the steamship, the railway, and the telegraph. More often than not, the notes would include an optimistic estimate of the contribution of such facilities to commercial development.[85] Allen believed that better means of transport and communications, as well as trade itself, would open up the minds of the Chinese while bringing them material well-being. But he also came to think that China needed other things as well.

China's need for education in science continued to absorb him. As he saw it, science could help the Chinese to appreciate the Christian truth and also enable them to deal with nature more adequately, through technology. Allen was sympathetic with the scholar official's concern for the wealth and strength of the Chinese state. "We Westerners regard science [*ko-wu*] as work on which wealth and strength depend," he wrote to a reader in April 1869. "This is where our principal scholarship lies. To talk about sincerity of thought and so on apart from *ko-wu* [literally, 'investigation of things'], I am afraid, is just empty talk without avail."[86] But important as was the problem of intellectual awakening, there were also the basic questions of health and livelihood.

The opium issue may well have been the catalyst of Allen's broadened concerns. At first he was primarily worried about opium smokers among the Christian converts.[87] But by August 1869, at least, Allen was thinking of opium as a national problem of the Chinese. He lamented the fact that some 80,000 chests were being imported every year and that, according to a Western investigator, about 40 percent of the "minor officials" of China, 70 or 80 percent of the yamen underlings, 20 or 30 percent of the army personnel, and 20 or 30 percent of the scholars were habitual smokers. Allen regretted that free trade made it impossible to stop the importation of opium, particularly when the Chinese demand created a vested interest in the drug in India. Four months before, the Cantonese Baptist Huang Mei had already made a proposal for severe laws prohibiting opium smoking. Allen added that the more Christian converts there were, the fewer addicts there would be.[88]

The flood famine in the fall of 1869, which agitated several Chinese contributors to the magazine, finally stirred Allen to make a systematic effort to present domestic news. In November he decided to publish in the *Chiao-hui hsin-pao* edicts and memorials from the *Peking Gazette* regarding famine conditions. The famine aroused Allen's interest in the rural economy, and the scope of his selections from the *Peking Gazette* widened. Documents on the rehabilitation of rural areas and on river conservancy were reprinted in full. Allen commended Tso Tsung-t'ang for his efforts at bringing relief to the war-torn northwest and Shen Ping-ch'en, the Chinkiang taotai, for his encouragement of sericulture.[89] The American editor seems to have been as impressed by the pronouncements made by some high Chinese officials as he was by the relief activities of Yü Chih. Yet he continued to believe that the machine offered the best hope for alleviating the economic plight of the Chinese populace. He continued to write articles on the railway and the telegraph, and he was particularly gratified in April 1870 when Governor Ting Jih-ch'ang used Western dredging machines to clear the rivers northwest of Shanghai, with a view to preventing the recurrence of flooding.[90]

In answer to criticisms that the *Chiao-hui hsin-pao* had received from more narrow-minded church members, Allen published a long editorial in December 1869. He was irked by complaints about the magazine's inclusion of "trivial news," such as Governor Ting's proscription of prostitution in Shanghai, and of strictly political reports, such as the news that the Muslim rebels in southern Yunnan had received pardon.[91] Some Christians even took exception to the documents of the P'u-yü t'ang benevolent association, regarding them as irrelevant to church affairs. Allen argued that "all good men and all good deeds should meet the approval of Jesus and should not be excluded simply because the men and the deeds are outside of the church." He defended the wide and comprehensive concern of his magazine. Stories about the ban on prostitution should be published, he argued, for they warned against licentiousness. The action of the government in pardoning the Yunnan rebels was commendable and should therefore be reported. Allen wanted his journal to be diversified as well as didactic. He would report on military and political measures if they were "good policies" (*shan-cheng*). "If we do not publish such news but confine ourselves to small talk and picayune matters, what interest is there in the publication?"[92]

This article marked Allen's commitment to a broad editorial approach. In mid-May 1870, the *Chiao-hui hsin-pao,* as we have seen, published its series of stirring essays proposing the prohibition of footbinding among young girls. And toward the end of the month, Huang Yun-sun, the Shanghai Episcopalian, raised the question of the best method for primary school teaching. While the airing of such issues was encouraged by Allen, in each case it was the Chinese writers who brought up the concrete proposals or inquiries. Within a few weeks, much space in the magazine was to be occupied by news of the massacre at Tientsin, which reminded all missionaries as well as Chinese Christians of the precariousness of their position. But in historical perspective, the significant event of 1870 was perhaps not the Tientsin massacre but the emergence of a magazine of opinion, within Chinese culture yet not of it, which began what was to be a major assault on the Confucian heritage of nineteenth century China.

PAUL A. COHEN

Littoral and Hinterland in Nineteenth Century China: The "Christian" Reformers

One of the great unworked themes in modern Chinese history has been the polarity between littoral and hinterland. Although this polarity can probably be traced to the sixteenth century, if not earlier, it became increasingly pronounced after 1842, as Western beachheads were established, first on the China coast, later along the Yangtze. In and around these beachheads, a culture grew up that was more commercial than agricultural in its economic foundation, more modern than traditional in its administrative and social arrangements, more Western (Christian) than Chinese (Confucian) in its intellectual bearing, and more outward- than inward-looking in its general global orientation and involvement. The center of gravity of Chinese civilization remained firmly rooted in the hinterland. But with the passage of time, the littoral became increasingly important as a stimulus to hinterland change—a "starter" in the bacteriological sense—and some of the foremost actors in modern Chinese history were products of the new coastal-riverine culture.

How these individuals came to be identified with the culture of the littoral varied from case to case, some having been born there, others having made their way to the littoral after the doors to advancement in the hinterland were shut. But once their roots in the littoral had been established, once they had become personally exposed to Western ideas, practices, and people, they found themselves in a strategic position to break out of traditional patterns and establish new ones. People in the hinterland, with few exceptions, were not placed in such a position until much later.

The significance of the men of the littoral may also be framed in broader historical terms. As a rule, sweeping cultural change takes place in two phases. The first phase belongs to the pioneers. These are the individuals who, through their writings and activities, transform what was once totally strange into something a little less strange, gradually desensitizing people to the newness of the new, making it less conspicuous, more palatable. Then, at some point, the culture moves into a second phase, in which broad acceptance is given to changes that a short time before would have been acceptable only on the acculturated fringes. This stage is dominated by the legitimizers—people who have been converted to the need for deep-seated change but who at the same time insist that such change be accompanied by some form of indigenous validation.

In the context of modern Chinese history, this two-phase process assumes the form of a succession of littoral assaults upon the hinterland, followed in each instance by hinterland attempts to legitimize the assaults through Sinicization. The first assault was the Taiping Rebellion. In the course of being Sinicized, however, the Taipings lost their original innovating spirit.[1] They began to look less like Christian revolutionaries and more like traditional Chinese rebels. It was different in the case of the second assault, that of the pioneer reformers (defined here as those reformers or reform-minded modernizers who were active or first achieved prominence prior to 1890).[2] The legitimation of this assault was carried out, initially, by the self-strengthening officials and, later on, by the hinterland reformers of the 1890s, reaching a peak in the Reform Movement of 1898. The leader of that movement, K'ang Yu-wei, was successful insofar as he preserved the reform impetus of the littoral while justifying it in hinterland (Confucian) terms. Where K'ang failed was in the realm of execution. The final assault from the littoral was Sun Yat-sen's revolutionary movement. Its legitimizing phase, successful in both conception and execution, was dominated by the figure of Mao Tse-tung.

So formulated, this sequence of assaults and legitimations is overly schematic and probably misleading. Yet the broad picture still stands. We have, in modern Chinese history, two largely separate and distinct cultural environments evolving side by side. Although to a high degree self-contained, these two environments interacted in strategic ways, each performing essential functions over time. In the nineteenth century, and for a while in the twentieth, the littoral assumed primary responsibility for the pioneering of change, the hinterland for its validation. Moreover, as long as neither could do what the other did (or at least not as well), this symbiotic relationship between the two cultures persisted. But once the hinterland, in addition to legitimizing change, also became the principal locus of innovation, the littoral atrophied. Shanghai and Canton, in the second half of the twentieth century, are still there, and they will always be "littoral" in a geographical and economic sense. Culturally, however, they have been absorbed into a new Chinese hinterland.

During the late Ch'ing period, Christian missionaries and their religion had a major shaping influence on the culture of the littoral, and many Chinese living there either became Christian or were conspicuously affected by Christian teaching. This Christian impact was particularly strong with respect to the three littoral assaults noted above. However, with the exception of the Taiping Rebellion, it has been almost entirely ignored.[3] Nowhere has the neglect of Christian influence been greater than in the case of the pioneer reformers. Certainly, in the nineteenth century as a whole, it is undeniable that the vast majority of reformers were neither Christian nor Christianity-inspired, though more than a few were strongly influenced by missionary writings on secular topics. However, in the pioneer phase of Chinese reformism, roughly during the 1870s and 1880s, a significant number of reformers, including some of the most radical, were at one time or another more than casually exposed to Christian influences.

Examination of the careers of eight of these men should serve to illuminate how their reformism was conditioned by the littoral, in general, and by Christianity, in particular. The eight were Yung Wing, Ho Kai, Wang T'ao, Ma Chien-chung, Ma Liang, Cheng Kuan-ying, Tong King-sing, and Wu T'ing-fang. To describe these individuals as "Christian" reformers is in some ways misleading. Three of them (Cheng Kuan-ying, Tong King-sing, and Wu T'ing-fang) may or may not have been baptized, and the degree to which Christianity informed the values and life styles of the remaining five varied greatly.[4] Furthermore, with one or two partial exceptions, the reform ideas and activities of the eight men were not defined by a characteristically Christian orientation.

From another standpoint, however, the adjective "Christian" seems clearly justified. All of these men were, in one way or another, products of the Western missionary effort in nineteenth century China. Six of them, as boys, attended missionary schools. Two worked closely with missionaries during portions of their adult careers. And at least five were, at some stage in their lives, bona fide practicing Christians.

The situation, then, was a rather anomalous one. Christianity for these individuals was an important dimension of the overall experience of acculturation. It helped them to wrench free from the old culture and was instrumental in enabling them to pioneer a reformist approach. When it came to specific reform ideas, however, the Christian contribution proved negligible. Indeed, it would be fair to say that intellectually the "Christian" reformers were scarcely Christian at all. For this reason, I shall take the precaution in the ensuing pages of surrounding the word "Christian" by quotation marks.

THE CAREERS OF THE EIGHT REFORMERS

Yung Wing (Jung Hung, 1828–1912) was a native of Hsiang-shan hsien, Kwangtung. As a boy, Yung received a thoroughly Christian education, first at a school operated by the wife of the Prussian missionary, Karl Gützlaff, and from 1841 to 1847 at the Morrison Education Society School in Macao and Hong Kong. The head teacher at the Morrison School was an American missionary, Samuel R. Brown,[5] and when Brown returned to the United States in 1847, he took Yung and two fellow students with him.[6] After studying for several years at Monson Academy in Monson, Massachusetts, Yung entered Yale. He received his degree in 1854, becoming the first Chinese graduate of an American university.

In the same year Yung Wing, now a naturalized American citizen, returned to China, where for the next decade he worked at a variety of jobs in Canton, Hong Kong, and Shanghai. In 1864 he again went to the United States, commissioned by Tseng Kuo-fan to buy machinery for what was to become the Kiangnan Arsenal. For his efforts, Yung was rewarded in 1867 by being made an official of the fourth rank.

Yung Wing is best known for his initiation and promotion of a project to educate Chinese youths in the United States. With the support of such powerful officials as Tseng, Li Hung-chang, and Ting Jih-ch'ang, the project got under way in 1872, with Yung as assistant commissioner. By the time that this pathbreaking educational venture was terminated in 1881—a casualty in part of conservative anxiety over the excessive Americanization of the students, in part of Chinese bureaucratic politics—over a hundred Chinese had received substantial training in a variety of technical areas.

While in America supervising the educational mission, Yung Wing was named associate minister to Washington, and in 1878 he took part in the opening of the first Chinese legation in the United States. At some point, possibly while still at the Morrison School, he became a convert to Christianity, and in 1875 he married an American woman. After a brief spell in China in the early 1880s, Yung settled down in Hartford, Connecticut. In 1895, however, he returned once more to his native land at Chang Chih-tung's invitation. During the next few years he was an active supporter of the reform movement and also became involved in several new modernizing schemes. None of these bore fruit, however, and in 1902 Yung went back to America.[7]

Ho Kai (Ho Ch'i, 1859–1914), a native of Nan-hai hsien, Kwang-tung, was the son of Ho Fu-t'ang (Ho Chin-shan), a businessman and former preacher affiliated with the Hong Kong branch of the London Missionary Society. After preparatory education at the Government Central School in Hong Kong, Ho continued his studies in Great Britain at Aberdeen University, St. Thomas's Medical and Surgical College, and Lincoln's Inn. Returning to Hong Kong in 1882 with degrees in both law and medicine and an English wife, Alice Walkden, Ho embarked on a long and distinguished career as barrister, public official, teacher, philanthropist, and reformer.

The most important of Ho's philanthropic endeavors was the founding of the Alice Memorial Hospital, which provided free care for Chinese patients. Named after Ho's deceased wife and, according to one source, largely funded with the inheritance she left him, the hospital was administered and controlled (on Ho's stipulation) by the

London Missionary Society. Ho was also the moving force behind the establishment of the College of Medicine for Chinese in Hong Kong, which was attached to the hospital and served as the nucleus for the University of Hong Kong. Ho Kai taught physiology and medical jurisprudence at the college, where one of his more promising students was the future revolutionary Sun Yat-sen.

Ho Kai was the British colony's most prominent Chinese resident, serving for three terms on the Hong Kong Legislative Council (1890–1914) and taking part in many other civic activities. In recognition of his services, he received from the British government the coveted honor of being named Companion of the Order of St. Michael and St. George, and in 1912 he was knighted.

Ho Kai's career as a political reformer in the larger Chinese context was launched in 1887 with an attack on the self-strengthening movement that was so trenchant that it stood as "a symbolic turning point in the reform movement."[8] Ho's essays on reform were all written in collaboration with Hu Li-yuan. Their principal themes were the importance of developing Chinese commerce and the need for basic governmental changes, including the introduction of some form of parliamentary system.[9]

Wang T'ao (1828–1897) came from a small town about fifteen miles outside of Soochow, in Kiangsu province. The son of a struggling teacher of the classics, he was educated in the standard Confucian curriculum, became a *hsiu-ts'ai* (first degree-holder) in 1845, but failed the *chü-jen* (second degree) examinations the following year. After his father's death in 1849, Wang, in order to provide for his family, took employment in Shanghai with Walter Henry Medhurst of the London Missionary Society. As Medhurst's "Chinese teacher," he had an important hand in preparation of the Delegates' Version of the *Old* and *New Testaments,* which in the second half of the nineteenth century enjoyed wider circulation than any other Chinese rendering of the Scriptures. In 1855 Wang was given the further task of revising and polishing all of the society's Chinese hymns, so that they would "not be repulsive to the ears of the most refined poetical genius." It is scarcely surprising to learn that the society missionaries, in announcing Wang T'ao's baptism the year before, entertained "great hopes of his usefulness" and anticipated "his proving a great blessing to our Mission."[10]

In the winter of 1861–1862 Wang T'ao was accused of furnishing gratuitous advice to the Taiping rebels, who were then threatening Shanghai. Wanted as a traitor by the authorities, he fled to Hong Kong with British help. During the rest of the 1860s he worked closely with another London Missionary Society member, James Legge, on the latter's translation of the Chinese classics. After spending two years (1868–1870) with Legge in Scotland, he returned to Hong Kong, where in 1874 he founded his own newspaper, the first successful Chinese-language daily to be wholly owned and operated by Chinese. Wang T'ao's outspoken editorials on current events and reform, along with his writings on the Franco-Prussian War, French history, modern science, and many other facets of Western culture, brought him fame as a foreign expert. His foreign expertise was enriched by a four-month stay in Japan in 1879 and by a large circle of foreign friends—Japanese, British, and American. Moving back to Shanghai in 1884, Wang became associated with John Fryer's Polytechnic Institution and Reading Room (Ko-chih shu-yuan). In the first half of the 1890s he was a regular contributor to the reform-oriented missionary periodical *Wan-kuo kung-pao* (Review of the times).[11]

Ma Chien-chung (1844–1900), a native of Tan-t'u hsien, Kiangsu, was born into a scholarly Catholic family that traced its intellectual descent to the great Sung scholar, Ma Tuan-lin, and its religious heritage to the days of Ricci. Although his formal education was carried on in Jesuit schools in Shanghai, where he acquired an early mastery of French, Greek, and Latin, Ma also received a solid grounding in the Chinese classical tradition. In 1877 Li Hung-chang, having learned of Ma's talents, sent him to France with a group of students studying ship construction. While in Paris, Ma studied government and international law at the École Libre des Sciences Politiques. In 1878 he became the first Chinese to receive the baccalaureate, and in the following year he was awarded the licentiate by the Faculté de Droit of the Université de Paris.

Back in China in the early 1880s, Ma Chien-chung quickly became one of the principal foreign affairs experts on Li Hung-chang's staff, performing such a varied assortment of tasks that Henri Cordier dubbed him "un véritable Maître Jacques." In 1881–1882 Ma undertook diplomatic missions for Li in India and Korea. From 1884 to 1891 he served as assistant manager of the China Merchants Steam Navigation Company. He went with Li to Shimonoseki in 1895 and accompanied him on his trip around the world the following year. The last period of Ma's life was spent in preparation of his influential grammatical study, *Ma-shih wen-t'ung* (Mr. Ma's grammar; 1904), described by a modern linguist as "the first Chinese grammar in the Western sense of the word."[12]

Ma Liang (Ma Hsiang-po, 1840–1939), the elder brother of Ma Chien-chung, was the more religious of the two. After completing his theological studies and probation, he became a Jesuit priest in 1870. Six years later, however, as a result of conflicts with his superiors, he returned to lay life. During the 1870s Ma served as principal of the Jesuit College of Ignatius in Shanghai, where he had studied as a boy. Around this time he also developed a serious interest in Western science and mathematics and did some translating.

After leaving the priesthood, Ma Liang began the second of his many careers, as an adviser on technological, financial, and diplomatic matters to prominent officials. In the late 1870s he served for a time as director of a machine factory in Shantung. At the request of Li Hung-chang, he also looked into that province's mining affairs. As counselor of the Chinese legation in Tokyo in 1882, Ma met Itō Hirobumi and began to study Japanese. Before long, however, Li Hung-chang sent him to Korea to help the Korean government reform its administration and army. After his brother's assignment to the China Merchants Company, Ma Liang served the company in a number of capacities, including that of auditor. At the invitation of Governor Liu Ming-ch'uan, he went to Taiwan, where in 1886 he advanced a plan for the island's development through foreign financial assistance. After returning to the mainland, he was sent by Li Hung-chang to the United States to negotiate a loan. The Ch'ing government, however, blocked both the loan and the Taiwan development project.

From 1887, the year of his arrival back in China, until 1896 Ma Liang concentrated on the study of science. His only official role during this period appears to have been a stint as Chinese consul at Nagasaki in 1892. In 1896 he became associated with Liang Ch'i-ch'ao, whose rise to prominence as a reformer was in part owing to Ma and his brother. Shortly after the turn of the century Ma Liang was instrumental in founding the Aurora Academy (later Aurora University) and, with Yen Fu, the Fu-tan Academy, serving for a time as principal at both schools. Ma's active involvement in Chinese educational, political, and religious affairs extended well into the twentieth century.[13]

Tong King-sing (T'ang Ching-hsing, T'ang T'ing-shu, Tong Chik, T'ang Chieh, 1832–1892) was born in Hsiang-shan hsien, Kwangtung. Tong, like his lifelong friend Yung Wing, was early immersed in a Christian environment at the Morrison Education Society School. After studying at the school for six years (1842–1848), he was enrolled in another missionary institution in Hong Kong. During the early and middle 1850s Tong, having acquired an excellent command of English, became an interpreter for the Hong Kong government. In 1858 he took up duties as interpreter and clerk with the Shanghai Maritime Customs. He also found time to publish (in 1862) a Chinese-English phrase book to assist Cantonese merchants in their transactions with foreigners. From 1863 to 1873 Tong was Shanghai comprador for the British firm of Jardine, Matheson, and Company. While serving in this capacity, he engaged in numerous investment activities of his own, and in 1872 he was elected a director of Jardine's China Coast Steam Navigation Company.

Tong King-sing's intimate knowledge of the shipping business attracted the attention of Li Hung-chang, and soon after the China Merchants Steam Navigation Company was formed, Li invited Tong to serve as its manager (1873–1884). Tong was also the principal organizer of the Kaiping Mining Company and served as the company's director from 1877 until his death in 1892. In 1874 Tong and Yung Wing founded *Hui-pao* (Repository), one of the earliest Chinese-owned newspapers. Tong thus had a leading hand in a number of China's pioneering modern-style enterprises. His knowledge of the West was extended by a tour of Europe in 1883, and he was much admired by the foreigners of the day for his ability, integrity, and desire to modernize China along Western lines.[14]

Cheng Kuan-ying (1842–1923) came from a family of moderate means in Hsiang-shan hsien, Kwangtung. His father was a schoolteacher and his early education was geared toward the examinations. At the age of seventeen, having failed to acquire the *hsiu-ts'ai* degree, he moved to Shanghai to enter trade. In Shanghai he studied English with an uncle and later with the prominent missionary translator John Fryer. For many years, beginning in 1860, Cheng worked as a comprador for two leading British firms, Dent and Company and Butterfield and Swire. Cheng's fund-raising activities in connection with famine relief in Shansi in 1878—1879 brought him to the attention of Li Hung-chang and marked a turning point in his career. Li asked Cheng to inaugurate the first Chinese-owned cotton mill, the Shanghai Cotton Cloth Mill. He also made him a manager of the Shanghai branch of the China Merchants Company in 1882. Cheng left the company two years later, but rejoined it in 1892 and was elected in 1907 to its first board of directors. During these years Cheng Kuan-ying also served as manager of several other *kuan-tu shang-pan* (government supervision and merchant operation) enterprises, including the Imperial Telegraph Administration, the Hanyang Ironworks, and the Kwangtung section of the Canton-Hankow railroad. Like Tong King-sing, Cheng acquired official rank by purchase, eventually becoming a taotai.

Better educated and more intellectually disposed than most compradors, Cheng Kuan-ying was an avid reader of missionary literature on reform, and the humanitarian sentiments pervading his own writings were very likely of Christian provenance. Cheng's essays on reform, emphasizing institutional change and commercial development, were initially published, probably in 1880, under the title *I-yen* (Easy words). A larger and more noted work, *Sheng-shih wei-yen* (Warnings to a prosperous age), first appeared around 1893 and so impressed the Kuang-hsu Emperor that he ordered it reprinted for official distribution.[15]

Wu T'ing-fang (Ng Choy, 1842—1922) was born in Singapore. However, his ancestral home was in Hsin-hui, Kwangtung, and his merchant father moved the family back to China when Wu was only three years old. Growing up in a suburb of Canton, Wu received his early education in the traditional Chinese curriculum. Finding this uninspiring, however, he began to study English at a mission hall near his home, and six months later at the age of thirteen he entered St. Paul's College in Hong Kong. Although St. Paul's had been founded by the Church Missionary Society some years earlier as a theological college, its curriculum had become quite secularized, and during his four years at the school Wu was able to concentrate on English, mathematics, and natural science.

From 1859, the year of his graduation, until 1874, Wu T'ing-fang worked as a translator at the Hong Kong Police Court. In 1860 he helped found the *Chung-ngoi san-po (Chung-wai hsin-pao;* Sino-foreign news), the first Chinese-language daily, and for some time thereafter he shouldered the paper's editorial responsibilities. In the early 1870s Wu took part in the establishment of at least two other Chinese-language newspapers, including Wang T'ao's *Tsun-wan yat-po (Hsun-huan jih-pao;* Universal circulating herald).

In 1874 Wu T'ing-fang went to London to study law. Three years later, after becoming China's first barrister, he returned to Hong Kong to launch a highly successful legal career. The governor of the colony appointed Wu to the post of acting magistrate and, in 1880, to membership on the Legislative Council—both firsts for Chinese in Hong Kong.

The turning point in Wu T'ing-fang's career came in 1882 when he left Hong Kong to join Li Hung-chang's secretariat. In the fourteen years that Wu spent working under Li, he tried with little success to push the governor-general in the direction of major institutional reform. Wu's principal contributions to Li's operations were in the fields of law, diplomacy, and railway management. He assisted in the negotiations terminating the Sino-French and Sino-Japanese wars and in 1887 was appointed director of the China Railway Company, which was charged with the construction of a rail line between Tientsin and Tangku. Wu became manager of the line upon its completion.

The autonomous phase of Wu T'ing-fang's public career began in 1897 with his appointment as minister to the United States, Spain, and Peru. After his recall in 1902, Wu became an active promoter of legal reform. When the court in Peking refused to consider sweeping changes in Chinese criminal procedures, however, he resigned his post as vice-president of the Board of Punishments. Although he served once again as minister to Washington from 1907 to 1909, by the end of his term Wu's disillusionment with the Ch'ing had become complete, and the Wuchang revolt found him solidly in the revolutionary camp. During the first decade of the republic Wu was a close follower of Sun Yat-sen and held a number of major offices.

As a reformer, Wu T'ing-fang was a consistent champion of political liberalism combined with cultural conservatism. He was also an exponent of physical fitness and wrote a book entitled *Yen-shou hsin-fa* (New methods for extending life). In his later years Wu was known to Westerners as a baptized Christian, and he may have entered the church as a youth. All that is certain on this point, however, is that Wu's connections with Christianity were close. His wife, who was the sister of Ho Kai, was all her life a devout Christian.[16]

CAREER PATTERNS AND WORLD OUTLOOKS

"Had he been born as a member of the governing class in Japan," Hu Shih once wrote of Wang T'ao, "he could have easily made himself an Ito, an Okubo, an Okuma, or at least a Saigo."[17] Hu's two-edged remark, praising Wang and damning the society that was unable to use him, serves as a fitting characterization of the "Christian" reformers in general and of the plight in which they found themselves in nineteenth century China. All of these men were extraordinarily gifted, yet none was able to convert his abilities into power and influence in the Chinese context. Quite the contrary, it seems that the closer they got to the sources of power, the more circumscribed they became as reformers. Power and innovation, in the late Ch'ing, were like fire and water.

Although the backgrounds, experiences, and outlooks of the eight reformers diverge in particulars, on a more general plane they exhibit a high degree of uniformity. Most striking, perhaps, is the presence in each instance of an uninhibited willingness to innovate, to pioneer, to do the unconventional. Half of the group received degrees from foreign universities, and of the remaining four all but Cheng Kuan-ying visited the West for extended periods before 1890. With the partial exception of Wang T'ao, all had a speaking knowledge of a European tongue, and at least six (Ho Kai, Yung Wing, Wu T'ing-fang, Tong King-sing, and the two Mas) could read one or more Western languages fluently.[18] Moreover, the occupations that the "Christian" reformers engaged in at one time or another—journalism, law, the priesthood, modern enterprise, diplomatic service—were for the most part unheard-of in China prior to the Opium War. Indeed, the career patterns of these men were more evocative of the China of the 1920s and 1930s than of the nineteenth century.

The main exception to this ultramodern look was the multiple careerism of the "Christian" reformers, which contrasted with a growing tendency toward occupational specialization among Western-educated Chinese of the twentieth century. The reformers' pursuit of multiple careers was in great measure a consequence of their special position as pioneers. As in most frontier-like situations, there was an acute shortage of certain kinds of human resources in nineteenth century China. People who had these resources were therefore called on to play a much wider assortment of roles than would have been the case in a more highly developed context. This tendency was especially pronounced in a society like China's where innovation was not accepted as a positive value. In such a society, modern expertise was defined more as a mental state, a matter of outlook, than as a product of specialized training, and the mere fact of being "modern-spirited" was often enough to qualify one for the gamut of modernizing tasks.

To be "modern-spirited" in this sense in the nineteenth century meant to be aware of the unprecedented character of the situation confronting China and to be receptive to the idea of fundamental change (modernization) as the only way to respond to the situation effectively. All of the "Christian" reformers were modern-spirited by this definition. To a man, they were tireless promoters of the blessings of Western technology. Ma Liang, Yung Wing, Cheng Kuan-ying, and Wang T'ao championed education in modern science. Wu T'ing-fang and Ho Kai were prominent advocates of legal reform. Cheng Kuan-ying, Ho Kai, Wang T'ao, and Wu T'ing-fang evinced an early enthusiasm for representative political institutions. And practically all of the "Christian" reformers were actively involved in the establishment of China's modern press.[19]

Implicit in the idea of fundamental change was a new vision of China's relationship to the rest of the world. The new world view shared by the "Christian" reformers had no place for the old assumptions of Chinese superiority and self-sufficiency. Instead, it was predicated on an earnest respect for Western civilization and a newfound willingness to see the civilization of China substantially transformed. The two most characteristic expressions of this new world view were an enthusiastic appreciation of the benefits to be derived from foreign commerce and, on the political side, a growing acceptance of nationalistic premises. Insofar as its two focal points were trade and nationalism, it was a mirror image of the contemporary Western world view. In one basic respect, however, it was not. The emerging world view of modern China incorporated from the outset a strong undercurrent of resentment and outrage—a sense, sometimes muted, of a score to be settled with the West.

Traditionally, Chinese had tended to regard agriculture as primary and commerce as secondary. Foreign commerce, in particular, had been viewed as unimportant, since in the official image China already had everything she needed. This image may have been warranted prior to the Opium War era. But by the latter half of the nineteenth century, the economic encroachment of the maritime West had begun to challenge the older conception of China's needs, and a new conception, shaped mainly by national power considerations, began to take hold. The "Christian" reformers were in the forefront of this development. Indeed, they were so prominently identified with it that Chinese Communist historians have defined Cheng Kuan-ying, Wang T'ao, Ma Chien-chung, Ho Kai, and Yung Wing in terms of their articulation of the economic demands of the nascent Chinese bourgeoisie.

The implication is that these men favored economic, and specifically commercial, development because they stood to benefit from it personally. Their class interests propelled them in this direction. This may or may not have been so. More to the point is the fact that, almost to a man, the "Christian" reformers identified commercial interests with national interests. The basic premise on which they operated was that a sizable portion of the profit made by foreigners in China was profit denied the Chinese themselves and constituted a drain of wealth from the country. The problem, therefore, was how to recover, maintain, or acquire control over sources of profit that had been, or were in danger of being, wrested from China by the West, and later Japan. Since the Chinese were prevented by treaty from raising the tariff rate on imports, the only approach left was to overcome their passivity and begin taking more initiative in their economic activities, cutting into the West's profit-making capacity at every conceivable juncture. This approach was applicable above all in the field of commerce, for it was here that the West was directly vulnerable to Chinese competition. With this in mind, Cheng Kuan-ying, Ho Kai, and Wang T'ao, in particular, called for greater protection and encouragement of commerce on the part of the Chinese government, higher social status for merchants, and a more energetic Chinese role in the overseas carrying trade and all its subsidiary operations.[20]

It is significant that early Chinese formulations of a rationale for economic modernization were dictated by considerations more of national strength than of popular welfare, though the latter too had a place, especially in the proposals of Cheng Kuan-ying. To the reformers of the 1870s and 1880s, China's goals of wealth and power were well-nigh inseparable, and among those who talked of Sino-foreign economic competition, there was the strongest predisposition to think also in terms of political rivalry with the Western nations. Viewed in this light, it is not surprising to find the "Christian" reformers among the first generation of modern Chinese to begin the transition to nationalism.

Sometimes this tendency was revealed in their actions. For example, Tong King-sing engaged in modern enterprise explicitly to compete with foreigners.[21] In 1873 Yung Wing investigated the conditions of Chinese coolie labor in Peru, of which he offered a scathing indictment.[22] Cheng Kuan-ying later took a prominent part in the boycott movement of 1905, protesting the discriminatory features of American immigration policy.[23] In 1899 Wu T'ing-fang negotiated a Sino-Mexican treaty in which China for the first time secured most-favored-nation status.[24] And the youthful Ma Liang announced, on turning down an offer of employment with the French consulate, that his knowledge of French would be placed at the service of his own country.[25]

The incipient nationalism of the "Christian" reformers was also expressed in their writings, where certain themes cropped up with great frequency. One such theme was the articulation of an acute sense of shame, long before the Sino-Japanese War had made such feelings fashionable.[26] Another theme was the overriding concern, common to many Chinese reformers after 1870, for national wealth and power. Still another, displayed most conspicuously in the essays of Cheng Kuan-ying, Wang T'ao, and Ho Kai, was the notion that the key to the Westerners' strength lay in the close, trusting relationship that existed between their rulers and people—a relationship all three men regarded as being due, at least in part, to the West's representative political institutions.[27] Wang T'ao drew the appropriate conclusion for China in a letter of late 1880, written at a point when war with Russia seemed imminent:

The fact that the countries of Europe, though no match for China in territory and population, are able to have their way throughout the empire is attributable to the unanimity of sentiment prevailing between ruler and ruled and to the sharing of governmental power between the sovereign and the people. The fact that the Chinese people, though more numerous than the people of any other country, are nevertheless treated with contempt by powerful neighbors and ruthless enemies stems from the failure of communication between ruler and ruled and the distance separating the sovereign and the people. On top all power is lodged in the hands of one man, while below the common people are unable to participate in the formulation of policies. If the system of the Western nations prevailed in China, the entire population would rise up and come to China's defense.[28]

One of the first Chinese reformers to supply a label for this phenomenon was Cheng Kuan-ying, who sometime prior to 1892 wrote, "The reason why China is poor and weak whereas the West is rich and strong lies in their different social customs—the familism (*chia-tsu chu-i*) of China and the nationalism (*kuo-chia chu-i*) of the West."[29]   In this statement Cheng also identified one of the great barriers to the emergence of nationalism in modern China: the centering of loyalties and attachments upon proximate, tangible institutions, such as family, clan, and village, rather than upon remote abstractions, like the state.

THE HONG KONG-SHANGHAI CORRIDOR

The "Christian" reformers, in their career patterns and world outlooks, diverged sharply from their Chinese contemporaries. This divergence is explained by a number of common features in the reformers' biographies, aside from their Christian affiliations. Most conspicuous, perhaps, were their geographical origins and the geographical loci of their educational and occupational careers. All eight men were born near, and spent considerable parts of their lives in, one or the other of the two primary zones of Western penetration in nineteenth century China: the Canton-Hong Kong-Macao zone and the Shanghai zone.[30] Their careers, moreover, bespoke an extraordinary degree of back-and-forth movement between the two zones, so great that one is tempted to describe a Hong Kong-Shanghai corridor. Wang T'ao, for example, worked in Shanghai during the 1850s, spent most of the period from 1862 to 1884 in Hong Kong, and then moved back to Shanghai. Conversely, Cheng Kuan-ying, Tong King-sing, and Yung Wing, although born and partially educated in the Canton-Hong Kong-Macao zone, spent substantial portions of their adult careers in Shanghai. The essential point was not the matter of movement per se—a phenomenon that was even more routine on the foreign side—but the degree to which Hong Kong and Shanghai represented interchangeable parts of a highly cohesive, self-contained littoral environment. In the final analysis, it was the common cultural and institutional character of the two zones that made physical movement between them natural.

The consequences for the "Christian" reformers of having spent much of their lives in these two zones were several. The most obvious, reinforced by their years abroad, was the simple fact of intensive, day-to-day exposure to Westerners, Western institutions, Western ways, and Western cultural and material influences. Inevitably, such exposure forced a different perspective on the world and unlocked the door to a host of fresh possibilities. The reformers became sufficiently detached from their own culture to detect the need for change and familiar enough with Western culture to discover new instrumentalities for effecting change. Shanghai and Hong Kong provided them with microcosms of the modernization process at work.

As urban environments, however, these two cities were neither unequivocally modern nor altogether Western. Both might better be described as intellectual and cultural frontiers, outposts of intercultural collision, where parochial (traditional) commitments were under constant challenge. Rhoads Murphey's characterization of Shanghai would do for Hong Kong as well: "Shanghai was a place where two civilizations met and where neither prevailed. To the foreigners, it was out of bounds, beyond the knowledge or supervision of their own culture, where each man was a law unto himself . . . Morality was irrelevant or meaningless . . . For the Chinese, Shanghai was equally off limits. Those who had chosen this new kind of life . . . were by that choice cut off from traditional China and from the sanctions which it imposed."[31] Shanghai and Hong Kong thus offered a unique moral climate, in which the social and psychological pressures that worked against innovation in the hinterland were in large measure neutralized.

Living in Shanghai and Hong Kong also had an immediate bearing on specific attitudes of the "Christian" reformers. The importance they attached to commercial competition with the West was one. This attitude derived not only from personal economic interest but also from a direct assessment of foreign fears. Wang T'ao, for example, wrote Ting Jih-ch'ang in 1875 that the British were in favor of China's adopting a policy of self-strengthening, because this would reduce the Russian threat and enhance the regional stability necessary for the conduct of trade. "What they dread," he went on, "is not our military power but our commercial power, for they are afraid that our country will use its commercial power to contend with them for mastery. Formerly, when the arsenal was established at Shanghai and the shipyard was built at Foochow . . . they had no misgivings whatever. But as soon as the China Merchants Steam Navigation Company was formed, everyone got all excited. This was only a first small step in the development of our commercial power, yet already they were starting to get apprehensive."[32]

Developments in Hong Kong in the 1870s and 1880s bore out Wang's observation. While British and other non-Chinese merchants had once dominated the colony's business, by 1881 seventeen of the twenty largest firms had come into Chinese hands. This steady growth of Chinese commercial interests was often accomplished at the expense of Westerners in the colony. British businessmen, already frustrated over the unexpectedly poor showing of the China market, began to feel threatened by their native rivals, and they grew so jittery by the mid-1880s that Hong Kong became rife with rumors of a "Chinese takeover."[33]

The colonial atmosphere of Hong Kong and Shanghai also made a direct contribution to the feelings of shame and inferiority that were crucial to the emerging nationalism of the "Christian" reformers. This worked in two quite different ways. First was the personal shame generated by collaboration with the enemy. All of the "Christian" reformers were connected at one time or another with foreign institutions—missionary societies, commercial firms, government organs, and schools. Insofar as they lived and worked with people who benefited directly from Western imperialism, they too, in some sense, became beneficiaries of this imperialism—"collaborateurs" in the French sense.[34] Such collaboration, from the standpoint of the hinterland Chinese, was the ultimate form of sellout. Its practitioners were labeled *han-chien* (Chinese traitors), and since few collaborators were so emancipated as to be entirely impervious to hinterland norms, feelings of shame inevitably developed. Nationalism, by restoring dignity and self-respect, provided the perfect antidote to such feelings.

In colonial (Hong Kong) and semicolonial (Shanghai) societies, shame was also directly aroused by the attitudes of the colonizer. If colonial society was amoral in one of its sides, it was hypermoral in another. Linda Shin has argued that the idealism, dogmatism, and hypocrisy that characterized middle-class Victorian society in England often redoubled in intensity in colonial settings. Thus, among the British residents of Hong Kong the unrelenting quest for social respectability gave rise to extreme snobbery and to the erection of rigid social barriers, leading in turn to the almost complete exclusion of Chinese from the colony's social and political institutions. Exclusion was only the polite form of discrimination; Yung Wing, Wang T'ao, and Cheng Kuan-ying catalogued less polite variants (such as having cotton balls tied to one's queue for a joke) that were rampant in their day in Shanghai.[35] The line between hypermorality and amorality was thus a fine one. In both Shanghai and Hong Kong, moreover, the injury of social discrimination was constantly abetted by the insult of the foreign penchant for glorifying Western civilization and power while denigrating the cultural traditions of China. In such a context, individual shame and national shame became indistinguishable, and feelings of personal hurt, insecurity, and inferiority served as a natural spawning ground for nationalistic passions.[36]

ACCESS TO THE HINTERLAND

Although in the twentieth century the distance between the hinterland and the littoral cultures narrowed appreciably, in the nineteenth century it was enormous. Not until the founding of the T'ung-meng hui (Revolutionary alliance) in 1905 did a true son of the littoral, Sun Yat-sen, succeed in bridging the gap on littoral terms. Prior to this, it had been bridged, if at all, only on terms set by the hinterland culture, with the consequence that much of the innovating potential of the littoral was vitiated. Such was the dilemma faced by the "Christian" reformers. If they were to exert influence beyond the confines of the littoral, they had to gain access to the hinterland power structure. But since this power structure was largely informed by traditional values, goals, and operating procedures, in becoming part of it, they risked the dilution, if not nullification, of their impact as innovators.

For people who were closely identified with the littoral, the primary access points to the hinterland power structure in the nineteenth century were those high officials with wide-ranging responsibilities in the foreign affairs area—men such as Tseng Kuo-fan, Ting Jih-ch'ang, Chang Chih-tung, Liu K'un-i, and above all, Li Hung-chang. For Chinese officials, these men were relatively open-minded. Overcoming their own prejudices and the scruples of the hinterland in general, they associated with the acculturated men of the littoral and even made room for them on their staffs. They badly needed foreign expertise, and prior to the turn of the century the littoral was almost the only source of this scarce commodity. For their part, the men of the littoral, in going to work for such officials, acquired the prestige and status of the hinterland but paid for it dearly in their freedom. As members of the Chinese bureaucracy, they had to play by the rules in order to succeed. Frustrated in their efforts to introduce comprehensive reform, the best they could hope for was to serve as instruments of limited, "defensive" modernization.

The period during which most of the "Christian" reformers were in their prime coincided roughly with the quarter-century of Li Hung-chang's domination of Chinese foreign relations and modernization efforts (c.1870—c.1895). The frequency with which Li served as their principal point of hinterland access was nonetheless extraordinary. Five of them—Wu T'ing-fang, Cheng Kuan-ying, Tong King-sing, Ma Liang, and Ma Chien-chung—were members of Li's personal retinue for varying lengths of time. A sixth, Yung Wing, performed a number of special missions under Li's direct authority. A seventh, Wang T'ao, apparently was invited to serve on Li's staff but declined, and the last and youngest, Ho Kai, worked for a period under Li's protégé, Sheng Hsuan-huai.[37]

The frustrations met by those reformers who chose to work in the bureaucracy were manifold. Yung Wing's problems with the educational mission to America have been noted. Wu T'ing-fang was forced to discard or modify his hopes for significant reform during the fourteen years he spent in Li Hung-chang's employ and was so distressed that on several occasions he thought of resigning.[38] Ma Liang, who did resign, years later described a revealing incident that took place during his service with Li. While passing through Hong Kong in 1885, Ma observed that the great development of British commerce since the colony's founding had been harmful both to Cantonese and to non-British foreign trading interests. It occurred to him that this situation might be rectified by transforming Kowloon, which lay opposite Hong Kong, into a major port of trade and connecting it by rail to Canton. Since Ma did not know the then governor-general of Kwangtung and Kwangsi, Chang Chih-tung, he asked a person from Chang's home place to deliver the proposal to him. Chang read Ma's memorandum and praised it warmly but did nothing more about it. On returning to Tientsin, Ma broached his plan to Li Hung-chang. Li, too, thought it an excellent idea, but he was unwilling to sponsor it himself, insisting that the initiative must come from Chang Chih-tung. "Thus," Ma concluded, "my plan evaporated into thin air!"[39]

Wang T'ao and Ho Kai had either more foresight or less patience. Wang, over the years, freely corresponded with the members of Li's entourage and certainly hoped to influence Li in this roundabout fashion, but he never accepted an official post. Ho Kai, after much persuasion by Wu T'ing-fang, consented to join Sheng Hsuan-huai's staff in 1896. His aversion for the corruption and inefficiency of official life was so strong, however, that he left his new post within a matter of weeks and hastened back to Hong Kong, more convinced than ever that reform within the Ch'ing bureaucracy was an impossibility.[40]

Was it a disaster for Chinese modernization that the littoral's main access point to the hinterland in the seventies, eighties, and early nineties was Li Hung-chang? Or was the system itself principally at fault? I find it hard to avoid the conclusion that it was the system. Certainly Li was *not* personally receptive to radical innovation.[41] Even if he had been, however, it would not have been possible for him to promote such innovation and still amass the power he acquired. Li's political genius enabled him to reach the pinnacle of Chinese bureaucratic power. But in mastering the system, he also became its creature. Tong King-sing is said to have remarked of his relationship with Li, "The viceroy leads, but I am the man that pushes."[42] The only thing to be added to this is that there were real limits to how far Li could be pushed without threatening his political position, and Li knew these limits better than anyone.

REFORMERS, REBELS, AND REVOLUTIONARIES

Although to operate within the confines of the hinterland framework was hard on the "Christian" reformers, it was not crippling. For to them the hinterland was much like a penitentiary without walls, which they could enter or leave at will. This freedom of movement had two aspects. It meant not only that they could withdraw physically from the hinterland when the pressures and frustrations of working there became intolerable, but also that they could change directions ideologically if the prospects for modernization through reform seemed hopeless. The line between reform, on the one hand, and rebellion or revolution, on the other, was much less sharply drawn in the littoral than it was in the hinterland.

One of the main reasons for this ideological fluidity lay in the Christian, largely Protestant background that pioneer reformers, modernizing rebels, and early revolutionaries shared in common. In the case of the Taiping Rebellion, the only rebel movement of the late Ch'ing with partial littoral origins and pretensions as a modernizing force, this Christian connection was clear. The founder of the movement, Hung Hsiu-ch'üan (1813–1864), received personal instruction from an American Baptist missionary in Canton in 1847. Also, Hung Jen-kan (1822–1864), the rebels' most articulate spokesman for Western-style reform, served as an evangelist for the London Missionary Society in Hong Kong in the 1850s. Through the influence of individuals like these and, even more, of Protestant writings, Taiping ideology acquired some of its most distinctive and iconoclastic features.[43]

Christianity was also a disproportionately prominent force in the earliest phase of the revolutionary movement. Not only was Sun Yat-sen baptized in Hong Kong in 1884, but most of the leaders of the Hong Kong Hsing-Chung hui (Society to restore China's prosperity), the inner circle of budding revolutionaries in the Canton-Hong Kong area at the turn of the century, were also Christians. These included, among others, Lu Hao-tung, Sun's boyhood friend; Cheng Shih-liang, a fellow medical student, also a Triad, who alerted Sun to the revolutionary potential of the secret societies; Ch'en Shao-pai, Sun's top lieutenant for the better part of a decade and editor of the first Chinese newspaper openly to advocate revolution; Tse Tsan-tai (Hsieh Tsuan-t'ai), an overseas Chinese from Australia;

Tso Tou-shan, the proprietor of a religious bookshop in Canton, which served as an important revolutionary hideout in 1895; Shih Chien-ju, a gentry revolutionary; and Wang Chih-fu and Ou Feng-ch'ih, two Chinese pastors.[44] Most if not all of these men were products of missionary educational institutions, one of which, Canton Christian College (later Lingnan University), was described by Harold Schiffrin as having "played a pivotal role in the early years of the revolutionary movement."[45] According to Schiffrin, the leadership in both the Canton plot of 1895 and the Canton phase of the Waichow uprising of 1900 was predominantly Protestant. Christians, moreover, accounted for some 30 percent of the insurgents in the Waichow campaign as a whole. Small wonder if, in the train of these events, nervous Chinese officials imagined that they were witnessing a resurrection of the Taiping movement.[46]

The fluid quality that distinguished relations among "Christian" reformers, rebels, and revolutionaries was apparent at both the intellectual and personal levels. The modernization proposals of the Taiping leader, Hung Jen-kan, for example, bore a marked similarity to those of some of the "Christian" reformers.[47] Two of the latter, moreover, were personally acquainted with Hung; Yung Wing had become friendly with him in Hong Kong in 1856, and Wang T'ao had come to know him in Shanghai two years earlier. After Hung joined the rebels in 1859, Yung and Wang separately made journeys into rebel territory, talked with rebel leaders, and submitted proposals designed to further the Taiping cause. Although these overtures came to nought, they signaled the willingness of both men to contemplate a nonreformist approach to Chinese modernization.[48]

Even more revealing was the ease with which the "Christian" reformers crossed the divide between reform and revolution. Here, the main point of contact was Sun Yat-sen. Sun had had a brief career himself as a "Christian" reformer. During his reformist years he had been directly influenced by his medical school mentor, Ho Kai, and probably also by the writings of Cheng Kuan-ying and Wang T'ao. The climax of this phase of Sun's career came in 1894, with his attempt to present a reform petition to Li Hung-chang. On his way north, he stopped off in Shanghai, where his fellow townsman, Cheng Kuan-ying, introduced him to Wang T'ao. Wang made some changes in the petition and provided Sun with an introduction to a friend in Li's secretariat. Sun's efforts, however, were shortcircuited by the outbreak of the Sino-Japanese War, and henceforth he became a committed revolutionary.[49]

Henceforth, also, the flow of traffic in this direction accelerated, as one "Christian" reformer after another, of those that lived, became converted to, or at least involved in, the revolutionary cause.[50] The first to take this step was Ho Kai, who as early as March 1895 joined in the deliberations of the Hsing-Chung hui high command and secretly assisted them in their revolutionary plotting.[51] Cheng Kuan-ying was also in contact with Sun's men at this time, though the part he played, if any, in the Canton plot is unclear.[52] Between 1900 and 1902 Yung Wing appears to have given his support to a number of projected uprisings against the government, and he was regarded by the revolutionaries as a prime candidate for a top government post in the event that they should be successful.[53] When they finally did succeed in 1911, Yung was too old to accept Sun Yat-sen's invitation to participate in the new government. However, Ma Liang and Wu T'ing-fang, both of whom were strongly committed to republican ideals, did accept official positions, the latter achieving prominence from the outset as the revolutionaries' chief representative at the negotiations that culminated in the Manchu abdication.[54]

Although the littoral was a better place to make revolution than the hinterland, it was far from ideal. Foreign officials, like their Chinese counterparts, placed a high premium on law and order, and more than a few revolutionary plots were broken up by the foreign constabularies of Hong Kong and Shanghai. This vigilance helps to explain the undercover nature of Ho Kai's involvement with the Hsing-Chung hui and also perhaps the obscurity of the revolutionary connections of Cheng Kuan-ying and Yung Wing. All of these men, after all, were prominent figures in the Sino-foreign world of the littoral, with positions and reputations to protect.

The littoral was enormously important, however, in facilitating the transition from reformer to revolutionary. Christian revolutionaries like Sun Yat-sen and "Christian" reformers like Ho Kai and Yung Wing could speak to one another, both literally, since so many of them hailed from the Canton area, and figuratively. They had common social and geographical backgrounds, common educational experiences, common world outlooks. And in the last analysis, these shared traits made them much closer to each other, in terms of social and cultural distance, than either group was to its ideological counterpart in the hinterland.

CHRISTIANITY AND THE "CHRISTIAN" REFORMERS

Apart from the role played by Christianity in lowering the ideological barriers that ordinarily separated Chinese reformers from Chinese rebels and revolutionaries, what, precisely, was its contribution to Chinese reformism in the nineteenth century? And why has this contribution been almost entirely obscured? The two questions are intimately related.

One outstanding feature of the interaction between foreign missionaries and native "Christian" reformers in this century was that it was more secular than religious in its practical consequences. The missionaries, playing Prospero to the Chinese Caliban, taught the reformers language—the language of Western civilization and the languages that provided direct access to its secrets. They also offered living examples of what it was like to be educated and non-Confucian, an upsetting new combination that, by contributing to the relativization of Confucianism, laid an intellectual basis for nationalism.[55] What the missionaries did not manage to convey, however, was a new spiritual outlook, one that would produce Christian solutions to Chinese problems.

This failure was owing only in part to the missionaries and much more to the intractability of the Chinese context. In Japan during this period, 30 percent of the Protestant converts were of samurai (elite) background. The samurai, unceremoniously deprived of their privileged station in Japanese society, were in a state of social, economic, political, and intellectual crisis. Christianity, by providing many of them with a new world view, helped to relieve this crisis. It contributed in a major way to the intellectual life of the Meiji period. It also helped to define a new ideology of radical dissent, which culminated in the birth of Japanese socialism.[56]

In China everything was different. The old leadership proved durable enough, in domestic political terms, to weather the onslaught of the West, and the old gentry elite, far from being destroyed, was actually strengthened by the dynasty as part of its response to the mid-century rebellions. Although the combined impact of the

Taipings and the Westerners threatened the elite's ideology, Confucianism, that ideology, when thrown on the defensive, became for a time less vulnerable than ever to foreign ideological inroads. The percentage of educated Chinese who became Christians in the nineteenth century was negligible. Christianity, as a religion, scarcely made a dent in the contemporary Chinese thought world. And among all social classes, but especially among the elite, resistance and hostility to the Western religion ran rampant.

The contrast between China and Japan may be stated in other terms. In Japan after the Meiji Restoration alienation became a core feature of the elite's outlook, whereas in China prior to 1890 elite alienation, whether from the traditional culture, the reigning regime, or both, was a peripheral phenomenon, confined for the most part to the littoral. Now if it is assumed that the acceptance of Christianity in China was apt to be greatest among the alienated, it is understandable that there should have been a relatively high percentage of Christians and persons influenced by Christian teaching within the emerging Chinese counterculture of reformers, revolutionaries, and modernizing rebels. However, the fact that reformers, unlike rebels and revolutionaries, were committed to working within the existing system, with its strong animus against Christianity, inevitably meant that their Christian associations would become an embarrassment.

The embarrassment was greatest for littoral reformers who still aspired to leave their mark in the hinterland context. Such people might convert to Christianity for reasons sincere or opportunistic. But whatever made them become Christians to begin with, and regardless of what kinds of Christians they turned into, one thing was clear. They were not about to parade their Christianity in the open. The published Chinese record, prior to the twentieth century, contains no hint that any of the eight reformers here dealt with had Christian affiliations. One discovers these affiliations, if at all, only in post-nineteenth-century Chinese works, in Western sources, or in unpublished Chinese manuscripts.

The case of Wang T'ao is especially instructive. Wang was by far the most prolific writer among the "Christian" reformers. Yet at no point in the entire corpus of his published writings was his Christian tie disclosed. In contrast, a diary kept by Wang in the 1850s and never published freely refers to his attending Sunday worship, taking communion, and distributing Bibles in the countryside around

Shanghai.[57] Before publishing his works, Wang deliberately edited out any phrasing that might identify him as a Christian, as is clearly shown by a comparison of the printed and manuscript versions of a letter he wrote to James Legge on the occasion of the latter's departure for England in 1873. The original text referred to Legge as "Pastor" (*mu-shih*), the printed text, as "Mister" (*chün*). At one point in the original Wang stated of Legge, "His main purpose was to preach the Gospel to bring salvation to the whole world and to lead men to eternal life, so that the light of the Christian doctrine could shine in every corner of the earth." In the printed version this sentence was replaced by another which made no reference whatever to Christianity. Only in the manuscript version, finally, did Wang reveal that the letter was written by him on behalf of the "members of the church of Hong Kong."[58]

It is impossible to determine at this juncture whether the other "Christian" reformers went to the same lengths as Wang T'ao to conceal their Christianity from public Chinese view. Three of them—Cheng Kuan-ying, Wu T'ing-fang, and Tong King-sing—may have had nothing to conceal. Yung Wing did not publish in Chinese. Ma Liang's writings from the last century remain largely unprinted.[59] And the Chinese publications of Ma Chien-chung and Ho Kai were of an impersonal nature, providing no occasion for discussing the writers' religious affiliations.

More important, in any case, is the fact that none of the "Christian" reformers seems to have shared the popular missionary conception that the primary purpose of reform was to build a future Christianized China. Nor could their modernizing philosophies and proposals be in any instance construed as extensions of a specifically Christian world view. As early nationalists, the "Christian" reformers aimed at the restoration of Chinese national strength and dignity, and as early modernizers, their outlooks were shaped chiefly by direct, intense exposure to modern Western civilization in all of its ramifications. Only occasionally, as in Cheng Kuan-ying's critique of the humanitarian shortcomings of Chinese society, did Christian teachings as such exert a noticeable influence.

As far as their reformism was concerned, then, it was of greater consequence that the "Christian" reformers were products of the littoral than that they were Christians. Whatever Christianity meant to them in their personal lives, it did not provide, as it did for many

Meiji Protestants and some Taiping leaders, a substitute world view, a replacement for Confucianism. Probably its greatest intellectual contribution was its clear demonstration of the fact that other world views, both legitimate and respectable, were possible. One did not have to be Christian, however, to arrive at such a discovery. Perhaps even here the crucial factor was participation in the secular culture of the littoral.

As non-Confucian values began to be taken seriously, the ecumenical pretensions of Confucianism became harder to sustain. Thus, even when the "Christian" reformers kept their commitment to Confucianism, as was sometimes the case, the nature of the commitment was altered. It became relativized. Wang T'ao spoke of *tao* (moral norms, the Way) as being a property of *human* civilization, not just Chinese, though he still insisted that it had achieved its most perfect expression in the teachings of Confucius.[60] Wu T'ing-fang, shortly after the Revolution of 1911, founded a society for the study of all religions, including Christianity and Confucianism, while vigorously denouncing the parochialism of those missionaries who showed open contempt for Confucianism.[61] Cheng Kuan-ying, who was also critical of the missionaries, relativized Confucianism in a still different way by contending that Taoism and Buddhism shared with it a common origin and should therefore be accorded equal status and treatment.[62]

How does one account for this lingering attachment to Confucianism? In the twentieth century, according to Joseph Levenson, radical young Chinese, seeing Christianity as the counterpart in Western culture to China's Confucianism, demanded rejection of the former as payment in kind for their abandonment of the latter.[63] The reverse may also have been true, as less radical Chinese, like Sun Yat-sen and Chiang Kai-shek, made up for their Christian connections by retaining an attachment, however tenuous, to Confucianism. Although on both sides it was certainly more complicated than this, some form of compensatory law probably did operate, and this law held for the nineteenth century as well. As the Chinese of the littoral became increasingly Westernized, the pressure on them to preserve or redefine their Chinese identities mounted, especially as racial difference and Western prejudice joined to make "passing" out of the question.[64] In these circumstances Confucianism acquired for some a new importance. This new importance, which Buddhism, Taoism, or even Mohism might share, lay in the plain fact that it was Chinese. Previously, before Confucianism had been assaulted by the Christian West, its Chineseness had been beside the point. Now it was the whole point. Confucianism, for many first-generation Chinese nationalists, thus became something to hold onto tightly, even as, in their modernizing capacities, they labored to make it obsolete by transforming the China that was its principal historical home.

PHILIP WEST

Christianity and Nationalism:
The Career of Wu Lei-ch'uan at Yenching University

Converts to Protestant Christianity in early twentieth century China included members of the intellectual elite, who saw Christian work as an outlet for expressing patriotic feeling. Christianity would make China strong. By the mid 1920s, though, rising nationalism, linked with the Anti Christian Movement, pressured converts to rethink their loyalties and to dissociate themselves from the foreign religion. A conflict was thus created in the minds of converts which was not resolved until the early 1950s after the Communist rise to power. The earlier appeal and the later conflicts are poignantly illustrated in the history of Yenching University. Founded by missionaries in 1916 and housed after 1926 on a beautiful campus northwest of Peking, Yenching is one of the best known examples of intercultural relations between China and the West.

The treatment of the university by historians and others has tended to fall roughly into one of two categories. First, there are the accounts of the missionary educators themselves who stress the contributions that Yenching faculty and graduates have made in the circles of education and politics in China, even to the present day. For them, the existence of the university on Chinese soil for thirty years is a solid vindication of the interracial, intercultural, and international ideals which lay at the heart of liberal Protestant thought.[1] Others, however, are inclined to dismiss the Yenching experience as a paradigm of "cultural imperialism" and would emphasize its negative effects on the thinking and lives of the Chinese people associated with it.[2] Neither of these approaches, as either success or failure, is a very meaningful way of understanding how the university was received and adapted to the Chinese scene. John Leighton Stuart (1876–1962), Yenching's president for more than a quarter century and the United States' last ambassador to China from 1946 to 1949, was certainly the pivotal figure of the university, as all historical accounts indicate. Yet for purposes of understanding the Chinese side of this intercultural relationship, it is useful to focus on the career of Wu Lei-ch'uan (1870–1944), Yenching's first Chinese vice-president and chancellor from 1926 to 1934.[3]

My aim is not to attempt a history of the university nor a full biography of Wu, but to indicate some of the important issues occupying his mind for roughly two decades in the 1920s and 1930s, during which time Yenching had reached its apogee in the circles of Chinese higher education. These include both his conversion experience and his perception of Christianity's crucial role in the task common to all educated Chinese at that time—national salvation. Furthermore, a number of significant changes occurred in Wu's faith when it appeared that national salvation required militant Sinification. Swept up in the tide of rising nationalism, Wu faced serious problems related to his Chineseness, his views of education, and most important, his relationships with Westerners, especially Stuart. Because Wu, unlike most of his Chinese colleagues, did not speak English and never went abroad, his experiences may be somewhat atypical for the Chinese faculty as a whole. Nevertheless, he is studied here because he keenly articulated the Chinese polarity in that missionary-convert, American-Chinese relationship.

NEW WINE AND OLD WINESKINS

Wu Lei-ch'uan's conversion to Christianity in 1915 and Yenching University's founding soon after occurred during the New Culture period, roughly 1915 to 1922. It was a time of intellectual and social fluidity. To many Chinese, old and young, in contact with Western missionaries at this time, Christianity appeared to be the wave of the future. The suppression of the Boxer War in 1900 by Western powers had temporarily discredited opposition to Christianity. By the mid-

1910s the Young Men's Christian Association had become one of the most popular organizations among students. YMCA secretaries in Peking boasted in 1913 that one hundred of the three hundred students at Tsinghua College were enrolled in YMCA-sponsored Bible study groups, while renowned scholars and officials such as T'ang Shao-yi, Yen Fu, Liang Ch'i-ch'ao, and Ts'ai Yuan-p'ei served on YMCA boards.[4] The number of converts to Protestant Christianity between 1911 and 1922, amounting to approximately 100,000, was almost equal to the number converted over the previous century.[5] And Ch'en Tu-hsiu, personification of the New Culture and later founder of the Chinese Communist party, in 1920 urged the readership of the influential *Hsin Ch'ing-nien* to study Christianity seriously and "knock at [Jesus'] door and ask that his lofty and magnificent character and his warm sympathetic spirit be united with us."[6]

The fact that Wu Lei-ch'uan was converted somewhat discredits the widely held belief, then and now, that Christianity had no appeal to the highly educated, for Wu had been a member of the Han-lin yüan or Hanlin Academy, the most prestigious position one could attain under the old examination system. From childhood to manhood he had poured his energies into the mastery of the Confucian classics and had gradually worked his way up the social ladder: *hsiu-ts'ai* at sixteen in 1886; *chü-jen* at twenty-three; *chin-shih* in 1898 in Peking after passing the metropolitan and imperial examinations; and shortly thereafter membership in the Hanlin Academy.[7]

As a result of Wu's intellectual absorption in the Confucian view of the world, he entered a period of deep personal confusion and intellectual rootlessness after the 1911 Revolution, which had decisively shattered the Confucian political order. In 1911, at the age of forty-one, he transferred his outward allegiance to the new order by serving as an official (*ch'ien-shih*, secretary, and later *ts'an-shih*, councillor) on the Peking Board of Education headed by Ts'ai Yuan-p'ei, but his life, as he later recounted, merely followed the "daily tide, partaking only of the joys of drinking and eating." In his search for an intellectual alternative, two friends encouraged him to take up Christianity. He bought a copy of the New Testament, attended Sunday services in a nearby church, felt moved by the serenity of the service, and a year and a half later, in 1915, was baptized into the Anglican faith. Eight years later he listed three factors accounting for his conversion: the "compassionate and patient nature" he had inherited from his mother; the strong sense of responsibility for society inherited from his long years of study for the examination system; and a deep sense of futility over his personal life and over the whole of Chinese society.[8]

After conversion, he continued to put up with the routine of bureaucratic work for the sake of salary but devoted all his spare time to spreading Christianity among the intellectuals in Peking. He seemed to be involved in most Protestant activity in Peking, especially that of the YMCA. In 1919 he joined the Life Fellowship (Sheng-ming hui), a group of key Chinese and Western figures in Peking who set out to direct the "Christian Renaissance," as they called it, and to create an indigenous theology, literature, and church in China.[9] The Life Fellowship included most of the early leading figures of Yenching University, and through it Wu eventually found his way into the life of the university, where he began teaching in 1922, first as a part-time lecturer in the school of religion, later as a professor in the department of Chinese. Despite these contacts with missionary figures, Wu seemed to be uncomfortable with Westerners and suspicious of their influence. In 1923 he organized a separate study group for Christian intellectuals, known as the Truth Fellowship (Chen-li hui), with membership open only to Chinese. For the next three years the Truth Fellowship's publication, the *Chen-li chou-k'an* (Truth weekly, 1923–1926), was kept separate from that of the Life Fellowship, the irregular *Sheng-ming* (Life journal, 1919–1926). But after 1926 these two publications merged into the *Chen-li yü sheng-ming* (Truth and life, 1926–1937), although for some time Wu still kept the meetings of the Truth Fellowship exclusively Chinese.[10]

After Wu's conversion the traditional and modern elements in his life and personality became gradually fused with a complexity that frequently baffled his Western colleagues. His choice of residence at Yenching after becoming the university's vice-president in 1926 was typical. He selected a little cottage just off the campus near a pond in a garden previously belonging to Prince Kung of the late Ch'ing dynasty. In the words of Grace Boynton, English teacher at Yenching and neighbor:

His manner of life is in true garden tradition. His floors are of stone, his windows of paper, his food the simplest provision of rice and vegetables. His gown is sober gray or black. He does not often wear silk . . . Although the modern world intrudes upon him for many hours through the day when he must be away from the garden, the old man returns to it as early as he may, and spends long hours with his books and writing brush. When evening comes, if the weather is warm and fine, an old table is sometimes moved out on the stone terrace above the stream and the Chancellor sips his rice wine under the moon in the company of one or two friends, for he has always young men about him.[11]

Boynton's portrait was that of a Westerner who loved China for its quaintness and serenity. But if Wu appeared serene on the outside, his writings revealed a spirit agonizing over the meaning of his own life and over China's future course. Westerners of the time did not seem to be aware of his writings and rarely got beyond his appearances. Yet until the late forties his writings provided some of the most stinging indictments of Western missionaries, church bodies, and theology ever to come from the pen of a Chinese figure within the Protestant church.

Throughout his religious experience and career at Yenching Wu struggled to root the Christian faith in Chinese society. The task, as he saw it, involved the rejection of major tenets of conservative Western theology, the fusion of Christianity with Chinese culture, and the emphasis on Jesus as a social reformer. In that task he was joined by other members, Western and Chinese, of the Life Fellowship and the university, but Wu appears unique in the urgency and thoroughness with which he posed the question of Sinification. Unlike other prominent Chinese figures, such as Liu T'ing-fang (T. T. Lew), Hsü Pao-ch'ien, Chao Tzu-ch'en (T. C. Chao), and Hung Yeh (William Hung), all of whom had spent years of study in the West, Wu appeared never to have gone through a "Westernizing" phase but remained intellectually rooted in the past. His conversion to Christianity, though, had made him more than a traditionalist. His hope was that Christianity would help to fill the spiritual and intellectual vacuum created by the discredited Confucian tradition. With Christianity, Wu claimed, the leaders in society would change their old concepts, gradually decrease their selfishness and profit seeking, and emphasize the public good, whereupon order would replace the current chaos. The people's sufferings would decrease, and the masses would turn from their worlds of superstition to face the problems of life before them.[12] For more than a decade after his conversion in 1915 Wu's major task, in effect, was to put new Christian wine in old Confucian wineskins.

In the 1920s Wu wrote prolifically, trying to fuse Christian theology with Confucian concepts. He argued that important Christian values had their Confucian counterparts: love was essentially the same as *jen,* "human-heartedness," of the classics; Christian prayer was similar to Confucian *hsiu-yang,* "self-cultivation"; and Christmas was a time of celebrating the birthdays of both Christ and Confucius.[13] He did not ignore the differences between Christ and Confucius, but in terms of strengthening Chinese society, he perceived them as playing a similar role, namely, to inspire the Chinese people to service and self-sacrifice.

The second aspect of Wu's faith was the criticism of Western theology. His arguments bore a striking resemblance to those articulated by non-Christian Chinese at the time, and he later argued his case with extensive quotations from the writings of Ch'en Tu-hsiu.[14] In reflecting on his conversion experience, Wu once admitted to three questions that he had never been able to answer to his satisfaction: What was Jesus' view of God? How was Jesus able to be Christ? And how was Jesus' death an atonement for mankind?[15] Other members of the Life Fellowship who followed Western thought patterns more closely had answers to these questions in one form or another, but Wu's admission was tantamount to missing much of the Christian faith as understood even by the liberals. Equally heretical, at least to evangelical missionaries, was his inability to accept the uniqueness of Christianity. In 1920 he wrote, "I believe that Christianity and every other kind of religion and even every school of thought are all of the same origin."[16] Throughout his adult life Wu remained a devout Christian and enthusiastically entered into the patterns of organized worship conducted regularly on the Yenching campus. Yet he strongly criticized the ecclesiastical tradition of the Western church brought to China by the missionaries. In 1920 he wrote, "I do not believe one can fully accept all the dogmas and teachings of the [Western] church. The regulations and liturgies of the church also do not need to be taken too seriously. The personality of Jesus alone is sufficient to serve as the center of our belief . . . From the orthodox point of view I must certainly be regarded as a heretic."[17] Wu was attracted to the Life Fellowship and to Yenching University because the theology and personalities in both groups were flexible enough to allow patriots such as himself to work out their own forms of religious practice.

The third and perhaps principal aspect of Wu's thought was the concept of Jesus as a social reformer. Like the liberal theologians, Wu demythologized Jesus and regarded him as a partner in an intimate and personal relationship and as the inspiration and model for carrying out social reform. The emphasis on Jesus' divine relationship with God, Wu insisted, "not only inadequately revealed Jesus' personality (*jen-ko*) but actually distorted it." If a man's "intentions and actions are predetermined, doesn't that amount to a mechanical existence? What then would there be to value? . . . If Jesus is merely divine and not human, and we are human and not divine, then how can we imitate him?" Salvation, he wrote, "is not eternal life after death. Rather it is getting rid of the sin of selfishness in this worldly life and sacrificing oneself to society." To Wu the greatness in Jesus' personality could be seen in his "dying in order to fulfill his life."[18]

During the New Culture period, Chinese members of the Life Fellowship considered themselves as leaders in the patriotic movement. They used the vocabulary of the day, words such as "love, freedom, equality, sacrifice, service, mutual help, adaptation, awakening, thoroughness." Like all major Chinese figures, they demanded change, and like most, they believed in reform. Liberal theology and the social gospel were viewed as relevant to the task of national salvation. But at the end of the New Culture period around 1922, they could no longer rest on past apologies or find answers in an alien Christian tradition. Nationalism began to force them to produce a new vocabulary and a new rationale. But the force of events was working against them, and the rationale came hard. "What we do not see in the Christian church," Chao Tzu-ch'en, one of Wu's colleagues at Yenching, lamented in 1925, "is a literature that has life, is touched by the throbbing Chinese heart, and can touch other Chinese hearts because it comes out of the subtle life materials of the ancient Chinese blood."[19]

THE ANTI CHRISTIAN MOVEMENT AND RELIGIOUS DECLINE

Nationalism as expressed through the Anti Christian Movement in the early 1920s closed the Christian so-called Renaissance.[20] The nationalist movement erupted in an unexpected and vigorous patriotic protest in 1922 against the meeting in Peking of the World Student Christian Federation. This protest precipitated a great swing of opinion, in which even friends of Yenching University, such as Ts'ai Yüan-p'ei and Chiang Mon-lin, joined students and political activists of all sorts in launching an attack on Christian groups in China. Converts were accused of being "half-foreign" (*pan-fan*), "foreign slaves" (*yang-nu*), and "the hairy ones once removed" (*erh mao-tzu*). Among those singled out for special attack were the YMCA and the Christian schools.

Most difficult for the Chinese Christians to bear was the charge by the activists of their loss of national character, or denationalization. Wu Lei-ch'uan painfully admitted that when many Chinese accepted Christianity, they "join a foreign church or mission and forget that China is a nation," and that Christian missions had "trained a group of students who do not love their own country."[21] The mental and spiritual agony caused him by the Anti Christian Movement was so deep that he never completely recovered the strength of his previous faith.[22] His friend in the Life Fellowship, Hsü Pao-ch'ien, also suffered a personal anguish to the point where he suffered insomnia for six months.[23] The Anti Christian Movement had become an intellectual and personal watershed, as shown by the writings of these Chinese converts, which after 1922 and into the 1930s frequently began with references to the Anti Christian Movement. Efforts by converts to define themselves as both Christian and Chinese had become problematic.

The Anti Christian Movement severely weakened Christianity as a force in the life of Yenching University. One indication was the rapidly declining percentage of Christians in the student body. Between 1924 and 1926, the earliest years for which figures are available, the percentage dropped off from 88 to 63. Before that time no figures on converts are available, although enrollment figures are extant, which may indicate the administration's assumption that almost all students were Christian. By 1935 the figure of converts had dropped to 31 percent of the students.[24] Changing enrollment patterns in the school of religion at Yenching also reflected the religious decline. Between 1917 and 1922 graduates from the school constituted more than one-sixth of the university's total, contrasting sharply with less than one-twelfth of the total between 1927 and 1931. And of the fifty-three graduates from the School of Religion in the latter five-year period, only three had received the B.D. degree, all others receiving short-course certificates, which often represented no more than one year of study.[25] President Stuart attributed this trend to the absorbing interest of the students in nationalism and to an "antiforeignism" that made the Chinese students "unwilling to give their services to organizations thought of by the Chinese as essentially foreign or controlled by the West."[26]

Perhaps more revealing than declining student interest in religion was the demise of the Life Fellowship itself. By the time of the Japanese occupation of Peking in July 1937, the Fellowship was in a state of collapse. The last issue of its journal, *Chen-li yü sheng-ming,* was published in June 1937. It had failed to lay the intellectual foundation and write the literature through which Christianity was to become a powerful force in saving the nation. Even Liu T'ing-fang, the tireless and ambitious guiding light in the early years of the Christian Renaissance, lost faith in the individualistic, character-building qualities of Christianity, let alone its contribution to national salvation. In 1931 he wrote, "Of course there are many who have been freed from sin through the help of the church. But the basis for spiritual training in daily life even among the church members who 'do good deeds' and are 'strong in faith' does not depend on the teachings of the church, but rather on the commonly held ethical norms within Chinese society, which in turn are the products of Confucian, intermixed with elements of Buddhist, thought."[27] Key Chinese figures in the group who had confidently worked to make Christianity respectable among intellectuals, had become by the summer of 1937 a disillusioned and tired band, united neither in purpose nor in action. They had come together as Chinese citizens and Christian converts to help save China, a task made all the more urgent by the Japanese invasion of North China and the coastal cities. But now Christianity seemed to speak only to individualistic concerns. It had little to contribute to national salvation.

LIBERAL ARTS AND NATIONAL SALVATION

Although Wu Lei-ch'uan was closely associated in the public eye with the liberal arts pattern at Yenching, his writings revealed marked differences in his views on education from those of his Western colleagues. To be sure, one cannot easily generalize about liberal arts even among Westerners, because the term has been as difficult to define as "nailing currant jelly to the wall." Even President Stuart vacillated in his educational purposes, stressing proselytizing in the earlier years and settling for more secular goals later on.[28] His refusal to define more precisely the goals of the university gave him precious flexibility in mediating between such disparate groups as the trustees, some of whom were still motivated largely by proselytizing, and the students, many of whom by the late 1920s had rejected the university's Christian purposes.

Wu's career in the field of education had begun in 1905 as headmaster of the Provincial College of Chekiang, where he served for the next four years. In 1909 he became director for a year of the *Chin-shih kuan,* a training program for *chin-shih* title holders who had not yet received official appointment, and in 1910 he again served as headmaster of a middle school in Hangchow.[29] He left teaching after the 1911 Revolution and for the next eleven years worked exclusively with government bureaus of education. When he returned to teaching in 1922 at the Yenching School of Religion, he explained to his students how difficult it was for him to understand the feelings of young people because of age and personality differences. Nevertheless, he had determined to work with them because he thought that youth held the key to the "future of China."[30]

Wu's evolving definition of education shifted according to changes in his search for national salvation. That search had led him to Yenching University, but at no point did he seem comfortable with the general understanding of liberal arts in the West. During his early years at Yenching, Wu's rather loose educational philosophy combined Confucian and Christian elements, which converged nicely around the phrase "character building." Although he criticized Christian schools for refusing to register with the government and for instilling in students the "desire for material things and pro-American thoughts," he nonetheless emphasized the efficacy of character

235

building provided by the schools and thus urged students not to join strikes and demonstrations.[31] Not that he opposed their being political—indeed, Wu saw education essentially in political terms—but he wanted the students not to dissipate their energies prematurely in acts of dubious political value. Rather, he urged them to pause for a few years and acquire the attitudes and technical skills necessary for national salvation as he saw it in the early 1920s. He argued that the Christian schools were better suited than government schools to the task of training youth because they offered better science courses, treated exams more seriously, attracted and cultivated more disciplined students, and provided teachers with more stable salaries. [32] During Wu's early years at Yenching he agreed with the missionary educators that the point of character building was to train students to become more effective leaders within the given political and social order.

Rising nationalism in the mid-1920s, however, forced Wu to reassess the role of Christian colleges and student politics. Summing up his views at the time of the Northern Expedition in 1926, he praised the youth as being the "most sensitive" to the humiliation inflicted on China by the Western nations, the "most concerned" as compared to the "hollow words and futile actions of their elders," and the "most daring" in having galvanized first themselves and later the labor and business communities in the patriotic activities of the 1920s. Although they had failed to change the minds of the Western powers, they had at least begun to awaken the masses. In striking against their own schools, the youth had destroyed the unexamined faith in the kind of education that knew only the "accomplishments of reading books," but which failed to "attack the problems at hand." The students had shown the importance of political action. In Wu's words, the students' "cries and activity are the vitality of the nation and deserve our understanding and support."[33]

By 1926, when Wu was assuming major administrative responsibilities as the vice-president of Yenching, he had considered four current theories tying education with national salvation. The first theory was that national salvation could be achieved through study, *tu-shu chiu-kuo*. He could not blame students for rejecting this notion, however, because their professors, while mouthing the slogan "In saving the nation don't forget study, and in studying don't forget national salvation," had nevertheless failed to see the urgency of

China's situation. The second theory was salvation through the influence of personality or moral example, *jen-ko chiu-kuo*. This theory was closely related to Wu's earlier emphasis on the personality of Jesus which, if imitated by enough people, would eventually influence the whole of China to service and self-sacrifice. A third theory, which had helped governments in the past, called for salvation through men of talent, *jen-ts'ai chiu-kuo*. But the question remained of how to create men of talent. Acknowledgment of the fourth theory, national salvation through struggle, *fen-tou chiu-kuo*, represented a new level of Wu's political awareness.[34]

True national salvation, Wu was convinced, could now come only with struggle, a view that represented a major inroad on his previous YMCA assumptions about the efficacy of gradual reform. But before students and intellectuals could assume responsibility for leading that struggle, they would have to go through a period of self-cultivation, *hsiu-yang*. Youth lacked experience and wisdom. They needed to maintain a clear and correct sense of purpose.[35] Therein lay the rationale for higher education at Yenching, which would incorporate the best of Christianity, of Confucianism, and of the Anti Christian Movement. The first three theories of national salvation, in other words, were insufficient by themselves. Struggle, which was offensive both to the missionary educators and to most of the Western-educated faculty at Yenching, would have to come. But the first three formulas, wrapped in the guise of higher education, were a necessary first step.

THE CHANCELLOR AND THE PRESIDENT

The radical departure in Wu's redefinition of Yenching's educational purpose coincided with growing conflicts in the university administration. One of the anomalies at Yenching was the existence of two heads in the university, Wu Lei-ch'uan, the chancellor, and John Leighton Stuart, the president. Their position and relationship differed according to which constitution one used, the English or the Chinese. Prior to 1928 the university had operated under a constitution approved by the trustees and written in English. But after 1928 the Nanking government required all private colleges to register with the ministry of education and carry out administrative changes according to a constitution based on government guidelines and written in Chinese. Wu Lei-ch'uan's major task as the vice-president was to work out the university's new arrangements with the central government.

Even Stuart endorsed the changes involved in meeting the requirements for registration. In 1927 he informed the trustees in New York that the university was faced with two crises: selection of a Chinese chancellor, and establishment of the "final authority of the board of managers [in Peking] in all matters affecting administration." He suggested that the board of trustees, all of whom were Americans working through New York, should reconstitute itself as the "American or Anglo-American Foundation," which would lease or entrust its property in Peking to the board of managers; relinquish all appointive powers over the university staff, except that of president; and arrange for all members of the board of managers to be completely Chinese, not because the terms for government registration required it, but because conducting its meetings in Chinese would help to "decrease the consciousness of the masterfulness of the Westerners." Stuart did not speak lightly. He said it was conceivable that a time would come when a Chinese board of managers might prefer to "sacrifice all support . . . rather than conform to the wishes of the Trustees, in which case the Trustees would have lost the institution completely anyway."[36] In the spring of 1928 Stuart traveled to New York to discuss matters further with the trustees, and soon after they adopted a revised English version of the constitution that conceded to the managers complete power of appointment over the faculty.

Meanwhile, during Stuart's absence, Acting President Howard Galt and Vice-President Wu Lei-ch'uan had called a special meeting of the entire faculty to "take into hand . . . needed changes in organization."[37] Wu and a faculty-appointed committee labored for several months producing a revised version of the constitution in Chinese, which was subsequently adopted by a general meeting of the faculty on May 28, 1928, just prior to Stuart's return to China in June. This Chinese version went much further than the English one. It granted the managers power to approve or revise the constitution (instead of the trustees and the four constituent mission boards); to appoint all administrative officers of the university, including the president and dean of women (not just the chancellor and dean of men); and to approve the annual budget (instead of the trustees).[38] For a moment it appeared the central government would enforce the Chinese constitution fully. But once in power, the Nationalist leadership chose not to risk antagonizing missionaries and other Western personalities. Chiang Kai-shek's ministers of education after 1928 were Western-educated and agreed on the importance of Western-style higher education in China. Chiang also turned to the West for economic and political support. In the late 1920s and early 1930s Stuart symbolized that cultural tie and became a valuable ally as the president of the most prestigious private university in North China.

On several occasions the board of managers, according to their English-language minutes, attempted to resolve the contradictions between the two constitutions by regarding the English version as both the "authoritative interpretation" and the "working document for the guidance of the constituent bodies of the university," while the Chinese one, formualted in accordance with the requirements of the Nanking Ministry of Education, was reserved for registration with the Nationalist governement.[39] But repeatedly Wu Lei-ch'uan reminded the managers that registration with the government required the use of the Chinese-language document. When he formally accepted the position as chancellor, *hsiao-chang* (literally "head of the school"), he took the occasion to remind the board that, according to government regulations, the chancellor assumed "full power and responsibility" over the life of the university.[40] The organizational chart drawn up by Wu and reproduced in the 1931 Chinese-language catalogue showed the chancellor's office occupying the top and central position in the administrative structure, while Stuart's position, *hsiao-wu-chang* (literally "official in charge of school affairs" but rendered "president" at Yenching), though mentioned in the organizational outline, was not even placed in the chart.[41]

Some who knew and worked with Wu argued that his differences with Stuart were owing to his preoccupation with "scholarly" pursuits and his lack of ability as an administrator. One prominent Yenching administrator, for example, described Wu primarily as a "patron-saint, a spiritual figurehead, an elder statesman." Others pointed out the sheer impossibility of establishing Wu's real, as opposed to nominal, headship because of Stuart's indispensability in securing money from America. Whatever validity there may be to the financial argument, people such as Howard S. Galt regarded Wu as a "veritable tower of strength in all administrative matters."[42] Whatever his administrative talent may have been, Wu was not just an eccentric scholar. His writings reveal unusual vitality and strength, probing social and political issues in the 1920s and 1930s as deeply as any other Chinese faculty member at Yenching.

There is no doubt that Wu wanted very much to be the real head but was convinced that Stuart would not allow it, despite the fact that as early as 1920 Stuart had lamented the "unduly large foreign elements in the institution" and urged an increased Chinese role in the "responsible control and in the shaping of our policies."[43] Stuart, in short, was willing to accommodate to Chinese demands for greater control, but only on condition that the university maintain its liberal and international outlook. He may have feared that Wu Lei-ch'uan, if given the power, would threaten to sever the American tie, even if it meant plunging the university into financial difficulties. Wu soon became embittered with his position. The board of managers, which by 1930 was two-thirds Chinese and according to the Chinese constitution was headed by Wu, in fact met in President Stuart's house and conducted its meetings in English. As a result, Wu stopped attending the meetings. He submitted his resignation as chancellor in May 1931, two years after his appointment, but the managers refused to accept it. He successfully resigned in May 1934.[44]

Wu Lei-ch'ian was not a cosmopolite in the sense that Stuart or most other members of the Life Fellowship or the Yenching board of managers were. He was less interested in building a "beloved community" of Westerners and Chinese than he was in helping China to achieve national salvation. By the mid-1930s it appeared that Wu had given up trying to "make Yenching Chinese."

FROM SOCIAL REFORM TO SOCIAL REVOLUTION

Wu Lei-ch'uan's departure in theology and education from the position of the missionary educators at Yenching was accompanied by a growing divergence in the realm of politics. Stuart serves as the most meaningful point of comparison. Throughout his tenure as president at Yenching he supported a gradualist, reformist, YMCA approach to social change and correspondingly remained a staunch opponent of revolutionary politics. Committed first and foremost to the educational enterprise, he supported whatever government happened to be in power, so long as the university was allowed to function. Thus, in the early 1920s Stuart cultivated personal friend-ships with all sides in the civil strife—with Tuan Ch'i-jui, Chang Tso-lin, Feng Yü-hsiang, and Wu P'ei-fu. In the late 1920s he quickly accommodated to the new Nanking government. Even in the fall of 1948, when liberation was imminent and reports indicated that Yenching would be allowed to continue, Stuart again urged accom-modation, this time to the Communist government.[45]

By contrast, Wu came to regard the institutional existence of the university as secondary to national salvation. Earlier in his career he had worked for various warlord governments, but by the late 1920s he had come to regard politics as central to national salvation and Chiang Kai-shek's government as the worst sort of politics. Soon after the establishment of the Nanking government he asserted that the Kuomintang leadership had completely lost the faith and in-creased the burden of the people, wasted millions of tax dollars, tried to destroy the Communists, who alone were concerned with "arous-ing the masses," and repressed the intellectuals.[46] Unlike other educators at Yenching, Wu never became seriously involved with the rural reconstruction projects of the 1930s. He was less interested in projects than in fundamental solutions.

Even before resigning as chancellor of Yenching, he had begun moving toward a more revolutionary interpretation of national salva-tion. Although his faith had always connected salvation with social reform, the double challenge of Marxist thought and the Anti Chris-tian Movement exposed the difficulties of the reformist approach to the problems of social and political change. Culminating a decade of anxiety, he wrote his most definitive statement on the relationship between Christianity and national salvation, *Christianity and Chinese Culture (Chi-tu chiao yü Chung-kuo wen-hua)*. The book underwent several printings and became a popular interpretation of the Christian faith in Protestant circles in China in the late 1930s.[47]

The central theme in Wu's emerging thinking was that the Christian faith and revolution were complementary. Wu argued that Jesus Christ was a revolutionary, and that the image of Christianity as a defender of the status quo was a distortion of the true faith. Wu had failed in 1923 to grasp the concept of Jesus as Christ. Twelve years later, still puzzled by the concept, he concluded that Jesus became Christ to the Jews through his promise to restore them as an independent nation. Jesus, Wu argued, knew that meaningful independence could come only after social injustices were corrected and the nation was unified. But political independence was nevertheless his ultimate aim.[48]

China's situation in the 1930s, according to Wu, was similar to that of the Jews at the time of Jesus in that both societies would achieve political salvation only after pervasive and deep social injustices had been corrected through social revolution. Wu saw only the Communists as embracing social revolution, and he warned the Chinese Christians, at a time when Christianity was rapidly waning, at least among intellectuals, that unless they supported the Communist program, the church would die. Marxist materialism posed no problem. Life, he argued, was essentially materialistic, and unmet physical needs, which were the result of social injustices, would always prevent the realization of Christian virtues.[49]

Wu amalgamated communism's stress on struggle, centralism, and the use of military force with the Christian hallmarks of "freedom and love" by arguing that the Christian was first and foremost concerned with truth. Citing Jesus' words, "You shall know the truth and the truth shall make you free" (John 8:32), Wu argued that freedom, in Jesus' mind, was conditional to truth and not the other way around. Furthermore, truth was not eternal but changed with the needs and conditions of the times. Thus, Wu wrote, "If one says that centralism and dictatorship are truths befitting the times, then our ideas of freedom and equality should be temporarily abandoned for the sake of truth. This is the spirit of Christianity."[50] As with many prominent Chinese before him, such as Liang Ch'i-ch'ao, Yen Fu, and Sun Yat-sen, Wu felt that freedom simply was not an issue compared with the pressing realities of the day.

With regard to the issue of love, Wu argued that Jesus was above all concerned with social justice. Love was important insofar as it helped to achieve that end, but by the 1930s he felt that justice could not be realized without social revolution, which necessarily required the use of force. Wu respected those who "esteemed pacifism" and would have preferred to avoid the use of "military force." But "realistically speaking, the reform of society required the seizure of power, which in turn required the use of military force. If Christianity insisted on avoiding the tragic costs of shedding blood in revolution, then would that not reduce the whole vision of reforming society to a mirage?" Jesus himself had anticipated "fighting, killing, and calamitous difficulties"; indeed, his early followers fully expected them to occur in their lifetime. Wu believed Christians should not shrink from supporting revolution just because of the strife and conflict.[51]

Another argument Wu used to support revolution was Jesus' teachings on private property and economic justice. He cited the parable of the rich man asking Jesus how to get to Heaven, whereupon Jesus told him to sell all that he had and give it to the poor. Wu believed that the problem of economic and social justice would be greatly reduced once private property was abolished.[52] Only the Communists, Wu wrote, were prepared to end the capitalist system. Social reformers might support the idea of economic justice in theory, but in the Chinese context, only social revolutionaries would be able to bring it about.

Wu's revolutionary interpretation of Christianity was sharply criticized by others in the Life Fellowship. Chao Tzu-ch'en, for example, regarded Wu's arguments as theologically naive and historically inaccurate. Social justice, Chao argued, was only one of Jesus' many concerns. Furthermore, Jesus' relationship to God was primarily spiritual and had nothing to do with the problems of society. Chao rejected Wu's tampering with materialism and argued with the help of extensive quotations from the New Testament that it was impossible to compromise Jesus' teachings about the primacy of the spiritual as opposed to the physical life. In Chao's thinking, communism and Christianity were irreconcilable.[53] Chao stated his arguments forcefully, yet he failed to answer the question of how one could still think primarily in liberal Protestant terms and still shoulder the burden of national salvation. Wu's revolutionary position in the 1930s foreshadowed the thinking of other Christian leaders, especially Wu Yao-tsung, another early member of the Life Fellowship. Even Chao Tzu-ch'en, moved toward Wu's position during the Communist takeover more than a decade later.[54]

Wu's preoccupation with the question of national salvation raises the question as to why he hung on to the Christian faith when it appeared to be largely meaningless among the students in whom he placed his confidence? His own writings do not provide a clear answer, but there are other clues. First, the speed of his original conversion experience in 1915 suggests that Wu's attachment to Christianity was rooted in the anxiety and existential despair caused by the shattering in the early 1910s of the Confucian value system. Second, Wu certainly felt that his critique of liberal Christianity was squarely within the teachings of Jesus and that the Christian-revolutionary synthesis was plausible, as Reinhold Niebuhr was arguing at precisely the same time and as other Western theologians have since argued. Finally, Wu's continuing loyalty to Christianity must be seen in terms of his belief that it still had a role to play, that the "national revolution needed the spirit of Christianity."[55] His view of the new man touched by the example of Jesus had a striking similarity to the vision of revolutionary leaders in China. It was the vision of a person devoted to the ideals of service and self-sacrifice. Wu continually asserted these ideals. The burden of proof, assuming the primacy of national salvation, lay not with those who attempted the Christian revolutionary synthesis but with those who insisted that the two approaches were irreconcilable.

A brief comparison in the mid-1930s with two other major Chinese groups at Yenching—the students and the board of managers—further illustrates the political dimensions of Wu's thinking. With regard to the students, Wu never succeeded in cultivating the friendship and loyalty of students to the same degree as Stuart, who was gifted in the art of personal relationships and who as late as 1933 could affectionately refer to the Yenching faculty as his "older children" and to the students as his "younger children."[56] Stuart always seemed present and available, while Wu seemed temperamentally remote. To be sure, they at times joined in supporting student protests. In December 1931 following the Manchurian Incident, for example, the two heads of Yenching, one a Hanlin and the other a missionary, led a patriotic parade of some 700 students and faculty through the towns and villages surrounding the Yenching campus.[57] But after resigning from the chancellorship in 1934, Wu appeared only remotely concerned with student politics and confined his energies to intellectual matters.

This distance between Wu and the students must not be over-emphasized, for it masked the definite converging of his political views with theirs. All available articles dealing with politics in the two major student publications, the *Yen-ta yüeh-k'an* (Yenta monthly, 1929–1934) and the *Yen-ta chou-k'an* (Yenta weekly, 1935–1936), revealed a strong commitment to social revolution and, implicitly an attack on the social reform approach to the problems of rural China and national salvation.[58] Kiang Wen-han, student secretary for the YMCA in Shanghai, described the political attitudes of students in Christian colleges generally in 1937: the more "thoughtful" students were "radical"; the outcry for individual development had changed to one for collective struggle; the worship of idealism and liberalism had changed to sheer realism and authority; the concern for an individual "way out" was replaced by actual identification with the masses; and solutions were no longer sought for minor adjustments but for fundamental changes.[59] Climaxing this political trend, Yenching student leaders led the famous December Ninth Movement (1935), dramatizing their disillusionment with the Nationalist government and their growing commitment to revolutionary solutions to the problem of national salvation.[60]

At the other end of the political spectrum at Yenching were the Chinese members of the board of managers. These prominent Chinese figures, such as K'ung Hsiang-hsi (H. H. Kung), Yen Hui-ch'ing (W. W. Yen), Ch'üan Shao-wen (S. J. Chuan), Chou Yi-ch'ün (Y. T. Tsur), and Sun Fo, were cosmopolitan and politically liberal. Fluent in English and comfortable with Westerners, they seemed almost as much at home in New York, where some retired after 1949, as in Peiping or Nanking. Most of them had strong ties with the YMCA and were frequently featured in missionary literature. They practiced a kind of pious and individualistic Christianity, which handled social issues no more seriously than Chiang Kai-shek's New Life movement in 1934–1936. One could examine their lives and discuss the content of their faith in the 1930s and hardly know that the Anti Christian Movement had occurred. As patriots they demanded from the trustees greater Chinese representation, greater authority, and above all racial equality at a time when antiforeign sentiment strongly influenced administrative policy at Yenching. They helped to "make Yenching Chinese" in Stuart's terms.

But even a Chinese-controlled Yenching was still a Western-style liberal arts institution whose underlying assumption was that needed social change would occur gradually. The managers were intellectually ill-equipped to handle the revolutionary approach to national salvation, and they had much to lose in case a real revolution were to occur. To Wu Lei-ch'uan and Yenching student leaders in the mid-1930s the board of managers represented Nanking's intellectual and political bankruptcy. Indeed, some of them were prominent officials in the central government. Upon graduation, most Yenching students did follow careers similar to the board of managers, in the YMCA and YWCA offices, the government, banks, schools, and journalism, but they were thinking different thoughts. Their home background and training in schools had made it difficult for them to do otherwise. But they were politically disaffected and were willing, even eager, to consider a revolutionary alternative.

Despite Wu's movement toward revolution, he returned to Yenching in 1936 to teach Chinese, write, and work with the Yenta Christian Fellowship. He made no effort to enter into administrative affairs. He continued to live in his small cottage. Following the Japanese attack on Pearl Harbor in 1941 and the closing of Yenching University the next day, Wu left the Yenching campus and moved into Peiping, where he died of apoplexy in 1944.

The career of Wu Lei-ch'uan illustrates both the appeal and the problems of Protestant Christianity among Chinese converts in the intellectual elite. For approximately a decade after his conversion experience Wu poured his energies into spreading Christianity among the intellectuals, especially the students in whom he placed his hopes for China's national salvation. Thus did he pursue his work as a teacher and administrator at Yenching University. But his identification with rising nationalism in the 1920s undermined the earlier confidence, increased his distrust of Western personalities and their theology, and caused him to move away from the more gradual programs of social change, as expressed in the educational purposes of the university, to a more revolutionary concept of national salvation. He tried as chancellor of Yenching to act on some of his redefinitions of the Christian faith and education, but the obstacles were too great, and he soon gave up. His calm, quaint, benign appearance notwithstanding, Wu Lei-ch'uan, through his life and thought, articulated the conflicts between Western expansion and Chinese nationalism, individualism and collectivism, reform and revolution—conflicts that confronted the missionary effort even during the high tide of Sino-Western relations in the 1920s and 1930s.

PART III

China Mission Images and American Policies

STUART CREIGHTON MILLER

Ends and Means: Missionary Justification of Force in Nineteenth Century China

A persistent theme that emerges from American missionary literature during moments of crisis in nineteenth century China is the conviction that normal diplomacy was unworkable with the Chinese because they only understood and responded to force. Such a belief was by no means restricted to missionaries. Many diplomats and traders echoed the belief that the "thunder of British batteries" was the ideal forensic in negotiating with the Chinese. At the end of the century as esteemed an educational leader as Jacob Gould Schurman, president of Cornell and chairman of the first Philippine Commission, advised President McKinley that "all Asiatic peoples have no trust in mere words without force behind them."[1] The evidence indicates that some American missionaries in China played an important role in the evolution of this "conventional wisdom."

Even before the first Opium War, the *Chinese Repository,* edited by the American missionaries Elijah Coleman Bridgman and Samuel Wells Williams, had published similar advice. Sometimes it took the form of an anonymous letter, strongly endorsed by the editors, explaining that the "imbecilic" Chinese "will insult so long as they meet no resistance, but when force is opposed to force, their courage fails." On other occasions an editorial directly advised an assault on Peking as the only honorable response by the British to Lord Napier's humiliation in 1834. The "more forebearance and indulgence" shown to the Chinese, the "more proud and overbearing they become," these missionary editors warned. Force alone would "break down their minds" and "compel China to a course more consistent with her rights and obligations," abandoning her "haughty isolation," which was "in open violation of the law—thou shalt love thy neighbor as thyself."[2]

These flagrant calls to arms were often mitigated by the editors' stipulation that they were not demanding an armed invasion—at least not immediately—but in the next breath they would point out that "the British flag has been insulted and British blood has been spilt. These hostile acts should be complained of, and reparation demanded and *obtained.*" Since on other occasions the *Chinese Repository* charged that "little can be expected from the good-will of the government in any negotiation," Bridgman and Williams appear to have anticipated that British complaints would go unheeded and would soon accelerate into an armed attack. Indeed, in the same editorial in which they clarified their aversion to warfare—"to prevent our being misunderstood"—they made eminently clear their expectations of the means that had to be used to obtain satisfaction from the Chinese government: "The Government of Great Britain could alone, were it necessary, dictate to the Chinese, and enforce any terms it pleased; and could by the exercise of its naval power effect the removal of all grievances which it is in the province of government to remove. This power we hope, will be speedily exerted and this effect produced. Recent injuries demand this. Humanity demands it. And justice will approve of it."[3]

Evidently the concept of national sovereignty was not applicable to the Chinese as far as these two missionary editors were concerned. When the American press criticized English demands for extraterritoriality, suggesting that China had the right to make her own laws, as well as to exclude foreigners if she so wished or to restrict their movement in the empire once admitted, Bridgman retorted angrily: "And why not ask: Have the banditti and pirates on the high seas a right to make their own laws? Have they a right to exclude 'foreigners' from what they choose to call their own dominions? And if those who do not belong to their own gang, are allowed to come among them, are they bound to obey their laws? The great Author of creation never intended, most surely, that any part of those dominions, given to man, should be appropriated exclusively either to this or that part of the human family."[4]

The government in Peking and its representatives in Canton apparently commanded no more respect from these American missionaries than would a gang of pirates. That government was, in their view, cruel and despotic, with laws that were obviously unjust. "And if laws are enacted requiring what is wrong, no one is bound to obey them," Bridgman declared.[5] Such a viewpoint encouraged missionaries to embark on illegal trips along the coast to distribute religious tracts and to preach to villagers. For example, the Reverend Edward Stevens and his English colleague, Walter Medhurst, bragged about physically pushing out of the way Chinese authorities who had attempted to restrain them on one such itinerary, and of disrupting schools and court proceedings to deliver their message of salvation.[6]

By 1838, however, the Reverends David Abeel and R. W. Orr were arguing that much more than civil disobedience was necessary to break down Chinese restrictions on their efforts to proselytize in the Celestial Empire. Nothing short of an armed invasion, hopefully carried out by an Anglo-American expeditionary force, would sweep away the hateful barriers to the gospel, resulting in "progress" for China and the world.[7] They did not have long to wait for a *casus belli*: a year later Commissioner Lin confiscated opium belonging to British merchants in Whampoa.

THE OPIUM WAR, 1839–1842

Since the Christian missionaries were unanimously opposed to the opium trade, many initially approved of Lin's action, and Williams expressed hope that the English would recognize the righteousness of this act, however much it violated the "so-called law of nations." Yet some of his colleagues hoped that England would respond by initiating their long-anticipated war, which would open up China to the gospel. "How long will England continue to wear the lion on her crest and yet play the part of the hare?" the missionary teacher Samuel Brown demanded when it appeared that war might not be immediately forthcoming. By 1840, Williams, too, was recommending for China "a hard knock to rouse her from her fancied goodness and security."[8]

When the Royal Navy finally materialized off China's coast, the Reverend W. J. Boone hailed her blockade as assurance that this time England was going to fight. "There is but one single barrier to the establishment of hundreds of missions among the literally perishing heathen idolators and that barrier is of a political nature which might be removed in a day," Boone declared. T. L. McBryde was also delighted that the English were "not mincing the matter at last," and "China will soon be open" to the gospel. When the English batteries began firing, America's first female missionary to China confessed, "How these difficulties do rejoice my heart because I think the English government may be enraged, and God, in His power may break down the barriers which prevent the gospel of Christ from entering China."[9]

Of course, it was still necessary for these missionaries to resolve the quandary presented by the evils of the opium trade as opposed to the need to break down, by force of arms, the restrictions placed on evangelical efforts in China. To answer such doubts, they often resorted to legalistic justifications for the war that avoided the opium issue altogether. Ironically, 1839 offered an important opportunity for the American missionaries to win the respect of Chinese officials if they had remained neutral. Lin even sought to use Williams and the medical missionary Peter Parker as intermediaries. Parker's biographers made vague reference to his efforts to "promote peace" by translating into Chinese "extracts from Vattel's 'Law of Nations' on international rights and upon war." But Vattel was more frequently used to prove that China's exclusive policies violated the rights of other nations seeking to engage her in peaceful intercourse. "In this struggle now going on we see the progress of freedom and Christianity over the opposition of ignorance and exclusion," Williams explained to Rufus Anderson of the American Board of Commissioners for Foreign Missions. It was essentially a struggle "for supremacy." The Chinese continually violated the rights of individuals by insisting that foreigners "must obey whatever is laid upon them, without the least contumacy . . . It needs no argumentation to prove that this principle must be given up before freedom of thought can make much progress among the Chinese," Williams reasoned.[10]

Not only were the rights of individuals and nations violated by the Chinese, but also those of God. In a printed circular, Bridgman, Abeel, and Williams declared, "In China we see a supremacy no less lofty and unjust in its pretensions, not only taking inalienable rights from man, but presumptuously encroaching on Jehovah's prerogatives, attempting to abrogate His laws and stigmatizing the religion of Jesus Christ as base and wicked.[11]

Once negotiations had broken down, England had every moral and legal right to make war on China, according to the thinking of these missionaries. "After many months had been occupied in vain attempts to negotiate, it became clear to every observer that in order to lay the foundation for free and friendly intercourse with this nation on safe and honorable terms, such as are recognized by all civilized states, recourse must be had to restraint and coercion," McBryde explained in a printed circular to Presbyterians back home.[12]

Missionaries became England's chief apologists in the United States and, in the case of Parker, England's unofficial lobbyist. Parker returned to lecture Americans, including the president, secretary of state, and a Congressional committee, on the "two common errors in American thinking": that the war was being waged "to perpetuate the opium trade," and that there was a "concealed object of conquest" on the part of England. "The real purpose of the war" was "indemnity for the past and security for the future," Parker insisted.[13]

Other missionaries, such as the Americans McBryde, Bridgman, Williams, Abeel, Ira Tracy, and J. Lewis Shuck, and the Prussian Charles Gutzlaff, hammered away at this theme in a series of letters to American religious and lay editors. Britain would seek nothing "beyond that which is just and right ... *simple redress for injuries sustained* with *ample securities* for the future." No less than "everyone in China" knew that "far higher principles were involved than the mere recovery of opium," and "England's victory" was "fraught with the highest benefit to commerce and civilization, and, indeed, the truest and best interests of the human race, and China especially."[14]

The opium question was never ignored, however. Forgetting his earlier recommendation for and justification of the English attack, Williams condemned the war as totally "unjust" in a letter to his father in 1841, because of its "intimate connections" with the opium trade. In publishing a speech of John Quincy Adams praising England for extending "her liberating arm to the farthest bound of Asia," the editors of the *Chinese Repository* also politely demurred over the elder statesman's contention that opium was no more a cause of the war than tea was the cause of the American Revolution. Opium was an issue, albeit "a lesser one." But these editors took solace in the observation that God's methods were strange and that "in His own chosen way" He would end the opium trade. This was a key rationalization for American missionaries during the Opium War (also known as the First Anglo-Chinese War). The "opium trade is deservedly regarded as inhuman," McBryde agreed; yet he reasoned that while God's ways "are dark and incomprehensible to our finite minds," they are "always perfectly understood by Himself." Thus, God could "make use of any means," even "His enemies for the advance of His glory. 'He maketh the wrath of man to praise Him.' Hence the opium trade—a direct violation of the laws of God—can serve Him." Parker even assured his sister that the war was in fact being fought to end the opium trade. Recognizing the paradoxical nature of this assertion, he hastily added, "But it has to be done in a manner that is peculiar to a nation that regards itself as the principal part of the world and all other nations as mere handfuls of men to share in its boundless compassion."[15]

Transcending the legalistic justification, therefore, was the will of God, who was, after all, the architect of nature and natural law. Indeed, between 1840 and 1900 every Western invasion of China was almost unanimously conceived of by these American missionaries as an act of Providence. In an ecumenical spirit, the Congregationalists Bridgman and Parker joined the Presbyterians Orr, Mitchell, and McBryde along with the Episcopalian Boone and the Southern Baptists J. Lewis and Henrietta Shuck in agreeing with Williams that the war in Asia was the scheme "of the God of nations . . . to open a highway for those who would preach the word." "I am constrained to look back upon the present state of things not so much as an opium or an English affair, as the great design of Providence to make the wickedness of man subserve His purposes of mercy toward China in breaking through her wall of exclusion," Parker concluded. "The hand of God is apparent in all that has transpired in a remarkable manner," Williams insisted, "and we doubt not that He who said He came to bring a sword upon the earth has come here and that for the speedy destruction of His enemies and the establishment of His own kingdom. He will overturn and overturn until He has established the

Prince of Peace." In describing the terrible slaughter of Chinese soldiers by the Royal Navy and Marines, Shuck calmly wrote in his journal, "I regard such scenes . . . as the direct instruments of the Lord in clearing away the rubbish which impedes the advancement of Divine Truth." Who else but God could break down such formidable barriers that had "kept his servants out of the stronghold of Satan," demanded McBryde.[16]

Lest questions be raised over God's choice of the Royal Irish to storm Canton, several missionary circulars assured their readers that "God has often made use of the strong arm of civil power to prepare the way for His kingdom—that kingdom which is righteousness and peace."[17] Bridgman further clarified the process: "The agency in these great moments is human; the directing power divine. The high governor of all the nations has employed England to chastize and humble China. He may soon employ her to introduce the blessings of Christian civilization and free intercourse among her millions." However, the means designed by God were a temporary expedient, the missionaries cautioned, and "in wrath He will remember mercy, bring order out of confusion, good out of evil, and make man's wickedness promotive of Divine Glory."[18]

Missionary militancy reached its heights at those moments when England hesitated or resorted to negotiations with the Chinese. Shuck was furious that the English were wasting time negotiating in 1839, giving the Chinese time to prepare defenses, and again in 1842 were bogged down in futile talks instead of marching straight to Peking. There could be no real settlement, he averred, except at "the door of the emperor's palace." In a similar manner, a printed circular letter of American Board missionaries in Macao in 1842 criticized England for giving up "high ground" already won in battle to "dilly dally in negotiations" with a government that was "unjust in letter" and "cruel in their action." McBryde expressed disbelief that England could have such patience, and China such arrogance, in still refusing to allow foreigners to trade in China "without restraint" during these negotiations.[19]

But there were also soul-searching moments when missionaries became at least partially aware of their confusion about ends and means. Boone confessed in a moment of candor, "We may err, but it is an error for which God will surely forgive us." Britain's conquests in Asia were "not righteous" in themselves, he explained, "but capable of deriving a good end." J. L. Shuck reasoned in the *Baptist Missionary Magazine,* "I deprecate war in all its forms, but the Chinese government is hostile, essentially and practically hostile, to the great God, and to the cause of His Son, and it would be no great cause of regret to me were the whole fabric soon to fall, to rise no more before the face of an offended heaven." On the pages of the same journal, Williams followed similar tortuous paths of protest and justification with regard to British aggression in China as an act of Providence: "Should England not feel herself called upon to demand explanations for past grievances, we [American missionaries] fear that the authorities will become still more overbearing and exclusive . . . Alas! Our hearts sink at the bare possibility of such a result. We deprecate war . . . While we pray, therefore, that if consistent with God's holy purposes, it may not be afflicted, ought we not to plead with even still greater importunity that if Great Britain pursues a peaceful policy, the pride and prejudice of this people may not swell into higher barriers, than they already oppose to our influence." [20]

When opium smuggling continued after the war, the missionaries' consciences were further stricken. "We have taught all Asia, if not to love us, at least to dread us . . . to acknowledge our power . . . let us now show that we are a nation of Christians," pleaded Boone. Two joint statements from American Board missionaries not only lamented the unabated continuance of opium traffic but also expressed the very practical concern that the Chinese, with typical "cunning," could seize upon this issue to rescind the rights recently gained by missionaries. The war was a failure on one more score, grieved Parker, Williams, Bridgman, and Dyer Ball: it had not changed the character of the people, whose hearts remained "unapproachable" and minds impervious to the teaching of Christ. [21]

American missionaries in China suffered some mild and indirect criticism for their support of Britain in the war, mostly from religious journals: "Strange that reflecting minds can ever believe that the wrath of man can work the righteousness of God: and still as strange that they can be brought to hope or desire that the gospel of Jesus Christ may be, or can be, brought to the minds of unbelievers by the sword, or that through the slaughter of thousands of our fellow mortals, the kingdom of the Prince of Peace is to be established." The *Christian Examiner* warned in an article on the Opium War, "While God may turn evil to good, the character of evil and the evil-doer remains unchanged." But only on the pages of the *Southern Literary Messenger* a few years later did the missionary in China get his first taste of the kind of criticism he was to suffer in greater abundance at the end of the century. In reviewing China's encounter with the West, the editor accused the missionaries of listening, "if not impatiently, at least anxiously, for the sound of the first gun. Well may the statesmen of China look suspiciously upon the efforts of religious missionaries, and regard them as covert designs to subvert the Chinese government . . . There they stand before the gates of the Chinese empire . . . with matches lighted and weapons bared, and cry as they knock: 'Peaceably if we may; but forceably if we must.' " [22]

THE *ARROW* INCIDENT AND THE SECOND ANGLO-CHINESE WAR, 1856–1860

Evangelical success continued to elude the missionaries in China following the Opium War. In 1853 the Taiping Rebellion offered a brief respite from the dismal conversion statistics and missionary hopes soared to almost ethereal heights at rumors that the rebels professed a Protestant Christianity. By the end of 1854, however, reports from missionaries who had visited the rebel camp carried shocking testimony of the blasphemous pretensions and arrogant xenophobia of the rebel leaders.[23] Perhaps as a function of their bitter disappointment over the Taipings, most American missionaries uncritically accepted the shabby pretext of the *Arrow* incident and called upon America to join England in an Anglo-Saxon crusade against Satan's stronghold in China.

The *Arrow* was a Chinese-owned "lorcha"—a Western type hull rigged in the Chinese manner—manned by a polyglot crew, commanded by an Englishman, and flying the British flag. The missionaries particularly despised the "lorcha" men, who served as middlemen plying the coast to peddle opium. In 1856, the Chinese government seized the *Arrow* for smuggling opium and harboring Chinese pirates among its crew. The *Arrow's* skipper had no right to fly the Union Jack, and the Chinese crew members arrested were wanted criminals. Nevertheless, when the English protested this alleged insult to their flag, the Chinese officials quickly apologized and released both ship and crew. Three of the more notorious Chinese crew members with long records of opium smuggling, however, had already been summarily executed by the mandarins before the decision to release them was reached. The English in turn escalated their ultimatum to the Chinese, demanding beyond an apology a guarantee that such a seizure would not take place in the future. Such an assurance would have been an open invitation to every opium runner along the coast to strike the Union Jack when being pursued by Chinese authorities. When such a guarantee was refused, the Royal Navy bombarded Canton and landed Royal Marines to take the city.[24]

While most American missionaries hailed England's decisive action, Williams acknowledged the weakness in England's case and even questioned her real motives for making war on China in 1856: "The English government as such has not the least interest in the progress of China in true religion." But once again Williams saw in the British assault "much to strengthen the hope that God is preparing to work mightily among the Chinese . . . for further triumphs." To Williams, the struggle would "break up the ground" for the missionary "to throw in the seed." The Reverend Daniel Vrooman also admitted that "some few things have been done which all good men regret, but in the main I think there is but one opinion in regard to all *general measures.*" That consensus, he made clear, was in support of the British invasion. Vrooman seems to have been reasonably correct in his assessment of missionary opinion; at least Boone, Parker, Dyer Ball, and the Reverend Samuel Bonney vociferously joined him in seeing "much more hope for China" as a result of an English invasion. "I sometimes feel," Vrooman added, "that God has taken the work out of our hands for the present and is carrying forward what we desire to attain by other instrumentalities than we were left to our option. But if we can do nothing more . . . we can pray for the overthrow of Satan and establishment of Christ."[25]

Bonney was ecstatic about the war, expressing no reservations over its origins or the underlying motives of the British. His main concern was that it might be limited to the Canton region rather than spreading to all of China. He saw no reason "the preaching of the glad tyding of salvation" should be "limited to five ports and vicinity." God's messengers would temporarily be clad in kilts and speak with bullets to open up China for His true messengers of peace, but "if the mild and gentle means which have been used for the last twelve years will not do it, perhaps they will yield to the scourge of war," he suggested. "In the meantime," Bonney concluded, "the servants of the Prince of Peace must retire and let Him work who is mighty in power and terrible to His foes. There must be more overturning in China before He whose right it is shall be supreme in the hearts of the people."[26]

In a second letter to Anderson a few months later, Bonney spelled out what most of his colleagues only implied: that the awesome power of British arms would not only intimidate Chinese officials and remove political restrictions on missionary movement in China, but would also break down the personal resistance on the part of the people to accept the missionary's truth: "O that this people were wise & would consider why these severe judgements are sent upon them. For the last fourteen years Christ's messengers have proclaimed that God which gives pardon, peace and prosperity. But the vast majority have returned only indifference and rejection to such kind offers. Now a scourge is applied, addressed to their fears. We pray that these calamities be short and overruled by God for the furtherance of the Gospel."[27]

On other occasions Bonney expressed more concern over "the loss of lives & much misery to thousands" that were attendant on destroying barriers to the gospel. But in the manner of Pontius Pilate, he washed his hands of any responsibility for decisions that were those of God: "We would that it could be obtained by milder measures but that is not for us to determine. All we desire is freedom to preach the gospel to this people & the influence of God's spirit making it effectual for their conversion." Vrooman declared with even more candor: "I would like to see China opened for the preaching of the truth & will not refuse to see it done by violence *if so it must be.* I pray for liberty unrestrained for God's word & servants and will not presume to *dictate* by what means it shall be secured, although I humbly pray that it may be done by the influence of truth and the operation of God's spirit upon the minds and hearts of men." Nevertheless, when the professed prayers for peaceful means went unanswered and God chose instead to rake Chinese bodies with English shot rather than to bombard their minds with truth and their hearts with love, these missionaries did not hesitate to cheer His decision. Vrooman's main concern was that American public opinion would again distort the real meaning of the British attack and relate it to opium and greed.[28]

At long last, the U.S. Navy seemed ready to respond to the

demands and prayers of many missionaries that their own nation join England and assume some of the burden of opening China to the gospel by force of arms. Not that the navy was ever reluctant to join its Anglo-Saxon cousins in the Royal Navy: U.S. Commissioner Robert McLane's aide, navy Captain Buchanan, had already earned the nickname "Old Million" because of his loud and frequent advice that the only way to deal with the Chinese was "to give them a million shot a minute." When a Chinese fort fired a few badly aimed rounds at the *U.S.S. Portsmouth,* its skipper, Commander Andrew Foote, was able to act on Buchanan's advice and quickly demolished the redoubt. While taking soundings preparatory to moving up in support of Foote, Commodore Armstrong's squadron was fired on by a second fort; one man was killed. Armstrong bombarded the fort and landed marines to complete the job. This action, plus news that the American consul in Hong Kong had joined the British assault on Canton and even carried Old Glory with him over the city's battered walls, raised the American missionary hopes.[29]

The Reverend R. S. Maclay was ecstatic over this turn of events and pleaded on the pages of the *Missionary Advocate* that America forsake isolationism and join England in its assault on China. Vroo- man explained to Anderson that, although "the assaults upon the flags of both countries" may "seem a small pretext," in contrast to which "the justice and propriety of the severe measures" undertaken by American and British naval commanders may appear "to those at a distance" extreme, it would be well for Americans to keep in mind that such "insults, though trivial in themselves, are of great moment as precursors of the future."[30]

Missionary hopes for American intervention were further enhanced by the fact that at the time Peter Parker was the U.S. Commissioner to China and was himself actively scheming with American business- men to get the United States involved in order to seize Formosa as an "American Hongkong." From his platform as the senior American diplomat, Parker was able to preach officially the missionary's max- im on Chinese character and the necessity of force. He made clear to a group of American businessmen that diplomacy in China was a waste of time. It was only from "influences more potent than those of the ablest diplomatist, that any changes are to be looked for in the relations subsisting between China and the Western nations."[31]

After Parker had been replaced by William B. Reed in 1857, the

United States was represented in China by a diplomat more scrupulously neutral than his predecessor. However, before Reed's arrival, he was filled in for briefly by Williams, who had been appointed the secretary of the U.S. Legation. Williams also used his diplomatic perch to propagate the time-worn missionary aphorism that, as he wrote back to America, the Chinese "would grant nothing unless fear stimulated their sense of justice for they are among the most craven of people, cruel and selfish as heathenism can make men, so we must be backed by force, if we wish them to listen." While conceding that the *Arrow* had "no right to fly English colors," Williams argued that England had no resort but war because treaties diplomatically arrived at were worthless in China: "A heathen people like the Chinese having no regard for truth . . . are ready to promise everything under pressure only to nullify it . . . [There is little] basis for a stable compact with this pagan, ignorant, conceited and weak people." [32]

The Reverend W. A. Macy, however, upset the apparent unanimity that had been enjoyed by American missionaries in 1840 by attacking England's lawlessness in the Second Anglo-Chinese War (also known as the Arrow War) and bitterly chastizing his colleagues in China for believing that Christianity stood to gain from the war: "Let Christians who are watching for the development of the present crisis remember that war and violence in themselves tend only to evil: the cannons which now roar speak not of brotherly affection but of hatred and ill-will. War many break down many barriers, it can never knit one band of union. This people will be broken and cowed, they cannot by fire, famine and sword be made to love." Macy's further complaint that the diplomatic roles played by Parker and Williams violated "the sacredness of high calling" enjoyed by missionaries was probably instrumental in forcing Anderson to ask for Secretary Williams' resignation as a missionary. Macy also criticized other colleagues who made no pretense at being neutral, openly collaborated with the British, and even assumed warlike postures. Vrooman armed himself with a cutlass when he accompanied English patrols into the countryside. Bonney and the Reverend C. L. Preston would follow closely British military expeditions in order to preach and distribute tracts in the wake of the fighting, much to Macy's disgust. Preston made no bones about the fact that such "systematic visitations of the country" were highly destructive. "It is generally believed that good will come of it—they burned one village which fired upon them," Preston reported first-hand to the Presbyterian Board, explaining that the Chinese "will learn by experience," which "is always a severe method but effectual."[33] Macy seems to have been the only missionary on record who understood how damning this close association with armed invaders was for the missionary enterprise in China.

The legalization of opium in the English treaty of 1858, which ended the conflict, angered the medical missionary J. G. Kerr, who called it "a disgrace not only to the nation that had brought it about but to all of Christendom." Kerr concluded his tirade, however, with the familiar rationalization: "Nevertheless God can make the calamities of war and all the evils growing out of it to work together for the accomplishment of His own gracious purposes of mercy to our fallen race." Macy, alone among his colleagues, seems to have sensed that original sin and God's transcending justice were convenient abdications of the missionary's moral responsibility in order to reap gains wrought by war. Another Presbyterian missionary, A. P. Happer, gleefully hailed the treaty of 1858, and a printed missionary circular declared of the pending treaty, "Christ our Lord desires it, claims it." Few missionaries besides Macy, Kerr, and Williams bothered even to mention the legalization of opium in their discussions of the treaty. In his diplomatic role, Williams reluctantly approved of it: "The honorable English merchants can now exonerate themselves from the opprobrium of smuggling this article. Bad as the triumph is, I am convinced that it was the best disposition that could be made of the perplexing question; legalization is preferable to the evils attending the farce now played and we shall be the better when the drug is openly landed, and opium hulks and bribed inspectors are no more."[34]

Indeed, several missionaries played crucial roles for the allied powers and the United States in negotiating new treaties at Tientsin in 1858. They were able to exploit their positions as interpreters and translators to win new privileges for the missionary community in China. Williams and W. A. P. Martin insisted that a religious toleration clause be inserted into the American treaty. It guaranteed the right to teach and practice Christianity for missionaries as well as for Chinese converts and ministers without any interference from the imperial government. Even the American envoy was uncomfortable with such a stipulation but reluctantly bowed to the persuasive pressure of his two missionary advisers. Later his fear proved to be justified when more militant missionaries capitalized on the vagueness of this clause to confer on their native congregations almost extraterritorial rights. An extraordinary coup by a French missionary, Father Delamarre, granted to missionaries the right to buy and lease property in the interior of China, outside the five treaty ports opened to all foreigners by virtue of other treaties. Delamarre extended this right to missionaries alone merely by inserting it into his Chinese translation of the French treaty, although his subterfuge should have been nullified by the stipulation in the treaty that in case of any discrepancy between the two texts, the version in the French took precedence.[35] Nothing appears to have been said about Delamarre's ruse at the time, but Bishop Boone's uneasy acceptance of this unusual special privilege for all missionaries under the most-favored-nation clause and Commissioner Reed's outright opposition to it were probably related to the manner in which it was acquired.[36] A little over forty years later Delamarre's action came back to haunt the missionary establishment when a San Francisco editor discovered the French missionary's deception at Tientsin in 1858 and charged American missionaries with being parties to "forgery" and "fraud" in China.[37]

Upon returning to Tientsin in 1859 with the ratified treaties, English, French, and American naval vessels found that the Chinese had erected new barriers in the Gulf of Chihli off the Pei-ho to replace those destroyed by the English a year earlier. Interpreting this as a hostile act, the Royal Navy once again began to destroy the barrier, only to find themselves in a murderous cross-fire at Taku. To the shock of the world, the Chinese, who reputedly could not shoot straight, sank five gunboats and repulsed an Anglo-French landing force with heavy casualties. Williams, who was on board Commodore Josiah Tatnall's flagship when the U.S. Navy rushed in to cover the retreating invaders, wrote home to his brother: "I never, I think, felt such a disappointment as when I saw the English defeated last June . . . I am sure that the Chinese need harsh measures to bring them out of their ignorance, conceit and idolatry; why then deplore the means used to accomplish this end so much as to blind our minds to the result which God seems to be advancing by methods whose inherent wrong He can punish at His own time."[38]

For almost the first time in the nineteenth century, however, a number of American missionaries voiced criticism of British aggressiveness and "recklessness" at Taku. The Reverend M. Simpson Culbertson, a West Point graduate and considered by his colleagues to be something of a military expert, charged the British with blundering into the wrong estuary; and Happer, Preston, and Boone joined him in criticizing the British for needlessly prolonging the war when all the desired gains had already been realized. But their criticism, unlike that of Macy and Kerr earlier, had no moral overtones; it was purely tactical in nature.[39]

Bridgman had no trouble in supporting the British action at Taku.[40] Preston wavered from anxiety over tactics to believing that one more punishment was needed to rub out the "ignorant" recalcitrance of the Chinese, then back again to a concern that another allied invasion might be too much of a good thing. "We may expect the pride and the haughtiness of these people will be manifested occasionally, but they suffered too much in the past three years to forget it too soon," Preston reasoned. But in typical fashion, he concluded his reflections by turning military affairs over to God, "whose power and wisdom are over all these things."[41]

Once the allied forces had returned in strength and marched on Peking in 1860, Happer forgot his earlier misgivings that a surfeit of suffering might create a reverse effect, and hailed the British and French victory as insurance of a completely open and more receptive China. Several American missionaries set out immediately with Admiral Hope to explore the Yangtze in a gunboat. Preston and Mrs. Kerr were delighted by their personal contacts with British soldiers, who were frequent visitors to missionary schools, hospitals, and compounds, and jokingly suggested that "certificates of American citizenship" be given these English friends.[42]

Bishop Boone remained unconvinced, however, that the missionary cause in China had not suffered irreparable damage in the minds of the Chinese as a result of permitting the gospel to be carried into that nation on the shoulders of "Tommy Atkins." "It will take us some time to live it all down," worried Boone in 1861. The Reverend J. M. Knowlton nevertheless appealed to his colleagues to concentrate on the future and to "make haste" in exploiting the new opportunities with plans to convert thirty thousand Chinese each day, or one million every month.[43]

THE BURLINGAME MISSION AND THE TIENTSIN MASSACRE, 1867–1871

While the missionaries realized their first significant evangelical success in China in the decade following the Second Anglo-Chinese War, the pace hardly lived up to Knowlton's sanguine expectations. Bitterness crept into the comments of some missionaries, and by 1868 C. L. Preston was suggesting another Western invasion of China. It would require a relatively small allied force, he maintained, to conquer all of China and to install "a new progressive government which by honesty and justice, would call forth the love and respect of the masses." Instead, however, the Western nations were busy negotiating new treaties with China, an exercise of which the missionaries were very suspicious. Of what value, demanded one missionary, was another treaty when China had so many times demonstrated "her incapacity to maintain treaties of reciprocity with civilized nations?" And once more a missionary repeated the tired dictum: China "must in that case be dealt with as other half-civilized and barbarous nations are," that is, with armed force.[44] To illustrate this maxim, the Reverend Hunter Corbett sent a news release from Yangchow describing disturbances against missionaries in 1868. Chinese officials were, as usual, being impossible until a "small squadron" of British gunboats appeared. Than "straight away all is changed," the bargaining over indemnity for destroyed mission property ceased, and the mission's full demands were immediately granted. How long would it take Americans to learn that the mailed fist was "the true method of dealing with such a nation," intoned an editorial in the *Chinese Recorder*.[45]

In 1861 ex-Congressman Anson Burlingame was appointed to represent the United States in China. He was an unabashed Sinophile, after a string of United States commissioners who had shared the view of most Westerners in China that the Peking government only responded to gunboat diplomacy. His was a voice of conciliation and moderation within the Western diplomatic community, which won him few friends among the missionaries. Upon retiring in 1867, Burlingame was asked by Peking to represent the imperial government and negotiate new treaties with the Western powers. His mission took him to Washington, London, and Paris in 1867, causing great concern among missionaries that the special privileges they had

gained in the treaties of 1858 might be jeopardized or even re-
scinded. These were, in fact, the first negotiations between China and
the Western nations over which the missionaries had little or no
influence.

The missionaries' anxiety was enhanced by their belief that China
was on the verge of extending officially to Christianity the same
tolerance it had granted to Buddhism centuries before. This expectation was based on a memorial to the imperial throne by Tseng
Kuo-fan which reasoned that Christianity offered no serious threat to
China because it attracted so few "supporters and converts." Sir
Rutherford Alcock upset this delicate situation when he demanded
that merchants be given the same rights as missionaries to purchase
and lease land anywhere in China under the new treaty. In order to
strengthen his case, Alcock argued that merchants were much less of
a threat to China's social tranquillity than were missionaries, who
preached a doctrine that could be "dangerous to the public peace."
Therefore, he demanded, "having accepted the greater [threat]
would it be wise for the government to refuse the lesser, and less
hazardous, venture in the interests of peace?" The missionaries were
outraged by Alcock's forensic betrayal and blamed him for the riots
of 1868 against Christian missions in the interior. They argued that
Chinese officials responded to Alcock's line of reasoning by deliberately stirring up the natives to harass the missionaries out of the
interior. It was a bewildering turn of events for the missionary
movement in China. On what they perceived as the threshold of
success, victory was snatched from their hands not by pagans, but by
fellow Christians, and Anglo-Saxon ones at that.[46]

The Burlingame Treaty with Washington in 1868 confirmed missionary suspicions. Article VIII, which "freely disclaims any intention or right to intervene in the domestic administration of China in
regard to the construction of railroads, telegraphs and other improvements," was labeled "a dangerous loophole" by one missionary
spokesman. Obviously Christianity was such an "improvement," and
this article would restore to Chinese authorities the control over it
that they had lost a decade earlier in the Tientsin treaties. By
conceding to the emperor "the reserved right to decide the time and
manner and circumstances of introduction of such improvements
within his domain," the treaty "emasculated" all foreigners in China.
According to this spokesman, the Chinese should have no control

over decisions affecting foreigners on their soil. That the naive officials in Washington could be taken in by such an "evil plot" was understandable, but less comprehensible was how the English, whose past policy of dealing forcefully with the Chinese had been so "correct," could also be taken in. As this writer lamented, "The Mongol had outmaneuvered the Saxon; the scow had got to the windward of the clipper."[47]

One missionary angrily denounced the treaty as "the greatest of humbugs," based on a premise that totally ignored the lessons of history: "The boasted progress China has made within the last fifty years, whatever it is, has been the result of force."[48] Others began a letter-writing campaign to editors back home, both lay and religious, The *New York Herald*'s James Gordon Bennett acknowledged that four-fifths of the letters from Americans in China were bitterly opposed to the Burlingame Treaty, charging that the West was being asked to lay down its arms with no real concessions from the Chinese. Western powers were being "bamboozled by the Yankee Chinaman without a tail [Burlingame]," and should immediately return to England's "old bulldog policy" in China, according to the letter writers. That most of them were missionaries was obvious. Not only did missionaries write much more prolifically than businessmen, but the letters' message was an old missionary refrain. Bennett, who favored the treaty, began in the same editorial an angry diatribe against the foreign missionary effort in China, calling it "a bad business." No stranger to vitriolic prose, Bennett mercilessly lampooned the missionaries in a series of editorials, calling them "apostles of Exeter Hall . . . venturesome ladies, Brahmapootra [sic] explorers, writers for the magazines and dabblers in the sale of naval stores." At the end of one tirade, Bennett demanded of his readers, "can we wonder" at "so few converts" after fifty years of Protestant effort in China, "when we see such ignorance, assumption and narrow-minded bigotry in these missionaries?"[49]

Ironically, the leading spokesman in China for the anti-Burlingame group was Burlingame's successor as United States minister to China, J. Ross Browne. Sounding more like a missionary than a diplomat, Browne reasoned that, as a "pagan state," China could not be expected to live up to treaty obligations. He emphatically denied that the Chinese were embarked on "a more enlightened policy" and publicly urged a vigorous, militant Anglo-American policy to wring more concessions from China. Bennett ridiculed what he called the "throat policy" of Browne and his missionary supporters: "There they are, God and Mammon side by side." When Browne was hastily recalled, missionaries were furious "that a minister having such a correct view of the relationship of China and European nations should be recalled at this juncture."[50]

Missionary opposition to the Burlingame Treaty was vindicated by the torture and murder of French nuns at Tientsin in 1870. The Reverend C. A. Baldwin charged the late Anson Burlingame and his confused supporters with the responsibility for this "unholy deed." It illustrated perfectly the point that missionaries had been making for decades: conciliation merely emboldened the Chinese. Almost immediately, Baldwin asserted, the concessions made in the Burlingame Treaty enhanced the "arrogant assumptions" of Chinese officials, and multiplied "the insults" to foreigners in China. When would America listen to their missionaries who knew the Chinese? "How the people of the United States were deceived and went into ecstasies over the oldest nation in the world sending a son of the youngest to represent it," Baldwin grieved.[51]

The *New York Times* was won over sufficiently by this line of reasoning to apologize belatedly to ex-Minister Browne for having been critical of his jingoistic advice. "We had as a nation been made the victims of overweening confidence and hopes, and the minister's statements were neither popular nor acceptable," the editor admitted sheepishly in 1871. But it was no time for quibbling over past mistakes, warned the *Chinese Recorder,* as the massacre presented a new opportunity for "England and America to stand shoulder-to-shoulder with their bereaved sister nation," particularly since the war with Prussia limited France's ability to retaliate in China. The editor regretted that the impulsive Napoleon III was no longer around when he was needed.[52]

The American missionaries Martin, Hattie Noyes, Samuel Dodd, E. W. Capp, and C. W. Mateer joined Baldwin in calling for armed retaliation and in hailing the Tientsin Incident as a golden opportunity for a final Anglo-Saxon invasion of China.[53] Mateer gloomily predicted, however, that the United States would not send troops. "We live here solely on the prestige of England and France, and when we get into trouble we can only appeal to them for help," he bemoaned with disgust.[54] Yet Mrs. Mateer was grateful that the

United States Navy had escorted missionaries back to a station they fled in 1870, and Capp made it clear that American naval officers in China had a better view of the situation than did their political superiors in Washington.[55] Yet these missionaries were rarely consistent on the issue of force in China, and in 1871 Happer denounced his fellow missionaries who "were anxious to fire the hearts of foreigners so as to make war on China," conveniently forgetting his own insistence only months before that the Chinese must be severely punished before they could be evangelized.[56]

ANTIFOREIGN RIOTS, 1871–1899

During the last three decades of the nineteenth century, riots against foreigners occurred in China with increasing frequency, and in the interior, missions bore the brunt of such attacks, being the most obvious symbols of Western cultural aggression. Yet the missionaries were not discouraged by this turn of events. On the contrary, the disturbances seemed to buoy a surprising optimism, as missionaries insisted that they were "no accident" but "part of GOD'S great plan for blessing China." A few missionaries innocently protested that they were uncertain just "how He may use them [the riots]." Others chose to veil their calls for armed invasion of China by euphemistically calling the riots "a golden opportunity" to "bless China" with "a much needed lesson." Anyone familiar with the missionary rhetoric had to know that such blessings in the past had been in the form of grapeshot and that the lessons were rather bloody. Other missionaries felt no need to be indirect and called outright for an Anglo-Saxon armed assault, to alter the "indifference and imbecility" of the mandarins and to "teach the Chinese that British and American blood is *sacred*." But whatever the manner in which these missionaries called for war, they all seemed to perceive the same process: a Western military invasion would create turmoil and weaken China's institutionalized resistance to Christianity. "We are not discouraged," the Reverend Arthur J. Brown exclaimed. "We believe the tumult will, in the Providence of God, break up the fossilized conservatism of China and result in the mighty enlargement of opportunity for the gospel."[57]

In order to illustrate this message further, some missionary journals featured a series of historical sketches from the Opium War to the

German activity in Shantung at the end of the century. As the Reverend H. V. Noyes concluded in one such sketch, China had "benefitted immensely" from past military invasions, and one more assault would be the "source of great blessing." His colleague William Ashmore was uneasy about including the Opium War as one of China's past "benefits" in his historical vignette of British assaults, because opium was "a real grievance" for the Chinese, however great the "towering insolence" that provoked the conflict.[58] Another missionary historian, B. F. Witt, left it up to her readers to judge whether the gains wrought for the gospel by this first war over the hateful opium trade justified Britain's aggression. But these authors ignored the opium issue in the Second Anglo-Chinese War, and Ashmore applauded in retrospect the actions at Taku in 1859: "Speaking in the interests of progress, it was just as well that the allies had to go back and complete the job," because the Chinese "had not learned their lesson," and the emperor himself "needed to be shaken out of his insufferable conceit of superiority." Nothing improved China's perspective of the world, Ashmore advised, better than "the dust kicked up by the brogans of British soldiers." As an outspoken anti-Catholic, however, Ashmore hesitated before including France as one of God's instruments in China: *"The French war was an instructive event in the period which had its lesson for the Chinese but which they have failed to profit by."* Clearly, Ashmore did not feel in 1898 that China had yet learned the "lesson" these missionaries had been so eager to have England teach her for three-quarters of a century.[59]

By 1895 a number of missionaries were even ready to accept Japan's invasion of China as an act of Providence. "Not by her own might and management, but by the arrangement of Providence, as we fully believe, Japan was used as a tool of the Almighty to shake China to its center," Ashmore declared. The English missionary Griffith John predicted in a letter quoted widely in American missionary journals that, whoever led the fight, "war is going to be a source of great blessing to China. It is awful chastisement, but China needed it, and will be the better for it." To add to the missionary's paradox of establishing the Prince of Peace in China through violence, God had now selected a pagan nation "to snap those cords which have bound her with an unbending conservativism to the old prehistoric civilization" and to impose on China the gospel message, which "she has heard for a century and yet persistently rejects." While ignoring the first paradox, another missionary reconciled the second by insisting that "God will interpose, and that the new Japan will be a Christian nation."[60]

Few American missionaries, however, joined their colleague, the medical missionary Henry Porter, in hailing the kaiser's retaliation for the murder of German Catholic missionaries in Shantung in 1897. Porter admired the swiftness with which the Germans had learned that the Chinese "as a whole are less trustworthy and less honorable than Westerners" and that they only respond to severe measures. "The German government deserves the admiration of all right minded men the world over," Porter declared. "At last there has appeared a providential hand to stay the marauding hand of irresponsible banditti." Germany's quick and decisive action was didactic for Americans, he pointed out, while the "immediate effect throughout Shantung Province is to strengthen every form of mission work." [61]

Most American missionaries made clear that they preferred to rely on the English, rather than the Japanese or Germans, to protect them and to pave the way for the evangelization of China. "Great Britain is especially the friend of the missionary as her power is felt by our Celestial brethren . . . for these people tolerate Christianity only because it is backed by standing armies and battleships. So far as we can see this is God's plan for us at present," wrote H. K. Shumaker. These missionaries also preferred that their own government join England in China, although by the end of the century they had given up hope that America would ever heed their pleas. Yet how Washington could sit idly by and witness "the cruelties of Satanic fiendishness on the part of the Chinese who slander, massacre and torture missionaries in Szechwan, Fukien and elsewhere" and still talk of diplomacy was unfathomable to them: "What is the diplomacy of our age good for if it is simply to smile and chatter over questions of etiquette while men and women are being put to the sword for righteousness' sake? What is the strong arm of Christian power worth among nations if it is to hang in flabby imbecility, while Turks and Kurds are slaughtering Armenian Christians and Chinese fanatics are holding high revelry over Christian blood . . . ? Let Christian public sentiment throughout England and America voice itself with no uncertain sound!"[62]

By 1899 there was also some missionary concern that the Anglo-

Saxon powers were too bogged down in South Africa and the Philippines to be able to heed the Lord's call in China. Under inept military leadership the British were besieged in Kimberly and Lady-smith. The Gordon Highlanders, to whom some missionaries liked to compare themselves as a spiritual counterpart, suffered a crushing defeat at Colenso. The initial American success against Aguinaldo proved illusory when the Filipino "insurrectos" began to launch a devastating guerrilla warfare. By the fall of 1899, practically the entire U.S. Army was in the Philippine archipelago as the war spread from Luzon to other islands. Ashmore, however, reminded his colleagues that the "Lord has other hammers in his forge," should the Chinese take advantage of England and America's temporary weakness and launch another wave of rioting against the missionaries. [63] Presumably these "hammers" were Germany, France, and Japan.

Between demands for armed retaliation during the final third of the nineteenth century, however, American missionaries also went through the usual soul-searching over the nature of the means being used to open China up for Christianity and the real motives of the British. European intervention in China was "wholly for selfish ends," Shumaker conceded. But it was equally "clear that as several of these powers extend their spheres of influence Christian missions are fostered and protected. How much rather we would stand supported by spiritual ideas ... [but] it appears that the hope of the rapid spread of evangelical effort is linked with the occupancy of heathendom by the Christian world-powers which despite their crimes, protect Christian missions." In similar fashion, Henry Blodget of the American Board attempted to answer the question as to whether force was ever to be used. "Certainly if employed, it should only be to put a stop to wrongs of a most manifest and flagrant manner," he pondered. But since Christianity was "the source of the greatest blessings to ... all nations, it is bound to use whatever influence it may to secure a favorable hearing for its message and to save it from being crushed out in its first beginnings by ignorance and prejudice." [64]

The editor of the *Chinese Recorder* insisted that no Westerner had "the right to force" Christianity or commerce on the Chinese, but only "a right to *offer* both." He made clear, however, that missionaries were not obliged to wait for a Chinese invitation to do so. "Did our Lord in His ministry wait for such invitations? Did His apostles?"

Another missionary editor wondered about the value of such bickering when it was clear that "the prompt and vigorous action of Great Britain" was the only "guarantee of safety" for American missionaries, and "China must learn at whatever cost, that treaty obligations are to be observed, and the citizens of other nations residing in her empire respected and protected."[65]

Like Bishop Boone earlier, some of the missionaries were concerned over possible dysfunctional characteristics that might accompany the use of force. While force opened China to the missionary, its use engendered a good deal of hatred for Christianity. Each military invasion "makes it more difficult to reach the individual," worried Shumaker, "but it makes it easier and more expeditious to herald the tidings to the millions yet in darkness."[66]

Apparently, few nineteenth-century American missionaries found it strange that Christ's glad tidings should be introduced to China by the skirl of pipes, the staccato message of Gatling guns, and the roar of Hotchkiss cannon. In fact, they liked to think of themselves in military metaphors, particularly British ones. "We are a company of God's army, and we fight against darkness and superstition, and like the Gordon Highlanders, we suffer defeat only to rally to win," explained a missionary in 1898. On another occasion American missionaries saw themselves as "the light brigade" at Balaklava, "closing the fight, and Confucius, Buddah and Lao-tsz shall surely go down before the Lord of Hosts." To yet another missionary, the "conquest of China" was "the storming of heathenism's Gibraltar," and he pleaded in the face of the Boxer setback to "Sound the advance!"[67]

THE BOXER CRISIS, 1900–1901

With the Boxer crisis, the sanguinary tone of American missionary cries for vengeance reached a new strident pitch. The final cable out of Peking before the siege from "a committee of American missionaries," which was blown up on the front page of the *New York World,* set the tone: *"Arouse the Christian World Immediately To Our Peril. Should This Arrive too Late, Avenge Us!"*[68]

Fortunately, many of the most vindictive statements and bellicose demands of the missionaries remained in private hands. After acknowledging widespread carnage by allied troops and concluding that "the Russians have fulfilled their dire reputation and the Germans have imperial authority for widespread destruction," Henry Porter praised the German soldiers as agents of God. Furious that American troops would not destroy Chinese cities, Porter protested: "It does not appear to any of us [missionaries] a matter of vengeance, but of simple justice that the punitive expedition should go to Pao Ting and destroy the city . . . I know of no one who is bloodthirsty, but there is a Mission for the army to do and if not done now it must be done later on. It is a source of great regret that Providence discards the United States in favor of the Germans. They will work out the plans of an overruling Providence, giving support to the right solution of the vast question now before China and the world." It is clear that, for Porter, the proper way of dealing with the Chinese was to burn, kill, and loot on such a scale as finally to get across the lesson that missionaries had been eager to teach China for so long. "Knowing Chinese methods as we do," Porter explained, "justice" should be quickly and summarily meted out to them by the military. There simply was no time for "civilian trials," and the effect would be destroyed by that slow-moving and discriminating process.[69]

Recognizing that this spirit seemed to be a far cry from that of the eponymic Nazarene, the Reverend D. Z. Sheffield explained that only "private revenge is unchristian." He suggested that a "more decidedly Christian" government in Washington would permit United States troops to be employed as were the Germans. "It is not bloodthirstiness in missionaries to desire to see further shedding of blood, but an understanding of Chinese character and conditions, and a realization that the policy of general forgiveness means the loss of many valuable native and foreign lives," Sheffield cautioned. Hence, to him, the calls for vengeance were justifiable on both theological and practical grounds.[70]

Given their absolute certainty of the righteousness of their position, some American missionaries were eager to get their views before the public. They readily granted interviews to correspondents and sent open letters to editors, lay and religious, and to the Associated Press, as well as copies of their petitions to Washington. Some of these public statements were so vindictive that they proved to be a source of embarrassment to their supporters and spokesmen in America.[71] An open letter from Martin chiding the Americans who were calling for "moderation and mercy in dealing with the Chinese" and arguing that "no punishment can be too severe" for "the murder of missionaries and innocent children" provoked unflattering headlines in San Francisco. Vindictive statements by two bishops returning from a tour of China evoked critical editorials. "It is worth any cost in money, it is worth any cost in bloodshed if we can make millions of Chinese true and intelligent Christians," one bishop had urged. "I would cut all the red tape in the world," he added, "and break all treaties ever made to place the armies of the United States in the fore, next to Great Britain." "These two bishops," the editor of San Francisco's *Call* countered with loathing, "make a sorry spectacle of the kind of Christianity that we seem to be exporting to Asia in carload lots."[72]

The same editor allocated most of his editorial page to answer Martin's letter. "Does he try to put himself in the place of China, overrun by foreigners, who enter a door opened by forgery [the French treaty of 1858] ... to attack the moral foundation of a nation whose system was ancient when other existing world religions were born?" the editor wondered. "How much slaughter" would balance Martin's "red ledger," he asked: "For every woman missionary sacrificed by the Boxers five hundred Chinese women have gone to torture and death. For every man ordained for martyrdom a thousand Chinese men have atoned with their lives. For every missionary child cut down in its innocence a hundred Chinese babies have been tossed and impaled on Cossack spears. For every missionary compound burned or sacked value a hundredfold has been looted in Tientsin and Peking. What more does the spirit of the Great Khan ask, through the body of President Martin of the New University of Peking?"[73]

In making their sentiments on the Chinese question known to the public, the missionaries had an incredibly bad sense of timing. Martin's letter followed the disclosure of mass murder, rape, and looting on the part of allied troops, particularly Russian and German soldiers. After screaming headlines had announced that the kaiser had ordered his troops "to give no quarter" in China, the *New York Sun* quoted an American missionary as saying, "the Germans have the right idea, punish the Chinese first and treat with them later." Even the correspondent felt it necessary to append an explanation: "Such a remark from a missionary might seem a bit surprising to persons away from Peking, but expresses the common sentiment here." A month later the Reverend W. S. Ament was again quoted as saying, "the soft hand of the Americans is not as good as the mailed fist of the Germans." He amplified his statement: "If you deal with the Chinese with a soft hand, they will take advantage of it."[74] This classic litany of the missionary on the Chinese national character and the necessity of force hit the streets of New York in 1900 on Christmas Eve, as carolers were no doubt proclaiming "Peace on Earth. Good will toward men."

More shocking than the timing or spirit of these statements was the revelation that Ament and his young assistant, the Reverend E. G. Tewksbury, had not been content to await the more slowly moving legal channels for vengeance and indemnification. Ament had cajoled American officers into permitting him to guide a squad of cavalry into the countryside in search of Boxers and their supporters. Since Ament was unfamiliar with this particular territory, the expedition got lost, and the villages they found were invariably deserted, the inhabitants having fled at the sight of foreign troops. But "Dr. Ament hustled around and kept the expedition from being a gloomy failure," the correspondent reported. That is, he "found houses which bore evidence of Boxer occupation and they were duly burned." Criticized by Ament for being "too lenient," Captain Forsythe, the unit's commander, later explained to his superiors that these "bloodthirsty" missionaries wanted him to shoot "suspected Boxers" on the spot "and burn down the towns in which they were harbored."[75]

The world of journalism was subsequently electrified by news that Ament, Tewksbury, and their native converts were looting Chinese palaces and extorting money from villages under the threat of sending in foreign troops. The *Springfield Republican* published a description by an American soldier of missionary families on the road loaded down with trunkfuls of loot. He claimed to have overheard a young girl in the caravan say to a friend, "Momma had to leave a lot of dresses and lace behind to make room for all the silk." Other reports described assaults on Chinese homes led by H. H. Lowrie and an English colleague, Georgina Smith of the London Missionary Society. Allegedly, the Tsung family was forced to rent a small house near their palace and to beseech Miss Smith to give them back their warmer clothes as winter approached. She accommodated the elderly, it was reported, but informed the sons that "when she recovered her lost clothes they would get theirs." Smith was also alleged to have used the Tsung palace as a collection point for Boxer suspects before delivering them to the British army for shooting. [76]

The *New York Herald* printed the testimony of an Englishman in Peking which shed doubt on Ament's claim that all the homes seized belonged to Boxer suspects. According to this report, Ament had also taken the opportunity to settle a few old scores in the process. On top of this, General Chaffee's report officially complained of a sliding missionary scale in their claims for indemnity, ranging from $17.50 per slain native Christian in one village to $350 for each dead convert in another. One Chinese citizen observed, according to the *New York Herald,* that "for a century to come Chinese converts will consider looting and vengeance Christian virtues."[77]

Such reports provoked the satiric pens of Mark Twain and Finley Peter Dunne into action, and the weapon of humor came crashing down on the missionary's already battered reputation. The "bald headed" missionary with "chin whiskers" from "Baraboo, Wisconsin" had been the butt of Dunne's humor before. Now "Mr. Dooley" described "the fine cillybration planned by th' mission'ries" when the relief columns got to Peking: "First day, 10 A.M., prayers be the allied mission'ries; 1 P.M., massacre iv the impress an' rile fam'ly; sicond day, 10 A.M., scatthren iv the remains iv former kings; 11 A.M., disecration iv graves gin'rally." The next few days were packed with such events as "burnin' iv Peking' and a "gran' pop'lar massacree." Dunne also pictured missionaries "fillin' packin' cases with th' undherwear iv th' Chinese imp'ror an' th' spoons iv th' impress. Th' air was filled with cries iv 'Hinnery, won't ye set on this trunk? I can't get th' lid down since ye put in that hateful idol.' " When Dooley worried about the future retaliation such behavior might provoke from the Chinese, he consoled himself with the observation: "Annyhow 'tis a good thing f'r us they aint Christyans an' haven't larned properly to sight a gun."[78]

While the missionary establishment wisely ignored Dunne, Judson Smith made the tactical error of attempting to justify the actions of Ament and Tewksbury in a rejoinder to Twain's sardonic piece on imperialism in the *North American Review,* despite the fact that only a small portion of Twain's article dealt with the missionary episode in Peking. Most of Twain's barbed wit was aimed at the atrocities committed by American soldiers in the Philippines and by the allied

troops in China. Not only did Smith's retort draw additional attention to Twain's damaging satire, underscoring his charges against the
two missionaries, but with his own words and quotations from
Ament's letters, Smith dug the missionary cause deeper into the mire
of un-Christian attitudes. Indeed, Twain's follow-up, "To My Missionary Critics," in the same journal proved to be more devastating
than his original commentary. It was less humorous and more like a
lawyer's brief, skillfully and systematically tearing apart the American Board's defense and using Smith's own admissions in that defense as damaging evidence against the entire missionary enterprise in
China.[79]

Ament himself was unable to retire quietly to lick his wounds
inflicted by Twain's pen. He insisted on granting the *Sun*'s correspondent an interview and rushed into print comments that should have
remained private, if not unsaid altogether. Abandoning any pretense
at objective journalism, the reporter was unable to conceal his own
contempt for Ament and the missionaries in China, reporting that he
found missionaries "vindictive and bloodthirsty in their desire for
vengeance." Ament did not disappoint him. He demanded "the
severe punishment of the law" for those Americans "who spread
rumors and falsehoods" about missionaries in China. As "Chairman
of the Committee on Confiscated Goods," he had worked directly
under Sir Claude MacDonald in administering the "loot auctions,"
Ament explained. A major portion of the money raised in this
fashion actually went to soldiers, and most of the goods sold were
not even looted but bought directly from allied soldiers or at even
lower prices from wealthy Chinese who were selling out for fear of
being looted. All this was "legitimate speculation," Ament insisted.[80]

In criticizing his government's conciliatory policy in China, Ament
once more repeated the standard refrain: "The Chinese do not
understand such leniency." Indeed, leniency had already encouraged
new riots since the Boxer trouble, he claimed. Missionaries understood "the situation and the Chinese," but by "expressing an opinion
. . . they are called vindictive and bloodthirsty . . . If there were any
moral obliquity of vision [in seizing houses and goods] . . . we fail to
discern it." But Ament must have suffered some doubts, because he
sounded one relativistic note that still rings strange in the mouth of
such a moral absolutist: "While believing that right is always right

and wrong is always wrong, yet there are many actions that are only relatively so."[81]

Editors in the United States had a field day with this interview, which was reported under such front-page headlines as "Man Whose Acts Furnished Testimony 'To the Person Sitting in Darkness' Defends His Conduct" and "Missionary Looter's Defense."[82] But still Ament could not be still, and on his return to the United States in May 1901, he granted more interviews until Judson Smith of the American Board finally silenced him. "Such words as 'seize' and 'take' in your explanations . . . give peculiar offense to certain sensitive consciences in this country," Smith cautioned. Ament seemed unaware that his last interview followed sensational headlines describing how some of the money he raised had gone into grain speculation and the purchase of expensive lands for future churches in Peking.[83] In the eyes of many editors, the missionary defense of looting in order to feed and shelter native Christian refugees was falling apart.

Whether the stories of looting and extortion were accurate or not, the sensational coverage they received in the nation's press was a fact. Possibly there was more malice than substance to these reports. Unquestionably, only a miniscule number of missionaries ever engaged in such activities. But rather than rest quietly on that plausible defense, missionary spokesmen were compelled to seek complete public vindication, and in this quest they only further stained their already tarnished image in the United States. The final apogee of arrogant self-righteousness was reached in an article by the celebrated missionary-author Gilbert Reid in *Forum* magazine, bearing the incredible title "The Ethics of Loot." Reid actually apologized for not having personally looted more. Loot was to Reid simply the spoils of war, and if the Chinese did not want to be looted, they should not have started the war. He made it clear that only white men could be entrusted with this delicate task, however, so the Indian troops serving Great Britain were not themselves permitted to loot in China, and English officers handled their share. Totally impervious to public opinion in the United States, Reid went on to describe how the "loot godowns and loot auctions . . . furnished popular relaxation" for Westerners after the trauma of the seige. He defended the German and French troops, although "their zeal may, perhaps, be excessive according to American ideas . . . and their punishments devoid of equitable discrimination," but such acts were justified by the conduct of the Chinese. Reid made it clear, a year after the uprising, that his need for vengeance was not yet satisfied. As negotiations dragged on "with defiance, disdain, callousness, and self compacency" marking every Chinese move, Reid questioned whether the sacking and burning of the entire city of Peking might not "have been the greatest good for the greatest number." In his most morally obtuse moment, Reid declared that "to confiscate the property of those who were enemies in war may be theoretically wrong, but precedent established the right." He concluded, "For those who have known the facts and have passed through a war of awful memory, the matter of loot is one of high ethics."[84]

The editor of the *Call* was flabbergasted by Reid's outrageous article. "It has long been apparent that what is called the 'missionary spirit' in its dealings with China has been anything but justice and Christian ethics, and the Western powers have taken their cue from its savage aggressions," the editor declared.[85] Reid seemed unprepared for the hostile reaction his article induced, but his reply to his many critics was wisely couched in generalities, avoiding any of the specifics that raised their ire. Missionaries, "especially British and Americans," were "the vanguard of Western civilization," and it was not "wrong to make converts in a country like China," even "if the outcome is to be trouble and perhaps war." In the middle of these banal *non sequiturs,* there was an implied apology for "German excesses," but looting was never mentioned.[86] Reid was more clever than Ament in bending with the criticism rather than standing up to it and thus providing his opponents with more damaging ammunition. At any rate, his original essay escaped being memorialized by Mark Twain's wit.

THE CELESTIAL DOMINO

Every crisis in nineteenth century China elicited from American missionaries the belief that the Chinese were incapable of understanding and responding to anything but force. Before 1870, however, their justification of British aggression reflected bitter despair over the lack of success in converting Chinese to Christianity in significant numbers. Having convinced themselves that the real barrier to China's conversion was political in nature, these missionaries were conditioned to expect dramatic results in the wake of each British and allied invasion. When success was not forthcoming, their euphoric expectations turned sour, and from this slough of angry disappointment they hailed the next armed attack as God's intervention to punish those tormentors who refused and mocked the gospel truth.

After 1870, however, the Protestant missionary movement in China was relatively more successful. Although almost 8000 converts in 1870 may seem small in terms of China's total population of more than 400 million, it represents twenty-two times the number of Protestant communicants in 1853. This ratio climbed dramatically over the next few decades, and there were close to 100,000 converts by the end of the century.[87] Cries of a "new era" were omnipresent in the missionary literature after 1870, and evidence that the tide had at last turned in China was ubiquitous. By injecting some statistical alchemy into the situation, missionaries convinced themselves that China's conversion was a mathematical certainty in the twentieth century. Antiforeign riots not only failed to shake their conviction that they stood on the threshold of evangelical success, but were even transformed into further proof of the imminence of victory. In such an optimistic mood, some missionaries accepted and even indiscreetly demanded one final temporal shove to move China over the glorious threshold into Christendom. Over and over again missionaries reassured their audiences that God could later correct the means used, as well as any attendant evils developed in the process, but first this pagan sloth had to be pushed into the Christian world.

These consistent justifications of, and frequent calls for, armed force must be understood in terms of an earlier "domino theory" about China that was operative in missionary thinking. China was the key to world-wide salvation. She was Satan's chief fortress, and the conversion of her huge population would topple pagan defenses elsewhere throughout the world and usher in the millennium. Scriptural warning that the devil's rout would involve turmoil and bloodshed made it that much easier to accept martyrdom as well as to convert the slaughter of countless thousands of "Satan's willing servants" by invading Western armies into actions divinely inspired and directed.

On another psychological level, the behavior of these missionaries in China offers a good illustrative case of the serious dangers involved in assuming a position of moral absolutism. History is strewn with examples of how morally indignant groups championing righteous truths have degenerated into a blind self-righteousness that obfuscated any distinctions between ends and means. Soviet slave-labor camps and the Orwellian rehabilitation programs on Chinese rice paddies are the products of other missionaries—ideological ones armed with secular truths pointing toward a *gens* community without injustice. On those occasions when the American sense of mission has deteriorated into an aggressive missionary impulse, we have carried out egregiously inhuman crimes, as against the peoples of the Philippine Islands seventy-five years ago and, more recently, against the Vietnamese in the name of freedom and social justice.[88]

Given the American penchant for a moralistic posture, particularly overseas, the missionary confusion between ends and means may also represent a cultural hazard. But whatever the explanation for the paradoxical justification of force in the name of the Prince of Peace offered by American missionaries to China in the last century, one thing is certain: Bishop Boone's anxiety in 1861 was, in retrospect, eminently perspicacious. It would indeed take some time for the missionary movement "to live it all down."[89] More than a century later, the term "missionary" still carries with it unpleasant connotations and imagery.

SHIRLEY STONE GARRETT

Why They Stayed: American Church Politics and Chinese Nationalism in the Twenties

It is at first easier to understand why several thousand American missionaries began to leave their posts in China late in 1926 than it is to see why they went back several months later. They left because there had been alarming antiforeign demonstrations in Szechwan, Yunnan, Kiangsi, Hunan, and elsewhere, and in March of 1927 several Westerners had to escape from Nanking under protective gunfire from American and British ships. With China erupting, it appeared safer for missionaries, safer for Chinese Christians, and more soothing to the nerves of American diplomats and admirals for missionaries to leave the interior for the haven of Shanghai or outside China.

The reasons that they were sent back were more obscure and complex. Some observers intimated that there had been no real need for them to leave in the first place, which they indignantly denied. The return also did not indicate that their mission boards never doubted China would resume its place as a missionary field, for there was great public controversy in the United States that mission boards could not ignore, and many people even within the evangelical churches loudly questioned whether China any longer wanted, needed, or deserved missionaries. In fact, the motivation for returning the missionaries to China was a complicated decision, reflecting not only the Chinese scene, but also denominational politics, financial necessities, and image making in the United States. The record suggests that by the late 1920s, sending the missionaries back was at least as necessary to the health of the churches in the United States as it was to the destinies of the churches in China. This imperative, unsuitable for public disclosure, had to be masked by more acceptable reasons. The search for such reasons led mission boards to formulate extravagant justifications about China and American responsibility, which left a deep imprint on American thought and feeling.

Such is the conclusion offered by a study of the two American denominations most prominent in China missionary work—the Methodist Episcopal Church, North, and the Presbyterian Church in the U.S.A. Their internal domestic problems in the 1920s suggest that the tenacious missionary bond to China originated not only in biblical mandates but also in bookkeeping ledgers and the emotions of American churchgoers.

THE METHODIST BOARD AND ITS PROBLEMS

Methodists were a commanding, though not the predominant, American denomination in the Chinese field. They were the largest single Protestant denomination in the United States, with some 4.7 million members, 25,000 churches, and 16,500 pastors. They were also a world-wide missionary organization, which had been in China since 1847. China was, except for India, the largest Methodist missionary field, accounting for one-third of the Methodist world force and four and a half million dollars (U.S.) in property. To support this enterprise, United States Methodists contributed about half a million dollars a year for missionary upkeep and work, to which sum was added the support of unmarried women missionaries pledged separately by the Women's Foreign Missionary Society.[1]

The administrative apparatus in the United States was crucial, since most of the money for China was raised in the United States. Major administrative decisions for the China missions were made by a Board of Foreign Missions located in New York, officially headed by a bishop but actually run by two corresponding secretaries and a staff that included an associate secretary for the Far East who had Asian missionary experience. This board had great powers. It set a budget for each country. It determined when and where buildings could be built or personnel allocated. It could establish a printing press or vote it out of existence, cut salaries, award furloughs, open schools or shut them. All mission funds were supposed to flow through its accounting ledgers. Thus, the philosophy and critical judgment of board members could and did affect the China program profoundly.

Although many of the board's judgments were shaped by the way in which it saw the local China situation, a key factor at home was money. In the financial sphere the board itself did not have complete autonomy but was part of an interlocking system, which lent credence to the Methodist belief that it was the most highly organized church body in the world outside of Roman Catholicism. To mediate among the many concerns competing for attention and funds, Methodists had created a World Service Commission as a central receiving and disbursing agency for foreign missions, home missions, the Epworth League for young people, the American Bible Society, the Temperance Society, and other special church responsibilities. Each year the World Service Commission set a quota for each board in order to ensure that fund raising did not become the kind of competitive solicitation that would pit an antirum group against a North China bishop, which was by no means an unknown circumstance. Enthusiasts sometimes solicited funds outside of regular channels, but this was frowned on. Total mission funds, therefore, depended to a large extent on World Service decisions, yet the totals for World Service were also somewhat affected by attitudes toward missions.

Apart from funds solicited from wealthy Methodists, which were not a large factor in the total picture, support came from collections in individual churches. Each year the World Service Commission allocated regional quotas, which were suballocated to districts and thence to individual churches. To raise this money, pastors were supposed to exhort their congregations through special prayer days, meetings, and other such events as their imaginations could conjure up. Although collections actually went into a pool, at their point of origin they could be specifically designated, with a children's Bible class, for example, contributing its pennies to Wuhu Hospital, a congregation taking on partial support of an Indian missionary family, or a Sunday school class mounting a campaign against liquor. What this procedure meant was that the fate of World Service, and within it the fate of China missions, depended not only on the state of the economy or of centralized decisions in New York, but also on whims, news headlines, and promotional techniques similar to those that surround any fund-raising campaign. The mechanics of World Service disbursement tended to protect each cause from severe fluctuation at any one time. But by the 1920s the entire Methodist money-raising operation was subject to factors that were beginning to affect all of their mission operations, including China.

One of these factors was the increasingly hazy notion of the purpose of foreign missions. By the mid-twenties American churchmen were still assuring the public that the United States was strongly religious, believing in God and attending church regularly.[2] Yet the former evangelical zeal for exporting Christianity had flagged, and among many Methodist leaders the new justifications for missions were vague. *The Story of Methodism,* for instance, a volume under preparation in 1925, defined as the duty of missions the task of representing God's love and righteousness among men.[3] The authors were Halford E. Luccock, an editor of the official Methodist organ *Christian Advocate,* and Paul Hutchinson, editor of *Christian Century*—both of whom were former members of the Board of Foreign Missions.

These were elusive concepts for churchgoers, the majority of whom had never seen a live missionary, and who gave their money mechanically to World Service collections or special drives. The concepts were elusive even for many pastors, who already had a staggering load of duties and obligations. Pastoral instructions adjured them to rise before dawn if possible, pray, visit the sick, preside over marriage and death, speak prudently to women, not cross their legs in public, and so on and on. Well down the list came the admonition to conduct vigorous mission campaigns. Devotion to invisible missionaries was an added burden to men who themselves were not always regularly paid, and rarely were adequately paid. It was little wonder that pastors were constantly being accused of apathy by missionary administrators and that many churchgoers were not systematically canvassed. The major exception was the women's groups, who were able to maintain a high level of enthusiasm within the emotional context of helping the women teachers and doctors whom they supported abroad. After a fashion, however, the collection procedures worked, and the constant accusation of lethargy was not always borne out by the figures. On the contrary, Methodists had by 1924 concluded such a burst of fund raising that they were suffering from a kind of battle fatigue that was affecting the entire missions field and was beginning to cast a shadow over China.

In the early 1920s an upsurge of internationalism and a vigorous promotional campaign had extracted huge sums of money from American Methodists celebrating the Centenary Campaign, which commemorated the first American mission to the Wyandotte Indians in 1819. Between 1918 and 1923 disbursements to foreign missions leaped from $2.1 million a year to $5.3 million, and 650 missionaries were sent abroad during the centenary program. But by 1924 the picture had abruptly changed, demonstrating that to get a pledge was easier than to get a check. In 1923 many people became so tired of giving that a growing percentage of earlier pledges were unfulfilled. Promotional expenses, such as a gigantic celebration in Columbus, Ohio, ran in the red, and a coincidental change in world exchange against the dollar raised the cost of overseas building and missionary maintenance. To meet its obligations, the board had to borrow from banks and other boards. Thus, by 1924 the Board of Foreign Missions found itself staring at a Himalayan structure known as the Centenary Debt, which it decided to start reducing immediately. The economizing entailed a sharp look at missionary costs everywhere. In 1924, Central China allocations were cut back 40 percent, and those in North China 35 percent, with other countries slashed even more sharply.[4] Within the United States, imposing churches continued to rise, and people continued to support their pet enterprises. But the mission boom was over, at least temporarily, and in 1925 the World Service Commission refused to authorize a special missionary appeal for Christmas.

It was therefore in an atmosphere of financial gloom and motivational confusion that the Methodist Board became aware of the outbreak of virulent nationalism in China. Beginning with the May Thirtieth Incident of 1925, events were reported in gloomy detail to the board by its own missionaries and administrators. These reports, despite occasional qualified admiration for the Nationalist movement, suggested that mission operations in China were moving into a time of jeopardy.

Some of the fears were generated by Frank Gamewell, who in 1925 was the board's associate secretary for the Far East, but before that had been a China missionary whose memory stretched back to the Boxer Rebellion. By chance, Gamewell and his wife (Uncle Frank and Aunt Mary, as they usually signed themselves) were in China just after the May Thirtieth uproar. On his return, Gamewell filed a pessimistic report cautioning against any new building or expansion. He even reported in strict confidence the remark of A. J. Bowen, president of Nanking University, that it might be time for missionaries to get out of China.[5] As subsequent correspondence indicated, Gamewell viewed with little joy the prospect of a revolutionary China. Because of his status as the board's Far Eastern expert, he was a key figure, able to play an important role in shaping board opinions in the ensuing months.

Other reports also came in from the three China bishops who administered Methodist affairs in the field. All three were American and were linked closely to the tight bureaucratic structure of the American Methodist organization. Two of them had arrived in China only the year before. Wallace Brown, assigned to the South China field with headquarters in Foochow, came from a series of pastorates, including a prominent one in Syracuse. An infrequent writer, Bishop Brown tended to produce missives of high spiritual tone that gave little practical indication of difficulties in the field but spoke to the moral sentiments of his readers. Bishop George Grose of North and West China, also a new arrival, had been president of De Pauw University. A prolific writer of articles and books, Grose displayed most markedly among his attributes a constant concern for financial soundness, which colored his whole picture of China missions. The senior bishop was Lauress Birney, who had been dean of the Boston University School of Theology for nine years before going to China in 1920. Birney's letters were less deanlike than they were military; he sounded as if he looked like Theodore Roosevelt, and was the kind of individual known in the clerical world as an "ordained general." Bishop Birney wrote frequently, at length, in declarative and exclamatory prose, on Chinese politics, student radicalism, fund raising, and the parlous state of American faith, despite the fact that he was often either recovering from pneumonia or coming down with tuberculosis. He seldom referred to God in his letters.

These men, especially Birney, were in constant touch with the New York Board, and their opinions bore weight because they were on the scene. From them emerged the picture of a China whose struggles to change were commendable, but which portended serious consequences for the mission movement. Bishop Brown was the least critical. The Nationalist movement, he explained to the New York Board, was not antiforeign; it was anti-injustice. Rights for China seemed to him to be inherent in the gospel, and he strongly urged Methodist support for abrogation of the unequal treaties. Birney, in contrast, was at first much more hostile. Markedly pro-British and anti-Soviet, he was by mid-1925 already shaping a picture of China manipulated by a Communist conspiracy. "I look straight across—at the red flag over Soviet headquarters," he wrote from his Shanghai office. "From that building . . . has emanated the chief trouble." Furthermore, the students before whom the city fathers had capitulated were "a bunch of youngsters who ought to be . . . spanked and sent back to school"[6] Nevertheless, the bishop came to feel that, despite all the undesirable features of nationalism, it represented the coming to maturity of a people, although his early suspicions still colored his later thinking.

The events of 1925 left the three bishops cautious rather than deeply perturbed. At a Shanghai bishops' meeting in September 1925, they formally recommended to the board that there should be no reduction in the missionary staff but great restraint in sending out new missionaries, that there should be no expansion in building, and that considerable care should be exercised in giving money directly to the Chinese.[7] Thus, the top administrators in China urged caution and possible retrenchment on the board in America.

At the end of 1925 the Methodist Board was therefore keenly aware from its own men on the scene that Chinese nationalism would present problems. This knowledge did not prod it into precipitate action, for, despite the kind of pessimistic remarks made by such men as Bowen, Gamewell assured the bishops that the board was not considering leaving the China field, especially as antiforeign demonstrations began to ease. Yet the financial squeeze at home combined with the China news to restrict expenditures. After a board meeting in the fall, Gamewell wrote the bishops that the board was as reluctant to continue large responsibilities in China as were the bishops to urge them. They must face up to facts, he wrote: "We cannot evangelize China, we cannot cure China's multiplied diseases, we cannot educate her multiplied millions or feed them. That is to say, there is a limit no matter how far we go to what we can do."

Since the Methodist Church clearly did not intend to meet the pledges made during the centenary campaign, the only thing to do was cut costs. But these observations were made in confidence. "I say none of these things at large," he ended.[8]

The disparity between Gamewell's private and public opinions was reflected in official reports. As 1925 came to an end, the board managed to convey in its annual report the news that things were both dreadful and promising in China. Since the report could not simply ignore news from the field, the China section contained excerpts from missionary letters that were both specific and unnerving, alleging the bayoneting of Bibles and abuse of missionary women. At the same time the report praised the new nationalist spirit and reaffirmed the board's belief that missions would have a place in the new China. There was much talk about high faith, optimism, and purification of the Christian movement in the face of adversity.[9]

At home, the general indifference to missions rather than the reaction to Chinese events remained the chief worry of fund raisers. The board was nevertheless anxious to avoid negative news from any source. Bad news from China might conceivably affect general finances, for many missionaries were now reported as saying that they ought to pull out completely from any country where the nationals were hostile.[10] Anxious to prevent pessimistic comments from spreading, the board decided to restrict distribution of the more exotic or outspoken letters that came through its office for dissemination to churches or the press. On March 11, 1926, a Miss L. Romer, charged with distributing missionary mail to supporting churches, noted her instructions to refer to Frank Gamewell all letters from China that were of a political nature. Romer recorded Gamewell's conviction that strictures on Chinese officials and the government should be removed from letters. The editors also scrutinized missionary mail for references to antiforeign, anti-Christian, or antimissionary controls, for though they knew the missionaries resented having the board hold back their letters, they did not want church members to get the impression that the time was coming when missionaries would no longer be needed in China. In May an outspoken letter from even so high a personage as President Bowen of Nanking University was held back for Gamewell's editing.[11]

This was a minor effort at news management, but it reflected the board's growing effort to fashion a favorable image at home to help its fund raisers. To stimulate interest in all World Service giving, the board enlisted the services of Bishops Brown and Grose as speakers when they were in the United States for regular home conferences. While Bishop Birney fretted in Colorado convalescing from pneumonia, the two other bishops moved busily about the country making literally hundreds of speeches for World Service, and sometimes a little clandestinely directly for China missions. The speeches, however, generated more cordiality than money. By the autumn of 1926 a prospective decrease in total collections threatened another cut for China, which was averted only at the last moment. The sagging collections were not yet attributed to the news from China, which was only one part of the vast World Service machinery.

MEETING THE CHINA CRISIS

Under the shadow of financial anxiety, the three bishops returned to a China where the cauldron of nationalism was reaching a boil. The Northern Expedition was moving through the Yangtze Valley. In September, fighting began in Kiangsi, then Fukien, then Chekiang. In December the Nationalists took Hankow, and in January mob violence broke out in Foochow. In the West, all Americans beyond Chungking were advised by their consul to leave. In March, Dr. John Williams of Nanking University was shot dead by a Nationalist soldier and Nanking was shelled by British and American gunboats. As the threat of physical violence increased, so did the pressures of Nationalist demands. Chief among these was the increasing insistence in Peking as well as in Nationalist-held provinces that Christian schools should register officially, abandon compulsory religious services or education, and install Chinese administrators and trustees. Even within the church, Chinese Christians were demanding a larger measure of control. How to handle these problems in China and how to explain them in the United States was a delicate question. Thus, the chief New York Board executive, Corresponding Secretary Ralph Diffendorfer, who had never been to China, scheduled a trip to assess the situation in person—a step also being taken by many other foreign mission heads. Diffendorfer reached Manila in March 1927, in time to hear a garbled account of the Nanking affair from a group of demoralized missionaries.

In the meantime the New York office was bombarded by reports from Grose and Birney. From Grose came gloomy accounts of the situation in both Peking and West China. With the Peking government melting away, Grose saw no firm protection for foreigners anywhere in China. On a field trip to the West, he found that in Chengtu foreign women were not safe on the streets, students were demonstrating, and the local warlord was running his army with Russian money. By autumn, the British were pulling out their missionaries. Except for his advice to keep all funds out of Chinese hands, Grose was agreeable to coming to terms with nationalism, which he feared less than disorder. His North China Conference had already agreed to register all secondary schools, and he worked to calm fears about Chinese demands for control or for the exclusion of missionaries. Even though he "did not presume" to advise that gunboats should be withdrawn at this time, he declared that gunboats did more harm than good for missionaries, whose only real weapon was the good will of the Chinese. Optimistic until the last moment, Grose did not tell his missionaries in the West to withdraw until urgent advice was sent by Consul Adams. By March 1, however, they had fled, many with only their clothes left to them. Even then, despite his insistence that the withdrawal was necessary, Grose maintained a long-range optimism about their return.[12]

From Birney, geographically closer to the Nationalist advance, came letters more concerned with political analysis and considerably more agitated. Although the bishop was not incapable of changing his mind, he held on to most opinions with a grip of iron. He had a passion for the clear-cut, which led him to see the Chinese scene in terms of good and bad, heroes and villains. The main criterion by which he tested events was their meaning for the missionary movement. These traits of personality and judgment swiftly led him to identify General Chiang Kai-shek as Protector of the Faith.

Before returning to China in November 1926, Birney had become wholly converted to the "southern" cause and to a belief that the Nationalist revolution was necessary for China, terming it a struggle between military feudalism and real democracy. Letters he received in Yokohama en route to Shanghai reinforced this opinion, with their accounts of an occupation of Nanchang in which a well-behaved, idealistic Nationalist army refrained from looting and harmed no missionaries. Their Bolshevism, he heard, was greatly modified, and he assured the board that the best thing for China would be the

South's complete victory. This did not mean that Birney approved of the immediate end of the treaty system or wanted to turn the church over to Chinese control; those matters rested in other compartments of his mind. His assurances did mean, however, that he was taking a semiofficial stand of approval toward the Kuomintang.[13]

A month later, while on a swing up river to Nanking and Nanchang, Birney began to realize that the left and right wings of the movement varied greatly. On his journey he received word of violent anti-Christian demonstrations in Changsha and of Russian influence with the Left. Convinced that a victory of the Left would spell the doom of missionary work, Birney thereafter vilified Hankow and its apologists in China or the United States.[14]

To use Birney's phrase, the good in the Nationalist movement still resided in "the real Kuomintang," a group that came to be symbolized for him by General Chiang. The love affair with Chiang was composed of several ingredients. Chiang assured Birney that no radical interference with missionary work or schools was on his mind. Chiang clearly recognized that the whole Nationalist movement might be ruined by Moscow. Chiang was willing to deal reasonably with Birney's favorite foreign country, Britain. Chiang had guaranteed Kiangsi missionaries complete safety. Chiang had ordered posted in leading cities a proclamation that all mission properties occupied by soldiers should be vacated at once, whereupon William Nast College had been evacuated. In Birney's reports of the situation appeared many adjectives characterizing the right wing of the Kuomintang as "right and reasonable," and their general himself as "really great," "fair," and "opposed to extremists." Even when Chiang produced a pamphlet indicating that the right or reasonable Kuomintang would regulate foreign activities rigorously when it took control, Birney insisted that with Chiang's victory, and only with his victory, could missionary work continue in its essentials. "These are really great days for China if the right wing of the movement can control the situation," he wrote in March, and someone, probably Gamewell, underlined the sentence for quotation.[15]

Guarantees notwithstanding, the wave of violence was also beginning to wash over Birney's area of responsibility in Central China. As reluctant as Grose to move missionaries, he had by February brought only mothers and children out of Kiangsi. But missionaries from the West were pouring into Shanghai, Brown's Fukien contingent had left, mostly for Manila, and by March 1927 Westerners were leaving Nanking in advance of its expected fall. Kiangsi Methodists were packed and ready to go. At the request of Bishops Grose and Brown, Birney prepared an article for distribution to the American churches insisting that the withdrawal of missionaries was only a precaution and that the situation was not as serious as it looked. Even a casual reader, however, could tell a retreat from an advance. Notably, Birney did not emulate his colleague Bishop Grose by scoffing at the need for gunboats.

While the missionaries were scurrying to safety, there was little the New York Board could do but wait for news. This was forthcoming not only from the China bishops but from many other sources, who explained China events in so varied a way as to add confusion to an already bewildering situation. The National Christian Council sent a group of speakers, including several American missionaries and T. Z. Koo of the Chinese YMCA, to explain the Nationalist revolution to congregations around the country. The *New York Times* printed daily bulletins that grew longer and ever more colorful. Board members and their fellow Methodists read *Christian Century* and the official Methodist journal, *The Christian Advocate*. Methodists consulted with Presbyterians and Baptists; the State Department was in constant touch. Board members in search of clarification found themselves in a crossfire of contradictory interpretation.

The source that managed to irritate or frighten almost everyone was the *New York Times*. Certainly the newspaper's reportage did nothing to calm apprehensions, for it gave considerable coverage to China events, including the tumultuous welcome for Michael Borodin in Hankow, the general strikes, the capture of Ichang, the Japanese move into Foochow, and the liberation of British missionaries at Sianfu. Headlines announced: "Reds Threaten an Attack on Foreigners," "All China in Ferment," "Peril in Foochow," "Semi-Bolshevization of Colleges in Shanghai," and "Official Reports Describe Necessity for Joint Foreign Action."

The *Times* also began to question the future place of missionaries in China. In December 1926 an editorial, otherwise kind and flattering, pointed out that China no longer seemed eager to welcome missionaries and questioned whether Americans would continue to finance the missionary enterprise if its supervision passed into Chinese hands. News dispatches throughout the winter further recorded

Chinese hostility by reporting the takeover of missionary colleges and the flight of missionaries from the interior. Later issues printed comments criticizing missionaries for leaving, including remarks by James Franklin, an observer for the Northern Baptist Conference, who pointed out that Catholics had not left.[16] By emphasizing Chinese violence but questioning missionary withdrawal, the *Times* managed to annoy conservative and liberal alike. It was soon evident that its reports were having a widespread effect.

Differences of opinion also generated wild controversy in the religious press, with conservative Methodists particularly infuriated by the loudly pro-Nationalist *Christian Century* and its Methodist editor Paul Hutchinson. The *Christian Century* took the stand that Nationalist demands were reasonable, especially those requiring that foreigners give up their treaty enclaves. The journal agreed that the movement was anti-Christian, but found it not hopelessly so. News from China claiming that the movement spelled doom to Christianity in that country was largely from "biased sources," a phrase sometimes replaced by the words "nerve-wracked Methodist bishop," both meaning Birney. The *Century* printed a long article by Koo asserting that China was not Communist and neither was the student movement. In February the journal proclaimed that China had made headway because she had learned to talk with guns, but conversely it attacked mission boards violently for refusing to repudiate force by the West in unequivocal terms.[17] Such talk elicited from Birney adjectives such as "vicious," but as John Edwards later wrote, many Methodist preachers throughout the country read and accepted the views of the *Christian Century,* and its influence could not be ignored.[18]

As a partial offset to *Christian Century* views, the *Christian Advocate* stressed the positive aspects of mission work and the desire by Chinese Christians to have that work continue. Even the *Advocate,* however, expressed sympathy with Nationalist demands and declared that a new type of missionary movement would have to arise in response to a changing China.

With such opinions issuing from the press, by March there was, according to Secretary John Edwards, an undercurrent of questioning as to whether the work for the Far East was worthwhile. The board, he wrote Birney, was trying to relieve the home church from a measure of misinformation that came through the secular press.

Board members were holding conferences, giving public addresses, and sending messages and bulletins to local church papers to keep the home church sympathetic with China's problems. One such message appeared in the *Advocate* of March 10. Headed "China: A Pledge of Loyalty" and signed by the recording secretary of the Women's Foreign Missionary Service, Jennie Brown Spaeth, it asked, "Do we withhold help for our country, our church and our children when they are in trouble?" and pledged that every dollar for support would be paid. The Board of Foreign Missions further distributed to every bishop, superintendent, and pastor a copy of a message called "Have Faith in China," which had appeared in the *Advocate* and the *Christian Century*. Missionaries were not fleeing, stated the message, and missions were not dead in China. Some Nationalist leaders had an anti-Christian bias, but there was no attempt to wipe out Christianity, and no missionary had left because of Chinese opposition to Christianity. Indeed, Bishop Brown called the Nationalist movement "anti-unchristian." Although Soviet influence was "uncomfortable here and there," it was temporary. The statement concluded that the Nationalist movement presented a great opportunity for missionaries and begged the church not to abandon them.[19]

These views represented a bland homogenization of opinion. Frank Gamewell did not believe for a moment that Soviet influence in China was minimal. Indeed, he had suggested to the former head of the Chinese YMCA, Fletcher Brockman, that Brockman ask Koo to guard against underestimating the influence of Communism in his speeches and articles. Bishop Brown was already becoming convinced that the movement was poisoned by Moscow. Edwards' own later correspondence indicated his general agreement with the Birney-Gamewell interpretation of events.[20] These anxieties were buried in the attempt to calm growing apprehension about China, for the same fears that haunted the board and the media were reflected church-wide.

But it was too late, for on March 24, the same day that "Have Faith in China" appeared in the *Christian Century*, Dr. Williams was killed and American and British gunboats shelled Nanking so that Westerners could escape from the city. Mission property was looted and Chinese Christians molested. Bishop Birney joined other mission heads in sending a cable to the State Department urging that Americans cooperate with the British in using force if necessary to restore order. In public and private the uproar mounted, assigning blame and assessing the future.

On the question of whether force had been necessary, comments ran true to form. "I stand by that cablegram," wrote Birney to Gamewell. The bishop felt that without the gunboats there would have been more trouble in Nanking and a massacre in Shanghai. Gamewell, as a veteran of mob uprising in China, agreed, believing that the gunboats should stay until China could offer protection to foreigners. Bishop Grose, however, wrote a strongly worded article for the *Christian Advocate* in which he deplored the use of gunboats. The *Christian Century* hotly denied that force had been needed at Nanking, and the *Advocate,* pinned between pro-Nationalist convictions and the need to present all sides of Methodist opinion, at one moment regretted that force had been used and at another denied that the shelling of Nanking had been like bombarding a defenseless city. Each point of view had its supporters. Methodist clergymen and many of their constituents agreed with *Christian Century* opinion, but many also were convinced that gunboats had been needed and would still be needed in the future. In Detroit one group of Congregational ministers attempted to get a petition against gunboat use and were rebuffed by church laymen.[21] Thus, China appeared kind and mistreated to some, hostile and untrustworthy to others.

The question as to whether missionaries should have left was also passionately argued. The *Christian Century* scoffed at their flight indirectly by singling out the missionaries who had stayed at their posts as "a Glorious Few." The statement rendered Birney apopleptic. What would Paul Hutchinson of the *Century* have had Nanking missionaries do when they were being robbed, stripped, shot, driven with the bayonet, and beaten like common criminals? In less scorching language Grose strongly defended his own withdrawals, declaring that consular requests had left him no choice.[22] The *Advocate* itself did not speak critically of missionary departures. The general implication that missionaries had behaved unlike Christian heroes, however, hovered in the air, an unspoken liability in a $75,000 emergency campaign launched in the *Advocate* to meet missionary losses.

The really compelling problem, though, was what to do now. The wounds that the missionary organism in China had sustained over two years seemed so deep that perhaps it might not survive. Should the missionaries go back? In the weeks and months following the

Nanking incident, no clear "yes" emanated from official Methodist sources or from the media. Instead, responses ranged from "not yet," to "not unless," to "maybe not at all."

Both publicly and privately Bishops Birney and Grose spoke of the withdrawal as temporary, and the *Advocate* printed their statement that the pullout had only been a short-term expedient to avoid any possible source of friction with the Chinese.[23] Birney soon wrote, however, that it might be two or three years before many of his people could go back, and Grose advised those of his missionaries going to the United States to look for jobs. In the summer of 1927 the "not just yet" appeared to be stretching out.

Christian Century writers saw no hope for the continuation of missions unless American mission boards relinquished paternalistic control and government protection. Missionaries should not go back, argued the *Century,* unless mission boards renounced the use of force and unless the boards turned over control of property and schools to the Chinese without delay. These conditions were tantamount to a long delay, for the boards in the United States showed no signs of hastening to meet Nationalist conditions. On the use of gunboats in the future, they maintained a silence that the *Century* considered disastrous.

The bluntest and most startling statement came from Ralph Diffendorfer. Shaken by what he had seen and heard in China, Diffendorfer prepared a none too optimistic report for the board. "We raise very definitely for consideration of the Board," he wrote, "not returning any missionaries yet and possibly withdrawing those there. This is aside from safety of life and property." He advised the board not to be influenced by the pleas for missionary return being made by Chinese who were financially dependent on them. To have the top executive of the board state the problem so baldly signified a deep doubt within Methodist circles. The doubt was reflected in progressively gloomier items appearing in the *Advocate*. A May editorial entitled "The Rebirth of the Missionary Spirit" declared that out of the turmoil in China "must and will be reawakened missionary passions, which is the very soul of Christianity." Two separate issues lauded a new book by George Grose, *The New Soul of China,* in which the bishop defended the need for missionaries with phrases such as: "Why missionaries in China? There are not many answers, only one: Christ, Christ, Christ." But the atmosphere grew somber,

and in the middle of June the *Advocate* noted that whether missionaries could go back or when, time alone would decide.[24] In the
meantime, the China Emergency Fund was failing dismally despite a
special day set aside for collections in the churches. It appeared that
the Methodists did not really care what happened.

Yet the implications of jettisoning the missionary movement in
China were enormous. Concern was voiced over what would happen
to Chinese Christianity if the Methodists from America left. From
Western observers of many denominations came the reassurance that
it would survive. The Baptist James Franklin, Ralph Diffendorfer,
and others had remarked admiringly on the way in which Chinese
Christians had kept the churches open and displayed heroic calm and
dignity in trying times.[25] Yet there remained an undercurrent of
belief that somehow Western missionaries still had a special contribution to make. In March, Harry Emerson Fosdick preached a sermon
at the Park Avenue Baptist Church declaring that the United States
had sent China its worst and should therefore send its best.[26]
Bishops Grose and Brown found China reeking with sin and superstition, in constant need of a missionary message.[27] Whether the gift
was to be evangelical or more broadly cultural, the intensely American feeling persisted that the missionaries had a gift to give China.
Even when the *Christian Century* began to question that gift, it did
so with an anguish of disbelief.

Less spiritual but nevertheless important was the question of what
would happen to all the property. Grose had made it clear ever since
his arrival in China that he did not trust the Chinese to administer
funds, and he had many supporters. Birney violently opposed transfer of church property in China except to a nation-wide group of
"responsible men," and protested any transfer at all of upper
schools, his reason being that local governments would tax property
too heavily.[28] If no missionaries were left, there would be no one
who could safely and efficiently administer a multimillion-dollar
enterprise. As for the schools, Chinese Christians would find it
difficult to keep them from becoming completely secular. The transfer of control was a tangled subject.

Equally tangled was the question of what effect a permanent
missionary withdrawal would have in the United States. It is startling
to find that the Methodists, but not they alone, were afraid to bring
missionaries back to the United States en masse. After an interde-

nominational meeting early in April, Gamewell confided to Birney that the Presbyterian Board had simply refused to bring back over four hundred displaced missionaries even though the China Board requested it. It was impossible, said the Presbyterians, to entertain the proposition of bringing home such a horde of people with varied messages and conflicting statements. Birney too expected that many of his people would go home for a while, but late in April Gamewell wrote him that Methodists should be cautious about using the returning men for cultivation of funds. On the one hand, there were men like President Bowen who with their tales of outrage were arousing anger against China. Although Gamewell agreed with many of their interpretations, they were certainly not goodwill ambassadors for the Chinese. On the other hand, there was the opposing contingent represented by such men as Paul Hutchinson and the missionary James Yard, who Gamewell and Birney felt would do anything to curry goodwill with the Chinese but who did it by sharply criticizing missionaries. Students speaking in churches were already doing so, and the influence of their critical statements, Gamewell wrote in May, would be disastrous.[29] Evidently, therefore, either an unworthy China or an unworthy missionary body could be equally damaging to public opinion.

A further fear was that the shock waves might spread not only to emergency relief or other China fund-raising but to a much larger area. No one said so explicitly or all at once, but to bring missionaries home, whether the fault was China's or theirs, would be to admit tacitly that the mission movement—not just in China but the whole mission movement—might be a mistake, a sentimental farce, a failure. For nowhere had the Methodists tried harder than in China. Nowhere had more labored, sacrificed, and died. Nowhere had they spent more money. How deeply the China news had offended church sensibilities became clear in the fall.

In October 1927, Ralph Diffendorfer remarked that in his many public appearances he had found a feeling throughout America that foreign missions were done with, the Christian movement in China had been a failure, and Methodists had wasted a lot of money. It was a dangerous omen, indicating that bad news from China was now bad news for missions as a whole. Even worse was the Grose affair. In George Grose's new book he had inserted a brief sentence criticizing what he considered the lavish overbuilding of schools in China beyond the Chinese ability to maintain them—the property lust, he termed it privately. A horrendous clamor went up, and Edwards and Gamewell both found that the statement had caused great harm, for many people had seized on it as an argument for withholding funds. Gamewell wrote Grose that probably no single thing had done greater damage to the cause of missions than the Grose assertion. The *Advocate* declared that certainly if any further argument were needed to discourage gifts to World Service, it was being provided by such statements from the field.[30] The tail was now wagging the dog. To protect World Service as a whole, they could not admit that China was lost, nor that the missionary operation had had drawbacks.

Such considerations prompted the board to discard the thought of pulling out. In November, Gamewell assured Birney that there was no thought of dismantling the operation, and the machinery for sending missionaries back to their posts began to move.[31]

The problem remained, however, to make the Chinese situation workable in China and palatable in the United States. The Diffendorfer Report tried to pass the burden on to the Chinese by calling for a statesmanlike document from them that would demonstrate Chinese leadership and also restimulate American interest. At Diffendorfer's suggestion the board recommended that an all-China conference be held in January, so that it could discuss issues arising from the Nationalist movement. In the meantime, there was work to be done at home to create a more favorable sentiment.

It was not really a coordinated public relations campaign that unrolled following the Nanking matter, planned to the last detail and emanating from a single source. Instead, the attempt to justify Chinese missions emerged from many sources as a wistful expression of deep emotion. There were many people who wanted China missions to have a reason to survive. The *Christian Century,* rail though it might against mission policies, applauded President Coolidge's declaration that missions were America's foremost interest in China. Gamewell had invested his life in China mission work. Birney and Grose felt deep humanitarian responsibility besides their evangelical convictions. Without prompting, they and others could be counted on to find virtues in a continuing effort. Thus, Dr. Williams' widow expressed her continuing faith in China if the right wing under Chiang should prevail.[32] Madame Sun Yat-sen stated that her faith in the Nationalist movement sprang from her Christianity, and the Kuomintang, wrote Stanley High, might be the agency to speed those tasks in China to which the Christian church was committed.[33]

Far from relying on occasional champions, however, the board and its colleagues concentrated on a few themes that might help the missionary cause. Many of these had been outlined by Birney a month after the Nanking affair. The effort to raise the morale of the church, Birney wrote John Edwards, needed to be Herculean. One absolutely necessary point to make was that the cause of things like the Nanking incident was Moscow. The board should stress that the China involved in the incident was not the real China at all. The real China was the group which opposed Moscow, that is, the right wing and Chiang. To these appeals Birney added one more: the heroic character of the Chinese church under the strain of these trying days.[34] Thus, in microcosm the bishop created what was to become the general approach of the board in the months ahead. The troubles in China had happened not in China at all but in a never-never land, a crypto-Russia. The real China was waiting to rise from the ashes under the leadership of a noble and pro-Christian general. The Chinese Christians were valiant heroes who could not be deserted.

These themes began to appear in press releases and speeches, some stressing Communist responsibility and others the heroism of Chinese Christians. A prize bit of Birney's prose appearing in the *Christian Advocate* in June illustrates the first. It read in part: "None dreamed that agents of Hankow's abysmal communistic darkness were inspiring units of that victorious army to deeds of brutality and loathsome indecency against that noble company of God's choicest souls." He ended this declaration with "pray for Chiang Kai-shek, chief hope of China's political redemption."[35]

The board used the Communist theme until the end of January 1928, when the apparent eclipse of the left wing decided Diffendorfer that there was no further need to stress Communist influence. Diffendorfer himself preferred to emphasize the heroism of Chinese Christians by using a fund-raising speech entitled "The Imperishable Message," devoted entirely to China. In it he declared that the spirit of Christianity lived in the hearts of Chinese Christians, hoping thus to prove that the mission movement had implanted permanent growth. In December he wrote the China bishops a long and significant letter. Not only Methodists, he stated, but all the mission boards had been staking their appeals for China on the heroism, devotion, stability, and ability of Chinese Christians in the present crisis. And a month later: "We've been basing our appeals on the evidence of Christlike spirit in the lives of Chinese—confident that this is still the best basis of appeal at this time." A thoroughgoing campaign of speeches and mailings to the churches carried these appeals. Diffendorfer also secured the speaking services of several attractive Chinese Christians, among them James Yen, William Hung, James Ding and his wife, and S. K. Hsu. After a few months of intensive speaking they were described as having worked "wonders" in helping to change American attitudes.[36]

Thus, the Methodists fashioned their new image of China, a country which, if free of the Communist scourge, would be devoted to moral ideals under a great leader and peopled by Christian saints. American Christianity had worked this miracle, and American Christianity could not now abandon responsibility.

Churchgoers would swallow only a limited amount of these tales, and the campaign was only a partial success. During the greater part of 1928 the board income continued to decline, owing to the feeling against continuing support for missionaries in a country where missionaries were not wanted.[37] In 1928 a windfall to World Service as a whole provided some relief, but in 1929 the mission receipts showed a decline of more than 20 percent from the corresponding months of 1928. China was responsible. In the minds of many people, wrote an associate secretary, in New York, Ernest Tuck, self-government and self-determination were inevitably linked with self-support.[38] Thus, China funds were slowly whittled down, and with the onset of the depression, great cuts occurred in all mission fields.

With the erosion of the China field, the men who had worked to preserve it also faded from the scene. In 1928 Bishop Brown returned home; in 1929 Grose, sick from bronchitis and complications, followed him. In the same year Birney developed tuberculosis and retreated to Switzerland to recover. Gamewell went back to China, where he was not happy at the changes that Chinese control were bringing about. A new administration faced the future of China missions with determination but now with increasing humility.

The China enterprise had continued to survive for many reasons related more to the American than to the Chinese scene. Conservatives and liberals alike had been averse to questioning the meaning of missionary work, which was the church version of foreign aid. To do so would have encouraged an admission of shrinking influence that was no easier for a church to face than for a state, and maybe harder. If Christianity was not a universal religion, its role in China was unclear. To prevent these questions from surfacing, the board had provided a rationale proving that the Christian message brought by missionaries had worked after all. The power of that message had transformed China into a special place with special people and a special relationship to Methodist affections. After such great efforts, no one could accuse the Methodists of infidelity. If the love affair should ever end, the fault would be someone else's.

THE PRESBYTERIANS: A COMPARISON

To generalize from the experience of the debt-ridden Methodists would be foolhardy without investigating other church groups. The Presbyterian experience is particularly interesting because Presbyterian support of China missions held steady throughout the late twenties. It was not just because they were solvent, nor that they had a greater faith in China. With Presbyterians, as with Methodists, domestic considerations played an important, perhaps decisive role in determining the fate of the China operation. In this case the determinant was theology rather than money, but in many ways the resultant rhetoric was the same.

Presbyterians as a whole seem to have paid little attention to the growing China crisis in the mid-twenties, despite the size of their operation. The Presbyterian Church in the U.S.A. was even more involved in China missions than were the Methodists, if comparative spending is an indication. Although well under half the size of the northern Methodists in the United States, the Presbyterian worldwide mission enterprise employed as many people and in the late twenties collected twice as much money. China accounted for one-third of all Presbyterian Western mission personnel, with some 537 missionaries in Hunan, Kiangsi, Yunnan, and the coastal provinces, supported by a million-dollar budget.[39] Administration was vested in a Board of Foreign Missions in New York, headed by the eminent Robert Speer, and in China by a China Council.

Generally there was an external similarity between the Methodist and Presbyterian response to the China situation. By the fall of 1926 Robert Speer had become enough concerned about China to head a mission that included the Reverend Hugh Thomson Kerr, publisher of the journal *The Presbyterian Banner,* and Mrs. Charles K. Roys, a board member. Kerr filed weekly articles, which grew more serious in tone as time passed, and the *Banner* also began to run a good deal of straight news about the China problem. In 1927, Presbyterians began to pull their missionaries out of potentially dangerous areas into Shanghai and then out of the country. The Presbyterians also had their Birney in the shape of Charles Patton, head of the China Council, who joined Birney in the telegram appealing to the American government for protection, and who was equally angry at Koo and the *Christian Century.* Like the Methodists, Speer and his mission also went to work preparing a lengthy evaluation on transfer of property to Chinese, school registration, and church control. These problems were common to all denominations.

THE THREAT TO UNITY

The China news was, however, a nuance rather than the main theme, for another problem was occupying the church's central attention. Throughout the 1920s the fundamentalist-modernist controversy had been raging steadily, and in 1927 there were still fears that it would split the Presbyterians apart. While the Methodists had their own fundamentalists, there was no real threat of schism in the denomination after the basic split between North and South in the Civil War. The primary targets of the Methodists were Roman Catholics and rum rather than each other. With Presbyterians, however, a serious theological and ecclesiastical tug of war had long been going on over such matters as the inerrancy of the Bible, the Virgin Birth, and the relative contributions of other religions. In 1922, Harry Emerson Fosdick, technically a Baptist, had created an uproar by inveighing against fundamentalism in a Presbyterian pulpit. Partly as a result of the Fosdick affair, an extreme conservative was elected moderator of the General Assembly in 1924. In 1925 extreme conservatives tried to get the assembly to throw out the entire presbytery of New York for disloyalty. Yet when an ultraconservative theologian, Dr. J. Gresham Machen, was nominated in 1926 to an important chair at Princeton Theological Seminary (where an earlier president had allegedly remarked, "I am not afraid to say that a new idea never originated in this seminary") a few directors and trustees managed to stall the appointment.[40] As one investigating committee followed another and invective piled upon venom, the controversy threatened to tear the church apart. There was ample precedent, for several Presbyterian denominations in the country had already split off on theological grounds. As an indication of the pre-eminence that the controversy held with ultraconservatives, the fundamentalist journal, *The Presbyterian,* barely mentioned China in the winter of 1926–1927, saving its pages for the war at home.

This controversy had already reached and threatened China missions. The primary reason for the huge mission enterprise was the denomination's profound evangelical sentiments. The Presbyterians had a large conservative component to whom a Presbyterianism without evangelical missions was unthinkable. Their efforts had helped to swell the coffers; Presbyterians contributed to the mission movement more than twice the sum per capita as the Methodists. Conservatives pointed out that Jesus' last words had been an admonition to develop foreign missions ("Go ye therefore and teach all nations," says the St. Matthew version). In celebrating January 1927 as Official Missions Month, *The Presbyterian* answered the question "Why missions?" with the simple statement, "Christ commands it."[41] For the conservative, Christianity without evangelical missions was like Christianity without Christ. Presbyterians conducted an enormous educational and medical missionary service, but leaders thought of the mission movement as evangelical rather than as a social-service unit.

In 1921 a clergyman speaking in New York had accused many unnamed China missionaries, including Presbyterians, of too great a liberalism in their work, by which he meant a neglect of evangelization and a Fosdick-like toleration of Oriental religions. Although the General Assembly affirmed its faith in the China personnel, the ultraconservative clamor was such that the assembly felt it wise to initiate an inquiry by the Board of Foreign Missions under Robert Speer.

Speer rose strongly to the defense of the China men and for several years thereafter produced long and spirited articles that defended missions in China and elsewhere.[42] At the same time he was writing on church problems as a whole, taking a position which, though clearly conservative, was by no means fundamentalist. Thus, the moderate elements in the church were also the China-mission supporters, and to display confidence in the China operation became in a sense a sign of moderation and the desire for church unity at home. This was particularly true when Speer began to emerge as the leading mediating figure in the domestic rift. As 1927 approached, he was widely regarded as an unbeatable candidate for moderator of the 1927 General Assembly. A vote for him could hardly avoid being a pledge of faith for the missions to which he had given his life, even if they were not the main issue.

Robert Speer was certainly a key figure in the destinies of the China operation and the domestic Presbyterian Church during the mid-twenties, a far more towering personality than any in the Methodist Board at the time. He was a staunch conservative, opposed to some of the airier justifications of Christianity: "We must keep Christianity as an institution with churches, not just a diffuse tendency," he declared. He nevertheless displayed enough flexibility so that he was widely seen as occupying the center in theological belief and ecclesiastical practice, a pragmatic conservative willing to come to terms with historical realities. His views toward China in 1927 are illustrative. A man with Asian missionary experience, a veteran of several trips to China, and secretary of the Board of Foreign Missions since 1891, Speer was firmly devoted to the tradition of evangelical missions. He said: "We have a great enginery in China . . . it ought to be directed for evangelical ends." To the wing of missionaries who thought of their work in China as broadly educational or humanitarian, Speer retorted: "I am a Christian propagandist and am going to be until I die."[43] Even accounting for his recognition of the need to reassure Presbyterians at home, there is no reason to discount his total sincerity. The remarks place him squarely in accord with traditional Presbyterian thinking.

At the same time, Speer was able to come to terms with the changing China perspective with more certainty and dispatch than the Methodists were showing. Ever since 1918 the Chinese Presbyterians had been working toward consolidation with the American Board into an Assembly of the Church of Christ in China, a move they were scheduled to make in the fall of 1927. Speer was able to view this move, as well as the transfer of some property to Chinese hands, with a degree of equanimity. He was willing to pledge continued support for the church even after such changes, particularly since to him they did not mean the end of a need for missionaries. This attitude by no means meant that Speer was ready for the total turnover of controls advocated by the more liberal wing. He dismissed such thinking with a biting remark, "The missionary bodies long for their own euthanasia."[44] It did mean that he was committed to staying in China and dealing with realities as best he could.

THE RESPONSE TO 1927

This spirit of pragmatism and commitment informed the Board of Foreign Mission's response to the events of 1927. When missionaries were withdrawn, the board issued comforting reports to the press. The evaluative report of the Speer mission under Speer's direction raised no questions about long-term withdrawals but pledged that Presbyterian missionaries would stay in China with home support. Speer's eminence as board secretary of itself carried much weight in having the report approved. Furthermore, when he was elected moderator for the 1927 Assembly by acclaim, China was an indirect beneficiary. The assembly adopted a resolution that was a triumph for his views: "As we believe that the religion of Christ is the only panacea for the woes of China and the only hope of her salvation, individually and socially, the Assembly sends to our missionaries and the Christians of China an expression of our abiding love and sympathy and confidence, and the Assembly believes that it is expressing the deep feeling of the church in making a solemn pledge to stand by China, to take up the work so rudely interrupted with greater faith and vigor than ever before."[45]

In a sense, therefore, the Presbyterian decision to stay in China was a foregone conclusion, for there is no indication that it was seriously questioned in 1927. Even *The Presbyterian,* when it finally noticed the China crisis, asked: "Shall we abandon China? No, we are there as witnesses for Christ."[46] There was no outward sign of the hesitation and confusion that characterized the Methodists. The battle to justify China missions had already been fought and won on theological grounds, and Chinese politics and warfare could not easily disturb the decision.

Yet there was an element of worry that the campaign against

missions might reopen. The board, therefore, soon became engaged in image making, to prove that China was worth the sacrifices being made by the noble band of Presbyterian missionaries. Like the Methodists, it attempted to prevent unfriendly reports from missionaries. After confiding to Frank Gamewell its reluctance to have hundreds of fleeing missionaries return home with conflicting messages, the board refused to let its mission treasurers in Korea, Japan, the Philippines, and Siam advance money to the refugees for passage home. It told the China Council not to make any public statements on China's internal and political matters, and edited China Council letters carefully for domestic release.[47] Its messages to constituents made some of the same points the Methodists were making, stressing that events in China did not represent the real China, that the violence in the Nationalist movement was only a passing phase owing to Communist influence, that the Chinese wanted missionaries. It emphasized the heroism of Chinese Christians in a time of travail. It equated the China cause with real Christianity, and indicated that to leave China was "to desert the cause of Christ at a very critical moment." As a testimony to its faith, the board sent its missionaries back to the field. This move was also, however, a testimony to its judgment of the situation at home, for one board member wrote to Charles Patton that keeping out missionaries for long would have a very bad effect on the home constituency.[48]

In short, the Presbyterians, like the Methodists, had to have China missionaries for many reasons unconnected with China. To ensure that the mission work would continue, they too stressed the special responsibility of Americans for China. After all, as their leaders told them, missionaries would be needed in China for the next hundred years. The work had scarcely begun.

The conversion of Chiang to Christianity and the rise of the Nationalist regime generated further unrealistic expectations about China among American churchgoers. With the Communist takeover, hope gave way to frustration, friendship to bitterness, and the collapse of the missionary era left a deep sense of betrayal. What effect the long emotional involvement had upon American attitudes and policies is still an enticing and unsolved problem for historians. It is certain, however, that China's repudiation of the missionary gift worked like a disease in the consciousness of many Americans, infecting the relationship between the two countries more than has yet been assessed. The connection is too subtle to be traced precisely, but it is nevertheless worth close attention, for it may indicate why the American passion for China turned to rage, and why for twenty years America blotted out the Chinese state from its map of the world.

PAUL A. VARG

The Missionary Response
to the Nationalist Revolution

Much of the writing on American missionaries in China during the Nationalist Revolution has focused on treaty revision. The missionaries have been made to appear as contestants seeking to move their own government to adopt more liberal policies toward China. A re-examination suggests that the cleavage was less sharp than at first appeared. Although distrust between missionaries and American government officials largely nullified the influence of the former on government policy, the two groups had more in common than they had differences. This was shown by the missionaries' reactions to developments in China after the Kuomintang seizure of control in 1927, and by the exchange of views between representatives of mission boards and the Department of State from 1927 to 1932.

The peak period of missionary agitation in favor of treaty revision came before the northern march of the Kuomintang forces and the Nanking incident of March 1926. After the incident, however, missionaries continued to sign petitions and mission boards likewise persisted in informing the Department of State that they favored revision. This support of treaty revision stemmed in part from goodwill for the Chinese and sympathy with their aspirations, but it owed even more to a realization that the continuance of missionary work and the future of Christianity in China depended on aligning the Christian effort with Chinese nationalist aspirations.

A majority of missionaries seem to have favored a surrender of treaty rights. The affirmative answer given by missionaries to the question of whether they favored revision probably meant in some cases little more than that they approved revision in the abstract and that they wished to win the favor of their Chinese constituents. Not all who signed petitions were of one mind as to when and under what conditions treaty rights should be surrendered. Searle Bates, one of the leading advocates of treaty revision, testified that he had to redraft petitions many times in order to arrive at a statement that any considerable number of missionaries were willing to sign. In some instances missionaries signed because of deep convictions that China must be supported; others undoubtedly signed because of some measure of intimidation both from their missionary colleagues and especially from their Chinese constituents. The signing of petitions did not necessarily mean that these American residents had the same faith as Chinese in the virtue of Chinese nationalism or in the justice of depriving the foreigner of special legal status.

The missionaries' advocacy of treaty revision is best understood within the broader context of Chinese charges against both the missionary and the institutions he had established. By 1927, many missionaries were of the same mind as Earl Ballou, a Congregational missionary of the North China station, when he spoke of their experience as a trip through purgatory. "The way of China's political salvation lies, so far as we can see," he wrote, "through a sane nationalism. But there begins to be grave doubt as to whether a sane nationalism will be given a fair chance."[1]

The revolution illumined the fact that those philanthropic enterprises in which Americans took greatest pride were in fact anathema to the Chinese. The practitioners of philanthropy, all 8000 of them, now labored under the charge of leading a cultural invasion. Their schools and hospitals, not long before welcomed as necessary to the modernization of China, now became the target of allegations that they denationalized their patrons.

CHINESE CHRISTIAN CRITICISMS

The criticisms set forth by Chinese Christians ranged from charges of racial superiority, unwillingness to turn over control of institutions to the Chinese, and bias in favor of their home governments, to failure to give priority to China's economic and social needs. Chinese Christians, no less nationalistic than other Chinese, vented their feelings in unsparing indictments in publications, in addresses before church groups, and in their day-to-day relations with missionaries.

T. L. Shen, a well-known Chinese Christian, contended that Chinese society had been undermined morally by the West. Traditional morality had its basis in Confucian teaching and in the social controls exercised by the family and the guild. These agencies of social control had been guided by the interests of society at large. Once China became involved in the world economy and commercial practices began to follow the Western pattern, the controlling social groups were transformed into competing units, each one seeking only its own enrichment. In the course of the transformation individuals were set adrift and, once free of control, made their own pleasures and interests the sole guides to behavior. The missionaries, wrote Shen, aligned themselves with a whole series of reactionary tendencies that were operating to prevent reform. Because missionaries lived in China under the protection afforded them by the unequal treaties, they were a party to the major barrier to China's solving her many problems.

In an even more severe indictment Shen contended that the church lacked vitality "in a consistent and uplifting life." "It is," he noted, "composed of too many 'eaters of religion' who have sought other advantages than the religious." "It has almost become a sort of economic institution by means of which certain classes of missionaries and Chinese have risen to a better economic life." The missionaries' feeling of superiority, he charged, made them unwilling to yield control of the Chinese church to the Chinese. But Shen's central accusation was directed at the missionaries' dependence on the toleration clause. To this he added the sweeping censure: "On the whole the Church as an institution does depend on and derive its support from the capitalistic order with its basis laid in the motives of profit and competition, which the Church cannot but denounce if it is actually following the lead of Jesus Christ. In so far as it is more or less standing aloof from the great surging tides of human need in China it is becoming a luxury rather than a necessity in China's national life."[2]

Djang Fang, a member of the National Christian Council, acknowledged that the pioneer missionaries deserved credit for introducing modern education, women's education, medical work, and the sciences. However, schools and hospitals now competed with government-supported institutions, and it was more proper for the government to provide for education and health. In the meantime, the missionary schools competed for funds and for students. Fang also deplored the methods of evangelization that placed a premium on conversion and then did nothing to train converts. "The Protestant Church in China," she wrote, "has been established for one hundred and twenty-one years, yet it is still not deeply rooted in the mind and the heart of the Chinese." It had, she continued, "neither been adapted to the needs of the common people or to the civilization of China. If a microscope could be invented which would reveal the contents of the cells of the human brain, [she wagered that] the cells of the Chinese brain would be found to consist of the moral teachings of Confucius, the passivity of the Taoist, and some of the superstitions of Buddhism." It would, she thought, show little in the way of Christian understanding.

Fang pointed an accusing finger at the emphasis placed on buildings and the comfortable homes of missionaries. She recalled that on a visit to the Drum Tower in Nanking, a friend looking out on the scene below remarked: "Look! To what country does our land belong? How can a person allow others to lie down on his cot?" She explained the reactions of the common people as they walked by "the magnificent Christian churches, educational institutions and beautiful homes. Every time they passed these buildings, the contrast between their level of living and that suggested by these Christian buildings is brought keenly home to them." They could only reflect, "How magnificent those buildings are and how ugly are our own." They asked themselves why they were condemned to live in bare and ugly huts. This, she thought, explained why in March 1927 the Chinese destroyed and looted in this section of Nanking.[3]

Missionaries encountered these criticisms in their daily work. To Helen Dizney, stationed at Taiku in Shansi, it seemed that the only reward missionaries received for all their efforts was "criticism of everything we do." She thought that at no place in the United States would they be subjected "to the same criticism of training, work, living conditions, attitude toward those we work with, as we do here now." William Leete, a young and liberal-minded missionary engaged in student work in Tientsin, told of the "wholesale criticism."

Chinese asked: "Why do missionaries spend so much on themselves? Why do they live in such luxury? Outsiders ask, wasn't Christ a poor man? Didn't He say to sell and give to the poor? Doesn't the standard of living which the missionaries have adopted prove them to be hypocrites?" Chinese asked further, according to Leete, why missionaries chose to live in compounds and to cut themselves off. "Why don't you live so that we may feel free to come in at any time without soiling your carpets and scratching your floors?" Leete quoted the disturbing Chinese question, "If you don't want to mix with us, why are you out here?"[4]

Leete, in revolt against his colleagues, clearly took delight in their discomfort. Others concluded that the heart of the problem lay in the fact that as foreigners, no matter what they did, they would fall under an avalanche of hostility. After a Sunday morning religious service Earl Ballou, although sympathetic with Chinese nationalism, wrote to his superior at home that the Chinese pastor "spent the last few minutes of his sermon laying into the benumbing and evil influence which foreign money, foreign houses and foreign gunboats, have had upon the spreading of the gospel." Ballou, tired of these tirades, confessed to "getting fed up on some things."[5]

MISSIONARIES' EFFORTS TO EXTRICATE THEMSELVES

Signing petitions calling for the surrender of treaty rights offered to missionaries the most readily available means of seeking to deflect the charges made against them. However, the Nationalist revolution extended far beyond the issue of unequal treaties. Treaty revision constituted only one minor aspect of the total revolutionary program for far-reaching political and social reform. Above all, it aimed at rooting out all that was alien to China and at creating a society that was both Chinese and powerful enough to establish itself as an equal among nations. Therefore, as the missionaries recognized, it would not suffice to side with the Chinese only on the treaty question. Hugh Hubbard of the Congregationalists had the situation fully in view when he wrote that the Chinese church "must align itself with this Nationalist spirit and become Chinese, or it will lose a great opportunity."[6] This broader approach to the challenge facing the missionaries somewhat reduced the importance of the treaty question.

The search for new adaptations of Christianity to the Chinese culture was also a product of the sharp setbacks that missionaries had experienced in the China parish. Rural churches were closing. Attendance at church services was falling off. Fewer students were attending missionary schools.[7] The YMCA suffered a 34 percent loss in membership between 1924 and 1928.[8] These difficulties alerted the missionary to the need for change.

Faced with criticism and failure, some engaged in self-mortifying criticisms. In the pages of *The Chinese Recorder* a few writers testified that they lived in more comfortable homes in China than they had in the United States. Others belabored the fact that, by living in compounds, they shut themselves off from the Chinese.

The more significant effort, however, involved the transfer of control of institutions to the Chinese. After the Nationalist uprising of 1927, the major denominations insisted that candidates for missionary work must be instructed in the importance of refusing administrative posts and of transferring control of churches, schools, and hospitals to the Chinese. The liberal social-gospel wing often sought to identify with Chinese needs by calling for greater emphasis on agricultural missions and the establishment of cooperatives. Hugh Hubbard, for example, moved to a small village some distance away from the North China mission of the Congregationalists, where he abjured all proselytism, forbade any mention of Christianity, and determined to restrict himself to lending a hand to the villagers wherever the need beckoned. Others sought ways of disassociating Christianity from the accretions of Western society so that its essence might find expression in purely Chinese forms.

These efforts, rather than the support of treaty revision, occupied the missionaries' major attention after 1927. At no time did the missionaries or any mission board at home call for the use of force or effective implementation of the treaties. Yet missionaries did have some second thoughts, for in the late 1920s there was not only much violence, but some political elements called for the killing of foreigners simply to bring about foreign intervention, which would in turn work to their political advantage. This development challenged earlier assertions by some missionaries that they would have nothing to fear if Western governments denied them protection. Bishop L. J. Birney of the Methodists expressed a fairly representative opinion when he said in December 1927 that he was wholly opposed to the gunboat policy, yet he thought that to remove all warships immediately could only result in chaos.[9]

Efforts to adjust to nationalism offered a new and peculiar trial of faith, which no previous generation had faced. The young people of China no longer saw Christianity as either challenging or exciting. Young Chinese found it irrelevant to the problems they faced. Few missionaries would have disagreed with Earl Ballou when he observed that for the next few years, "China will continue to be in the grip of what, to my mind, are forces absolutely beyond the control of the Christian enterprise as it exists here."[10] This healthy fatalism enabled many missionaries to recognize that China was destined to pursue her own peculiar course and that the efforts of neither private foreign philanthropies nor powerful Western states could greatly influence the final outcome.

MISSIONARY VIEWS OF THE COMMUNISTS AND THE KUOMINTANG

Both the missionaries and the boards at home avoided taking public stands on Chinese domestic political issues, but they conveyed their estimate of the China situation and how they felt about the two major political parties in letters to the mission boards. Insofar as the missionaries did write for the religious press, they placed developments in the best possible light and encouraged the public to believe that the new Nationalist government was making progress.

The proclaimed enmity of the Communists toward missionaries was confirmed by their widespread experience of ruthless persecution in Communist-dominated areas. George W. Shepherd of the Shaowu Mission of the Congregational Church in South China informed the secretary of his board in March 1927 that two prominent parties were "engaged in a death struggle for the control of power around Shanghai, which is the richest of all the spoils of war." Shepherd, already strongly anti-Communist, warned that if the Communists should win, "we are in for trouble." However, if the liberals should win, Shepherd thought, the missionaries could expect to go about their work as usual. Another missionary of the same mission, writing in October 1927, reported that he did not know of "a single place where the new government has improved political conditions especially in the rural districts." He acknowledged that the southerners had a few idealistic leaders, but most of them were simply brigands. He also noted that the government lacked control over many of those who were serving under its name. "There is no central authority. Both military and naval commanders did exactly as they pleased. A Congregationalist stationed in Shansi in May 1927 wrote: "Most of us are hoping that the conservative wing of the Nationalist Party will win out, and will be able to overthrow the destructive, communistic elements, and ultimately bring to pass a unified body of leaders from all over the country."[11]

However, hostility to the Communists did not blind some of the leaders to their strength. In October 1927, Frank Rawlinson estimated that the Communists were far from subdued, although they had been prevented from taking over the reins of government. He believed that the Communists, the Kuomintang, and the reactionaries had reached a stage of equilibrium. During that same month an English missionary leader, Dr. Henry T. Hodgkin, secretary of the National Christian Council, observed that the Communists had a "spirit of fanatical devotion." The party, wrote Hodgkin, "is kept alive by the intense enthusiasm of a small group whose convictions are hard to shake. They are deeply convinced that communism is the solution to China's troubles and are prepared to sacrifice anything for it. The conduct of some communists who have been executed has inspired the witnesses with the feeling that these men and women have found something that was capable of filling them with courage even in the hour of death." The party, Hodgkin continued, might well take over eventually if the present government failed to establish internal order. More fighting could only bring more suffering and despair, out of which would come a general turning to Communism.[12]

In January 1928, the Methodist bishop in Shanghai, L. J. Birney, expressed pleasure over Chiang Kai-shek's return to power and noted with approval that he was squarely and strongly against the Communists. But Birney, uneasy about the future, reported that as some of the Soviet officials were about to leave China, they were heard to say: "Never mind, we will be back, by and by. Moreover, the seed has been sown so widely and deeply that it will come to harvest itself." The bishop noted, "We feel that there is some truth in that prophecy."[13]

Missionaries never tired of citing the Communist denunciation of religion as the opiate of the people. Their publications recited gruesome tales of murder and kidnapping. No distinction was drawn between Communist party policy and the actions of the troops. Yet the more thoughtful recognized the popular appeal of the Communists' social and economic program, and of its all-encompassing doctrine of redemption whereby immutable historical forces made inevitable the victory of the proletariat in the unfolding of time. In October 1932, Frank Cartwright, secretary of the Methodist Board of Foreign Missions, wrote: "Now as to the Communist tendency in China. Judging from snatches selected from various letters from different parts of the country, I am inclined to believe that Communism is gaining in its influence, as seems to me almost inevitable in a country where general chaos prevails in politics and with great misery continuing among the common people."[14]

One missionary captured by the Communists in 1932, the Reverend Oscar Anderson, confided to a Chinese friend that he and the women accompanying him had been well treated by General Ho Lung, commander of the Communist army north of the Yangtze River. He wrote of Ho: "He was very friendly and assured the ladies that no harm would come to them. He explained earnestly that he was not a bandit, but a leader of an organized Communist army." Anderson further observed that the soldiers were well disciplined. Those who violated regulations, including the strictures against the use of opium, were summarily shot.[15]

In November 1932 Rawlinson, upon receiving an article on the Communists from a Chinese friend, decided to publish it, but the Chinese printing firm refused, fearing to get into trouble with the government. Rawlinson then forwarded the manuscript to A. L. Warnshuis in New York, explaining what had happened and suggesting that it would be useful to forward copies "to a private list." The article described the extensive indoctrination program, the people's courts, the policy for redistributing land, and discipline in the army. It stated that the Soviets desired friendly foreign relations and treated foreigners cordially but insisted on the abolition of special privileges for foreigners. The author found that "there is little or no evidence that help comes from Russia in funds or men. The seed may have been Russian, but the present Communist Crop has grown on rich Chinese soil." The central government, noted the author, was in jeopardy. It had recently denied relief to the victims of famine in Hupeh on the ground that it had no further funds for this purpose.

"Already," he wrote, "Hankow is like an island upon whose shores the waves of Communism are encroaching like an ever rising tide." The previous February the garrison in Hankow, because the soldiers had not been paid, would have gone over to the Reds had not the local Chamber of Commerce stepped in to pay the arrears.[16]

The missionaries' attitude toward the Kuomintang during the years 1927–1931 was not representative of their attitudes during the remainder of the 1930s or during the war years. Two later developments brought favor to the party in the eyes of the missionaries. First, although the conversion of Chiang to the Christian faith in 1930 did not immediately strengthen his credentials, as the years passed, the act won him support among both missionaries and the churchgoing public in the United States. Second, beginning with the Japanese invasion of Manchuria in September 1931, the missionaries almost uniformly rallied to China's support, and thereafter they manifested a greater interest in the defense of China than they did in the domestic side of Chinese affairs.

Missionaries generally wished the Kuomintang success. In spite of strong strains of antiforeignism and antireligious feelings within the Kuomintang, it was the only party offering any hope of tolerating Christianity. In short, to many missionaries the Kuomintang was clearly the lesser of two evils, but they also took hope in the fact that more than two hundred Christians occupied government posts.[17] They saw in the Kuomintang the only possibility of bringing to an end the years of civil war and of avoiding a more radical regime.

Arthur J. Bowen of the University of Nanking, in one of his early letters to the Methodist Board after Chiang Kai-shek's rise to power, cited two weaknesses. Chiang had made a serious error in marching north to take control before dealing with the Communist forces at Wuhan. Second, the presence of many Communist soldiers and officers in the Nationalist army meant that Chiang did not have full control. This accounted, as Bowen saw it, for the continued occupation of mission properties by Nationalist troops.[18]

Approximately a year later Bowen continued to hope that the Nationalists would be successful. The highest officials, he thought, were doing as well as any group could under the circumstances. Yet the government, because of lack of experience, was making many mistakes. The leaders confronted a serious problem in party organization; underlings in the government, like the yamen runners of old, were self-seeking and corrupt. There was a lack of political understanding among the merchants, who failed to grasp that a modern government must have revenue. As a result, merchants failed to support the regime.[19]

At the close of 1928 Bowen wrote that there had been no significant change in the situation, and he had no great confidence in the Nationalists' staying power. If they could survive the party conference scheduled for the coming March, Bowen believed, "the hopes for a longer lease of life will be much brighter." He took the long view: the government would need a period of at least ten years to demonstrate its constructive capacities. As the job would be huge, long, and difficult, "continuity and time are absolutely essential." Then he pointed to the weaknesses. "One gets the impression," he wrote, "that the party organization and party members outside of the regular ministries and bureaus are a serious handicap and liability to the men actually in office." Furthermore, outside of Kiangsu and part of Anhwei, the authority of the central government was only nominal. He cited reports that at the time only five provinces were supplying revenue to the central authorities. As a result, the government had to move cautiously. It did not have a free hand.[20]

Fred Brown, a Methodist missionary stationed at Nanchang, exhibited the same restrained optimism. The behavior of the Nationalist troops who were occupying all of the mission buildings at his station did not nourish any admiration for the newly established authority. Yet Brown, acknowledging the difficulties, avoided harsh judgments. Viewing the situation from a broad perspective, he saw three strong forces at work, which he chose to label Anglo-American, Slavic, and Mongol. These were engaged in the struggle to shape the Chinese civilization of tomorrow. The first represented a reformed capitalism and the second communism. Between these two, the first sought to raise everyone to the level of the more privileged groups, while the second was engaged in lowering everyone to the level of the poorest classes. "Hence," wrote Brown, "while we denounce imperialism and freely criticize capitalism, we are nevertheless Anglo-American in our viewpoint, not Slavic." Looking beyond the immediate failures and successes, Brown thought it might be useful to establish a program that would bring individual Americans of ability and goodwill to China, where they would travel widely, learn about conditions at first hand, and strive sympathetically to understand the viewpoint "of these young leaders and patiently interpret our viewpoint to them." The goal should be a "spiritual linking together of our two great countries so that the future will find two mighty friends facing each other across the Pacific."[21]

Bishop L. J. Birney, who was at Shanghai during the early months of Chiang's rise, expressed great hopes for the new government and was particularly pleased that the Russian representatives had been sent home. In October 1928 he wrote to Dr. Frank D. Gamewell in New York: "While there are some problems yet existing in the National Government, they seem to be getting hold of the situation and for the most part are moving in the right direction." He believed some of the plans being discussed would benefit the entire country. He also reported the dark side, however: the government had launched a large-scale road-building program and in scores of cities had robbed the people of their property, in most places not paying a single cent of remuneration.[22]

By January 1929 Birney, clearly discouraged, emphasized the difficulties facing the government. There was, he said, "a very grave possibility of further communistic upheavals." Birney attributed the declining confidence in the Nationalist government to a number of factors. One was the removal of the capital from Peking to Nanking. Northerners viewed the new government as a southern government, most of whose officials actually came from the central and southern sections. The move thus gave new life to the old antipathy between these two sections. The poor economic conditions prevailing in the north added to the hostility. Peking had "practically subsisted economically upon the income from the vast army of officials." These former officeholders were now in abject poverty, and hundreds of shops in the former capital were closed. In addition to the economic difficulties in Peking, the northern provinces were suffering from devastating famines. Birney also attributed the decline in confidence in the government to its foolishly high taxes. He noted with sadness that war was already underway in West China and that the central government had the support of only six provinces.[23]

The bishop gave way to further foreboding by May of 1929. At that time Chiang was engaged in war with the Christian General Feng Yü-hsiang. Missionaries, long since disillusioned with Feng as a religious man, continued to give him credit for holding his troops to high standards of conduct and, unlike most of the warlords, for refusing to enrich himself. In addition, Feng championed a program of social and economic reform. Birney's sympathy was with Feng, "because he is protesting against the graft and squeeze and imperialism and luxury of the present government. There is absolutely no doubt that his accusations in this respect are well founded." Birney believed that he had accurate information from Chinese friends, and "some of these friends say, (to foreigners; they dare not say it to the Chinese lest they be reported and they be stood up against a stone wall the next morning at dawn) 'It is the "rottenest" government we have had for 500 years from the standpoint of graft and squeeze.' " Yet at the close of 1929, Birney, although still highly critical of the extreme arbitrariness of the government, observed, "yet we wish it to stand because it is absolutely certain that if it is overthrown the next one will be far more radical and communistic than the present one."[24]

In the early years of the Kuomintang government no one opinion concerning its strengths and weaknesses prevailed among the Congregationalists. In January 1928, Earl Ballou expressed skepticism: "As to the Nationalists, or any other party with power at present, I am completely from Missouri. I suppose there is still a chance that they *are* genuinely 'sacrificing' for something other than themselves, but I have got to be shown. They have started something which is beyond them to control." Ballou observed that the fire was underground everywhere, ready to break out anywhere. He thought it likely that in the end the Kuomintang would be "squeezed out between the militarists and the communists." In contrast, Harold Matthews, a Congregational missionary teacher in Shantung, was optimistic. He was impressed, for example, with the simple life style and friendly attitude of a local magistrate. Although he acknowledged that there had been few visible signs of progress, he had found signs of a new spirit. Roads had been repaired, and temples had been renovated for use as markets, museums, and schools. The party was supporting an antifootbinding campaign, discouraging gambling, promoting equality between the sexes, and encouraging the boycott against Japan. The principles laid down by Sun Yat-sen, he noted, were on everyone's lips.[25]

The ever-optimistic Frank Rawlinson, editor of *The Chinese Recorder,* who was oriented to the liberal side of politics, placed his hopes in the Kuomintang, although in his private correspondence he also called attention to its weaknesses. In his periodical, however, he carefully avoided questions of Chinese internal politics.[26] Watching the political scene during late 1927, Rawlinson concluded that the Chinese intelligentsia had yet to decide which form of government would best meet the needs of China. The strength of the militarists worried him, for they had managed to retain a dominant position. As early as October 1927, Rawlinson reported that the Communists were not finally "squelched," and he noted the beginning of a wave of disillusionment with the Kuomintang. Then, in typically optimistic fashion, he professed to see the emergence of a new spirit and of a search for new and better solutions to political, economic, and social problems.[27]

In March 1928 Rawlinson forwarded a detailed analysis to his old friend Warnshuis in New York. The country lacked experienced and outstanding leaders, while the mass of people were suffering severe hardships. The Chinese Christians, he wrote, were still nationalistic, but they no longer looked to the existing party to meet current problems. In April he told Warnshuis that, although the Chinese people continued to favor nationalistic principles, they were discouraged by recent failures and the submergence of officialdom in graft.[28]

A year later, in the spring of 1929, Rawlinson thought that the prestige of the government had grown considerably over the past year. He was particularly pleased that at the party conference held in Nanking in January moves had been made to reduce the size of the armies. However, the one-party rule of the Kuomintang disturbed him. His words had the ring of prophecy: "Of course, I might raise the question as to how long the one party can carry on the government and exclude the left or a modified communist party. Here I may only venture a conjecture or two. Undoubtedly the communists are still active under the surface, and furthermore, the leftists are not satisfied, they want a more direct voice in government . . . On the other hand, I am personally convinced that the elements of the left will eventually have to have a voice in the government and that it will have to be a two party rather than a one party affair."[29]

The failures of the Kuomintang did not cause missionaries to lose faith in Chinese nationalism. They still wished to see a strong China. However, the kind of China that they longed to see was the remotest of probabilities. In a country where almost 80 percent of the population was illiterate, where more than half of the population lived below the poverty line, and where nationalism gained much of its strength from the prevailing hatred of the foreigner, any loosening of old bonds or revolution would almost inevitably catapult the society into an upheaval in which neither Anglo-Saxon traditions of law, respect for the individual, nor standards of personal integrity would or could prevail. Given the breakdown of traditional controls imposed by the family and guilds, the surviving tradition of squeeze, and a callousness toward the suffering of others, the revolution degenerated into a situation where groups having power exploited the surrounding disorder to enrich themselves. The new China appeared to retain the worst of the old and to include only enough idealism to keep hope for reform alive.

The missionaries, being idealists who were originally dedicated to the nurture of individual lives, reacted negatively to the denial of their own ideals. Even those who shared the vision of a new society were, in terms of twentieth century revolutions, conservative. G. W. Sheppard, a Congregationalist in the Shaowu Mission, in an article entitled "The Church of Tomorrow—Its Faith in the Bible," wrote: "Amid the drastic changes which have taken place around us, even the most optimistic among us, those most in sympathy with China's recent national movements, can hardly view with equanimity some of their aspects and directions. This ancient nation, formerly characterized by rigid conservatism, by persistent and almost slavish loyalty to traditional customs, has in these recent years swung violently to the opposite extreme; abandoned its former reverences; set its hopes on sweeping and peremptory external reforms; paying homage to policies and maxims, which, it seems to us, those who advocate them little understand." He concluded, "The ultra-revolutionary spirit which would make a clean cut from the past as though wisdom was born with this generation, is not only folly, but fatal to progress itself."[30]

Missionaries correctly analyzed the weaknesses of the Kuomintang, its narrow political base, its determination to preserve one-party rule, its failure to implement many of the social aspects of its program, its inability to mobilize society so as to undermine the power of the provincial warlords, and its susceptibility to corruption. These views did not differ in essence from the interpretations placed on Chinese developments by American diplomats, many of whom knew China as well as the old hands among the churchmen.

MISSIONARIES AND THE DEPARTMENT OF STATE

The United States government responded to the Chinese revolution with some of the same ambivalence as did the missionaries. From 1925 until 1928 the State Department placed major emphasis on two considerations. First, since the Washington Conference of 1921–1922 the United States had adhered closely to a cooperative policy whereby no action was taken without seeking agreement with the other major powers having an interest in China. Because the other governments had much more at stake in the way of both trade and investment, they moved with great caution. This was particularly true of France, whose ambassador in Washington, Paul Claudel, constantly discouraged any yielding of treaty rights. Second, the Department of State, prior to 1928, professed to be troubled by the question of which government or factions in China the United States should negotiate with. Nelson T. Johnson, assistant secretary of state, argued that none of the several governments could speak for the whole of China or commit it to a treaty. Moreover, for the United States to choose one faction as the most representative and then yield to it on the unequal treaty question would be to bestow undue prestige on that faction.

Both of these considerations fell into abeyance in July 1928 when Secretary of State Kellogg departed from the cooperative policy and negotiated a treaty with the Nationalists in which the United States yielded on the question of the treaty tariff. Prior to the new treaty of 1928 and the simultaneous recognition of the Nanking government, the Department of State and the Foreign Missions Conference of North America had been in close communication. In January 1928 the Foreign Missions Conference, representing most Protestant denominations having missionary work in China, adopted a series of resolutions urging the government to undertake revision of the treaties as soon as possible. These resolutions were agreed to only after prolonged study of reports provided by the Department of State.

On April 25, 1927, shortly after the Nanking incident, the Consultative Group on China of the Foreign Missions Conference had discussed a series of cablegrams received by the Department of State

326

from consuls in China, copies of which had been furnished by Nelson T. Johnson. They failed to agree on any one course of action. Consequently, the Consultative Group merely authorized A. L. Warnshuis, secretary of the conference, to communicate with the State Department as opportunity might offer. The committee noted, however, "that the policy of the Government, as expressed by the President, was in favor of strictly refraining from any interference in the internal political affairs of the Chinese people and the use of military force only in the case of extreme emergency and only for the protection of life." In transmitting a copy of the action taken to Johnson, Warnshuis informed the assistant secretary that he had suggested to missionaries in China that they refrain "from public discussion of Chinese party politics." This, he wrote, did not apply to questions of relations between China and the foreign powers. Warnshuis stated further that the Consultative Group approved of the government's policy of refraining from the use of military force except for the protection of lives, then added: "The missionary interests in China are the largest American interests and we shall be glad if knowledge of the attitude of this group will strengthen your hands in carrying forward the policy that we understand you are following."[31]

At this juncture the missionary groups were content to endorse the government policy of restraint in employing force. The Department of State could scarcely regard this action as reason for moving with haste on the question of treaty revision. Nor was there any great pressure from other directions. An official in the department, analyzing the mail received by the White House as of May 12, 1927, reported to Johnson that 126 form letters had been received carrying 157 signatures. An effort had been made to classify them according to geographical location of the senders, but 62 carried no return address. Of the others, 81 came from New York, New Jersey, and Pennsylvania; another 14 from Maryland, the District of Columbia, North Carolina, South Carolina, Florida, Mississippi, Michigan, and Iowa. One had been received from each of six educational institutions.[32] This was scarcely a sufficiently imposing array of letters to demand the attention of the decision makers.

Nor did Johnson, the key figure in the formation of China policy, accede to missionary suggestions readily. Johnson had on many public occasions spoken in friendly terms of the missionary effort in

China. To have done otherwise would have been impolitic. However, in a lengthy interview with William R. Johnson, a returned missionary, he bristled with hostility. The missionary urged that the United States assist the Nationalist movement. Only by so doing, he averred, could Americans restore themselves in the favor of the Chinese. In turn, the assistant secretary asked "whether he believed that American missionary schools and other missionary enterprises would be allowed to flourish if the Government took some action in this matter." His caller stated that he was convinced that this would be the case.[33]

Johnson took sharp issue. Missionary enterprises, he said, had never been the direct concern of the government, but the government had, when requested to do so by missionary organizations, written into the treaties provisions for their protection. The Protestant missionaries, he said, would never have covered so wide an area in China "if it had not been for the stand which governments had taken in their treaties, although the American Government had never meddled directly in missionary work." Now the situation had changed. The schools, chapels, and other works must now stand or fall "according as they had won a place for themselves in the estimation of the Chinese." The assistant secretary then made his major point: "If the Chinese needed them, they would continue in spite of anything that the government could do. If the Chinese did not need them and did not want them, there was no way in which the government could force these institutions upon the Chinese or continue their life."[34] Clearly American policy was not to be formulated with the objective of rescuing the missions.

Johnson also expressed direct criticism of the attitude of the missionaries. The difficulties they faced in China were not owing to the policies of the American government but to "the standoffish attitude of the missionary institutions." In a tone that betrayed not a little irritation, Johnson's account of the interview continued:

> I reminded him that at Shanghai there was Nanyang College, a national Chinese institution, and St. John's University, an institution conducted by Americans; that likewise in Nanking there was the Southeastern University, a national Chinese institution, and the missionary institution called Nanking University, and I pointed out to him that through the years, intercourse between these competing establishments, one under the American flag and the other

under the Chinese flag, had been of the stiffest and most formal kind and that I knew from conversation with the faculty of the missionary institution that they had a low opinion of the faculty employed in the Chinese institution and that I had heard from Chinese that they had a very low opinion of the mental training of the average faculty member in a missionary college or school.[35]

So strong were the feelings between these institutions that the students of the Chinese and missionary schools seldom associated, and it was impossible to have athletic competition between them.

Hostility, Johnson pointed out, was increased by the different levels of financial support. The American schools had what they needed in the way of supplies and equipment, whereas the Chinese institutions, because of the political chaos, lacked even books. The Chinese naturally resented this situation. The assistant secretary went on to criticize the education offered by the American schools. Their instructors often lacked any knowledge of the economy of China, and they were not able to train their students for functioning in the Chinese environment. "As a result, the missionary schools were becoming training places for youths who wanted jobs in the foreign settlements rather than training places for Chinese youths who intended to go back to their home places to bear the responsibilities of home life."[36]

This was not the only occasion on which the Department of State assumed a critical attitude. Several months after Herbert Hoover had become President, a delegation from the Foreign Missions Conference, headed by A. L. Warnshuis, called on the President in an effort to convince him of the importance of appointing people to the Foreign Service who were friendly to the missionary cause. According to Warnshuis, the President manifested great interest and asked him to prepare a memorandum stating the ideals and purposes of the missionaries, which he would then circulate to the members of the Foreign Service. When Warnshuis informed Johnson of this interview, Johnson seized the occasion to state some of his own views on the missionary effort. He professed to having a number of friends among the missionaries and to an appreciation of their work, but he stated in blunt fashion that the misunderstanding between missionaries on the one side and businessmen and diplomats on the other was in part the fault of the missionaries. Johnson reported: "I pointed out that my experience in China had been that the missionaries generally felt that they were dedicated to the other world and they looked upon business people as being dedicated to this world; that the business people reacted to this idea by taunting the missionaries with the fact that dedicated though they were to the other world they found reasonable pleasure in the flesh pots whenever they could get at them or had a reasonable interest in the comforts of this world as enjoyed by the ordinary merchant whenever the missionary could come near such comforts and between the two groups there was rarely any agreement."[37]   Johnson thought that the missionaries had taken a holier-than-thou attitude.

A lack of mutual confidence between missionaries and Foreign Service officers also showed itself in the relations between J. V. A. MacMurray, the minister to China during this period, and the missionaries. MacMurray showed no sympathy with the missionaries in their advocacy of treaty revision, which he dismissed as nothing more than an effort to redeem themselves with the Chinese. Hugh Hubbard was so distrustful of MacMurray that after the Nanking incident, when the minister called on the missionaries to withdraw, Hubbard believed he simply wanted to get the missionaries out of the way so that the American government could embark on a large-scale invasion. This absence of cordiality was no secret. Frank Rawlinson observed that while the diplomats were quite willing to talk, "they do not pay much attention to what missionaries have to say."[38]

American missionaries, however, were not sharply at odds with their government. They found much in government policy to approve. Three steps in particular caused them to have confidence in the good intentions of Washington: the refusal of the United States to join with other powers in taking military action after the Nanking incident, the negotiations of 1928 leading to the new tariff treaty and recognition of the Nationalist government, and Kellogg's and Stimson's standing offer to negotiate on the question of extraterritoriality subject to the understanding that the yielding of rights should be gradual and limited. Whether the pressure from missionaries and church mission boards caused the Coolidge and Hoover administrations to take these steps, or even whether these groups wielded any influence at all, the documents neither affirm nor deny, but it appears reasonable to believe that the support of the missionaries and the churches at least made it easier to take these steps.

Nevertheless, a careful reading of the scores of memoranda prepared by Johnson and Stanley Hornbeck of the Department of State indicate that they acted in accordance with their own view of developments in China.

The spokesmen for the missionary interests and the officers in the Department of State arrived at essentially the same position after 1927.[39] In 1930 and 1931 representatives of both governments, in Nanking and in Washington, sought to reach agreement on extraterritoriality. Their efforts came to naught, because the Chinese insisted on immediate and complete abrogation, whereas the American representatives insisted that extraterritorial rights could only be yielded gradually and in certain categories. By early 1931 some officials in the Department of State were prepared to surrender extraterritorial rights everywhere outside of Shanghai.[40] The chief obstacle to further concessions was fear on the part of MacMurray, Johnson, and Hornbeck that, given the Chinese hostility to foreigners, Americans would find themselves facing lawsuits inspired by vindictiveness and encountering hostile judges moved by political considerations. The Chinese, in turn, deeply resented demands for special guarantees and argued that Americans were unreasonable in insisting that the judicial system be flawless. Quite understandably the Chinese reasoned that if foreigners chose to come to China, they must be prepared to adjust to prevailing conditions.[41]

By 1930 Warnshuis, although in favor of yielding on extraterritoriality, favored some curbs on the Chinese judicial system. Medical missionaries had expressed fear that in the event of mishaps or failures in surgical cases they might face lawsuits. Warnshuis, in an interview at the Department of State, conceded that the Chinese would not accept a special provision for this category of cases. However, he pressed more firmly for a provision that missionaries who had criticized the Chinese government prior to the pending treaty should not be prosecuted. He was assured that such a provision was already included in the American draft. A third provision sought by missionaries related to rights to immovable property, and again the pending treaty provided for protection. Finally Warnshuis expressed concern over the question of taxation of church property, but he accepted the position of the Department of State that this was a matter for the Chinese government to decide.[42] In brief,

Warnshuis and the Department of State both accepted the necessity for a new treaty but insisted that the new treaty contain some legal safeguards.

The coming together of the missionaries' views and the government position on extraterritoriality had its parallel in the identity of their response to the more general political situation in China. In April 1931, J. W. Ballantine, consul-general at Canton, presented a forty-page dispatch giving a history of the missionary encounters with bandits, Communists, and troops of the Kuomintang. He told of hospitals and schools closed by strikes fomented by Communist-controlled unions demanding large financial contributions, of the persecution of missionaries in isolated areas, and of the occupation of mission properties by Nationalist troops.[43] Ballantine praised the missionaries for their courage and for their intelligent adaptation to new conditions. F. P. Lockhart, consul-general at Hankow in early 1931, provided a similar picture of developments in his area. The complaints of both consuls and missionaries stressed that the Nationalist government had no effective control over its own officials and its own troops. A Catholic missionary, the Reverend Lawrence D. Curtis, stationed in Kiangsi, deplored the ineffectiveness of the Nationalists in dealing with the Communists. Either the government did not realize the danger, or it was powerless to cope with the problem. Another Catholic, the Reverend Thomas W. Megan, ridiculed the Nationalist government for its weakness and charged that "some of the biggest bandits in China are among the military contingents. When one has seen things in their naked reality in China this chatter about abolition of extraterritoriality and kindred privileges in China makes one shudder." Megan cited the endless skirmishes with the military, "who by their numbers and revolvers try to occupy your residence," and he wondered "what Nanking stands for except 'good words.' "[44]

Neither Ballantine nor Lockhart questioned the severe indictments. However, while individual consular officers and missionaries emphasized the weakness of the government and the chaos existing in many areas of China, the Department of State and the major missionary bodies at home took a larger view and accepted the fact that China was still in revolution. In February 1931, Hornbeck of the Division of Far Eastern Affairs, in a memorandum on extraterritoriality, stated that it was unrealistic to adhere to the Strawn Commission's requirement that China must establish a judiciary "protected against any unwarranted interference by the executive or other branches of the Government" and complete and put into force a civil code, commercial code, banking law, bankruptcy law, patent law, land expropriation law, and law concerning notaries public. "Their fulfillment cannot," he wrote, "be required as a condition precedent to the abolition of extraterritoriality." In a spirit of realism Hornbeck concluded: "We are dealing with a situation. The most forceful fact in the situation is the development of 'nationalism' in China. Regardless of treaty provisions, of desiderata, of recommendations, and of their unpreparedness both in the political and in the legal field, the Chinese will abolish extraterritorial rights, with or without the assent of the powers, before very long,—unless the powers choose to use force, in combination, to prevent."[45] Hornbeck was not prepared to use force, and he saw the necessity of compromise. Perhaps, he noted, the best that could be hoped for was the preservation of extraterritorial rights in Shanghai.

Few Westerners were able to confront realities without reservations. One of these was William Leete, who as early as 1925 saw Chinese nationalism eventually pushing the missionary enterprise off the map, about which he observed: "But we must be glad to suffer whether justly or unjustly that the cause of the people may win." Seven years later, Walter A. Adams, then consul-general at Hankow, in response to an inquiry concerning land titles, showed some of the same realism. He cited the growth of the Communist movement, the establishment of soviets, and the certainty that these soviets would destroy land titles. The Nationalist government, he observed, was seeking to eradicate communism by means of military drives, but the use of military force would not suffice. "The soviet movement in this area is deeply rooted in economic distress," Adams wrote. "Its eradication will be possible only through an appropriate change in the conditions which give rise to it." He concluded, "So far as I have been able to ascertain, the Chinese Government is not now effectively executing any program which will result in such appropriate change."[46]

The Americans failed to meet the Chinese expectations on treaty revision, although they went further than the British and well beyond the French. They acknowledged that the Chinese held the upper hand and could readily abrogate the treaties. They were likewise aware that no Chinese government could withstand the popular pressure in favor of abolition. But awareness of these facts was not equivalent to taking appropriate action. Whether foreign "rights" would be protected in the courts of China to the satisfaction of Westerners was of no concern to the Chinese. What mattered to the Chinese was achieving a status of equality. Neither missionaries nor diplomats were in fact ready to concede what history had already wrested from their hands.

The basic point of conflict between China on the one hand and the missionaries on the other lay in the difference between China's conception of her own interests and the outsiders' interpretation of their "rights." A willingness to accept Chinese aspirations and to subordinate foreign interests within China, when such subordination meant almost certain loss, succumbed to the foreigners' general reluctance to face the uncertainties of that course of action.

Superficially it would seem that missionaries, who in their own terms went to China with the aim of serving the Chinese people, and Foreign Service officers and officials in the Department of State, who looked upon their assignment as serving the interests of the United States, would inevitably clash on questions of treaty revision and differ in their attitudes toward the Chinese Nationalist revolution. The analysis of the years 1927 to 1932 suggests the reverse. It is true that there was an absence of cordiality between American government officials and missionaries, and it appears certain that neither missionaries nor mission boards significantly influenced government policy during this period. However, in spite of their other differences, missionaries and government representatives responded in similar fashion. Both showed considerable sympathy toward and understanding of the Chinese point of view, and both were disturbed by the antiforeignism of the revolution and by what the missionary Earl Ballou called the departures from a sane nationalism. Perhaps this was no more than a reaction against the violence and the almost casual use of force by undisciplined soldiers who took the law into their own hands. Or perhaps the common response of both missionaries and American government officials represented something deeper, namely, a common inability to share the Chinese view that the extreme price paid to achieve Chinese Nationalist goals was not too great. Certainly those goals were more important to the Chinese than to the Americans, who in spite of their sympathies were essentially mere observers of the scene. The Americans were intellectually able to understand the humiliation that the Chinese had experienced at the hands of Westerners, but they had not themselves experienced it. Moreover, the Americans were conditioned to believe that change could be brought about through legislative processes and legal procedures in an orderly manner. The Chinese, in contrast, saw no way to achieve change except through violence. Although they too would have preferred to achieve their goals by peaceful means, they had little reason to believe that, short of the use of force, the Western nations would ever yield the privileges which, indeed, the same Western nations had gained by the use of force.

ARTHUR SCHLESINGER, JR.

The Missionary Enterprise
and Theories of Imperialism

For nine centuries European civilization has been engaged in the process of entering and altering non-European societies. The question arises of the relationship of Christian evangelism to other modes of Western penetration and dominion; and my aim here is to show how the Christian missionary enterprise, and more specifically the American Protestant missionary enterprise, fits into general theories of imperialism.

During eight of these nine centuries the process of European expansion took place without benefit of theory. Imperialism did not even appear as a word until the 1840s. Its first use in English came in application, not to overseas colonialism, but to the Second Empire of Napoleon III.[1] Its contemporary meaning emerged in the wake of the renewal of territorial acquisition by European states in the late nineteenth century. It is only since then, in the ninth and last century of Western expansion, that a literature has arisen to explain the phenomena of colonial or neocolonial empire. This literature, while considerable, is also discordant and confusing. By 1919 J. A. Schumpeter could write, "The word 'imperialism' has been abused to the point where it threatens to lose all meaning."[2]

The abuse is, if possible, worse today. One can, however, divide the analytical theories of "imperialism" (I shall ignore the apologetic theories) into three broad categories: economic interpretations, soci-

336

ological interpretations, and political interpretations. Ironically, though the evangelical compulsion was one of the first and strongest motives in the expansion of the West, the classical theories of imperialism have generally ignored the missionary.

CLASSICAL ECONOMIC INTERPRETATIONS

Marx wrote voluminously if unsystematically on colonialism but paid little attention to the evangelical enterprise. However, he did leave missionaries a potential role in his analysis by condemning the traditional religions of Asia as obstacles to modernization. He also took polemical relish in noting the manifold ways in which the Christian colonizers violated the tenets of their own faith. He thus implied that the propagation of Christianity might be a means of change against the Asians and a means of restraint against the Europeans.

In Marx's view, Oriental society lacked the internal stimulus necessary to set the historical dialectic in motion. Therefore, external stimulus was necessary, and this, as Marx saw it, was the historic function of the European intrusion. "England has to fulfill a double mission in India," he wrote in 1853, "one destructive, the other regenerating—the annihilation of the old Asiatic society, and the laying of the material foundations of Western society in Asia." The old society, he continued, was buttressed by religions that "restrained the human mind within the smallest possible compass, making it the unresisting tool of superstition, enslaving it beneath traditional rules, depriving it of all grandeur and historical energies." The result was an "undignified, stagnatory, and vegetative life," which evoked in reaction "wild, aimless, unbounded forces of destruction, and rendered murder itself a religious rite in Hindostan." By subjugating "man to external circumstances instead of elevating man to be the sovereign of circumstances," Asian religion "transformed a self-developing social state into never changing natural destiny, and thus brought about a brutalizing worship of nature, exhibiting its degradation in the fact that man, the sovereign of nature, fell down on his knees in adoration of Hanuman, the monkey, and Sabbal, the cow." European imperialism, by shattering this traditional social and religious structure, became the necessary condition of Asian revolution. The question, Marx said, was whether mankind could "fulfil its destiny without a fundamental revolution in the social state of Asia? If not, whatever may have been the crimes of England she was the unconscious tool of history in bringing about that revolution."[3]

There would have been fewer crimes, Marx added, if the English imperialists had obeyed the dictates of their own faith. "While they combatted the French revolution under the pretext of defending 'our holy religion,' did they not forbid, at the same time, Christianity to be propagated in India, and did they not, in order to make money out of the pilgrims streaming to the temples of Orissa and Bengal, take up the trade in murder and prostitution perpetrated in the temple of Juggernaut?" After describing British plunder and atrocity in India, he asked sarcastically, "What is the influence of the Christian religion on a nation . . . which can lift such thieves to the highest places of hereditary honor . . . make them the privileged landowners, fountains of patronage, mirrors of morals and manners, models for aspiring ambition?"[4]

But these were rhetorical flourishes. In the end, Marx, seeing European criminality as an indispensable agency of Asian change, welcomed the Western assault on traditional Eastern society. He congratulated the British for introducing the railroad and the telegraph, for encouraging a free press, and for training Indian military and administrative elites on the Western model. It could only have been by accident that he failed to congratulate the missionaries for their associated work in undermining Asian religions. Engels summed up this Marxist attitude when he wrote of the French advance into the Magreb: "The conquest of Algeria is an important and fortunate fact for the progress of civilisation."[5]

Oddly, later "Marxist" interpretations abandoned the founders' belief in imperialism as a necessary stage of development. Lenin even denounced H. Cunow for "clumsily and cynically" arguing that "imperialism is modern capitalism, the development of capitalism is inevitable and progressive; therefore imperialism is progressive."[6] Subsequent versions of the economic interpretation, including Lenin's, derived less from Marx than from the British Radical J. A. Hobson, who emphasized the need of capitalist industry for foreign markets and investment outlets.

Yet Hobson by no means denied the autonomy of other motives in expansion. Imperialism, he took care to say, contained "clearly distinguishable threads of thought and feeling," and among these certain "genuinely social and humane motives stand prominent,—the desire to promote the causes of civilisation and Christianity, to improve the economic and spiritual condition of lower races, to crush slavery, and to bring all parts of the habitable world into closer material and moral union."[7] This effort, Hobson said, though honest, was based on major fallacies.

One fallacy was the assumption by missionaries and their supporters that "religion and other arts of civilisation are portable commodities which it is our duty to convey to the backward nations, and that a certain amount of compulsion is justified in pressing their benefits upon people too ignorant at once to recognize them." An even graver fallacy was the self-deception that resulted when "the selfish forces which direct Imperialism . . . utilize the protective colours of these disinterested movements." Even this, Hobson conceded, might not be totally cynical. Politicians, soldiers, and company directors "who push a forward policy by portraying the cruelties of the African slave raids" might not "deliberately or consciously work up these motives . . . They simply and instinctively attach to themselves any strong, genuine elevated feeling which is of service, fan it and feed it until it assumes fervour, and utilize it for their ends."

As for the evangelists themselves, Hobson affirmed their independent role in the process. He was, he said, "well aware that most British missionaries are quite untainted by admixture of political and commercial motives, and that they set about their work in a single spirit of self-sacrifice, eager to save the souls of the heathen, and not a whit concerned to push British trade or 'sanctify the spirit of Imperialism.' Indeed, it is quite evident that, just in proportion as the suspicions of worldly motives appear in missionary work, so the genuinely spiritual influence evaporates."[8]

Lenin, when he transformed what Hobson saw as an option for capitalism into an iron necessity, did not mention missionaries. No doubt he subsumed them in "the non-economic superstructure which grows up on the basis of finance capital, its politics and its ideology."[9] However, contemporary Soviet writers have repaired the omission, in particular A. A. Volokhova, in the recent work *Inostranny Missionery V Kitae, 1901–1920 (Foreign Missionaries in China, 1901–1920)*. Observing that Soviet historical literature had paid little attention to missionary activity, and that "Chinese authors practically never treat it," Volokhova portrayed missionary organizations as "important ordnance in the arsenal of contemporary colonialists . . . the first to penetrate many countries of Asia and Africa and prepare the ground for further colonial expansion." By teaching "submission, humility, and nonopposition to foreign aggression," by indoctrinating their students and getting them jobs in government, missionaries became "the means whereby the imperialist monopoly tries to preserve its influence in Afro-Asian states."

Although Volokhova's detailed narrative indicated that the change in missionary strategy in China after 1880 took place in part for internal reasons within the evangelical community, the thesis laid major stress on conscious external manipulation by monopolists and eager cooperation by missionaries. The notion that saving souls might have remained an independent motive received little consideration. Denying that the religious movement could be separated from imperialism, Volokhova concluded that "the activities of the missionaries were a part of foreign aggression," at least in the twentieth century.[10] Contemporary Leninist analysis would therefore regard the missionary as the accomplice of the capitalist, divesting his role of autonomy and even of ambiguity.

CLASSICAL SOCIOLOGICAL AND POLITICAL INTERPRETATIONS

Where the economic approach perceived imperialism as a response to the internal dislocations of the capital market, the sociological approach perceived it as a response to the internal dislocations of the social structure. The sociological interpretation has therefore been less interested in what imperialism was than in who the imperialists were and what drove them to the far corners of the earth. Schumpeter and Hannah Arendt both saw imperialism as the work of men displaced in their own societies, "superfluous men" in Arendt's phrase, who could not, according to Schumpeter, "find a solid footing at home." Although this insight could have been most usefully applied to missionaries, both Schumpeter and Arendt confined it essentially to adventurers, desperadoes, and scum, "the Bohemians of the four continents," to use J. A. Froude's phrase, who shipped "somewheres east of Suez, where the best is like the worst,/Where there aren't no Ten Commandments, an' a man can raise a thirst." The Eldorado Exploring Expedition in *Heart of*

Darkness distilled the type—"reckless without hardihood, greedy without audacity, and cruel without courage."[11]

Yet even those whose purpose in shipping east of Suez was precisely to plant the Ten Commandments and make the worst the best may also have included some inclined to foreign travel because they could not make it at home. Or so at least astute observers thought, not least Herman Melville, who mused in *Typee:* "May not the unworthiness or incapacity of those who assume apostolic functions upon the remote islands of the sea more easily escape detection by the world at large than if it were displayed in the heart of a city?"[12] This remains a possibility worth considering but not yet systematically examined by proponents of the sociological approach.

The political interpretations, passing lightly over the economy and the social structure, understood imperialism as primarily a specific response to the needs of the state itself. The modern state, quite regardless of systems of ownership or ideology, was, according to this interpretation, intent on self-preservation and self-aggrandizement and therefore exposed to dangers or temptations when confronted by disparities of power. This was the view broadly held by such writers as W. L. Langer, Hans Morgenthau, A. J. P. Taylor, Geoffrey Barraclough, D. S. Landes, and D. K. Fieldhouse. Although some of these writers took the narrowly strategic argument more seriously than others, most have tended to explain imperialist manifestations as the consequence of competition among states for power and status, often preemptive or preclusive in nature and stimulated, in Morgenthau's phrase, by "the existence of weak states or of politically empty spaces."[13]

Political interpretations, less dependent on dogmatic and sweeping formulas than economic and sociological interpretations, have no conceptual problem about making room for the missionaries. They point out that missionaries create political claims, collaborate with or oppose native governments, request or resist the intervention of their own governments, and provide pretexts for government action on other grounds. But in the main, political interpretations have been descriptive rather than analytical in their treatment of the missionary role—that is, when they have mentioned the missionary at all. John K. Fairbank hardly exaggerated when, in discussing the work of American historians, he called the overseas missionary "the invisible man of American history."[14]

The classical theories of imperialism, in short, tell little about the missionary. When they note his existence, they see him as subordinate to, even if not a witting part of, the economic or political machine. For the missionary to lose his invisibility, the historian must not only reconstruct the details of his life and activity but place his role in intelligible analytic relation to the broad process of Western expansion.

To do so, one must begin by acknowledging the autonomy of the missionary impulse. Indeed, though such autonomy is often minimized or ignored, it is not often finally denied, not even perhaps by A. A. Volokhova. Whatever links the missionary enterprise might develop along the way with traders or bankers, politicians, generals, or diplomats, however much it might express in its own way the aggressive energies of the West, the desire to save souls remains distinct from the desire to extend power or to acquire glory or to make money or to seek adventure or to explore the unknown. If this autonomy is conceded, then it is possible to identify the areas where more knowledge is needed before moving toward a general theory of the missionary role in the expansion of the West.

THE MISSIONARY AND THE ECONOMIC INTEREST

Expansion, like most historical processes, tends to be, in the Freudian sense, "overdetermined"; that is, the actors involved may be responding to a number of motives, even though one motive, on the principle of William of Ockham, might be sufficient to explain the act. Prince Henry the Navigator was thus Grand Master of the Order of Chivalry of Our Lord Jesus Christ; but this hardly implies that, when he was navigating, he was not also challenged by the mystery of *terra incognita* and inspired by visions of personal and dynastic fame. When Vasco da Gama sailed into the harbor of Calicut, someone asked what he was looking for. He replied, according to the old tale, "Christians and spices," and unquestionably meant both. Bernal Diaz, explaining why he and his comrades sought the Indies, said "To serve God and his Majesty, to give light to those who were in darkness and to grow rich as all men desire to do."[15]

It may well have been increasingly true of the secular adventurers that, as Ogier Ghiselin de Busbecq wrote in the sixteenth century, "Religion supplies the pretext and gold the motive." But the desire to save souls and the desire to make money were still separate—a fact plainly demonstrated when the two motives came into conflict. Such conflicts have been recurrent in the history of Western empire. In Spanish America, Franciscan and Dominican friars, like Las Casas, strove perseveringly to defend the Indian from the conquistadors. In the Philippines, Miguel Lopez de Legaspi informed Philip II, "If this land is to be settled . . . in order to civilize its inhabitants and bring them to the knowledge of our holy Catholic faith . . . it cannot be sustained by way of trade, both because our articles of barter have no value among them, and because it would be more expense than profit."[16]

This was the sixteenth century, but such quotations can be matched in every century since. The Colonial Office in London in the nineteenth century was under constant pressure from the missionaries and the Aborigines Protection Society to save the natives from the settlers. In China, an American diplomat saw missionaries as "the only barrier between the unhesitating advance of commercial adventure and the not incongruous element of Chinese imbecile corruption"; while a British consul, more favorably disposed to commercial adventure, told London wistfully, "Immense services might be rendered to our commercial interests if only the members of the various missions in China would co-operate with our Consuls in the exploitation of the country, and the introduction of commercial, as well as of purely theological ideas to the Chinese intelligence." In Polynesia, missionaries sturdily opposed the depredations of white traders and planters. As Robert Louis Stevenson wrote of them: "whether Catholic or Protestant, with all their deficiency of candour, of humour, and of common sense, the missionaries are the best and the most useful whites in the Pacific." In Hawaii, the American consular agent complained in 1823, "Trade will never again flourish at these Islands until these emmissaries from the Andover mill are recalled . . . O that Providence would put a whip in every honest hand to lash such rascals naked through the world." Half a century later Mark Twain remarked that there were now 3000 whites in the Sandwich Islands—"sugar-planters, merchants, whale-ship officers, and missionaries. The missionaries are sorry the most of the other whites are there, and these latter are sorry the missionaries don't migrate." In the United States, when land-hungry Georgians persuaded the state government to expel the Cherokee Nation from the territory assigned to it by treaty, the missionaries stood nobly by the Indians; and when two missionaries were imprisoned for defying Georgia law, the evangelicals carried the case of *Worcester v. Georgia* to the Supreme Court. "To this day," wrote Sarah Gertrude Millin about South Africa in 1933, "the missionary is to the Boer the fundamental traitor, the white man who stands for black against white."[17]

Not only did the evangelists find themselves in frequent opposition to acquisitive whites, but some were even ready to identify the acquisitive impulse itself as an enemy. Of all Christianity's adversaries, George Cookman told the Methodists in 1830, the most formidable have been "your cool, prudent, calculating common sense men, who would reduce the question to a mere sale of profit and loss." Josiah Thompson added in 1857, "Commerce cannot be entrusted with the moral interests of mankind: she has no principle that can withstand a strong temptation to her insatiable cupidity." "As soon as the faithful missionary of the cross has begun to succeed in turning the miserable heathen from his idols," said the Episcopalian John Seely Stone, "... modern commerce, with its four great maces, war, slavery, intemperance, and disease, beats to the earth the work of heavenly benevolence, and knocks the head of the new-born hopes of regenerated tribes!" Perry Miller has noted "the peculiarity, more striking in America than anywhere else in Christendom, of a continuous admonition to the merchant classes, who contributed the finances for missionary endeavors, that they were at heart the secret foes of the sacred enterprise." In short, at least in particular times and places, missionary zeal was strongly at war with the secular interest in acquisition and exploitation. Writing in 1908, Archibald Cary Coolidge, the first American diplomatic historian, could speak of "the permanent antagonism between the business community and the missionaries."[18]

The idea has nonetheless evolved that the missionary enterprise served, consciously or not, as a means of easing the job of traders and capitalists. In the words of the laymen's Commission of Appraisal, organized under the chairmanship of William Ernest Hocking to "rethink" missions in 1930–1932, "The Protestant missionary of the eighteenth and nineteenth centuries followed in the wake of trade."[19]

It is true enough that religion could be used to justify expansion as well as restraint. In Gen. 1:28, God enjoined Adam and Eve to "be fruitful, and multiply, and replenish the earth, and subdue it" which no less a moralist than Saint Thomas More read as giving his Utopians the right to seize lands that others were not putting to productive use. "The whole earth," wrote John Winthrop of Massachusetts, "is the lords Garden." It was therefore covered by the injunction of Genesis, "that wch lies common & hath never been replenished or subdued is free to any that will possesse and improve it." Indians were on notice. What A. K. Weinberg in his neglected book *Manifest Destiny* has called "the destined use of the soil" was a powerful justification of expansion; John Quincy Adams called it, though Henry Clay laughed, "the best argument we had."[20]

When missionaries went overseas, they often had a free passage on merchant ships. In some regions they helped, as interpreters, to complete business transactions. Funds for missionary work came largely from the business community; and some missionaries did not hesitate to hint that the Christianization of heathen lands would produce much commercial benefit, either because they believed this, or because they wanted to stimulate business donations, or probably both. The Reverend R. S. Storrs said in a sermon of 1850 before the American Board of Commissioners for Foreign Missions, "If the manufacturers of our country find their way to Africa and China, to the Sandwich Islands and India, in increasing abundance, and produce correspondingly remunerative returns, it is because the herald of salvation has gone thither, seeking the welfare of the people, changing their habits of life, breaking down their prejudices, and creating a demand for comforts and wealth before unknown." Ten years later, before the same audience, the Reverend Samuel Fisher displayed the confusion of commercial and religious appeals: "What is to hinder us from ascending to a position where we shall command the markets of the world, and give laws to commerce, and possess resources sufficient to sustain more missionaries than we now have population?" Reversing the dictum of the Hocking Commission, the Social Gospel preacher Josiah Strong put it succinctly: "What is the process of civilizing but *the creating of more and higher wants?* Commerce follows the missionary." Diplomats like Charles Denby in China agreed: "Missionaries are the pioneers of trade and commerce . . . The missionary, inspired by holy zeal, goes everywhere, and by degrees foreign commerce and trade follow."[21]

345

There is a point in all this, and the question requires detailed investigation; but the evidence of occasional missionary support for mercantile endeavor qualifies more than it refutes the earlier picture of the missionary enterprise as in restraint of trade. There was not much parallelism between the routes of evangelism and of commerce. When the American Board chose Burma as its first target, it did so, not because Salem merchants were dreaming about the great Burma market, but because American missionaries were looking for territory beyond the jurisdiction of British missionary societies. When the American Board entered the Middle East, it did so not to advance trade but to redeem the Holy Land; indeed, investment in foreign missions in the Ottoman Empire, Clifton Phillips reported, greatly exceeded commercial investment.[22] This was undoubtedly true in other parts of the world. American business interests were not conspicuous in India, Ceylon, the South Pacific, or Africa; nor, for that matter, were American missionaries conspicuous where American merchants were busiest.[23] If from time to time the missionary effort facilitated the capitalist effort, the missionaries themselves remained a force independent of, and often at odds with, both the white trader and even more the white settler.

THE MISSIONARY AND THE POLITICAL INTEREST

The Christian mission to the pagan world was, in theory, the propagation of an eternal, transcendent, and universal faith, beyond nation and beyond history. But Christian missionaries were the products of particular nations, and they were rarely the more cosmopolitan representatives of their national cultures. Many were filled with patriotic as well as evangelical ardor. This was perhaps especially true in the new democratic republic in North America, so intensely concerned in the early nineteenth century with asserting its own sense of national identity.

Tocqueville, visiting America in 1831–1832, encountered "societies formed by Americans to send out ministers of the Gospel into the new Western states, to found schools and churches there." These Yankee missionaries, he discovered, did not pursue their calling only to save souls from damnation. They were also worried "lest religion should be allowed to die away in those remote settlements, and the rising states be less fitted to enjoy free institutions . . . Thus religious zeal is perpetually warmed in the United States by the fires of patriotism." Chatting with them, Tocqueville found it hard to sort out the disparate motives of nationalism, republicanism, and Christianity. "If you converse with these missionaries of Christian civilization, you will be surprised to hear them speak so often of the goods of this world, and to meet a politician where you expected to find a priest . . . The Americans combine the notions of Christianity and of liberty so intimately in their minds that it is impossible to make them conceive the one without the other."[24]

By "politician" Tocqueville did not mean that his missionary friends were Jacksonians or National Republicans. He meant that they were partisans of democracy and America. Nor was he inaccurate in his observation. When the Reverend Adoniram Judson, in his eagerness to get into the field, threatened to sign up with the London Missionary Society, his colleague the Reverend Samuel J. Mills exclaimed in shocked protest: "Is England to support her own Missionaries and ours likewise? O for shame . . . I do not like this dependence upon another nation." Mills's national patriotism was more representative than Judson's supranational piety. In the year of Tocqueville's arrival in America, a twenty-three-year-old student at Andover Theological Seminary, where the American Board had been founded twenty-one years earlier, wrote the words for the anthem known to later generations as "America" ("My country 'tis of thee"). Later the Reverend Samuel Francis Smith, as editorial secretary of the American Baptist Missionary Union, also wrote the famous missionary hymn "The Morning Light Is Breaking" as well as books like *Missionary Sketches* and *Rambles in Mission-Fields*. Patriotic and evangelical emotions often ran together. "How can we better testify our appreciation of her free institutions," the Reverend John Codman said of his native country in a sermon before the American Board four years after Tocqueville's departure, "than by laboring to plant them in foreign lands?" "Our Heavenly Father," said the Baptist William R. Williams in 1845, "has made us a national epistle to other lands." The Presbyterian clergyman and educator Philip Lindsley summed it up: "Why should not *American Christian* become the characteristic distinct appellation of our people? . . . and he would be joyfully hailed as the missionary of liberty and light, of religion and peace, of mercy and salvation, to an oppressed, benighted, and perishing world."[25]

In 1816 the American Board defined its goal for the American Indians as making them "English in their language, civilized in their habits, and Christian in their religion." American Christian missionaries in the early years often brought along farmers and mechanics to assist, as Dr. Rufus Anderson put it, in settling "the savages of the wilderness . . . in communities like our own."[26] In the same spirit missionaries abroad tried for a time to uproot their protégés from the indigenous culture, making them learn English words, read English books, dress in Western clothes, and even, as a final assault on identity, take American names.

Inasmuch as missionaries were Americans as well as Christians, they could propagate political as well as theological doctrine; they could even, without betrayal of their mission, aid the state as well as the church. John Quincy Adams was the first President to make this point. In one of his last presidential acts, he informed King Kamehameha of Hawaii that "a knowledge of letters and of the True Religion—the Religion of the Christian's Bible . . . are the best, and the only means, by which the prosperity and happiness of nations can be advanced." American missionaries in Hawaii responded with alacrity to the hint that they could simultaneously serve Hawaii, the United States, and God. Sir George Simpson of the Hudson's Bay Company, visiting the islands in 1842, alleged to London that the missionaries could be considered "a political Engine in the hands of Government of the United States."[27]

Missionaries elsewhere often found themselves mixed up with diplomacy as translators and copyists. William B. Reed, the American minister plenipotentiary who negotiated the Treaty of Tientsin in 1858, noted, "Without them as interpreters, the public business could not be transacted . . . There is not an American merchant in China . . . who can write or read a single sentence of Chinese."[28] In the Mediterranean, missionaries enjoyed amiable relations with the commanders of American warships. This was less true in the Pacific, where missionaries too often tried to spoil naval fun ashore.

Local crises, moreover, began to lead missionaries to request the direct aid of their governments in the interests of the evangelical enterprise. Often missionaries were ahead of traders in clamoring for protective intervention and thereby affording home governments pretexts for territorial expansion. When French armed forces went into the Saigon delta and seized the three eastern provinces of

Cochin-China in 1858—1862, it was to gain not trading advantages but missionary guarantees; Vietnam was thus a missionary legacy to the twentieth century. Nor did American missionaries hesitate to solicit diplomatic or even military intervention by Washington when, as in the eastern Mediterranean, foreign governments impeded or harassed American missionary activity, or when, as in the Far East, they forbade it altogether. During the Ottoman troubles of 1876, according to James A. Field, Jr., the Navy Department was even prevented by missionary pressure from moving its squadron base out of the eastern Mediterranean.[29]

The case of China, which combined an exclusion policy with internal weakness, particularly tempted missionaries to invoke the secular power in order to break down barriers to salvation. As Peter W. Fay suggested, whereas foreign merchants could do well enough with limited access to the Chinese interior, for foreign missionaries "the opening of China was the indispensable precondition to their doing anything at all." The truculence of Protestant missionaries in China in the nineteenth century often exceeded that of both foreign merchants and governments. S. C. Miller pointed out that during the Tientsin negotiations of 1858, the Reverend Samuel Wells Williams, whose book *The Middle Kingdom* had a decade earlier demonstrated scholarly sympathy with China, observed privately that "nothing short of the Society for the Diffusion of Cannon Balls" would bring the Chinese to their senses; "they are among the most craven of people, cruel and selfish as heathenism can make men, so we must be backed by force if we wish them to listen to reason." Williams was responsible for the insertion into the treaty of the "religious toleration" clauses, protecting native converts as well as foreign missionaries and, as Paul A. Varg noted, making the American government in effect a partner in the missionary enterprise.[30]

In due course American missionaries in China began to doubt whether treaty provisions unaccompanied by physical intervention could accomplish much. In 1869 the missionary journal *Chinese Recorder* asked how long it would take Americans to understand that the mailed fist was "the true method of dealing with such a nation." "Between 1840 and 1900," S. C. Miller wrote, "every Western invasion of China was almost unanimously conceived of by some American missionaries as an act of Providence." Even the Opium War was taken in stride as God's way of opening up China;

obviously He could be counted on to deal with the evils of the opium traffic in the fullness of time. Henrietta Shuck, the first American woman missionary to China, observed when the trouble began, "How these difficulties do rejoice my heart because I think the English government may be enraged, and God, in His power may break down the barriers which prevent the gospel of Christ from entering China." Those whose hearts were not rejoiced by opium could still believe, as Marx had in the case of India, that the British in spite of themselves were performing a necessary historical task. "The English government as such has not the least interest in the progress of China in true religion," said Williams in 1856, but British military intervention must "strengthen the hope that God is preparing to work mightily among the Chinese . . . for further triumphs."[31] If force broke the ground, religion could plant the seed. Given such attitudes, it is hardly surprising that so many American missionaries in China moved by gradual steps from the chapel to the chancellery.

THE MISSIONARY AND THE CULTURAL INTEREST: GRACE

So the American Protestant missionary enterprise contained within itself from the start strong drives toward political, national, and technological as well as religious evangelism. But some participants in the enterprise began early to wonder whether the central purpose of opening souls to the grace of God was not endangered when, in Tocqueville's phrase, priests turned into politicians. Thus, in 1823 the American Board instructed its missionaries to "abstain from all interference with the local and political views of the people. The Kingdom of Christ is not of this world; and it especially behooves a missionary to stand aloof from the private and transient interests of chiefs and rulers."[32]

This was above all the view powerfully expounded by the Reverend Rufus Anderson who, as corresponding secretary of the American Board from 1832 to 1866, was a dominating influence among American missionaries (and through his friendship with Henry Venn of the Church Missionary Society, on British missionaries too) and who used his influence to withdraw the evangelists from everything but their essential duty of saving souls. In a sermon of 1845 on "The Theory of Missions to the Heathen," Anderson warned that the "very perfection of our own social religious state" led Christianity to be identified "with the almost universal diffusion . . . of the blessings of education, industry, civil liberty, family government, social order, the means of a respectable livelihood, and a well ordered community." As a result, he said, *"our* idea of piety" among the heathen "generally involves the acquisition and possession, to a great extent, of these blessings; and *our* idea of the propagation of the gospel by means of missions is, to an equal extent, *the creation among heathen tribes and nations of a highly improved state of society, such as we ourselves enjoy."*

It was against this illusion that Anderson directed his argument; or more precisely, it was against the illusion that such a vast intellectual, moral, and social change could take place in a short time, that "the first generation of converts" could be expected "to come into all our fundamental ideas of morals, manners, political economy, social organization, right, justice, equity." The office of the missionary was not, he emphasized, "the reorganizing, by various direct means, of the structure of that social system, of which the converts form a part"; it was, simply and sublimely, "that of *reconciling immortal souls to God."* Evangelism should therefore have "as little to do with the relations of this life and the things of this world and sense, and as few relations to the kingdoms of this world, as is consistent with the successful prosecution of its one grand object."[33]

Anderson thus set his face against the mission as an agency of social or political reform. He stopped the dispatch of farmers and mechanics as part of the mission team, called for vernacular instead of English schools, and recommended the translation of the Scriptures into native languages. He opposed the entry of missionaries into the service of foreign governments. "As a missionary society and as a mission," he said in 1847, "we cannot proceed on the assumption, however plausibly stated, that the Saxon is to supersede the native races." In 1845 the American Board in this spirit even opposed missionary association with "secular embassies." Any benefits growing out of such connections, the board declared, rarely compensated in the longer run for the diversion of the missionaries from their "more appropriate labors" and for the confirmation of native suspicions that "after all missionaries are agents of the governments of their own countries."[34]

In the early and middle nineteenth century, most missionaries accepted the policy, as Anderson put it, of keeping "the missionary and political currents of the world as distinct as possible." J. R. Bodo, after careful research in the years 1812–1848, reported, "So far as we could ascertain, no missionary in our period ever expressed the hope that their work abroad might prepare the way for American colonization or even pave the way for American influence."[35] Although exceptions might be made to the last phrase, certainly the Anderson program of self-restraint expressed the prevailing mood.

Yet even Anderson, for all his austere logic, was not immune to the temptations of the *mission civilisatrice*. Rather, he saw the process in phases: first the evangelist, the soldier of the cross, continually moving on to new fields of conquest; then the pastor, the shepherd of the flock, staying with and improving the life of his community. In time, after "two or three generations," the Christian seed must burst into social flower. The missionary could well believe that, once "the alienated heart" was reconciled to God, "the principle of obedience implanted, and a highly spiritual religion introduced, a social renovation will be sure to follow." In his most expansive mood, Anderson could even expect "the Anglo-Saxon race to fill the myriads of sunny islands on the bosom of the broad Pacific; and the genius of American and English enterprise to preside in great commercial cities, (other New Yorks, or even Londons,) reared on the Sandwich Islands, New Zealand and Australia."[36]

THE MISSIONARY AND THE CULTURAL INTEREST: REFORM

That Rufus Anderson should himself harbor such dreams testifies to the strength of the forces within American Protestantism working to undermine his own program of self-denial. If the American Board insisted that the Kingdom of Christ was not of the world, the doctrine of that Kingdom still had considerable potentiality for application in the world. The rising millennial fervor rendered such application more urgent by contending that the day of judgment might well be at hand. "As the time shortens," the Reverend Joseph Harvey observed in 1815, "the work will be hastened."

By 1827, even the American Board in its eighteenth annual report defined the task of foreign missions as "no less than the moral renovation of a world. Wars are to cease. All the domestic relations are to be sanctified. Every village is to have its school and its church." The Reverend Lyman Beecher had warned the year before that the human race would not experience "moral renovation" without considerable changes in "the civil and religious conditions of nations." He laid down various secular specifications: "the monopoly of the soil must be abolished . . . the monopoly of power must be superseded by the suffrages of freemen . . . the rights of conscience must be restored to me." He added, "To accomplish these changes, a great example is needed . . . Some nation, itself free, must blow the trumpet and hold up the light."[37]

The idea of the regeneration of secular society thus lay latent within the doctrine of the Kingdom of God. Then, as H. Richard Niebuhr explained, that doctrine gradually evolved under the pressures of nineteenth century America from an individual to a social dispensation. The abolitionist crusade helped to charge the evangelical gospel with immediate social content. More and more, preachers began to see the Kingdom of God as something not just to be anticipated in heaven but to be pursued on earth. After the Civil War, Lyman Beecher's son Edward could declare, "Now that God has smitten slavery unto death, He has opened the way for the redemption and sanctification of our whole social system."[38] America was at last preparing to blow the trumpet and hold up the light.

The missionary enterprise had in the meantime been faltering. But the growing determination to save societies as well as souls both widened the range and diversified the tools of missionary effort. All pagan society was now the target. Nor was it any longer enough to win individuals to Christ if the environment remained non-Christian; individual conversion, indeed, was seen increasingly as a means to social reform. Other factors contributed to the revival of foreign missions: a new surge of millennial enthusiasm in the wake of Dwight L. Moody's revival of the revival; a tempering of dogma to replace a God of wrath by a God of mercy and especially to relax the old Calvinist insistence on the irrevocable damnation of all persons dying impenitent; and a growing belief among missionaries in the field that a more humane approach would bring success after so many sour years of frustration.[39] Above all, the missionary enterprise doubtless provided one more outlet for abounding national vitality, generated by economic and demographic growth and now shooting off in a diversity of directions and fields around the planet.

As confidence revived in the missionary enterprise, the identification of Christianity with American nationalism became more explicit, a process much assisted by Darwinian injunctions about the necessity for the more favored races to succeed in the struggle for survival. The Reverend Austin Phelps, professor emeritus of sacred rhetoric and homiletics at Andover, argued in his introduction to Josiah Strong's *Our Country* that apostolic success responded not to sentiment—how poorly Christian missionaries had done in Palestine—but to power. "Success in the work of the world's conversion has, with rare exceptions, followed the lines of human growth and prospective greatness ... [Christianity] has allied itself with the most virile races. It has taken possession of the most vigorous and enterprising nations. The colonizing races and nations have been its favorites ... By natural sequence, the *localities* where those elements of powerful manhood are, or are to be, in most vigorous development, have been the strategic points of which our religion has taken possession as by a masterly military genius." Military metaphors, always convenient in a vocabulary of spiritual and moral conquest, rushed more than ever to the fore. "The principles of such a strategic wisdom should lead us to look on these United States as first and foremost the chosen seat of enterprise for the world's conversion ... As goes America, so goes the world."[40]

Strong himself agreed that the "Anglo-Saxon" race had been "especially commissioned to prepare the way for the full coming of God's kingdom in the earth." In his notorious phrase, God was "not only preparing in our Anglo-Saxon civilization the die with which to stamp the people of the earth, but ... also massing behind that die the mighty power with which to press it." But to do Strong justice, he insisted more on social than on racial interpretations of the Kingdom. "An enthusiasm for humanity means far more than a strong desire to save as many individual souls as possible. It means a longing for the uplifting and perfecting of humanity as a whole, for the saving of society."[41]

The Social Gospel made reform almost as urgent a Christian duty as conversion. It thereby repealed the self-denying ordinances of Rufus Anderson and licensed a much greater sweep of interference, both missionary and secular, into the affairs of benighted peoples. In China particularly, missionaries moved on to ever more systematic attack on social as well as religious heresy—on foot binding, concubinage, and other aspects of the subjection of women, on opium, gambling, and squeeze, on non-Western educational and medical practices. Such intervention was not only righteous but exultant, drawing strength from a complex mixture of rectitude, duty, and power.

At home the Social Gospel was prepared to invoke the secular government in order to rescue the powerless, so the tactic seemed plausible abroad too. It appeared the best way to save the natives from local tyranny or foreign exploitation. Moreover, missionary property, now embracing schools, clinics, hospitals, and residences as well as chapels and printing presses, was becoming a sizable vested interest of its own. This development gave missionaries themselves a new and sometimes avid property consciousness and created a further claim for protection by their governments. The alliance of progressivism and imperialism, exemplified in the United States by Theodore Roosevelt and Herbert Croly and in England by Joseph Chamberlain, Sidney Webb, Bernard Shaw, and the Fabians, no doubt confirmed missionary faith in political, even in military, intervention as a means of both individual and social salvation.[42] The responsibility of stewardship over backward peoples would in turn, it was supposed, call forth the highest moral virtues. "From the muscular Christianity of the last generation to the imperial Christianity of the present day," wrote J. A. Hobson, "is but a single step."[43]

So the social euphoria of progressive Protestantism had the ironic effect of promoting a deeper Christian intrusion into non-Christian societies and strengthening the ties between the missionary and his government. The Turkish massacre of Armenians in 1894–1895 thus led to a clamor in American religious circles for American intervention. Hearing that missionaries were about to be expelled, Lyman Abbott's *Outlook,* a progressive Christian journal, said it was the duty of the United States government to protect them "and, if necessary, to spend its last dollar and call out its last soldier for that purpose."[44]

The new mood swelled as the United States found itself on the verge of a war with Spain. "Great people have great responsibilities," said the Episcopalian *Churchman* in 1897; " . . . They must—or be recreant to all that makes them grand or free or worth dying for—stand by the weak and defend the helpless, and advance the banner of mercy and justice over the world." Six months later the Presbyterian *Evangelist* declared, "If it be the will of Almighty God, that by war the last trace of this inhumanity of man to man shall be swept away from this Western hemisphere, let it come!" With victory over Spain, the religious community saw shining new evangelical opportunities in territorial acquisition. To refuse "the Ladrone, the Caroline, and the Philippine Islands, and even Cuba, Porto Rico, and the Canaries," said the *Religious Telescope,* " . . . would be to render the nation guilty of a great crime in the sight of high Heaven. The times are ripe for us to extend the blessings of free government to all those portions of the earth which God and the fortunes of war render it reasonably obligatory upon us to extend them to." Judson Smith, secretary of the American Board of Foreign Missions, sent the State Department petitions from American missionaries in China calling for the annexation of the Ladrone, Caroline, and Pelew Islands. "Wherever on pagan shores the voice of the American missionary and teacher is heard," said the Reverend J. H. Barlow, "there is fulfilled the manifest destiny of the Christian Republic." The Reverend Alexander Blackburn, a Baptist with missionary interests, wrote in the *Standard* of the "Imperialism of Righteousness." When the *Boston Herald* in 1900 queried five occupational groups in fifteen cities on their attitudes toward expansion, ministers led the list of supporters in every city. In a new book, *Expansion under New World-Conditions,* Josiah Strong, after a survey of secular forces pressing the nation toward expansion, called on the nation "to adopt a political ethics which will not outrage Christian ethics." He concluded, "It is time to dismiss 'the craven fear of being great,' to recognize the place in the world which God has given us, and to accept the responsibilities which it devolves upon us in behalf of Christian civilization."[45]

In the years before the war, the Far East had overtaken the Levant as the leading area of missionary endeavor, and after the war, China bulked largest of all nations in the missionary mind. China was, according to the young Sherwood Eddy, "the goal, the lodestar, the great magnet that drew us all." Both religious and national interests were believed to require the Protestantization of China before it was either Russified or modernized under native and non-Christian auspices. "Is the Anglo-Saxon or the Slav to command the Pacific and therefore the world's future?" asked Strong; and others, like Bishop Charles H. Fowler of the Methodists, echoed the fear: "If Russia appropriates and assimilates China, we are face to face with the most powerful Empire ever known among men."[46]

As for the alternative possibility, a non-Christian modern China, this was threatening too. "The work of the missionaries tends to avert revolutionary disturbances in China," wrote Theodore Roosevelt in 1908; " . . . *Now* is the time for the west to implant its ideals in the Orient, in such fashion as to minimize the chance of a dreadful future clash between two radically different and hostile civilizations." "Modern civilization has been already admitted," Strong had said in 1900, "and cannot be cast out. The liberated genie can never again be imprisoned. I look for the fulfillment of General Grant's prophecy that 'in less than half a century Europe will be complaining of the too rapid advance of China.' " General Grant's friend Mark Twain also mused, but in a different vein, about the notion of Christianizing the Chinese: "Leave them alone, they are plenty good enough just as they are; and besides, almost every convert runs a risk of catching our civilization. We ought to be careful. We ought to think twice before we encourage a risk like that; for, *once civilized, China can never be uncivilized again.*"[47]

As usual in millennial circles, time was short, and a sense of urgency may have appeared to justify a resort to what conventional minds might have regarded as methods alien to the Prince of Peace. In 1900 the Boxer Rebellion included the foreign missions as a major target. When Western armies marched on Peking and put down the uprising, missionaries applauded the troops. For some missionaries, it seemed, the more brutal the liberation, the better. The Reverend William S. Ament of the American Board told the *New York Sun:* "The soft hand of the Americans is not as good as the nailed fist of the Germans:—If you deal with the Chinese with a soft hand they will take advantage of it." After the Western victory, the missionary demand for condign punishment struck less sanctimonious observers as a thirst for vengeance. Ament roamed the countryside, accompanied by an American cavalry troop, blackmailing peasants into delivering up "indemnities," whether or not membership in the Boxers could be proved, and burning houses when peasants were unavailable. Some servants of the Lord even moved into Peking palaces, auctioning off goods and furnishings left behind by frightened Chinese. Toughness, missionaries told the American minister, must be the policy in the future; in general, they wanted an even tougher policy than did the businessmen. The Presbyterian Devello Z. Sheffield, a former president of the China Educational Association, explained to Judson Smith of the American Board, "It is not 'blood-thirstiness' in missionaries to desire further shedding of blood, but an understanding of Chinese character and conditions." In 1907 this same moralist published a book entitled *Principles of Ethics*. The Presbyterian Gilbert Reid, director of the International Institute of China, in a piece airily entitled "The Ethics of Loot" wrote, "Personally, I regret that the guilty suffered so little at my own hands," and added that, after six months of reflection, he was not sure but that razing Peking to the ground "would have been for the greatest good of the greatest number." It is little wonder that W. W. Rockhill of the State Department noted in a China dispatch: "That our Protestant missionaries require restraining in their ardor there can be no doubt. How is it going to be done? The Lord only knows."[48]

Still, as the missionaries themselves had contended when the international expeditionary force burned and sacked Peking, the Lord could use wondrous instruments to achieve his purposes. This time His choice evidently fell on Mark Twain, who laid into the unfortunate Ament and his defenders in the American Board with relish in two devastating pieces in the *North American Review*. In private jottings Mark Twain fulminated about the "reverend bandits of the American Board" and the achievement of the missionary movement in having "loaded vast China onto the concert of Christian Birds of Prey" (the pun was no doubt deliberate). The more bishops who, like the Methodist Earl Cranston, declared it "worth any cost in bloodshed if we can make millions of Chinese true and intelligent Christians," the more ludicrous and appalling the missionary position became.[49] Lay comment in America and Britain supported Mark Twain, and even the board began to wonder about its representatives in the field. The reaction against the excesses of 1900–1902 was rapid and definite.

Even before these voices of restraint, Josiah Strong himself had warned against racism: "I do not imagine that an Anglo-Saxon is any dearer to God than a Mongolian or an African." He therefore contended that the main missionary work "must be done for Africa by negroes and for China by Chinamen. Men of the same race can better endure the climate and can more easily establish close relations than men of foreign blood."[50] Although this idea got nowhere, prudent evangelists, recognizing the growth of nationalism in the non-Western world, laid increasing emphasis on the need for national churches, staffed and run by converts. Yet most missionaries, their careers bound up with their superior status abroad and their condescension toward converts unimpaired, tended, until very late in the day, to favor the nationalization of churches more in theory than in practice.

The theological thaw of the late nineteenth century even produced a certain awareness that non-Christian religions might have a use and dignity of their own. From the publication of the first volume of James Freeman Clarke's *Ten Great Religions* in 1871, comparative religion became an issue in the United States. Clarke, as a Unitarian, was easily dismissed by the evangelical community; but a sense of respect for other faiths continued to grow, encouraged perhaps by their capacity for resistance and, in England, by the Colonial Office's interest in using heathen prelates to thwart nationalist politicians. Liberal theology promoted efforts to redefine Christianity in order to reduce its points of friction with other faiths—efforts that divested Christianity of much of its historical and theological content and reduced it to ethical pieties, like George A. Gordon's "pure idea of self-sacrifice" and Henry Churchill King's "reverence for personality."[51]

Missionaries now retreated from the view that faith could be served by force or that missions shared a common cause with national states. Confronted by anti-Christian riots in Nanking in the 1920s, missionaries opposed American military intervention and, by calling for a revision of the unequal treaties, signified a readiness to renounce special diplomatic protection.[52] By the 1930s the Hocking Commission said it was "clearly not the duty of the Christian missionary to attack the non-Christian systems." He should "look forward, not to the destruction of these [other] religions, but to their continued co-existence with Christianity." In an exhortation that the Fundamentalists could only regard as unabashed syncretism, the Commission called on the modern mission *"to know and understand the religions around it, then to recognize and associate itself with whatever kindred elements there are in them."* In 1935 a professor at the University of Chicago Divinity School could even write a piece for *The Christian Century* stirringly entitled "I Don't Want To Christianize the World!"[53]

TOWARD A CULTURAL INTERPRETATION

Once recovered from the social euphoria of the nineties, missionaries in general returned to the position of Rufus Anderson. The Hocking Commission declared "with conviction" that the Protestant missionaries it had studied around 1930 were "in no sense apologists for, nor promoters of, any political or economic system, or interest."[54] Yet if missionaries were rarely conscious promoters of Western political or economic systems, they remained quite conscious promoters of Christianity and thereby of a most penetrating, powerful, and alien structure of ideas and values. In the reforming mood of the Social Gospel and even in the self-denying mood of Rufus Anderson, they were inescapably involved in a deadly assault on central ideas and values in the lands to which they carried the evangelical crusade.

Today, with the Europe-centered world contracting to its actual geographical boundaries, the Christian missionary enterprise seems in retrospect not only incredibly audacious and ambitious but also incredibly arrogant. This arrogance, however, was the simple-hearted expression of a strength of faith—a faith that galvanized the will of conquest and no doubt contributed to more secular forms of imperialism. The Faustian optimism about Western man's ability to change the world explains in part why the Christian adventurers were not only intrepid but victorious. J. H. Parry, reflecting on the collapse of the Aztec and Inca empires before a handful of Spanish Christians, suggested that in contrast to Christianity the Amerindian religion was "profoundly pessimistic, the sad acquiescent faith of the last great Stone Age culture . . . The Indian believed that his religion required him to fight and if need be to die bravely. The Spaniard believed that his religion enabled him to win."[55]

The evangelical crusade enlisted men and women of clearly delineated and aggressive psychological cast. By definition, missionaries were so persuaded of their possession of absolute truth that they would risk anything and destroy nearly anything to assure its propagation. Savers of souls, as William James noted, had specific characteristics: asceticism, humble-mindedness, steadfastness, charity, patience, and self-severity. But, he added, "all these things together do not make saints infallible. When their intellectual outlook is narrow, they fall into all sorts of holy excesses, fanaticism or theopathic absorption, self-torment, prudery, scrupulosity, gullibility, and morbid inability to meet the world. By the very intensity of his fidelity to the paltry ideals with which an inferior intellect may inspire him, a saint can be even more objectionable and damnable than a superficial carnal man would be in the situation." Moreover, James wrote, "narrowness of mind" could not always be blamed on the individual, "for in religious and theological matters he probably absorbs his narrowness from his generation."[56]

Though there were men of broad intellectual outlook among American Protestant missionaries, James's description could well have applied to the majority, especially in the early days. As the archetypal missionary saw it, he was preserving the heathen from the unutterable torment of eternal damnation. Along the way he might condemn the economic and political aggression practiced by his fellow whites. But he placed no limits on his own spiritual aggression, that is, his right to challenge ancient custom and authority, to denounce traditional rituals, creeds and gods, to deprive the pagans of their spiritual inheritance and identity. "A missionary sermon," as Santayana wrote, "is an unprovoked attack; it seems to entice, to dictate, to browbeat, to disturb, and to terrify; it ends, if it can, by grafting into your heart, and leaving to fructify there, an alien impulse, the grounds of which you do not understand, and the consequences of which you never have desired."[57]

The Hocking Commission itself was constrained to acknowledge that missionaries sometimes displayed "the impulse to dominate or to impose one's type of mind on others, the 'predatory temper,' the will to power." Indeed this was the prevalent image in literature, from the "rapacious hordes of enlightened individuals who . . . clamorously announce the progress of the Truth" described by Melville in *Typee,* to Somerset Maugham's Reverend Davidson in "Miss Thompson" (the short story from which John Colton and Clemence Randolph drew the play *Rain*). Melville in particular raged at the missionaries for their determination to impose New England's Blue Laws on the hapless Tahitians. On Sundays, for example, they sent out constables to whip the natives into Sabbath service, while "on week days, they are quite as busy . . . These gentry are indefatigable. At the dead of night prowling round the houses, and in the daytime hunting amorous couples in the groves." Dancing, kite flying, flute playing, and the singing of traditional ballads fell under the missionary ban, all of which, in Melville's strangely modern phrase, was "denationalising the Tahitians."[58]

Many missionaries, even after the theological thaw, expressed condescension if not contempt for the depraved and unrepentant people whose souls they are trying to save, "debased," as Lyman Beecher had put it in an earlier time, "by their own superstitions." Thus, one Protestant chaplain in Hong Kong declared: "The Chinese are a lying, thieving, licentious race, defiling everything which comes in contact with him, deceiving from a natural instinct to deceive." British missionaries often felt the same way about the Indians, as did the French about the Polynesians. Nor were converts necessarily more highly regarded. "The position of these uprooted Christians," the Hocking Commission conceded, "was the more unhappy since their tutors in the faith were seldom inclined to admit them to social equality." Sometimes condescension and contempt grew into racism, the powers of darkness claiming the missionaries as they had claimed Conrad's Kurtz. "By the simple exercise of our will," Kurtz had written, almost in the accents of an evangelist, "we can exert a power for good practically unbounded." But after what Conrad described as Kurtz's "magnificent" peroration filled with "burning noble words" came the scribbled cry of his unconscious, "Exterminate all the brutes!"[59]

Or, if extermination was too much, transform them. Leave the native, in the words of Winwood Reade, "nothing of the African except his skin." The Andersonians might disclaim this goal, but even they sought to save the heathen by plucking his soul out of the intricate religious and moral web of his traditional society. "It is a most strange vocation, the missionary's," Mark Twain observed, four years before he encountered Dr. Ament. "There is no other reputable occupation that resembles it . . . In all lands the religious deserter ranks with the military deserter; it is considered that he has done a base thing and shameful. It is the mish's trade to make religious deserters."[60] And the effort to make religious deserters struck at the heart of the native culture.

Even when missionaries might in the Anderson style renounce the transformation of cultures as a conscious aim, it remained an unconscious result. "Even if they carefully refrain from teaching disloyalty," A. C. Coolidge wrote of the missionary enterprise in Turkey, "the whole spirit of their instruction . . . the mere presence of these protected strangers, the representatives of a higher and freer civilization, must stimulate aspirations which the Turks regard with aversion." The creation of missionary communities in the American style, the introduction by missionaries of the idea of change, the exemplification by missionaries of such explosive notions as the worth of the individual, "the dignity of labor, the status of women, the values of literacy, the virtues of honesty, and the importance of technology"—all these tended to disorient static societies. "I assure you," said Sir Bartle Frere, "that ... the teaching of Christianity among the one hundred and sixty millions of civilized industrious Hindus and Mohammedans in India is effecting changes, moral, social, and political, which, for extent and rapidity of effect, are far more extraordinary than any thing you or your fathers have witnessed in modern Europe."[61]

In spite of the panic among the pious at home over the geological account of the age of the earth and later over Darwin, missionaries in undeveloped lands came on as modernizers—as apostles not only of Western religion but of Western science and technology. When Elijah C. Bridgman explained the United States to China in his vernacular manual of 1838, he laid stress on science and technology as proud achievements of Western civilization.[62] After another half-century, Josiah Strong described science as "destined to become the great iconoclast of the heather world," adding, "The church ought to leap for joy that in modern times God has raised up these new prophets of his truth." A question asked by the Turkish sultan about the American engineer demonstrating the telegraph to his court in 1847—a question reported to America by Cyrus Hamlin—summed up the point: was he "one of those American missionaries who were turning the world upside down?"[63]

In his way, therefore, the missionary was an agent of the Western assault on non-Western societies. But his way was evidently not the way laid out in the classical theories of economic and political imperialism. The historian, seeking to explain the role and impact of Christian evangelism, must move on to the idea of "cultural imperialism." Cultural imperialism means purposeful aggression by one culture against the ideas and values of another. The mere communication of ideas and values across national borders is not in itself imperialism—except in the view of Communist states that fear the idea of "ideological coexistence." Such communication becomes aggression only when accompanied by political, economic, or military pressure.

Classical theories of imperialism were essentially concerned with the imperialists rather than the imperialized. They sought to show how economic, sociological, or political compulsions within Western civilization produced intrusions into the non-Western world. Whatever the specific causes adduced, the process was characteristically seen through Western eyes. But the penetration of the non-Western world by one of the most dynamic of Western ideas—nationalism—began in time to bring about a radical shift in perspective. Nationalism led to the insistence that the imperial process be considered in terms less of the sending than of the receiving country. As American historians, belatedly interested in the poor and powerless, now talk of writing history "from the bottom up" instead of "from the top down," so new interpretations of imperialism sought to portray the Western impact on the East not "from the outside in" but "from the inside out." The new perspective affected some of the classical theories. The economic interpretation, for example, became a way of explaining the persistence not only of Western capitalism but also of non-Western underdevelopment. The most striking result was to throw the idea of cultural imperialism into separate and sharp relief.

Cultural aggression did not necessarily parallel political or economic aggression. As missionaries sometimes opposed political or economic controls imposed by fellow whites, so white administrators and entrepreneurs, however activist in government and business, often sought to protect the native culture, including the traditional religion, against unnecessary Westernization. Thus, Warren Hastings wrote Lord Mansfield in 1774 that he "desired to found the authority of the British Government in Bengal on its ancient laws" and "to rule the people with ease and moderation according to their own ideas, manners and prejudices." In this spirit the East India Company banned missionaries until in 1813 the pious at home forced a change in policy. The great myth-maker of British imperialism, Rudyard Kipling, told a Protestant minister in 1895 how "cruel" he found it that white men should "confound their fellow creatures with a doctrine of salvation imperfectly understood by themselves and a code of ethics foreign to the climate and instinct of those races whose most cherished customs they outrage and whose gods they insult." Lord Cromer, after conceding "the material benefits derived from Europeanization," added, "But as regards the ultimate effect on public and private morality the future is altogether uncertain. European civilisation destroys one religion without substituting another in its place."[64]

Literary men influenced by the romantic myth of native innocence also joined the critique of cultural aggression. Asking what "the Polynesian savage" has to desire at the hands of civilization, Melville answered grimly, "Let the once smiling and populous Hawaiian Islands, with their now diseased, starving, and dying natives, answer that question." Western civilization in his view gave a hundred evils for its every benefit. "The fiend-like skill we display in the invention of all manner of death-dealing engines, the vindictiveness with which we carry on our wars, and the misery and desolation that follow in their train," he wrote, "are enough of themselves to distinguish the white civilized man as the most ferocious animal on the face of the earth." The word "savage," Melville thought, was applied to the wrong side. "So far as the relative wickedness of the parties is concerned, four or five Marquesan Islanders sent to the United States as Missionaries might be quite as useful as an equal number of Americans despatched to the Islands in a similar capacity."[65]

The thesis that the native should be assimilated to Western political or religious values was particularly challenged by the proponents of indirect rule in England and of association in France. The anti-assimilationists believed in disturbing native political and religious institutions only to the extent necessary to facilitate tasks of administration or plunder. Some genuinely respected the inherent worth of the native culture, but more were probably racists who believed the natives genetically incapable of rising to the standards of Western civilization. Ironically, it was the missionaries who, in order to prove the native's spiritual equality, were most prepared to destroy his cultural identity.

Political and economic forms of imperialism thus did not reach so deep as cultural into the soul of native societies. Political and economic imperialism were essentially utilitarian and assumed little more than that one state or economy was stronger than another. Cultural imperialism maintained that one set of values was better than another, and this was far more demoralizing. As nationalism spread through the non-Western world, its edge of bitterness came in the end more from cultural than from political or economic wounds. "The most humiliating kind of defeat," Jean-François Revel pointed out, "is a cultural defeat. It is the only defeat that one can never forget, because it cannot be blamed on bad luck, or on the barbarism of the enemy. It entails not only acknowledgment of one's own weakness, but also the humiliation of having to save oneself by taking lessons from the conqueror—whom one must simultaneously hate and imitate."[66]

Of all forms of cultural defeat, the religious defeat would presumably be most humiliating of all. As Wen Ching observed at the turn of the century in *The Chinese Crisis from Within,* "We cannot wonder that the Chinese officials should hate the missionaries. Their Church is an *imperium in imperio,* propagating a strange faith and alienating the people from that of their ancestors." By that time antimissionary riots were common in China. In April 1899, Wu T'ing-fang, the Chinese minister to the United States, tried to persuade the American Academy of Political and Social Science to see the missionary invasion through Chinese eyes. Suppose, he said, that the Chinese had sent Confucian missionaries to America, that these missionaries had established themselves in New York, Philadelphia, and San Francisco, and that they had built temples, held public meetings, opened schools, and gathered round them a mass of converts. "If they were to begin their work by making vehement attacks on the doctrines of Christianity, denouncing the cherished institutions of the country, or going out of their way to ridicule the fashions of the day, and perhaps giving a learned discourse on the evil effects of corsets upon the general health of American women, it is most likely that they would be pelted with stones, dirt and rotten eggs for their pains." Imagine what would happen, he continued, if they then called in the police and demanded official interference from Washington. "I verily believe that such action would render the missionaries so obnoxious to the American people as to put an end to their usefulness, and that the American government would cause a law to be enacted against them as public nuisances."[67]

For a season the growing missionary concern with education and medicine may have diminished native hostility. In 1931, for example, Gandhi, who ascribed his own "fierce hatred" of child marriage to Christian influence, endorsed the philanthropic side of the missionary enterprise, though only the philanthropic side. "If instead of confining themselves purely to humanitarian work such as education, medical service to the poor and the like," Gandhi added, "they would use these activities of theirs for the purpose of proselytizing, I would certainly like them to withdraw . . . I hold that proselytizing under the cloak of humanitarian work is, to say the least, unhealthy."[68]

The next generation of nationalists, however, rejected Gandhi's distinction. They saw both humanitarian and proselytizing efforts as forms of cultural aggression—the philanthropic form being perhaps the more insidious because it was the more plausible. Nothing, for example, could seem more benign than the introduction of Western medicine. Yet from another viewpoint there could hardly be a more diabolical way of unraveling the web of native folkways. Frantz Fanon, a black born in Martinique, trained in psychiatry in France, and transformed into a revolutionist in Algeria, wrote that to the native "the doctor always appears as a link in the colonialist network, as a spokesman for the occupying power." In China traditional medicine went underground until the Maoists relegitimized it as part of the national revival, and eventually even retaliated by exporting acupuncture to the West.

At first glance the efforts to end the foot binding of women in China and to encourage the women of the Magreb to take off their veils certainly seem "progressive." Yet in Fanon's view the second, at least, was an attempt to make native women allies "in the work of cultural destruction." The French officials, "committed to destroying the people's originality, and under instructions to bring about disintegration, at whatever cost, of forms of existence likely to evoke national reality," were simply striking at the weakest, namely the least defensible, links in the native culture. "Converting the woman, winning her over to foreign values, wrenching her free from her status, was at the same time achieving a real power over the man and attaining a practical, effective means of destructuring Algerian culture." Every veil that fell from a woman's face demonstrated that "Algeria was beginning to deny herself and was accepting the rape of the colonizer. Algerian society with every abandoned veil seemed to express its willingness to attend the master's school and to decide to change its habits under the occupier's direction."[69]

From the inside out, education seemed another malign technique of cultural subversion. So the Chinese Communists condemned the use of the American Boxer indemnity to Westernize Chinese students. As for missionaries, they made a vital contribution, Fanon charged, to the "work of calming down the natives" by presenting as models "all those saints who have turned the other cheek, who have forgiven trespasses against them, and who have been spat on and insulted without shrinking." The white man's church, he added, "does not call the native to God's ways but to the ways of the white man, of the master, of the oppressor." Even the Christian assertion of the dignity of man seemed an act of aggression, for individualism was a Western heresy and when natives threw off their bonds, Fanon argued, "the idea of a society of individuals . . . is the first to disappear." At every point it was necessary to reject the values of the occupier "even if these values objectively be worth choosing."[70]

Such arguments suggest the shift in perspective involved in the cultural interpretation. The cultural approach did not necessarily exclude economic, sociological, or political interpretations, any more than any of these necessarily excluded another. But it viewed the problem from a new angle, thereby bringing to the fore points that in the past had figured mainly in literary portrayals of the imperial relationship. Indeed, a surprising amount of the analysis of cultural imperialism has taken off from the first great literary rendition of that relationship, *The Tempest*. Shakespeare, in his drama of Prospero and his island, identified salient themes of the imperial situation. Prospero's subjects included the good native Ariel and the bad native Caliban. "You taught me language," Caliban reproached Prospero, "and my profit on 't/Is, I know how to curse." But Caliban, for all his dreams of freedom, really wanted a master; to dissident whites whom he enlisted in a putsch against Prospero, he said, "I'll show thee every fertile inch o' th' island;/And I will kiss thy foot. I prithee be my god."[71]

Pursuing Shakespeare's themes three and a half centuries later, Ottare Mannoni, the French ethnographer, wrote the first sustained exercise in the cultural interpretation, called in English translation *Prospero and Caliban: The Psychology of Colonization*.[72] Mannoni argued that the colonial relationship was rooted in the respective psyches of the colonizer and the colonized as shaped by their drastically different social experiences. The colonizer, fleeing from competitive Western society, had an inferiority complex requiring assuagement by the experience of domination. This complex was matched in Mannoni's view by the "dependence complex" of the native, generated by the conditions of a static and traditional society.

Colonization could not exist without the twin needs for domination and dependence: "Not all peoples can be colonized; only those who experience this need. Neither are all peoples equally likely to become colonizers." When white men succeeded in establishing colonies, "it can safely be said that their coming was unconsciously expected—even desired—by their future subject peoples. Everywhere there existed legends foretelling the arrival of strangers from the sea." Prospero and Caliban, the inferiority and dependence complexes, Mannoni suggested, were "symmetrically" opposed to each other, "and these two different psychological climates serve to characterize two different types of personality, two different mentalities, two different civilizations." Nor was compromise between them possible. Europeans thought that man could change his customs by a simple act of will, but "archaic personalities . . . exist only by virtue of the well-defined place they occupy in an unchanging whole, and it is that place which is instrumental in giving them their form." Assimilation meant that "the personality of the native is first destroyed through uprooting, enslavement and the collapse of the social structure."[73]

Mannoni drew his material from his experiences as a white French official in Madagascar. Although he made prodigious efforts to transcend his race and nationality, subsequent analysts from the colonial side, especially Fanon and Albert Memmi, a Tunisian Jew educated in Algiers and Paris, discovered white condescension in major parts of his argument, particularly the dependence complex. Yet both Fanon and Memmi were nonetheless influenced by Mannoni, particularly by his concepts of the cultural destruction of the colonized by the colonizer and of the totality of the conflict between the colonizing and the native cultures.

Thus, Fanon saw "the enterprise of deculturation . . . the liquidation of its systems of reference, the collapse of its cultural patterns," as basic in the process by which white men established control. Colonialism, Fanon argued, was not satisfied merely with political and economic domination. It wanted to empty the native's brain of all form and content, to condemn his language, his food habits, his sexual behavior, his way of sitting down, of resting, of laughing, of enjoying himself, to divest him of his past and of his history.[74]

Furthermore, the conflict of cultures was integral and complete. Fanon repeatedly emphasized "the impossibility of finding a meeting ground in any colonial situation." When the world of the colonizer acquired moral dominance, the native underwent a crisis of his own identity, compelled to "a choice between a retraction of his being and a frenzied attempt at identification with the colonizer." As Memmi added, the colonized could "never succeed in becoming identified with the colonizer, nor even in copying his role correctly." Confused in his own sense of selfhood, he was more and more at the mercy of the aggressor.[75]

This was the analysis that led Fanon to insist on violence as the means of reclaiming native identity. Colonized people, he believed, must react to cultural aggression "in a harsh, undifferentiated, categorical way." It was impossible to "attack this or that segment of the cultural whole"—as, for example, by introducing Western medicine into a colonial culture—without endangering the whole culture. But "violence, like Achilles' lance, can heal the wounds that it has inflicted." When the native's rage boils over, "he rediscovers his lost innocence and he comes to know himself in that he himself creates his self." Collective violence opens up the opportunity for integration in a group; "the colonized man finds his freedom in and through violence." And "at the level of individuals, violence is a cleansing force. It frees the native from his inferiority complex and from his despair and inaction; it makes him fearless and restores his self-respect." Only violence could restore the integrity of the native culture; and once this was done, then an attack on tradition would be possible within the native's own framework. "The people who take their destiny in their own hands assimilate the most modern forms of technology at an extraordinary rate."[76]

The psychohistory of imperialism has been largely developed on the basis of the experience of French Africa. It requires testing in other realms of European expansion. Frances FitzGerald, for example, thought that the Mannoni analysis worked for Vietnam, and R. H. Solomon referred, in a somewhat different context, to a "politics of dependency" in China.[77] Much depends on the depth and intensity of the Western intrusion. Some non-Western countries underwent intense colonization; some, limited colonization; some, notably China and Japan, were never colonies at all. Yet insights derived from conquest may throw light on milder Western penetrations of non-Western societies.

As cultural interpretations are further considered, the idea of the totality of the cultural conflict may well undergo modification. The supposed homogeneity of native societies was perceived more from without than from within. Native societies were not gardens of innocence and tranquillity. Many rested on systems of hierarchy and oppression maintained at the expense of the intellectually innovative, the women, the poor, and the low-caste. And the missionary enterprise was seriously effective only when it touched nerves in the native culture.

Conversion, therefore, often had a social or even a political dimension; that is, converts in many cases were receptive to strange gods precisely because they were frustrated, disoriented, or exploited in their own societies. This was true, V. G. Kiernan noted, in the South Pacific. D. A. Low, describing Buganda, reported the way that Christianity for some "solved the immense spiritual and intellectual confusion" into which the Kabaka's court had fallen. The Taiping rebellion in China showed how the Christian doctrine of the brotherhood of man became the means of social protest against an unequal society. For others, Christianity appealed as an instrument of modernization. Thus, Y. C. Wang wrote that Hsü Ching-ch'eng advised Lu Cheng-hsiang "to become a Christian in order to Westernize himself thoroughly." Christianity, in short, was not just a faith imposed by external force. On occasion it answered questions or filled needs in native societies. Many converts suffered grievously for their faith. Their martyrdom, as Father Martin Jarrett-Kerr said, had "a stamp of authenticity which proves that they were genuinely looking for, and found, something which their whole being craved."[78]

Nor is Fanon's theory of the universally disintegrating impact of the slightest Western touch—medicine, for example, or the unveiled woman—altogether convincing. The idea of total deculturation is hard to visualize. Some native cultures are very tough and resilient and have shown a considerable ability (especially when they have not been subjected to an intensive colonial experience) to select out and absorb Western techniques and values. Fanon's further argument that only changes brought about by and within the native culture are legitimate, and that all changes brought from outside, no matter how valuable in themselves, must be resisted, is also less than convincing. Given the fact that traditional cultures were so often committed beyond memory to a static existence, it may well be that Marx was more to the point in contending that external stimuli were necessary to create internal revolutionary energies.

China would seem to be an impressive example both of the use by the native culture of external stimuli for its own purposes and of the role of such stimuli in encouraging native revolution. It is hard to suppose, for example, that the Chinese revolutions, both Nationalist and Communist, were not forwarded in a diversity of ways by missionary pressures on traditional Chinese society—both in conformity with some pressures (such as values of equality, democracy, change) and in sharp reaction against others. The ferment stirred by the missionaries, the challenges they embodied to traditional structures and values, their elevation of the individual as against the family and of equality as against hierarchy, their courageous attack on what they saw as national vices (opium, foot binding, the subjection of women, the marriage of children), their devoted work in fostering the institutions of modernization (schools, universities, clinics, hospitals, magazines, agricultural stations), and in general their moral claims, their social hopes, and the extraordinary examples they offered of personal sacrifice and heroism—all had a revolutionary effect. Professional revolutionaries understood this. Malraux quoted Borodin's remark to a *Hong Kong Times* interviewer: "You understand the behavior of the Protestant missionaries, don't you? Well, then, you understand mine!"[79]

The missionaries wanted to shatter the pagan order for their own purposes. But when one undertakes the demolition of traditional societies, one can never be sure of concluding with the revolution one intended. "We are incapable of implanting our civilisation," Hobson wisely noted; " . . . we are only capable of disturbing their civilisation." The missionaries ended as another "unconscious tool of history," in Marx's phrase, helping to bring about an Asian revolution. So, ironically, did the European Marxists. Borodin, at the close of his career as a Soviet agent in China, mused: "I came to China to fight for an idea . . . But China itself, with its age-old history, its countless millions, its vast social problems, its infinite capacities, astounded and overwhelmed me."[80] This could serve equally as an epitaph for the Christian missionaries.

The missionary impact on the American mind may have been more profound than its impact on the non-Western mind. Cultural aggression not only threatened the self-image of the violated nation but fed the self-righteousness of the intruders. Americans had long seen themselves as in some sense, first religiously and then politically, a chosen people. The Founding Fathers supposed that America would spread its influence by example rather than by intervention. But missionaries saw their responsibilities more urgently. Where traders wanted only to make money or politicians to make treaties, missionaries wanted to change souls and societies. Their evangelical spirit helped to infuse the American role in the world with the impulses of a crusade. Many things contributed to the disaster in Indochina, but one element was surely the notion that Americans had a special capacity and duty to "build" nations—an illusion strengthened by the experience of military occupation after the Second World War and especially by the experience of occupied Japan. Vice President Humphrey defended the Vietnam policy in 1966 in missionary accents: "We ought to be excited about this challenge, because here is where we can put to work some of our ideas . . . nation building, of new concepts of education, development of local government, the improvement of the health standards of people, and really the achievement and the fulfillment of social justice."[81] It required but one step more to the idea, which missionaries had already held on occasion for themselves, that America was commissioned to play the role of judge, jury, and executioner for a sinful world. In a double sense, Vietnam can be seen as a missionary legacy, not only because the French went in to protect the missionary enterprise, but also because the Americans went in to achieve the missionary goal.

Cultural aggression in the end rebounded upon the aggressors, but not without affecting the pagan peoples who were the objects of the evangelical zeal. The cultural factors in the East-West encounter are complex and elusive. Nonetheless, as we contemplate the variety of ways in which cultures threaten, violate, and transform each other, and as representatives of these cultures analyze their own experience and anguish, it may be possible to begin to formulate a cultural interpretation of imperialism, in which the missionary will find his most fitting place.

Notes
Glossary
Index

ABCFM	American Board of Commissioners for Foreign Missions
ABMU	American Baptist Missionary Union
ABP	Papers of the American Board of Commissioners for Foreign Missions, Houghton Library, Harvard University
AM	Alleniania Memorabilia, Robert C. Woodruff Library for Advanced Studies, Special Collections, Emory University, Atlanta, Georgia
ARBFM	*Annual Report of Board of Foreign Missions of the Methodist Episcopal Church*
CHHP	*Chiao-hui hsin-pao*
FMCNA	Foreign Missions Conference of North America
LMM	Laymen's Missionary Movement
SCA	*Southern Christian Advocate*
SVM	Student Volunteer Movement for Foreign Missions

NOTES

JOHN K. FAIRBANK, "THE MANY FACES OF PROTESTANT MISSIONS IN CHINA AND THE UNITED STATES"

1. James A. Field, Jr., *America and the Mediterranean World, 1776–1882* (Princeton, Princeton University Press, 1969), notes their interaction and characterizes their peculiar expansiveness.

2. These figures are taken from Jessie Gregory Lutz, *China and the Christian Colleges, 1850–1950* (Ithaca, 1971), p. 202; M. Searle Bates, *Missions in Far Eastern Cultural Relations* (New York, 1943), p. 11.

3. A systematic survey of topics and research materials is offered in Kwang-Ching Liu, *Americans and Chinese: A Historical Essay and a Bibliography* (Cambridge, Harvard University Press, 1963).

JAMES A. FIELD, Jr., "NEAR EAST NOTES AND FAR EAST QUERIES"

1. The history of American relations with the Near East, like that of American foreign missions, has until recently been pretty much ignored. The best guides to the literature are John A. DeNovo, "American Relations with the Middle East: Some Unfinished Business," in George L. Anderson, ed., *Issues and Conflicts: Studies in Twentieth Century American Diplomacy* (Lawrence, University of Kansas Press, 1959), pp. 68–98; John A. DeNovo, "Researching American Relations with the Middle East: The State of the Art, 1970," in Milton O. Gustafson, ed., *The Archives of United States Foreign Relations* (Athens, Ohio University Press, forthcoming). For the general history of American-Near Eastern relations, see James A. Field, Jr., *America and the Mediterranean World, 1776–1882* (Princeton, Princeton University Press, 1969); John A. DeNovo, *American Interests and Policies in the Middle East, 1900–1939* (Minneapolis, University of Minnesota Press, 1963); there remains something of a hiatus for the eighties and nineties. On the missionary and philanthropic effort, see Robert L. Daniel, *American Philanthropy in the Near East, 1820–1960* (Athens, Ohio University Press, 1970).

2. In the Mediterranean and Near East, American sympathy for self-determination showed itself, inter alia, in individual or group support for Greece, Egypt, Crete, Bulgaria, and the Armenians against Turkey; Turkey against Russia and Great Britain; Tunis against Italy; Egypt and Persia against Great Britain. Economic determinists may note how often the lesser trading partner was supported against the greater. Field, *Mediterranean World*, passim; DeNovo, *American Interests*, passim.

3. Ernest R. May, *Imperial Democracy* (New York, Harcourt, Brace and World, 1961), pp. 27–29, 53–54, 60; Elting E. Morison, ed., *The Letters of Theodore Roosevelt* (Cambridge, Harvard University Press, 1951–1954), II, 823. In 1909 Roosevelt wrote that he thought Constantinople "the most important and most interesting diplomatic post in the world" (VII, 18).

4. Field, *Mediterranean World*, passim; John K. Fairbank, *The United States and China*, 3rd ed. (Cambridge, Harvard University Press, 1971), pp. 284–286.

5. Walter LaFeber, *The New Empire: An Interpretation of American Expansion, 1860—1898* (Ithaca, Cornell University Press, 1963), p. 5; Robert A. Divine, Foreword, in Warren I. Cohen, *America's Response to China* (New York, Wiley, 1971), p. vii.

6. Charles O. Paullin, *American Voyages to the Orient, 1690—1865* (Annapolis, U.S. Naval Institute, 1971), pp. 10—11, 33—34; Dudley W. Knox, *A History of the United States Navy* (New York, G. P. Putnam's Sons, 1948), pp. 49, 100.

7. *Historical Statistics of the United States: Colonial Times to 1957* (Washington, D.C., Government Printing Office, 1960), p. 543.

8. John T. McCutcheon, *Drawn from Memory* (Indianapolis, Bobbs-Merrill, 1950), pp. 95—100. The case of the *McCulloch* is the more remarkable, as her intended destination was not the Far East but the United States west coast. The high price of coal in South American ports balanced out the greater distance of a globe-girdling cruise. On the navy's problems, see William R. Braisted, *The United States Navy in the Pacific, 1897—1909* (Austin, University of Texas Press, 1958); Braisted, *The United States Navy in the Pacific, 1909—1922* (Austin, University of Texas Press, 1971).

9. The question of orientation depends a good deal on convention, cartographic or other. In early nineteenth-century atlases the standard hemispheric or "globular" projection placed the eastern hemisphere, comprising Europe, Africa, and Asia, to the east (i.e., right) of the western hemisphere. In the latter part of the century the picture changed as the increasingly popular Mercator projections placed the Americas in the center, with Asia to the west and Europe to the east. By the 1930s China seems in some sense to have faced west toward the United States. James C. Thomson, Jr., *While China Faced West: American Reformers in Nationalist China, 1928—1937* (Cambridge, Harvard University Press, 1969). In the 1950s, presumably, it faced east toward the Soviet Union.

10. *Historical Statistics*, pp. 550, 552; Mira Wilkins, *The Emergence of Multinational Enterprise: American Business Abroad from the Colonial Era to 1914* (Cambridge, Harvard University Press, 1970).

11. See Thomas J. McCormick, "The State of American Diplomatic History," in Herbert J. Bass, ed., *The State of American History* (Chicago, Quadrangle Books, 1970); Ernest R. May, "The Decline of Diplomatic History," in George A. Billias and Gerald N. Grob, eds., *American History: Retrospect and Prospect* (New York, The Free Press, 1971); James A. Field, Jr., "Transnationalism and the New Tribe," in Robert O. Keohane and Joseph S. Nye, Jr., eds., *Transnational Relations and World Politics* (Cambridge, Harvard University Press, 1972).

12. On the difficult question of motivation, see Clifton J. Phillips, *Protestant America and the Pagan World* (Cambridge, East Asian Research Center, Harvard University, 1969), pp. 1—31; Field, *Mediterranean World*, pp. 68—84; R. Pierce Beaver, "Missionary Motivation Through Three Centuries," in Jerald C. Brauer, ed., *Reinterpretation in American Church History* (Chicago, University of Chicago Press, 1968), pp. 113—151; Max Warren, *The Missionary Movement from Britain in Modern History* (London, SCM Press, 1965), pp. 36—55. The frequent suggestion that missionary recruitment benefited from the promise of upward social mobility seems unlikely, at least for ordained men in the early years, given the opportunities for the college-educated at home. For women, however, this opening field of professional endeavor was undoubtedly attractive. Page Smith, *Daughters of the Promised Land* (Boston, Little, Brown, 1970), pp. 181—201. The numerical preponderance of women in overseas missions, a phenomenon startling to the receiving societies, is barely hinted in Tables 3 and 4, which include data only for the major boards and neglect the women's groups, which

by 1890 maintained about a thousand workers abroad. *The Encyclopaedia of Missions*, ed. E. M. Bliss (New York, 1891), II, 479, 631–632.

13. To the long-time secretary of the ABCFM, India "was the pivot on which the lever of Providence . . . seemed to move" in opening up the heathen world. Rufus Anderson, *Foreign Missions: Their Relations and Claims* (New York, 1869), p. 2.

14. See articles on "Asia," "China," "Owhyhee," "Turkey," etc., in William Guthrie, *A New Geographical, Historical, and Commercial Grammar*, 12th ed. (London, 1790); *Encyclopaedia; or, a Dictionary of Arts, Sciences, and Miscellaneous Literature* (Philadelphia, 1798); Jedidiah Morse, *The American Universal Geography*, 3rd ed. (Boston, 1801); John Pinkerton, *Modern Geography* (Philadelphia, 1804).

15. *Encyclopaedia*, II, 393; IV, 693; IV, 665; Pinkerton, *Modern Geography*, II, 73. Later works seem equally even-handed. George F. Seward's article on "China" in *The American Cyclopaedia*, ed. George Ripley and Charles A. Dana (New York, 1873), considers Chinese pride wholly understandable, notes much of interest in Chinese culture, and sees no problems in Chinese immigration; a similar view is presented in the ninth edition of the *Encyclopaedia Brittanica* (New York, 1878). Although *The Encyclopaedia of Missions* discusses such matters as Chinese mendacity and the low status of women, the overall impression is one of judicious assessment, and the Chinese are described as being, in general, the "finest of the Asiatic races." These descriptions, so different from the American image of the Chinese presented in Stuart Creighton Miller, *The Unwelcome Immigrant* (Berkeley, University of California Press, 1969), suggest the persistence of two coexisting (and often contrapuntal) currents of opinion, the one exemplified by standard reference publications and the other by local and transitory yelps of alarm. Is it not possible that historians, recognizing no encyclopedist since Diderot and concerned either with the events of the day or with the "China shelf," have tended to overlook the significance of such reference works as basic sources of information for men of affairs?

16. *Memorial Volume of the First Fifty Years of the American Board of Commissioners for Foreign Missions* (Boston, 1861), pp. 227–241; Phillips, passim.

17. Kenneth S. Latourette, *Missions and the American Mind* (Indianapolis, National Foundation Press, 1949), p. 32.

18. Phillips, *Protestant America*, pp. 236–239; *Memorial Volume*, p. 172.

19. Phillips, *Protestant America*, pp. 240–242.

20. Phillips, *Protestant America*, pp. 35, 94; *Memorial Volume*, pp. 229–232.

21. For sketches of Anderson, see *The National Cyclopaedia of American Biography* (New York, 1898––), XXIV, 153; *Appleton's Cyclopaedia of American Biography*, ed. James Grant Wilson and John Fiske (New York, 1888), I, 71. For his influence on the American Board, see R. Pierce Beaver, ed., *To Advance the Gospel: Selections from the Writings of Rufus Anderson* (Grand Rapids, W. B. Eerdmans, 1967), pp. 13–38; Phillips, *Protestant America*, passim; Field, *Mediterranean World*, passim. Anderson's matured views on the calling to which he devoted his life appear in his *Foreign Missions*.

22. Anderson, *Foreign Missions*, pp. 96–98, 113–115, 118; Field, *Mediterranean World*, pp. 190, 354–355. The limits of Anderson's willingness to civilize may be inferred from his instructions of 1833 to the first American Board missionary to Africa. *Memorial Volume*, pp. 235–240, esp. p. 239.

23. Field, *Mediterranean World*, pp. 204, 351–355; Phillips, *Protestant America*, passim. On medical missionaries, see *Encyclopaedia of Missions*, II, 49–57.

Women's liberation began with the departure of the first missionary couples. In the Farewell Sermon of February 5, 1812, the Rev. Jonathan Allen pointed out to the young wives about to embark for India the "arduous work" that awaited them in teaching the women "to whom your husbands can have but little, or no access . . . that they are not an inferior race of creatures; but stand upon a par with men." R. Pierce Beaver, ed., *Pioneers in Mission* (Grand Rapids, W. B. Eerdmans, 1966), pp. 276–277. The more institutionalized forms of "Woman's Work for Woman" appear to have derived from an 1834 suggestion of David Abeel. *Encyclopaedia of Missions*, II, 470–523. On deracination and emigration, see Daniel, *American Philanthropy*, pp. 31, 39, 78, 108, 122, 277; A. L. Tibawi, *American Interests in Syria, 1800–1901* (Oxford, Clarendon Press, 1966), pp. 238, 278–280, 299–301.

24. *Memorial Volume*, pp. 282–285; Anderson, *Foreign Missions*, pp. 110, 112, 117; Field, *Mediterranean World*, pp. 74–75, 200. For the expectation of the self-perpetuating chain reaction, see Norman A. Etherington, "An American Errand into the South African Wilderness," *Church History* 30:62–71 (1970).

25. Ezra Stiles, *The United States Elevated to Glory and Honor* (New Haven, 1783), p. 52.

26. *Memorial Volume*, p. 231.

27. Eli Smith, *Researches of the Rev. E. Smith and Rev. H. G. O. Dwight in Armenia* (Boston, 1833; London, 1834); Edward Robinson, *Biblical Researches in Palestine, Mount Sinai, and Arabia Petraea* (Boston, 1841); S. W. Williams, *The Middle Kingdom* (Boston, 1848); David O. Allen, *India, Ancient and Modern* (Boston, 1856); J. Leighton Wilson, *Western Africa* (New York, 1856); Phillips, *Protestant America*, pp. 304–306.

28. Thomas Laurie, *The Ely Volume; or The Contributions of Our Foreign Missions to Science and Human Well-Being* (Boston, 1885), pp. 174–176 and passim. This grab-bag volume is a must for the student of cultural interchange.

29. Field, *Mediterranean World*, pp. 201–239; Phillips, *Protestant America*, pp. 276–277.

30. End-of-the-century assumptions are well displayed in J. S. Dennis, *Christian Missions and Social Progress*, 3 vols. (New York, Fleming H. Revell, 1898–1906).

31. *Encyclopaedia of Missions*, articles on "Commerce and Missions," I, 308–312; "Liquor Traffic and Missions," I, 548–550; "Opium in China," II, 193–195; Field, *Mediterranean World*, pp. 189–192.

32. Field, *Mediterranean World*, pp. 209–210, 285–287. The persistence of the non-national attitude is reflected in the titles of such missionary biographies as W. E. Griffis, *Verbeck of Japan: A Citizen of No Country* (New York, Fleming H. Revell, 1900); Basil Mathews, *John R. Mott, World Citizen* (New York, Harper & Brothers, 1934).

33. Phillips, *Protestant America*, pp. 103–105, 110; Jonathan Elliot, *The American Diplomatic Code* (Washington, D.C., 1834), II, 679–680; Mediterranean Squadron Letters (Naval Records Collection, National Archives), Morgan to Latimer, May 17, 1850; Morgan to Sec. of Navy, Nov. 1, 1850.

34. Field, *Mediterranean World*, pp. 285–297.

35. Squadron Letters, Worden to Sec. of Navy, Oct. 25, 1876.

36. Daniel, *American Philanthropy*, pp. 116–121, 148–170; Joseph L. Grabill, *Protestant Diplomacy and the Near East: Missionary Influence on American Policy, 1810–1927* (Minneapolis, University of Minnesota Press, 1971). The

increasing involvement of government, the result of developments in both the Near and Far East, is suggested by the inclusion of an article on this "matter of great perplexity, difficulty, and importance" in *The Encyclopedia of Missions*, 2nd ed., ed. H. O. Dwight, H. Allen Tupper, Jr., and E. M. Bliss (New York, Funk and Wagnalls, 1904), pp. 270–273; no discussion had been deemed necessary in Bliss's 1891 edition. Six years later the Edinburgh World Missionary Conference published a small volume on *Missions and Governments* (Edinburgh and London, Oliphant, Anderson & Ferrier, 1910). The American members of the reporting commission included John W. Foster and Alfred Thayer Mahan.

37. John K. Fairbank, " 'American China Policy' to 1898: A Misconception," *Pacific Historical Review* 39:409–420 (1970). For other areas of Anglo-American cooperation, see Frank Thistlethwaite, *The Anglo-American Connection in the Early Nineteenth Century* (Philadelphia, University of Pennsylvania Press, 1959).

38. It seems quite possible that knowledge of Canning's successes in Turkey lay behind the pressures brought by the Protestant missionaries in Shanghai on Lord Elgin in 1858. Kenneth S. Latourette, *A History of Christian Missions in China* (New York, Macmillan, 1929), p. 359.

39. Field, *Mediterranean World*, passim; Phillips, *Protestant America*, passim; *Encyclopaedia of Missions*, "Missionary Conferences," II, 104–110; Warren, *Missionary Movement*, pp. 149–159. That the transnational aspect of the missionary enterprise was not limited to Anglo-American cooperation was early shown in the career of Charles Gutzlaff, a Prussian sent to China by a Dutch society, who worked closely with both British and Americans. By the century's end Norwegian, Swedish, Finnish, and French Protestants had joined British, Americans, and Germans in far places.

40. The greater British concern with power is suggested by the contrast between President Adams' message to Kamehameha, with its emphasis on "prosperity and happiness," and Sir Harry Johnston's speech to the Basoga of Uganda: "We were like you long ago, going about naked . . . with our war paint on, but when we learned Christianity from the Romans we changed and became great. We want you to learn Christianity and follow our steps and you too will be great." Warren, *Missionary Movement*, p. 66.

41. Field, *Mediterranean World*, passim. Before assuming command of the East India Squadron, Commodore Tattnall had three tours of duty in the Mediterranean.

42. There seems to be no very good name for this phenomenon. The nineteenth century lived comfortably with the term "Anglo-Saxon civilization," a usage dating from the 1840s, when the packet *Anglo-Saxon* was launched by Donald McKay and when Hollis Read, in *The Hand of God in History* (Hartford, 1849), made much of these transnational folk and of their culture. But the term has now been so firmly tied in with myths about social Darwinism and conventional misapprehensions about John Fiske and Josiah Strong that it has lost most of its value. This is perhaps a pity, for if the Anglo-Saxons are what Strong said they were—"all English-speaking peoples"—the concept is a useful one. Josiah Strong, *Our Country*, ed. Jurgen Herbst (Cambridge, Harvard University Press, 1963), p. 202.

43. Charles B. Davenport and Mary T. Scudder, *Naval Officers: Their Heredity and Development* (Washington, D.C., Carnegie Institution of Washington, 1919). It may be noted that the *Harvard Guide to American History* (Cambridge, Harvard University Press, 1954) has no entry under "genealogy."

44. *Memorial Volume*, p. 82; Phillips, *Protestant America*, pp. 2—3, 191; Field, *Mediterranean World*, pp. 88, 249—250, 377.

45. Although rare, cases of intertheater transfer and of families involved in more than one field were not unknown. In 1868, after twenty-nine years in India, Phineas Hunt was transferred to Peking, where he established the first foreign printing office. Cyrus T. Mills served in both Ceylon and Hawaii. In 1849 a younger brother of S. Wells Williams joined the Syrian Mission.

46. Daniel, *American Philanthropy*, pp. 72—83, 100—102; Grabill, *Protestant Diplomacy*, pp. 23—24, 30, 42, 128; Field, *Mediterranean World*, p. 428. As the examples of the Gulicks in Hawaii and Japan, the Scudders in India, and the Underwoods in Korea make clear, the dynastic phenomenon was not limited to the Near East. Nor, indeed, did all missionary descendants remain steadfast in the Hopkinsian faith. Rufus Anderson's best-known son became a New York lawyer and clubman and an Episcopalian; that son's son was an early president of the Automobile Club of America and owner of a yacht big enough to be taken over by the navy in 1917.

47. Daniel, *American Philanthropy*, pp. 150—165; Grabill, *Protestant Diplomacy*, p. 128 and passim.

48. Daniel, *American Philanthropy*, pp. 79, 89—92, 144, 189; Grabill, *Protestant Diplomacy*, pp. 24, 27, 70—71, 86—89; Merle Curti, *American Philanthropy Abroad* (New Brunswick, Rutgers University Press, 1963), pp. 148—149, 154—156, 164—165. The first Stokes to settle in America had been one of the thirteen founding members of the London Missionary Society. Anson G. Phelps, founder of the metal importing firm, in 1853 left $100,000 to the American Board. Their granddaughters, Olivia and Caroline Phelps Stokes, were important supporters of the American College for Girls at Constantinople.

49. Grabill, *Protestant Diplomacy*, pp. 94, 128, 138, 143—144, 262; Latourette, *Christian Missions*, p. 586. Prosopographical evidence in William R. Hutchison, "Cultural Strain and Protestant Liberalism," *American Historical Review* 76: 408—409, Table E (1971), reinforces the notion that there was something special about clergymen with a mid-Atlantic Presbyterian, Princeton background. For a Princeton family whose connection with Near East missions antedated even that of the Phelpses and Dodges, see E. D. G. Prime, *Notes Genealogical, Biographical, and Bibliographical of the Prime Family* (New York, 1888).

50. Robert L. Daniel, "The Friendship of Woodrow Wilson and Cleveland H. Dodge," *Mid-America* 43:182—196 (1961); Daniel, *American Philanthropy*, pp. 154—155; Grabill, *Protestant Diplomacy*, pp. 80—89 and passim.

51. Grabill, *Protestant Diplomacy*, pp. 45, 71, 96—97.

52. That the Chinese missionary interest had a bright future was suggested in 1913 by Wilson's tender of the Peking legation to John R. Mott, a leader in the international YMCA and Student Volunteer movements, and his regret when that "robust Christian" declined the post. R. S. Baker, *Woodrow Wilson, Life and Letters* (Garden City, Doubleday, Doran, 1931), IV, 31; A. S. Link, *Wilson: The New Freedom* (Princeton, Princeton University Press, 1956), p. 98.

VALENTIN H. RABE, "EVANGELICAL LOGISTICS: MISSION SUPPORT AND RESOURCES TO 1920"

1. Adoniram Judson to Luther Rice, July 13, 1836, in Francis Wayland, *A Memoir of the Life and Labours of the Rev. Adoniram Judson, D.D.* (London, 1853), I, 35.

2. Melanchthon's assurance that the apostles had fulfilled Christ's Great Commission (Matt. 28:19–20, Mark 16:15) had made Protestant leaders apathetic if not hostile to evangelization by human effort in the non-Christian world. Commission of Appraisal, William E. Hocking, Chairman, *Re-thinking Missions: A Laymen's Inquiry after One Hundred Years* (New York, Harper and Bros., 1932), p. 8. Others had rationalized that the promise of salvation made to Israel did not extend to the colored races, since they were the descendants of Ham. J. H. Bavinck, *An Introduction to the Science of Missions*, trans. D. H. Freeman (Philadelphia, Presbyterian and Reformed Publishing Co., 1960), p. 277. Even the twentieth century has produced no clear imperative for the mission to distant peoples. A committee at the 1952 Willingen World Missionary Conference determined that there was as yet no such thing as a theology of missions. Wilhelm Andersen, *Auf Dem Wege zu einer Theologie der Mission*, vol. 6 of *Beiträge Zur Missionswissenschaft und Evangelischen Religionskunde*, (Gütersloh, Carl Bertelsmann Verlag, 1957), pp. 7–8. The executive secretary and historian of America's oldest foreign mission board came to the same conclusion in surveying 150 years of world-wide activity. Fred Field Goodsell, *You Shall Be My Witnesses* (Boston, ABCFM, 1959), p. 276.

3. Quoted in Herbert W. Schneider, *The Puritan Mind* (Ann Arbor, University of Michigan Press, 1958), p. 216.

4. Oliver Wendell Elsbree, *The Rise of the Missionary Spirit in America, 1790–1815* (Williamsport, Pa., Williamsport Printing & Binding Co., 1928), p. 141.

5. Schneider, *Puritan Mind*, pp. 230–231.

6. H. Richard Niebuhr, *The Kingdom of God in America* (Hamden, Conn., Shoe String Press, 1956), p. x.

7. Niebuhr, *Kingdom of God*, pp. 21–23, 105.

8. *A Cyclopedia of Missions*, ed. Harvey Newcomb (New York, 1860), pp. 546, 643, 112.

9. Joseph Tracy, *History of the American Board of Commissioners for Foreign Missions* (New York, 1842), p. 451.

10. Goodsell, *Witness*, pp. 13–18.

11. Fred Field Goodsell, comp., "Receipts and Expenditures, 1810–1956," ABP.

12. Goodsell, "Receipts," passim. I am indebted to James A. Field, Jr. for pointing out the apparent inconsistencies between these income figures and the increase in gold expenditures of the ABCFM and the Northern Presbyterian Board, 1865–1880, demonstrated in his article in this volume. The differences are probably owing to Goodsell's and my failure to distinguish between contributions made in gold and in depreciated greenbacks prior to specie resumption in 1879. To some extent they also reflect the notorious incompleteness of mission society financial reports, owing to the exclusion from annual statements of gifts for special objects and other types of income. Valentin H. Rabe, "The American Protestant Foreign Mission Movement, 1880–1920" (Ph.D. diss., Harvard University, 1965), app. 3.

13. Goodsell, *Witness*, p. 290.

14. Jesse T. Peck, *The History of the Great Republic Considered from a Christian Stand-point* (Boston, 1877), p. 550.

15. ABCFM, *Fifty-fifth Annual Report* (Boston, 1865), p. 29; ABCFM, *Sixty-second Annual Report* (Boston, 1872), p. xxi.

16. ABCFM, *Seventy-first Annual Report* (Boston, 1881), p. xiv; Goodsell, *Witness*, p. 215.

17. Arthur T. Pierson, *The Crisis of Missions, or, The Voice out of the Cloud* (New York, 1886), p. 273.

18. John R. Mott, *Five Decades and a Forward View* (New York, Harper and Bros., 1939), p. 4.

19. Pierson, *Crisis of Missions*, p. 356.

20. Samuel B. Capen, "The Necessity of Making the Financial Plans of the Church Commensurate with the Magnitude of the Task of the World's Evangelization," in *World-Wide Evangelization, The Urgent Business of the Church* (New York, SVM, 1902), p. 177; Samuel B. Capen, "The Responsibility of the Laymen for the Promotion of the Foreign Missionary Enterprise," in *Students and the Present Missionary Crisis* (New York, SVM, 1910), p. 475.

21. ABCFM, *Thirty-third Annual Report* (Boston, 1842), p. 66.

22. *American Board Almanac of Missions, 1916* (Boston, ABCFM, n.d.). p. 30.

23. Isaac Taylor Headland, *Some By-products of Missions* (Cincinnati, Jennings and Graham, 1912), p. 198.

24. Richard Hofstadter, "Manifest Destiny and the Philippines," in Daniel Aaron, ed., *America in Crisis* (New York, Alfred A. Knopf, 1952), p. 183.

25. For the biographical survey on which these generalizations are based, see Rabe, "Foreign Mission Movement," app. 1.

26. "Position Description; Executive Secretary, Laymen's Missionary Movement of North America, Inc.," undated typescript, Missionary Research Library, New York.

27. Trevor P. Bowen, "Causes for Withdrawal of Missionaries," in *Home Base and Missionary Personnel*, vol. 7 of Orville A. Petty, ed., *Laymen's Foreign Missions Inquiry, Fact Finders' Reports* (New York, Harper and Bros., 1933), pp. 51, 59.

28. John R. Mott, "The Commitment of Life and How God Leads Men," in Milton T. Stauffer, ed., *Christian Students and World Problems* (New York, SVM, 1924), p. 63; Sherwood Eddy, *Eighty Adventurous Years* (New York, Harper and Bros., 1955), p. 35.

29. *Men and Missions* 10.4:100 (December 1918).

30. H. E. B. Case, "Number of Missionaries of the American Board of Commissioners for Foreign Missions, 1900–1929," typescript, file AB12Z9, ABP.

31. Charles H. Fahs, "Recruiting and Selecting New Missionaries," in *Home Base and Missionary Personnel*, p. 17.

32. *Foreign Missions Conference of North America, Being the Report of the Twenty-first Conference of Foreign Mission Boards in the United States and Canada* (New York, FMCNA, 1914), p. 75.

33. ABCFM, *One Hundred and Sixth Annual Report* (Boston, 1916), p. 15.

34. In 1925, 1475 ordained men were outnumbered by 2357 wives and 2538 unmarried women or widows, followed by 1293 unordained men. Harlan P.

Beach and C. H. Fahs, eds., *World Missionary Atlas* (New York, Institute of Social and Religious Research, 1925), p. 76.

35. Both single women and ordained men's wives were generally designated as missionaries. Wives, however, were compensated only indirectly through adjustments in their husband's subsistence allowance, and single women were long restricted to the types of activities considered appropriate by male secretaries and superiors. Personality differences and variant methods of decision making at individual mission stations make generalizations difficult, but women before the 1920s seem generally to have had an equal voice only in such matters as were directly related to their own work and responsibilities. The American Board, for example, which seems to have been ahead of general practice when it decided in 1894 that women should henceforth have an equal voice and vote with men at meetings in the field, restricted this privilege to the "consideration of questions touching their own work." ABCFM, *Eighty-fourth Annual Report* (Boston, 1894), p. 5.

36. The American Board, for example, supported 1269 "Indigenous Workers" in 1880, 3472 by 1900, and 4941 in 1920. A far more significant increase in this area followed World War II. Goodsell, *Witness*, p. 291. The American Baptist Foreign Mission Society increased its total of native workers from 1200 in 1884 to nearly 6200 in 1914, while its missionary force barely doubled. H. B. Grose and F. P. Haggard, eds., *The Judson Centennial, 1814–1914* (Philadelphia, American Baptist Publication Society, 1914), p. 300.

37. Harlan P. Beach, *A Geography and Atlas of Protestant Missions* (New York, SVM, 1903), p. 23.

38. Of 6633 missionaries supported by North American societies in 1909, 2086 were ordained men, 2169 were missionary wives, 1754 were unmarried women, and 624 were laymen. J. Campbell White, *Our Share of the World* (New York, LMM, n.d.), p. 7.

39. *North American Students and World Advance*, ed. Burton St. John (New York, SVM, 1920), p. 62; Mott, *Five Decades*, pp. 12–22.

40. ABCFM, *Seventieth Annual Report* (Boston, 1880), p. xxi.

41. Fahs, "Recruiting New Missionaries," pp. 22–24. Between 1906 and 1930, thirty major colleges and universities, including most of the Ivy League and Big Ten, never produced more than 12.5 percent of the volunteers who sailed, and the contribution dipped to 6.7 percent in the postwar decade. Fahs, "Recruiting New Missionaries," pp. 19–21.

42. Chauncy J. Hawkins, *Samuel Billings Capen* (Boston, Pilgrim Press, 1914), p. 187.

43. ABCFM, *Annual Report for 1880*, p. xxi; ABCFM, *Annual Report for 1916*, p. 16.

44. *Re-thinking Missions*, p. 10.

45. John F. Goucher, "The Strategic Importance of the Student Volunteer Movement to the World's Evangelization," in *Students and the Modern Missionary Crusade* (New York, SVM, 1906), p. 175.

46. Clifton J. Phillips, *Protestant America and the Pagan World: The First Half Century of the American Board of Commissioners for Foreign Missions, 1810–1860* (Cambridge, East Asian Research Center, Harvard University, 1969), p. 30.

47. ABCFM, *Annual Report for 1880*, p. xxi.

48. F. F. Ellinwood to the Shantung Mission, Nov. 9, 1888, reel 233, vol. 70,

no. 59, Presbyterian Board of Foreign Missions Correspondence, Presbyterian Historical Šociety, Philadelphia.

49. *The Student Missionary Enterprise*, ed. Max W. Moorhead (New York, 1894), pp. 71, 77. The following regional distribution was reported for 7500 volunteers carried on the SVM rolls in 1892:

Central States 2345
Western States 1680
Middle Atlantic 1440
Southern States 845
New England 650
Canada 480
Pacific States 60

The Western States included none further west than South Dakota. Ohio, Illinois, Indiana, and Michigan formed the predominant Central States region. Illinois led the nation with 809, producing more volunteers than either New England or Canada. John R. Mott, *The Student Volunteer Movement for Foreign Missions*, vol. 1 of *The Addresses and Papers of John R. Mott* (New York, Association Press, 1946), pp. 277–278.

50. A reluctance by Southern denominations to participate in the national and interdenominational organizations of the mission movement was only slowly overcome by 1920. The Fundamentalist issue of the late twenties provided new cause for remaining aloof and working through independent or Southern organizations.

51. See, e.g., Courtenay H. Fenn, *Over Against the Treasury* (New York, LMM, 1910), pp. 12–13.

52. See, e.g., Herbert H. Smith, "Millionaire Borden's Decision," reprinted from *The Continent* in *Men and Missions* 4.4:25–26 (December 1912). Borden was a recently ordained Chicago multimillionaire who had surrendered all to serve Christ and China.

53. The American Board, e.g., was informed by one of its most promising candidates that he would pay his own salary and expenses but would be forced to apply to another society if not sent to the North China mission he had selected. Horace T. Pitkin to the Secretaries of the American Board, Aug. 12, 1894, ABP, ser. 6, vol. 45, no. 258.

54. Nellie M. Cheney to Charles H. Daniels, Feb. 6, 1894, ABP, ser. 6, vol. 41, N. M. Cheney file.

55. R. P. Mackay, "Qualifications of Missionary Candidates," in *Report of the Seventh Conference of Officers and Representatives of the Foreign Mission Boards and Societies in the United States and Canada* (New York, 1899), p. 27.

56. Frank A. Waples to James L. Barton, July 3, 1892, ABP, ser. 6, vol. 47, no. 83.

57. George R. Grose, *James W. Bashford* (New York, Methodist Book Concern, 1922), pp. 55–56.

58. Life Sketch of Bertha Harding Allen, enclosed in B. Allen to D. Brewer Eddy, Jan. 29, 1916, ABP, ser. 6, vol. 75, B. H. Allen file, no. 14; Life Sketch of Earle Holt Ballou, enclosed in Ballou to the Prudential Committee of the ABCFM, May 6, 1915. ABP, ser. 6, vol. 79, E. H. Ballou file, no. 6; Bowen, "Causes for Withdrawal," p. 55. Of 151 active missionaries polled at the same time, over 85 percent had acted because of the "relatively greater need of the foreign field." Fahs, "Recruiting New Missionaries," p. 38.

59. Eddy, *Eighty Adventurous Years*, pp. 27–28.

60. David Abeel, *Journal of a Residence in China* (New York, 1836), p. 34.

61. James Stuart Udy, "Attitudes Within the Protestant Churches of the Occident Towards the Propagation of Christianity in the Orient: An Historical Survey to 1914" (Ph.D. diss., Boston University, 1952), p. 384.

62. Paul Varg, *Missionaries, Chinese, and Diplomats* (Princeton, Princeton University Press, 1958), p. 323.

63. *The History and Program of the Laymen's Missionary Movement* (New York, LMM, 1912), p. 17.

64. Samuel B. Capen, *The Uprising of Men for World Conquest* (New York, LMM, 1909), p. 3.

65. *History and Program of the LMM*, p. 15.

66. Samuel B. Capen, *The Next Ten Years* (Boston, ABCFM, 1910), p. 25.

67. From 1810 to 1918, out of the total ABCFM receipts of $49,853,487, the Congregational Women's Boards formed only during the late 1860s contributed $10,403,236 besides paying their own administrative and promotional expenses. Goodsell, *Witness*, pp. 165, 167.

68. Wilson T. Hogue, *History of the Free Methodist Church of North America* (Chicago, Free Methodist Publishing House, 1915), II, 257–259.

69. *American Board Almanac of Missions, 1891* (Boston, 1890), p. 32.

70. That other factors are involved in the contrast between evangelical and liturgical church mission interest is demonstrated by the fact that in 1913 the Protestant Episcopal Church, with its largely native-born and reputedly upper-class membership, maintained only 168 missionaries in the field with contributions of $677,975. Despite a slightly smaller membership, the Congregational Churches contributed $1,044,688 for the support of 615 ABCFM missionaries. *American Board Almanac of Missions, 1914* (Boston, ABCFM, 1913), p. 30. Even more puzzling are variations among the evangelical denominations. For example, over 40 percent of the United Presbyterian Church's total contributions in 1916 were dedicated to work in the foreign field, compared to 28 percent for the Northern Presbyterian and 27 percent for the Southern Presbyterian branches. Compare these figures to other major denominations: Northern Baptist, 16 percent; Southern Baptist, 13 percent; Protestant Episcopal, 19 percent. Only two other bodies exceeded the 40 percent mark in 1916: the Congregational Churches (47.5 percent) and the Seventh-day Adventists (47.1 percent). Bureau of the Census, *Religious Bodies, 1916* (Washington, D.C., Government Printing Office, 1919), II, 99–100.

71. *Men and Missions* 9.3:68 (November 1917).

72. David McConaughy, *Money the Acid Test* (New York, Missionary Education Movement, 1918), p. 3.

73. Luther P. Powell, "The Growth and Development of the Motives and Methods of Church Support with Special Emphasis upon the American Churches" (Ph.D. diss., Drew Theological Seminary of Drew University, 1951), II, 383.

74. John E. Lankford, "Protestant Stewardship and Benevolence, 1900–1941" (Ph.D. diss., University of Wisconsin, 1962), pp. 19, 426–428.

75. McConaughy, *Money*, p. 95.

76. David Riesman, Nathan Glazer, and Ruel Denny, *The Lonely Crowd* (New York, Doubleday, 1953), p. 139.

77. McConaughy, *Money*, pp. 7–8, 12.

78. Judson Smith, "The Cry of the Pagan World," in ABCFM, *Eighty-first Annual Report* (Boston, 1891), p. xxix.

79. ABCFM, *Forty-third Annual Report* (Boston, 1852), p. 22; Samuel B. Capen to John R. Mott, June 13, 1908, Capen file, John R. Mott Collection, Day Missions Library, Yale Divinity School, New Haven.

80. An insignificant increase of $162,651 set a predepression high point in foreign mission contributions in 1921. C. H. Fahs, *Trends in Protestant Giving* (New York, Institute of Social and Religious Research, 1929), pp. 6, 46.

81. White, *Our Share*, p. 5. Of a total income of $38,922,822 received by 412 Protestant foreign mission societies during 1915, $18,055,836 represented the income of 128 United States agencies, $13,819,340 the receipts of 92 societies in Great Britain and Ireland. Harlan P. Beach and Burton St. John, eds., *World Statistics of Christian Missions* (New York, FMCNA, 1916), p. 54.

82. William B. Millar, *The Advance of a Decade* (New York, LMM, 1916), p. 25.

83. *Ninth Conference of Officers and Representatives of the Foreign Mission Boards and Societies of the United States and Canada* (New York, FMCNA, 1902), p. 28.

84. Fahs, *Trends*, p. 53.

85. Lankford, "Protestant Stewardship," p. 410; Fahs, *Trends*, pp. 27–28.

86. C. M. Clark, "The Brethren, A Chapter in the History of the American Board," typescript, 1893, ABP.

CLIFTON J. PHILLIPS, "THE STUDENT VOLUNTEER MOVEMENT AND ITS ROLE IN CHINA MISSIONS, 1886–1920"

1. Clarence P. Shedd, *Two Centuries of Student Christian Movements: Their Origin and Intercollegiate Life* (New York, Association Press, 1934), pp. 52–74; Clifton J. Phillips, *Protestant America and the Pagan World: The First Half Century of the American Board of Commissioners for Foreign Missions, 1810–1860* (Cambridge, East Asian Research Center, Harvard University, 1969), pp. 20–28.

2. John R. Mott, *History of the Student Volunteer Movement for Foreign Missions* (1892), pp. 6–10. This summer Bible school is sometimes referred to as the first Northfield Conference, though it was held a short distance from Northfield in the small community of Mount Hermon. See the contemporary announcement in the YMCA Historical Library, New York City: "Suggestions for Delegates to the College Student Summer School for Bible Study, To Be Conducted by D. L. Moody, at Mount Hermon, Mass., July 7 to August 1, 1886."

3. For brief accounts of the SVM, see Shedd, *Two Centuries*, pp. 243–320; C. Howard Hopkins, *History of the YMCA in North America* (New York, Association Press, 1951), pp. 294–304, 629–630; Paul A. Varg, *Missionaries, Chinese, and Diplomats: The American Protestant Missionary Movement in China, 1890–1952* (Princeton, Princeton University Press, 1958), pp. 57–63, 147–149, 156–161. The only extended study is William H. Beahm, "Factors in the Development of the Student Volunteer Movement for Foreign Missions" (Ph.D. diss., University of Chicago Divinity School, 1941). Beahm divided his subject into

three phases: establishment and acceptance, 1886–1900; expanding achievement, 1900–1920; and confusion and decline, 1920–1936.

4. By 1916, China had displaced India as the mission field with the highest concentration of Protestant foreign missionaries. The foreign staff in China that year numbered 5750, compared with 5465 for India. The United States and Canada were represented in the China field by 50 societies and 2862 foreign staff members, while Great Britain had 21 societies and 1252 staff. Harlan P. Beach and Burton St. John, eds., *World Statistics of Christian Missions* (New York, FMCNA, 1916), pp. 63–65. In 1920 the budget for the China missions of all North American Protestant sending agencies was $19,075,741, compared with $17,917,394 for India missions. Interchurch World Movement of North America, *World Survey* (New York, Interchurch Press, 1920), II, 158–159.

5. Phillips, *Protestant America*, pp. 7–12; Ernest R. Sandeen, *The Roots of Fundamentalism: British and American Millenarianism, 1800–1930* (Chicago, University of Chicago Press, 1970), pp. 42–58.

6. Sandeen, *Fundamentalism*, pp. 167–187.

7. Arthur T. Pierson, *The Crisis of Missions; or, the Voice out of the Cloud* (New York, 1886), pp. 24–25, 27.

8. Pierson, *Crisis of Missions*, pp. 349–364; Arthur T. Pierson, "Can This World Be Evangelized in Twenty Years?" *Missionary Review*, 4:437–441 (1881).

9. Arthur T. Pierson, "The Evangelization of the World in This Generation," *The Student Missionary Enterprise: Addresses and Discussions of the Second International Convention of the Student Volunteer Movement for Foreign Missions* (Boston, 1894), pp. 105–115. Cited hereafter as *Report of the Second International Convention of the SVM* (1894).

10. See Robert E. Speer, "The Evangelization of the World in This Generation," *The Student Missionary Appeal: Addresses at the Third International Convention of the Student Volunteer Movement for Foreign Missions* (New York, 1898), pp. 201–216. Cited hereafter as *Report of the Third International Convention of the SVM* (1898).

11. Both these positions were in fact represented in addresses before the second SVM convention in 1894. Judson Smith, "The Intellectual Preparation of the Volunteer," in *Report of the Second International Convention of the SVM* (1894), pp. 19–26; J. Hudson Taylor, "The Spiritual Needs and Claims of China," *Report of the Second International Convention of the SVM* (1894), pp. 46–54.

12. Shedd, *Two Centuries*, pp. 232–237; James F. Findlay, *Dwight L. Moody: American Evangelist* (Chicago, University of Chicago Press, 1969), pp. 339–355.

13. J. Leighton Stuart described in his autobiography the soul struggle he had experienced as a college and seminary student in Virginia during the 1890s when SVM leaders were attempting to convert him to a foreign mission career. Stuart, *Fifty Years in China: The Memoirs of John Leighton Stuart, Missionary and Ambassador* (New York, Random House, 1954), pp. 23–28.

14. Apparently the first revivalist to use pledge cards was Edward P. Hammond in the 1870s. Moody made some use of them in his later campaigns, but the most consistent advocate was B. Fay Mills, who asked his converts to sign a card inscribed, "I have an honest desire to lead a Christian life." William G. McLoughlin, *Modern Revivalism: Charles Grandison Finney to Billy Graham* (New York, Ronald Press, 1959), pp. 156–157, 264, 334–335.

15. Robert E. Speer, "The Volunteer Movement's Possible Perils," *The Stu-*

dent Volunteer, 1:41 (1893); John R. Mott, "Three Years of Progress," *Report of the Second International Convention of the SVM* (1894), pp. 66–70.

16. In 1891, out of 6200 volunteers registered, only 321 had sailed for the mission field. The discrepancy was greatly narrowed in succeeding years, but after 1898 the executive committee reported only the number of "sailed volunteers," not the total number of those who signed pledge or declaration cards. Beahm, "Factors," p. 112.

17. Beahm, "Factors," pp. 97–120. These items are now located in the SVM Archives, Yale Divinity School Library, New Haven.

18. John R. Mott, "The Report of the Executive Committee," *North American Students and World Advance: Addresses Delivered at the Eighth International Convention of the Student Volunteer Movement for Foreign Missions* (New York, 1920), p. 70.

19. Beahm, "Factors," p. 129. As early as 1894 Mott noted a "falling off" in missionary interest in New England colleges and reported that most volunteers were coming from the Middle West. John R. Mott, "Three Years of Progress," p. 17.

20. Hopkins, *History of the YMCA*, pp. 271–294.

21. Hopkins, *History of the YMCA*, pp. 295–296, 328–347.

22. Shedd, *Two Centuries*, pp. 163, 214–228.

23. Shedd, *Two Centuries*, pp. 347–354.

24. Shedd, *Two Centuries*, pp. 355–372; Hopkins, *History of the YMCA*, pp. 630–634. See also John R. Mott, *The World's Student Christian Federation: Origin, Achievements, Forecast* (New York, 1920).

25. In 1920 Mott claimed that the SVM had "for some time" supplied 75 percent of the men and 70 percent of the unmarried women sent out by North American Protestant sending agencies, figures that are probably somewhat too large. John R. Mott, "Report of the Executive Committee," p. 62.

26. Basil Mathews, *John R. Mott: World Citizen* (New York, Harper and Bros., 1934), pp. 225–226.

27. Mott, *History of the Student Volunteer Movement*, p. 9.

28. *Report of the Second International Convention of the SVM* (1894), p. 1; John R. Mott, "What of the War?" *Report of the Third International Convention of the SVM* (1898), pp. 274–275.

29. *World-Wide Evangelization the Urgent Business of the Church: Addresses Delivered Before the Fourth International Convention of the Student Volunteer Movement for Foreign Missions* (New York, 1902), p. 28.

30. Charles C. Hall, "The Responsibility Resting on Christian Colleges and Theological Seminaries in View of the Student Missionary Uprising," *Report of the Third International Convention of the SVM* (1898), p. 185.

31. One of the strongest demands for this kind of thorough training came from Judson Smith of the ABCFM in an address at the 1894 SVM convention. Smith, "Intellectual Preparation," pp. 19–26.

32. John R. Mott, "The First Two Decades of the Student Volunteer Movement," *Students and the Modern Missionary Crusade: Addresses Delivered Before the Fifth International Convention of the Student Volunteer Movement for Foreign Missions* (New York, 1906), p. 59. Cited hereafter as *Report of the Fifth International Convention of the SVM* (1906).

33. J. Leighton Stuart candidly described his own aversion to street preaching

in Hangchow and his happiness in transferring to seminary teaching in Nanking a few years later. Stuart, *Fifty Years*, pp. 35–41.

34. The number of women volunteers multiplied rapidly in the second decade of the twentieth century, accounting for over 60 percent of the "sailed volunteers" by 1920.

35. Smith, "Intellectual Preparation," p. 24.

36. Luther D. Wishard, "The Volunteer Movement among Students in Non-Christian Lands," *Report of the Second International Convention of the SVM* (1894), p. 96.

37. Ernest D. Burton, "The Demand for Men and Women of Education in the Orient," *Students and the World-Wide Expansion of Christianity: Addresses Delivered Before the Seventh International Convention of the Student Volunteer Movement for Foreign Missions* (New York, 1914), pp. 400–404. Cited hereafter as *Report of the Seventh International Convention of the SVM* (1914).

38. W. M. Forrest, "Christian Colleges in Mission Lands," *Report of the Fifth International Convention of the SVM* (1906), p. 532.

39. Mott, "First Two Decades," p. 43; Mott, "Report of the Executive Committee," pp. 61–62.

40. The following incomplete list of missionaries and former missionaries who contributed scholarly publications to the field of Chinese studies is extracted from the published rosters of "sailed volunteers" during the period 1906–1923: John Lossing Buck, Thomas F. Carter, George B. Cressey, Homer H. Dubs, Henry Courtney Fenn, Luther C. Goodrich, William J. Hail, Arthur W. Hummell, Daniel H. Kulp, Kenneth Scott Latourette, Harley F. MacNair, Carroll B. Malone, Mary A. Nourse, Ida C. Pruitt, Arnold Rowbotham, John K. Shryock, George Nye Steiger, and Nancy Lee Swann. *Report of the Sixth International Convention of the SVM* (1910), pp. 513–538; *Report of the Seventh International Convention of the SVM* (1914), pp. 641–670; *Christian Students and World Problems: Report of the Ninth International Convention of the Student Volunteer Movement for Foreign Missions* (New York, 1924), pp. 496–533.

41. Gilbert Reid, "China: Her Possibilities," *Report of the Second International Convention of the SVM* (1894), pp. 235–236; Henry Kingman, "The Need of Men and Women of Literary Tastes in China," *Report of the Second International Convention of the SVM* (1894), pp. 242–243.

42. A. P. Happer, "The Educator's Opportunity," *Report of the Second International Convention of the SVM* (1894), p. 247; Robert R. Gailey, "The Students of China," *Report of the Fifth International Convention of the SVM* (1906), pp. 192–194.

43. John R. Mott, "An Unprecedented World-Situation," *Report of the Seventh International Convention of the SVM* (1914), pp. 85–98; Sherwood Eddy, "The Awakening of Asia," *Report of the Seventh International Convention of the SVM* (1914), pp. 195–200. Eddy published a popular book on his tour entitled *The New Era in Asia* (New York, Missionary Education Movement of the U.S. and Canada, 1913), and Mott had some of his letters privately printed as *Experiences and Impressions During a Tour in Asia in 1912–1913* (New York, 1913).

44. John R. Mott, "A Quadrennium in the Life and Work of the Student Volunteer Movement," *Report of the Sixth International Convention of the SVM* (1910), p. 34.

45. C. T. Wang, "The Part of Oriental Students in the Evangelization of the Far East," *Report of the Sixth International Convention of the SVM* (1910), pp. 45—47. Wang was not the first Chinese student to address an SVM convention, for a Mr. Lien, a protégé of Gilbert Reid who was attending DePauw University, gave a brief message in 1898. *Report of the Third International Convention of the SVM* (1898), p. 340.

46. John R. Mott, "Obligations Resting on Chinese Students for the Evangelization of China," *Report of the Seventh International Convention of the SVM* (1914), p. 559; Abram E. Cory, "Our Present Responsibility in China," *Report of the Seventh International Convention of the SVM* (1914), p. 258.

47. John R. Mott, "The World Opportunity," *Report of the Eighth International Convention of the SVM* (1920), p. 17.

48. Some of these factors are suggested in Beahm, "Factors," pp. 306—318, who summed it up: "But the heart had gone out of the early argument for foreign missions" (p. 317).

WILLIAM R. HUTCHISON, "MODERNISM AND MISSIONS: THE LIBERAL SEARCH FOR AN EXPORTABLE CHRISTIANITY, 1875—1935"

1. Robert E. Speer, *Christianity and the Nations* (London, Fleming H. Revell, 1910), p. 33.

2. W. O. Carver, "Baptists and the Problem of World Missions," *Review and Expositor* (Southern Baptist) 17:327 (July 1920).

3. See also W. R. Hutchison, ed., *American Protestant Thought: The Liberal Era* (New York, Harper and Row, 1968), pp. 1—14.

4. Shailer Mathews, *The Faith of Modernism* (New York, Macmillan, 1924), pp. 34—35.

5. Sydney E. Ahlstrom, *The American Protestant Encounter with World Religions* (Beloit, Beloit College, 1962), text corresponding to nn 52, 32—37.

6. Ahlstrom omits mention, for example, of S. Wells Williams, *The Middle Kingdom* (New York, 1848).

7. *Annual Report of the American Board of Commissioners for Foreign Missions* (Boston, ABCFM, 1900), pp. iii-xii; Edward C. Moore, *The Vision of God: Annual Sermon Before the ABCFM, Delivered at St. Louis, Mo., October 10, 1900* (Boston, ABCFM, 1900), pp. 5—6.

8. See, e.g., George A. Gordon, *The New Epoch for Faith* (Boston, Houghton, Mifflin, 1901).

9. [Emily Smith Clarke], William O. Stearns, et al., *William Newton Clarke: A Biography, with Additional Sketches by His Friends and Colleagues* (New York, Charles Scribner's Sons, 1916), pp. v-vi, 129, 152—158, 217; William Newton Clarke, *A Study of Christian Missions* (New York, Charles Scribner's Sons, 1900), pp. 192—194, 171.

10. Clarke, *Missions*, pp. 171—174, 182—183.

11. Clarke, *Missions*, pp. 174, 178—179.

12. Clarke, *Missions*, pp. 184—185; Francis Peabody, *The Mission of Christianity to the Far East: Addresses at the First Unitarian Missionary Conference, Channing Hall, Boston, November 11 and 12, 1913*, pamphlet no. 1 (Boston, n.d.), p. 3.

13. Clarke, *Missions*, pp. 243, 19.

14. George E. Burlingame, review, *Biblical World* 17:384–386 (May 1901).

15. Some of these views—for example, those involving doubts about Western or American culture—were echoed in conservative theology; conservatives were very likely to see the home culture as morally declining or bankrupt. On other points, professedly conservative missionary leaders gradually found the liberal approach less menacing than they had supposed, so that they were able to make its proposals their own. Given those qualifications, the configuration of ideas just described can be linked directly with the rise and establishment of liberal theology.

16. Newman Smyth, *Dorner on the Future State: Being a Translation of the Section of His System of Christian Doctrine Comprising the Doctrine of the Last Things, with an Introduction and Notes* (New York, 1883), pp. 33–37.

17. Egbert Smyth, "Christianity and Missions," in Egbert C. Smyth et al., eds., *Progressive Orthodoxy* (Boston, 1885), pp. 186, 155, 153–190 passim.

18. George A. Gordon, *My Education and Religion: An Autobiography* (Boston, Houghton Mifflin, 1925), p. 330; Smyth, "Christianity," p. 178.

19. *David Swing's Sermons* (Chicago, 1874), p. 43; George A. Gordon, *The Gospel for Humanity: Annual Sermon Before the American Board of Commissioners for Foreign Missions, Delivered at Brooklyn, New York, October 15, 1896* (Boston, 1895), pp. 5, 9, 7.

20. Gordon, *The Gospel*, pp. 12–14, 17.

21. R. Pierce Beaver, ed., *To Advance the Gospel: Selections from the Writings of Rufus Anderson* (Grand Rapids, Eerdmans, 1967), pp. 16, 38. Anderson's advocacy of native churches, moreover, did not entail liberality toward ethnic religions, for he "had no respect for Oriental, Pacific, and African cultures and religions" (pp. 35–36).

22. Clarke, *Missions*, pp. 50–60, 62–63.

23. Dorothea Muller has argued that Strong himself was a case in point, since his expansionism was religious rather than racist and he was sharply critical of American society. Dorothea Muller, "Josiah Strong and American Nationalism: A Reevaluation," *Journal of American History* 53:487–503 (December 1966). See also Jurgen Herbst, editor's introduction to Josiah Strong, *Our Country: Its Possible Future and Its Present Crisis* (Cambridge, Harvard University Press, 1963), pp. ix-xxvi. For examples of greater assurance about the credentials of American or Anglo-Saxon Christendom, see the ABCFM sermons by Nehemiah Boynton, *The Commission of a Recovered Life* (Boston, 1897), and by Washington Gladden, *The Nation and the Kingdom* (Boston, 1909).

24. Dores R. Sharpe, *Walter Rauschenbusch* (New York, Macmillan, 1942), pp. 358, 150–151; Walter Rauschenbusch, *Christianity and the Social Crisis* (New York, Macmillan, 1907), pp. 317–318.

25. Henry Churchill King, *The Moral and Religious Challenge of Our Times; The Guiding Principle in Human Development: Reverence for Personality* (New York, Macmillan, 1915), pp. 344, 348.

26. King, *Challenge*, pp. 348–360, 361.

27. King, *Challenge*, pp. 371, 384; see also pp. 363–372.

28. King, *Challenge*, p. 365.

29. Smyth, "Christianity," p. 189; Clarke, *Missions*, pp. 40–49; Douglas C. Macintosh, "The New Christianity and World-Conversion," *American Journal of Theology* 18:337–354, 553–370 (July, October 1914). An increase was re-

corded in American missionary personnel from 2500 in 1886 to 10,000 in 1914. "Native communicants" attached to American missions increased from 300,000 to 1,500,000 (rounded figures). *Missionary Review of the World* 9:552–553 (November-December 1886); vol. 29 (March 1916), charts facing p. 168.

30. See, e.g., John Horsch, *The Modernist View of Missions* (Scottsdale, Pa., Fundamental Truth Depot, 1920); W. H. Griffith Thomas, "Modernism in China," *Princeton Theological Review* 19:630–671 (October 1921); John Gresham Machen, *Modernism and the Board of Foreign Missions of the Presbyterian Church in the U.S.A.* (Philadelphia, privately printed, 1933).

31. "A Committee of the Presbytery," ed., *The Trial of the Rev. David Swing* (Chicago, 1874), p. 71.

32. Cyrus Hamlin, "The New Departure and Missions," *Bibliotheca Sacra* 43:769 (October 1886).

33. Hamlin, "New Departure," p. 769; Charles A. Bowen, "A Message from Missions to the Modern Ministry," in A. C. Dixon et al., eds., *The Fundamentals: A Testimony to the Truth* (Chicago, Testimony Publishing Co., 1910–15), IX, 96–102.

34. A. A. Hodge, review of A. V. G. Allen, *The Continuity of Christian Thought*, in *Presbyterian Review* 6:563–564 (July 1885).

35. Thomas, "Modernism," pp. 670–671.

36. Albert H. Plumb, "Dr. George A. Gordon's Reconstruction of Christian Theology," *Bibliotheca Sacra* 53:357, 353–354 (April 1896).

37. Commission of Appraisal, William Ernest Hocking, chairman, *Re-Thinking Missions: A Laymen's Inquiry after One Hundred Years* (New York, Harper and Brothers, 1932).

38. *Re-Thinking Missions*, pp. 49–59, 29–48.

39. Archibald G. Baker, "Reactions to the Laymen's Report," *Journal of Religion* 13:379–398 (October 1933).

40. See Robert T. Handy, *A Christian America: Protestant Hopes and Historical Realities* (New York, Oxford University Press, 1971), pp. 128–139. Handy stressed the self-confidence of the missionary movement as a whole at the turn of the century, and its failure—despite efforts in this direction—to distill a purely religious message for the world. He also contributed to a more sympathetic or rounded understanding of spiritual "imperialists" with a quote from Josiah Strong: "I do not imagine that an Anglo-Saxon is any dearer to God than a Mongolian or an African. My plea is not, Save America for America's sake, but Save America for the world's sake" (p. 147).

41. Henry W. Frost of the China Inland Mission, underlining the primacy of love for Christ as a missionary motive, told the heartening story of a Miss Stayner, whose only apparent disqualification for missionary service in China was that she disliked the Chinese: "They are so ignorant and dirty." "This was a real obstacle," Frost allowed, "especially as she had been working among the Chinese." But Stayner did love the Lord, and Frost admonished her that she therefore had no choice but to go to China. Frost, "What Missionary Motives Should Prevail," in *The Fundamentals*, XII, 93–94. For Eddy's view of Speer's conservatism, see Handy, *A Christian America*, p. 132.

42. Speer, "Foreign Missions or World-Wide Evangelism," in *The Fundamentals*, XII, 76–77, 84. Cf. Clarke, *Missions*, pp. 10–11, 107–108.

43. Speer, "Foreign Missions," p. 31; Machen, *Modernism*, p. 3; Lefferts Loetscher, *The Broadening Church: A Study of Theological Issues in the*

Presbyterian Church since 1869 (Philadelphia, University of Pennsylvania Press, 1957), pp. 150–151.

44. Ahlstrom, *Encounter,* text corresponding to nn 65–71. For direct statements of neo-orthodox attitudes toward world religions, see also John A. Mackay, "Christianity and Other Religions," in Arnold S. Nash, ed., *Protestant Thought in the Twentieth Century: Whence and Whither?* (New York, Macmillan, 1951), pp. 275–296; Reinhold Niebuhr, *Beyond Tragedy* (New York, Charles Scribner's Sons, 1965), esp. pp. 28–29: "Man . . . is not content to be merely American man, or Chinese man . . . He wants to be man. He is not content with his truth . . . He seeks *the* Truth . . . But . . . the truth man finds and speaks is, for all of his efforts to transcend himself, still his truth."

45. Dr. Harry Denman, addressing a Methodist gathering in 1971, assailed American churches as social clubs and American society as flaccid: "In the Thirties, individuals went on welfare. Today, corporations are going on welfare." He continued, "I may be too pessimistic, but I don't think the United States can evangelize the world. We are imperialist, we are militant, and we are still dropping bombs." All in all, Denman argued, the proper mission field for American Christianity was America. Denman, quoted in typescript of televised news report, Oct. 17, 1971, Massachusetts Council of Churches, Boston.

46. The case for an exemplary rather than proselytizing Christianity has been offered in many theological contexts. James Luther Adams paraphrased H. Richard Niebuhr's suggestion that it may be unfitting for Christians "to vaunt the alleged superiority of their norms, their obligation being rather to allow others peradventure to observe" such superiority as may be there. Adams, editor's introduction to Ernst Troeltsch, *The Absoluteness of Christianity and the History of Religions* (Richmond, Va., John Knox Press, 1971), p. 19.

47. See, e.g., Clifford Geertz, "Religion As a Cultural System," in Michael Banton, ed., *Anthropological Approaches to the Study of Religion* (New York, Frederick A. Praeger, 1966), pp. 1–46.

M. SEARLE BATES, "THE THEOLOGY OF AMERICAN MISSIONARIES IN CHINA, 1900–1950"

1. Statistical data are derived from Harlan P. Beach, *Geography and Atlas of Protestant Missions* (New York, SVMFM, 1906), pp. 19, 23–24; James S. Dennis, Harlan P. Beach, and Charles H. Fahs, *World Atlas of Christian Missions* (New York, SVMFM, 1911), pp. 83, 87–88; Joseph I. Parker, *Interpretative Statistical Survey of the World Mission of the Christian Church* (New York, International Missionary Council, 1938), pp. 86–88; Edwin C. Lobenstine, "China," in Parker, *Survey,* p. 27. See also Harlan P. Beach and Burton St. John, *World Statistics of Christian Missions* (New York, FMCNA, 1916), pp. 63–64; Charles H. Boynton, *Handbook of the Christian Movement* (Shanghai, 1936), pp. viii-ix; H. Paul Douglass, "Some Major Problems of the Christian Evangelization of China," in Orville A. Petty, ed., *Laymen's Foreign Missions Inquiry: Fact-Finders' Reports,* vol. 5, supp. ser., pt. 2, of *China* (New York, Harper, 1933), esp. pp. 4, 89. No data after those for 1935–1936 are of sufficient significance to warrant similar consideration. The situation changed repeatedly and irregularly, forming no pattern.

2. For this period, see Milton B. Stauffer, ed., *The Christian Occupation of China* (Shanghai, 1922); Boynton, *Handbook*. For earlier stages, see *China Centenary Missionary Conference Records* (Shanghai, 1907)—cited hereafter as *CCMCR;* Donald MacGillivray, ed., *A Century of Protestant Missions in China, 1807–1907* (Shanghai, 1907). For the disordered and poorly reported later stages, see "Directory of Protestant Missions in China, 1948, 1949, 1950" (January 1950), mimeo. National Christian Council, Shanghai; *World Christian Handbook*, ed. E. J. Bingle (London, World Dominion Press, 1952); Frank W. Price, *China, Twilight or Dawn?* (New York, Friendship Press, 1948).

3. *CCMCR*, pp. 437–439.

4. *CCMCR*, pp. 474–475.

5. *CCMCR*, pp. 353–363.

6. *CCMCR*, pp. 393–403.

7. *CCMCR*, pp. 403–405.

8. *World Missionary Conference, 1910* (New York, Revell, 1910), p. iv; *The Missionary Message in Relation to Non-Christian Religions*, vol. 4: *Chinese Religions*, p. 68.

9. *The Bulletin of the Bible Union of China*, becoming *The Bible for China* (Shanghai, 1921–1937), statement of Nov. 25, 1920, no. 2 (April 1921).

10. *Statement of Policy* (Shanghai, China Inland Mission, 1928), p. 1.

11. Phyllis Thompson, *D. E. Hoste: A Prince with God* (London, China Inland Mission, 1947), p. 215; F. Howard and Mary G. G. Taylor, *"By Faith ... " Henry W. Frost and the China Inland Mission* (Philadelphia, China Inland Mission, 1938), pp. 262–264; Stanley Peregrine Smith, pamphlets privately published in Shanghai, 1916–1919, now in Missionary Research Library.

12. Leslie T. Lyall, *A Passion for the Impossible. The China Inland Mission, 1865–1965* (Chicago, Moody Press, 1965).

13. *The Chinese Church As Revealed in the National Christian Conference ...* (Shanghai, 1922), pp. 693–694.

14. For documents of the Church of Christ in China, see *China Christian Year Book*, app. B, 15:405–412 (Shanghai, National Christian Council, 1928). For a history of that body, see Wallace C. Merwin, *Adventure in Unity: The Church of Christ in China* (Grand Rapids, Eerdman, 1974).

15. See Lewis S. C. Smythe, "Changes in the Christian Message for China by Protestant Missionaries" (Ph.D. diss., University of Chicago, 1928); C. William Mensendiek, "The Protestant Missionary Understanding of the Chinese Situation and the Chinese Task from 1890 to 1911" (Ph.D. diss., Columbia University, 1958).

16. For the most representative statement of American missionary theology in relation to Chinese society and culture, see Frank Rawlinson, *The Naturalization of Christianity in China* (Shanghai, Presbyterian Mission Press, 1927).

ADRIAN A. BENNETT AND KWANG-CHING LIU, "CHRISTIANITY IN THE CHINESE IDIOM: YOUNG J. ALLEN AND THE EARLY *CHIAO-HUI HSIN-PAO*, 1868–1870"

1. Suzanne Wilson Barnett, "Protestant Expansion and Chinese Views of the West," *Modern Asian Studies* 6.2:129–149 (April 1972).

2. Allen to George W. Yarborough, Feb. 19, 1897, AM; Allen, "Notes from Emory," Jan. 24, Nov. 9, 1856, AM; James Caughey, *Methodism in Earnest* (Nashville, E. Stevenson and F. A. Owen for the Methodist Episcopal Church, South, 1854); W. J. Townsend, H. B. Workman, and George Eayrs, *A New History of Methodism* (London, Hodder and Stoughton, 1909), p. 545.

3. Allen, "At Emory College, 1857," AM.

4. Allen, "Young J. Allen, Missionary to China," Jan. 11, 1896, p. 2, AM; Harold Mann, *Atticus Greene Haygood* (Athens, University of Georgia Press, 1965), pp. 21–22; H. M. Bullock, *A History of Emory University* (Nashville, Parthenon Press, 1936), p. 98; "Allen to Dr. Young," Apr. 12, 1884, in the *Christian Advocate* (Nashville, May 31, 1884), p. 11.

5. Allen to Mrs. J. W. Talley, May 30, 1861, in Warren A. Candler, *Young J. Allen: The Man Who Seeded China* (Nashville, Cokesbury Press, 1931), pp. 73–76.

6. Allen to George F. Pierce, Jan. 1, 1864, AM; Allen, Diary, Jan. 14, 1864, AM.

7. Allen to George F. Pierce, Jan. 1, 1864, AM; Allen, Diary, Apr. 7, 1864, AM; Allen to Edward W. Sehon, Dec. 7, 1866, AM; Allen, Diary, Mar. 19, June 19, 1867, AM.

8. Allen, Diary, Feb. 24, 1864, AM; Knight Biggerstaff, *The Earliest Modern Government Schools in China* (Ithaca, Cornell University Press, 1961), pp. 160–164.

9. Allen, Diary, Jan. 9, Feb. 11, 12, Apr. 13, 1864, AM.

10. Allen, Diary, Nov. 25, 1864; Allen to Edward W. Sehon, Dec. 7, 1866, AM.

11. Allen to unknown, June 15, 1870, in Candler, *Allen*, p. 82; Mellie Allen Loehr, "Young J. Allen," p. 9, AM; W. B. Nance, *Soochow University* (New York, United Board for Christian Higher Learning in Asia, 1956), p. 17.

12. Allen to Edward W. Sehon, Dec. 7, 1866, AM; Allen, Diary, Apr. 13, 1864, AM.

13. Soon after Allen had assumed superintendency of the China mission of the Methodist Church, South, in 1881, he initiated a three-tiered educational system. At the first level he planned a primary school for boys and one for girls. Two high schools formed the second level. At the third level was a college, which together with the high schools was known as the Chung-hsi shu-yuan (Anglo-Chinese School). The schools offered instruction in English, Chinese classics, religion, and sciences. Over one hundred and forty students were admitted to the Anglo-Chinese School, and the number remained constant at least until 1895, when Allen resigned the presidency of the institution.

14. "Missionary Intelligence," *The Missionary Recorder* 1:15 (April 1867); Allen, Diary, Apr. 2, 1867, AM.

15. Long Loh Chi [Lin Lo-chih, Young J. Allen], "A Few Notes on Cotton Production in China," *The Missionary Recorder* 1:56–58 (July 1867). In the October issue of *The Missionary Recorder* the article was criticized by James Meadows of Ningpo as being too secular for a missionary magazine. Allen later expanded his ideas on the role of cotton production in China's economy in a series of notes published in the *Wan-kuo kung-pao* 9:247 a-b (Dec. 16, 1876), 9:260 (Dec. 23, 1876), 9:331 (Jan. 27, 1877).

16. Allen, Diary, Mar. 4, Apr. 20, 29, May 20, Sept. 29, 1867, AM.

17. Allen, Diary, Feb. 5, Dec. 5, 1867.

18. Allen, Diary, Mar. 13, Apr. 25, 1867; Allen to E. H. Myers, *SCA* (Aug. 16, 1867), p. 130; Allen to Myers, *SCA* (Mar. 20, 1868), p. 46.

19. Allen to E. H. Myers, Jan. 1, 1868, *SCA* (Mar. 27, 1868), p. 50; Allen, "Mental Memorandum, 1868," AM.

20. Allen, Diary, May 1, 1868, AM; Roswell S. Britton, *The Chinese Periodical Press, 1800—1912* (Shanghai, Kelly and Walsh, 1933), pp. 49, 52; Allen to E. H. Myers, Dec. 9, 1868, *SCA* (Feb. 26, 1869), p. 34.

21. *CHHP* 4:120b (Feb. 10, 1872).

22. I. G. John, *Methodist Handbook of Missions* (Nashville, Southern Methodist Publishing House, 1893), p. 197. John quoted an Allen letter written sometime in the 1870s.

23. Rudolf Lowenthal, *The Religious Periodical Press in China* (Peking, The Synodal Commission in China, 1940), p. 77.

24. For the *Chiao-hui hsin-pao* articles not otherwise noted, see Adrian A. Bennett, comp., "Research Guide to the *Chiao-hui hsin-pao* and the Early *Wan-kuo kung-pao*, 1868—1883" (in preparation).

25. These reports cover in particular Methodist, Presbyterian, Baptist, and Congregational societies, both British and American, as well as Anglican and Episcopal missions.

26. *CHHP* 2:2b-3 (Sept. 4, 1869). Thirteen treaty ports, Hong Kong, Peking, Soochow, and Hangchow, as well as "miscellaneous places" with negligible returns, are included in the following figures: ordained Chinese pastors (*mu-shih*), 19; unordained Chinese preachers (*chiang-shu*), presumably including teachers, 316; preachers in surrounding villages and townships, 306. *CHHP* 1:4a-b (Sept. 5, 1968).

27. *CHHP* 1:3b (Sept. 5, 1868).

28. *CHHP* 1:146b (Apr. 24, 1869).

29. Besides Hsu Wei-ts'an, one other southern Methodist convert, using the pseudonym Ch'ih-p'ing shou, frequently wrote for the *CHHP*. Two other converts of the mission contributed less frequently.

30. *CHHP* 1:22a-b (Oct. 10, 1868). Hsu Wei-ts'an wrote under the name Wei-ts'an tzu; for his surname, Hsu, see *CHHP* 1:91b (Jan. 30, 1869). The English table of contents of the Oct. 10, 1868, issue contained a reference suggesting that Hsu was a native of Nanking and was teaching in one of the two small mission schools established by Allen and Lambuth in 1867 in Shanghai.

31. *CHHP* 1:25b (Oct. 17, 1868).

32. *CHHP* 1:33b—34a (Oct. 31, 1868).

33. *CHHP* 1:41a-b (Nov. 14, 1868). Yates wrote under the name "Yen Chiao-shih of the Southern Baptist Convention, Shanghai." For his identification, see *CHHP* 1:18b (Oct. 3, 1868); Alexander Wylie, *Memorials of Protestant Missionaries to the Chinese* (Shanghai, American Presbyterian Mission Press, 1867), p. 167. The discussion here is based on the nine replies to Chieh-yü tzu that appeared November 1868—May 1869. Later the magazine published a further reply by Wang Kuang-ch'i. *CHHP* 2:201b-203 (June 8, 1870).

34. *CHHP* 1:45b (Nov. 21, 1868), 1:71b (Jan. 2, 1869), 1:121 (Mar. 20, 1869). See James Legge, trans., *The Chinese Classics* (Hong Kong, Hong Kong University Press, 1966), I, 357. Wang Kuang-ch'i, also known as Wang I-hua, was a scholar in his sixties and the author of two books on Christianity, including *T'ien-tao ming-teng* (The bright lamp of heaven's way). *CHHP* 1:170b (May 29, 1869), 2:204 (June 18, 1870).

35. Among the authors of the replies to Chieh-yü tzu, the only one who adopted a disrespectful tone regarding the concept of *hsiao* (filial devotion) was Liang Chu-ch'en from Kwangtung, who stated, "Father and mother are no more than husband and wife; in the beginning God made husband and wife but not father and mother." *CHHP* 1:151 (May 1, 1869). This iconoclastic rhetoric was not typical of the writers in the *Chiao-hui hsin-pao*.

36. *CHHP* 1:54b (Dec. 5, 1868).

37. *CHHP* 1:131 (Apr. 3, 1869).

38. *CHHP* 1:45b (Nov. 21, 1868).

39. *CHHP* 1:54b (Dec. 5, 1868), 1:58b (Dec. 12, 1868), 1:62b (Dec. 19, 1868), 1:106 (Feb. 27, 1869).

40. *CHHP* 1:76 (Jan. 9, 1868), 1:106b (Feb. 27, 1869), 1:58b–59 (Dec. 12, 1868), 1:116 (Mar. 13, 1869), 1:67a-b (Dec. 26, 1868), 1:76b (Jan. 9, 1869).

41. *CHHP* 1:33 (Oct. 24, 1868).

42. See esp. *CHHP* 1:134 (Apr. 3, 1869), 1:141 (Apr. 17, 1869), 1:146, 149 (Apr. 24, 1869).

43. See, e.g., *CHHP* 1:140b (Apr. 27, 1869), 1:161b–162 (May 15, 1869), 2:25b (Oct. 2, 1869), 2:103b–104 (Jan. 22, 1870). Beginning in the winter of 1869–1870, under pressure of anti-Christian agitation, the magazine published a few articles arguing that Christian precepts were also taught by the Confucian classics.

44. *CHHP* 1:151 (May 1, 1869), 1:215b (Aug. 7, 1869). Chang Ting also styled himself Chih-fei tzu. Ch'üan-shan tzu was reported as writing from Chefoo.

45. *CHHP* 1:161 (May 15, 1869), 1:201b (July 10, 1869).

46. Hsu's article on the concepts of *wu-yin* and *kuang-ai* had stimulated an enthusiastic response from Cheng Pi-teng, a Baptist convert in Chefoo, who mentioned that he was engaged in "[maritime] customs affairs." Cheng wrote that the two concepts enabled him to see the essence of biblical teachings. *CHHP* 1:81 (Jan. 16, 1869).

47. *CHHP* 1:95b (Feb. 6, 1869), 1:107 (Feb. 27, 1869). Hsu Wei-ts'an used the name Ai-kuang sheng for both articles. On another occasion when using the same pseudonym, he further identified himself as Huai-yuan, a variant name he had used earlier. *CHHP* 1:22b (Oct. 10, 1868), 1:136 (Apr. 10, 1869).

48. *CHHP* 1:166b (May 22, 1869), 2:50 (Nov. 6, 1869).

49. *CHHP* 2:60a-b (Nov. 20, 1869).

50. *CHHP* 1:166b (May 22, 1869), 2:60a-b (Nov. 20, 1869).

51. *CHHP* 2:19b (Sept. 25, 1869), 1:161b (May 15, 1869). On Allen's exhorting converts and missionaries to respect Chinese law, see *CHHP* 1:221 (Aug. 14, 1869), 2:77b (Dec. 18, 1869).

52. *CHHP* 1:86b–87 (Jan. 23, 1869), 1:91b–92b (Jan. 30, 1869), 1:116b–117 (Mar. 13, 1869), 1:130b (Apr. 3, 1869), 1:136a-b (Apr. 10, 1869).

53. *CHHP* 1:137b (Apr. 10, 1869), 1:172 (May 29, 1869).

54. See, e.g., *CHHP* 2:87a-b (Jan. 1, 1870), 2:91b (Jan. 8, 1870), 2:97a-b (Jan. 15, 1870), 2:106a-b (Jan. 29, 1870), 2:191a-b (June 4, 1870).

55. *CHHP* 1:128 (Mar. 27, 1869), 1:218a-b (Aug. 7, 1869), 1:229 (Aug. 21, 1869).

56. *CHHP* 1:199b (July 3, 1869).

57. *CHHP* 1:140–141 (Apr. 17, 1869), 1:176b–177 (June 5, 1869). Huang Mei was the only Chinese Christian writer cited in this article known to have

been abroad. He had gone to San Francisco, converted to Christianity in 1855, and become a preacher in 1857. He returned to Kwangtung in 1859 and was associated with the southern Baptist missionaries there, including Issachar J. Roberts. *CHHP*, 1:140b (Apr. 17, 1869).

58. *CHHP* 1:137b (Apr. 10, 1869).

59. *CHHP* 2:46 (Nov. 6, 1869), 2:53b (Nov. 13, 1869). Pien-cheng tzu composed a song exhorting the refugees to abandon their Buddhist or Taoist beliefs. *CHHP* 2:46b (Nov. 6, 1869).

60. *CHHP* 2:59b—60 (Nov. 20, 1869).

61. *CHHP* 2:90b (Jan. 1, 1870), 2:155b (Feb. 12, 1870), 2:177b (Feb. 19, 1870).

62. *CHHP* 2:13 (Sept. 18, 1869), 2:17 (Sept. 25, 1869).

63. *CHHP* 2:92b (Jan. 8, 1870).

64. *CHHP* 2:13 (Sept. 18, 1869).

65. Yü Chih, ed., *Te-i lu* (Having got hold of what was good: an anthology), 16 chüan (Soochow, Te-chien chai, 1869; Taipei reprint, 1969), postface, 2. Compiled by Yü as early as 1849, the book was not published until 1869, when Yü received for the purpose the financial assistance of four friends, including Tong King-sing, the comprador of Jardine, Matheson & Co. Tong had benefited in his youth from a missionary school and was now a principal backer of the P'u-yü t'ang.

66. *CHHP* 2:92 (Jan. 8, 1870); Legge, *Chinese Classics*, I, 389.

67. *CHHP* 1:215b (Aug. 7, 1869).

68. *CHHP* 2:4 (Sept. 4, 1869), 2:20a-b (Sept. 25, 1869).

69. *CHHP* 2:158a-b (Apr. 10, 1870).

70. *CHHP* 2:105b—106 (June 18, 1870).

71. *CHHP* 2:178b—179 (May 14, 1870).

72. *CHHP* 2:179b (May 14, 1870), 2:182—183 (May 21, 1870).

73. *CHHP* 2:178 (May 14, 1870), 2:182b (May 21, 1870).

74. *CHHP* 2:206a-b (June 25, 1870).

75. *CHHP* 2:36b—37 (Oct. 23, 1869).

76. Allen, "Our China Mission," June 10, 1880, AM.

77. Allen to E. H. Myers, Jan. 17, 1868, *SCA* (Mar. 27, 1868), p. 50; Allen to E. H. Myers, Dec. 21, 1869, *SCA* (Feb. 11, 1870), p. 20.

78. *CHHP* 1:86b—87 (Jan. 23, 1869), 1:91b—92b (Jan. 30, 1869).

79. *CHHP* 2:28b—30b (Oct. 9, 1869), 2:32—33 (Oct. 16, 1869).

80. *CHHP* 2:216—217 (July 9, 1870).

81. *CHHP* 2:70a-b (Dec. 4, 1869), 2:74—75b (Dec. 11, 1869), 2:84a-b (Dec. 25, 1869), 2:94—95 (Jan. 8, 1870).

82. Allen also encouraged Chinese Christian writers to collect sayings from the Confucian classics to support Christian precepts. *CHHP* 2:73b—74 (Dec. 11, 1869), 2:107b—108 (Jan. 29, 1870).

83. *CHHP* 2:167b—168 (Apr. 30, 1870).

84. *CHHP* 2:185a-b (May 21, 1870).

85. See, e.g., *CHHP* 1:77—78 (Jan. 9, 1869), 1:102a-b (Feb. 20, 1869).

86. *CHHP* 1:144b (Apr. 17, 1869).

87. *CHHP* 1:167 (May 22, 1869).

88. *CHHP* 1:219a-b (Aug. 7, 1869).

89. *CHHP* 2:53b—54 (Nov. 13, 1869), 2:57b (Nov. 20, 1869), 2:116b—117 (Feb. 19, 1870), 2:137b—138b (Mar. 19, 1870).

90. *CHHP* 1:182b—183 (June 12, 1869), 2:38a-b (Oct. 23, 1869), 2:153b (Apr. 9, 1870), 2:165b (Apr. 23, 1870).
91. *CHHP* 2:54b—55 (Nov. 13, 1869).
92. *CHHP* 2:73 (Dec. 11, 1869).

PAUL A. COHEN, "LITTORAL AND HINTERLAND IN NINETEENTH CENTURY CHINA: THE 'CHRISTIAN' REFORMERS"

1. For the Sinicization of the Taipings, see So Kwan-wai and Eugene P. Boardman, assisted by Ch'iu P'ing, "Hung Jen-kan, Taiping Prime Minister, 1859—1864," *Harvard Journal of Asiatic Studies* 20:292—294 (June 1957).
2. Although not all pioneer reformers were products of the littoral, many were, and the majority of those who were not had important conditioning experiences in either the littoral (Feng Kuei-fen in Shanghai), the West (Kuo Sung-tao, Hsueh Fu-ch'eng), or Meiji Japan (Huang Tsun-hsien). I have dealt with Feng, Kuo, Hsueh, and Huang in an expanded, and somewhat different, version of the present chapter. See Pt. IV of my *Between Tradition and Modernity: Wang T'ao and Reform in Late Ch'ing China* (Cambridge, Harvard University Press, 1974).
3. Chinese historians have tended to discount the significance of the Christian impact even in the case of the Taipings. For a noteworthy exception, see Jen Yu-wen (Chien Yu-wen), *The Taiping Revolutionary Movement* (New Haven, Yale University Press, 1973).
4. Tong King-sing and Wu T'ing-fang probably were baptized, Cheng Kuan-ying probably was not. Cheng's eventual interest in popular Taoism is not germane here, but rather the paucity, compared to the seven other reformers, of his known contacts with the missionary community and the lack of any presumptive evidence in favor of baptism.
5. Brown's annual reports to the directors of the society showed the development of the school's curriculum. He detailed the efforts made, both in class and out, to achieve the pupils' conversion to Christianity, which he viewed as being "the only perfectly satisfactory result of our labors." These efforts included encouraging the boys to participate in morning and evening devotions in the Brown home and to observe the Sabbath. Also there were daily readings from the Bible with explanatory comments. See, e.g., the third, fourth, seventh, and eighth annual reports, in *The Chinese Repository*, 10.10 (October 1841), 11.10 (October 1842), 14.10 (October 1845), 15.12 (December 1846).
6. The two fellow students, Wong Shing (Huang Sheng) and Wong Foon (Huang K'uan), may be classified as second-rung modernizers, who performed significant pioneering functions but who never achieved fame in nineteenth century China. Both Wongs were Christians, who in later life had close connections with the London Missionary Society. Wong Shing returned to China in 1848 because of ill health. After learning the printing trade, he was for twenty years superintendent of the London Missionary Society Press in Hong Kong, where he supervised the printing of Legge's *Chinese Classics*. In the early 1870s he helped Wang T'ao, with whom he had earlier collaborated in the production of a book on modern firearms, to purchase the press's equipment and found the *Tsun-wan yat-po (Hsun-huan jih-pao;* Universal circulating herald). Wong Shing

was the first Chinese to sit with Englishmen on a jury. In 1874 he returned to the United States in connection with the Chinese educational mission and was later appointed interpreter to the new Chinese legation in Washington. Wong's son, Wong Wing-sheung (Huang Yung-shang), was an early follower of Sun Yat-sen and took part in the formation of the Hong Kong Hsing-Chung hui (Society to restore China's prosperity). The Wong family, originally from Hsiang-shan hsien, Kwangtung, was related to Ho Kai. Roswell S. Britton, *The Chinese Periodical Press, 1800—1912* (Taipei, Ch'eng-wen Publishing Company, 1966), p. 45; Ch'en Hsueh-lin, "Huang Sheng—Hsiang-kang Hua-jen t'i-ch'ang yang-wu shih-yeh chih hsien-ch'ü" (Wong Shing: A distinguished Chinese in early Hong Kong), *Ch'ung-chi hsueh-pao* (Chung Chi journal) 3:226—231 (May 1964); Harold Z. Schiffrin, *Sun Yat-sen and the Origins of the Chinese Revolution* (Berkeley, University of California Press, 1968), pp. 48—49; Wang T'ao, *Huo-ch'i lueh-shuo* (Introductory treatise on firearms), first preface (*ch'ien-hsu*), Aug. 24—Sept. 2, 1863, reproduced in Wang T'ao, *T'ao-yuan wen-lu wai-pien* (Supplement to *T'ao-yuan wen-lu*), 10 original chüan (Hong Kong, 1883) and two subsequently published chüan (Hong Kong, n.d.) 8:9—11.

Wong Foon (1828—1878), also a native of Hsiang-shan, after completing his secondary school education, earned a medical degree at the University of Edinburgh, becoming the first Chinese doctor to be trained in the West. He returned to China in 1857 under the auspices of the London Missionary Society. For the next twenty years Wong Foon practiced medicine in Canton. Around 1860 he was appointed by Li Hung-chang as a medical adviser, but disliking administrative work, he quit the position after six months. In 1863 Wong was named the Customs Medical Officer for Canton, a job he held until his death. During the last years of his life, from 1866 to 1878, he taught medicine at the Canton Hospital Medical School, an Anglo-American missionary institution directed by Dr. John Kerr. K. Chimin Wong and Lien-teh Wu, *History of Chinese Medicine*, 2nd ed. (Shanghai, National Quarantine Service, 1936), pp. 371—372, 391, 395, 405; William Warder Cadbury, *At the Point of a Lancet: One Hundred Years of the Canton Hospital, 1835—1935* (Shanghai, Kelly and Walsh, 1935), pp. 52, 116—117, 121—123, 127, 164, 175—176; Yung Wing, *My Life in China and America* (New York, Henry Holt, 1909), pp. 32—33; Thomas E. La Fargue, *China's First Hundred* (Pullman, State College of Washington, 1942), p. 21.

7. For a biography of Yung Wing (under Jung Hung), see Arthur W. Hummel, ed., *Eminent Chinese of the Ch'ing Period* (Washington, D.C., Government Printing Office, 1943—1944), I, 402—405. Yung's retrospective account, *My Life in China and America*, must be used with caution because it is self-serving and marred by inaccuracies. The most detailed scholarly account of Yung's career is Lo Hsiang-lin, *Hsiang-kang yü Chung-Hsi wen-hua chih chiao-liu* (Hong Kong and Sino-Western cultural interchange; Hong Kong, Chung-kuo hsüeh-she, 1961), pp. 77—134. There is an English edition of Lo's book, *The Role of Hong Kong in the Cultural Interchange Between East and West*, 2 vols. (Tokyo, The Centre for East Asian Cultural Studies, 1963), but since the translation is quite poor, I have not cited it. On Yung's educational mission, see La Fargue, *China's First Hundred*; Otake Fumio, "Shindai ni okeru Chūgoku no gaikoku ryūgakusei" (Chinese who studied abroad during the Ch'ing dynasty), in Hayashi Tomoharu, comp., *Kinsei Chūgoku kyōikushi kenkyū* (Studies in the educational history of modern China; Tokyo, 1958), pp. 309—328. For Yung's years in America, see Edmund H. Worthy, Jr., "Yung Wing in America," *Pacific Historical Review* 34:265—287 (August 1965).

8. Lloyd Eastman, "Political Reformism in China Before the Sino-Japanese War," *Journal of Asian Studies* 27:698 (August 1968).

9. Biographical information on Hu Li-yuan (c. 1847–c. 1916) is sparse. Born into a merchant family from San-shui hsien, Kwangtung, he lived in Hong Kong from an early age. His educational background was both Chinese and Western. He competed unsuccessfully in the civil service examinations and was a graduate of Queen's College in Hong Kong. A prosperous merchant and close friend of Ho Kai, Hu served from 1879 to 1881 on the translating staff of Wang T'ao's *Tsun-wan yat-po*. He visited Japan at the time of the Sino-Japanese War. Lu T'ing-ch'ang, "Hu I-nan hsien-sheng shih-lueh" (A sketch of Mr. Hu Li-yuan), in Hu Li-yuan, *Hu I-nan hsien-sheng ch'üan-chi* (The collected writings of Hu Li-yuan; 1920), ts'e 1; *Hsun-huan jih-pao liu-shih chou-nien chi-nien t'e-k'an* (Special volume commemorating the sixtieth anniversary of the *Tsun-wan yat-po*; Hong Kong, 1932), p. 14; Jen Chi-yü, "Ho Ch'i Hu Li-yuan ti kai-liang-chu-i ssu-hsiang" (The reformist thought of Ho Kai and Hu Li-yuan), in *Chung-kuo chin-tai ssu-hsiang-shih lun-wen chi* (A collection of essays on modern Chinese intellectual history; Shanghai, 1958), p. 75.

For biographical material on Ho Kai, see Schiffrin, *Sun Yat-sen*, pp. 20–26 and passim; Brian Harrison, ed., *University of Hong Kong: The First Fifty Years, 1911–1961* (Hong Kong, Hong Kong University Press, 1962), pp. 6, 11, 35; Arnold Wright, ed., *Twentieth-Century Impressions of Hong Kong, Shanghai, and Other Treaty Ports of China* (London, Lloyds Greater Britain Publishing Co., 1908), p. 109; Linda P. Shin, "China in Transition: The Role of Wu T'ing-fang (1842–1922)" (Ph.D. diss., University of California at Los Angeles, 1970), pp. 131–134; Wu Hsing-lien, *Hsiang-kang Hua-jen ming-jen shih-lueh* (Sketches of famous Chinese of Hong Kong; Hong Kong, Wu-chou shu-chü, 1937), supp., pp. 1–2; Lo Hsiang-lin, *Hsiang-kang yü Chung-Hsi wen-hua chih chiao-liu*, pp. 135–178; Lo Hsiang-lin, *Kuo-fu chih ta-hsueh shih-tai* (Sun Yat-sen's university days; Chungking, 1945), pp. 7–16.

For the reform thought of Ho Kai and Hu Li-yuan, see Eastman, "Political Reformism," pp. 695–710 passim; Hsiao Kung-ch'üan, *Chung-kuo cheng-chih ssu-hsiang shih* (A history of Chinese political thought; Taipei, 1961), VI, 795–803; Jen Chi-yü, "Ho Ch'i Hu Li-yuan ti kai-liang-chu-i ssu-hsiang," pp. 75–91; Onogawa Hidemi, "Ka Kei Ko Reien no shinsei rongi" (The "Hsin-cheng lun-i" of Ho Kai and Hu Li-yuan), in *Ishihama sensei koki kinen Tōyōgaku ronsō* (Oriental studies in honor of Juntaro Ishihama on the occasion of his seventieth birthday; Osaka, 1958), pp. 121–133; Watanabe Tetsuhiro, "Ka Kei Ko Reien no shinseiron" (The administrative reform proposals of Ho Kai and Hu Li-yuan), *Ritsumeikan bungaku* 11:939–955 (November 1961).

10. *The Report of the Directors to the Sixty-first General Meeting of the Missionary Society, Usually Called the London Missionary Society, on Thursday, May 10th, 1855* (London, 1855), p. 53. Wang is identified in this report as Wang-lan-King (i.e., Wang Lan-ch'ing), his courtesy name at the time.

11. For biographical information on Wang T'ao, see Cohen, *Between Tradition and Modernity*; Hummel, *Eminent Chinese*, II, 836–839; Henry McAleavy, *Wang T'ao: The Life and Writings of a Displaced Person* (London, The China Society, 1953); Wu Ching-shan, "Wang T'ao shih-chi k'ao-lueh" (A brief examination into the life of Wang T'ao), in *Shang-hai yen-chiu tzu-liao* (Materials for the study of Shanghai; Shanghai, 1936), pp. 671–691. For Wang's writings and the abundant secondary literature on his career, see Paul A. Cohen, "Wang T'ao's Perspective on a Changing World," in Albert Feuerwerker, Rhoads Murphey, and

Mary C. Wright, eds., *Approaches to Modern Chinese History* (Berkeley, University of California Press, 1967), pp. 133–162; Paul A. Cohen, "Wang T'ao and Incipient Chinese Nationalism," *Journal of Asian Studies* 26:559–574 (August 1967); Cohen, *Between Tradition and Modernity.*

12. Biographical information on Ma Chien-chung is scattered. See Henri Cordier, *Histoire des relations de la Chine avec les puissances occidentales, 1860–1902* (Paris, Félix Alcan, 1901–1902), II, 499–500; Stanley Spector, *Li Hung-chang and the Huai Army* (Seattle, University of Washington Press, 1964), pp. 282–283; Y. C. Wang, *Chinese Intellectuals and the West, 1872–1949* (Chapel Hill, University of North Carolina Press, 1966), pp. 80–81; Kenneth Folsom, *Friends, Guests, and Colleagues: The Mu-fu System in the Late Ch'ing Period* (Berkeley, University of California Press, 1968), pp. 139–140; Chang Jo-ku, *Ma Hsiang-po hsien-sheng nien-p'u* (A chronological biography of Mr. Ma Liang; Shanghai, 1939), passim; Li Chi, trans. and ed., *"A Provisional System of Grammar for Teaching Chinese" with Introduction and Commentary* (Berkeley, Center for Chinese Studies, Institute of International Studies, 1960), pp. 173–176. For Chinese Communist studies of Ma's thought, see Jen Ching-wu, "Ma Chien-chung tsai *Shih-k'o-chai chi-yen* li so piao-hsien ti ssu-hsiang" (Ma Chien-chung's thought as displayed in *Shih-k'o-chai chi-yen*), *Kuang-ming jih-pao*, Nov. 4, 1953; Jen Chi-yü, "Ma Chien-chung ti ssu-hsiang" (Ma Chien-chung's thought), *Chung-kuo chin-tai ssu-hsiang shih lun-wen chi*, pp. 66–74.

13. For a biography of Ma Liang, see Howard L. Boorman, ed., *Biographical Dictionary of Republican China* (New York, Columbia University Press, 1967–1971), II, 470–473. Much interesting detail on his life is also furnished in Chang Jo-ku, *Ma Hsiang-po.* Despite the fact that by the end of the Ch'ing, Ma Liang was over seventy and could already look back on an extremely active and unusual career, he has been completely overlooked by students of the late Ch'ing. Hummel, *Eminent Chinese*, does not mention him. Another leading Ch'ing scholar, after briefly describing the modernizing activities of Ma Chien-chung's brother, S. P. Ma, confessed an inability to provide fuller identification. Ma Liang, as it happens, was best known by his courtesy name, Hsiang-po, which in nineteenth-century English-language materials would probably have been transliterated Siang-po; hence, the S. P. Albert Feuerwerker, *China's Early Industrialization: Sheng Hsuan-huai (1844–1916) and Mandarin Enterprise* (Cambridge, Harvard University Press, 1958), pp. 142, 284n147.

14. For biographical material on Tong, see Liu Kuang-ching (Kwang-Ching Liu), "T'ang Ting-shu chih mai-pan shih-tai" (Tong King-sing: His comprador years), *Ch'ing-hua hsueh-pao* (Tsing Hua journal of Chinese studies), new ser., 2.2:143–183 (June 1961). For his involvement with the China Merchants Company and the Kaiping Mining Company, see Feuerwerker, *China's Early Industrialization*, pp. 110–111; Ellsworth C. Carlson, *The Kaiping Mines (1877–1912)*, 2nd ed. (Cambridge, East Asian Research Center, Harvard University, 1971), pp. 5–8, 31, 38, and passim. See also Folsom, *Friends*, pp. 144–146; Hummel, *Eminent Chinese*, II, 956; Yen-p'ing Hao, *The Comprador in Nineteenth Century China: Bridge Between East and West* (Cambridge, Harvard University Press, 1970), pp. 196, 199, and passim.

15. For biographical information on Cheng, see Feuerwerker, *China's Early Industrialization*, pp. 116–117; Hao, *Comprador*, pp. 186–187, 196–197, 201–206, and passim. For his thought, see Liu Kuang-ching, "Cheng Kuan-ying *I-yen*—Kuang-hsu ch'u-nien chih pien-fa ssu-hsiang" (Cheng Kuan-ying's *I-yen*:

Reform proposals of the early Kuang-hsu period), *Ch'ing-hua hsueh-pao*, new ser., 8.1–2:373–425 (August 1970); Wang Yung-k'ang, "Cheng Kuan-ying ch'i jen chi ch'i ssu-hsiang" (Cheng Kuan-ying: The man and his thought), *Shih-hsueh yueh-k'an* (Historical studies monthly) 1:34–40 (1958); Chou Fu-ch'eng, "Cheng Kuan-ying ti ssu-hsiang" (Cheng Kuan-ying's thought), *Chung-kuo chin-tai ssu-hsiang shih lun-wen chi*, pp. 99–109. The various editions of Cheng's writings are unraveled in Ichiko Chūzō, "Teĭ Kannō no *Ekigen* ni tsuite" (On Cheng Kuan-ying's *I-yen*), in *Wada hakushi koki kinen Tōyōshi ronsō* (A collection of essays on Oriental history presented to Dr. Wada on the occasion of his seventieth birthday; Tokyo, Kōdansha, 1960), pp. 107–115.

16. For a biography of Wu T'ing-fang, see Boorman, *Dictionary*, III, 453–456. Shin's study is much more complete and, in the case of discrepancies with Boorman, more authoritative. Boorman, for example, has Wu attending the British Central School in Hong Kong rather than St. Paul's. Shin, in a letter to me of June 22, 1971, indicates that Wu was probably baptized even before going to Hong Kong to study at St. Paul's, though the evidence is circumstantial. See also Cyril Pearl, *Morrison of Peking* (Sydney, Angus and Robertson, 1967), p. 234, where Wu is described as "a baptized Christian with two concubines."

17. Hu Shih, *The Chinese Renaissance* (Chicago, University of Chicago Press, 1934), pp. 11–12.

18. Although Wang T'ao appears to have spoken some English, there is no evidence that he could read it. In Liu Kuang-ching's opinion, Cheng Kuan-ying "probably did not learn enough English to read this language easily." Liu, "Cheng Kuan-ying *I-yen*," p. 418.

19. Ho Kai had a part in the founding of *Hua-tzu jih-pao* (Chinese mail). Ko Kung-chen, *Chung-kuo pao-hsueh shih* (History of Chinese journalism; Peking, 1955), p. 74. Cheng Kuan-ying, possibly acting on a suggestion first advanced by Wang T'ao around 1876, made an abortive effort to launch a Western-language newspaper for the purpose of publicizing the Chinese side in Sino-Western disputes. See Wang's letter to Tong King-sing, in *T'ao-yuan ch'ih-tu* (Letters of Wang T'ao; Peking, 1959), p. 126; Ko Kung-chen, *Chung-kuo pao-hsueh shih*, p. 104; Cheng Kuan-ying, *Sheng-shih wei-yen hou-pien* (Warnings to a prosperous age: second part) (Taipei, 1969; original preface dated 1909), III, 1720–1723.

20. For Cheng Kuan-ying's developed ideas on commerce, see his *Sheng-shih wei-yen tseng-ting hsin-pien* (Warnings to a prosperous age), rev. and expanded ed. (Taipei, 1965), II, 677–802, esp. the essay, "Shang-chan" (Commercial warfare), pp. 753–766; Hao, *Comprador*, pp. 204–205. For Cheng's earlier economic views, see Liu Kuang-ching, "Cheng Kuan-ying *I-yen*," pp. 398–410, 422–425. For the evolution of Wang T'ao's economic thought, see his essays: "Li-ts'ai" (Financial management), in Wang T'ao, *T'ao-yuan wen-lu wai-pien* 12:31b-33; "Hsing-li" (The promotion of wealth), in Wang T'ao, *T'ao-yuan wen-lu wai-pien*, 2:14–16b; "Lun i hsing chih-tsao i kuang mao-i" (On the need to promote manufacture in order to expand trade), *Wan-kuo kung-pao* (The globe magazine) 45:2b–4 (October 1892); "Lun i she shang-chü i wang shang-wu" (On the need to establish a bureau of trade for the promotion of commerce), *Wan-kuo kung-pao* 49:6–7b (February 1893). For Ho Kai's economic thought, see Onogawa Hidemi, "Ka Kei Ko Reien," pp. 132–133; Watanabe Tetsuhiro, "Ka Kei Ko Reien," pp. 943–946.

21. Hao, *Comprador*, p. 194.

22. Yung Wing, *My Life*, pp. 191–196.

23. Hao, *Comprador*, pp. 205–206.

24. Boorman, *Dictionary*, III, 454.

25. Fang Hao, "Ma Hsiang-po hsien-sheng shih-lueh" (A sketch of Mr. Ma Liang), in Fang Hao, ed., *Ma Hsiang-po hsien-sheng wen-chi* (The collected writings of Mr. Ma Liang; Peiping, 1947), p. 2.

26. Cohen, *Between Tradition and Modernity*, ch. 8; Cohen, "Wang T'ao and Incipient Chinese Nationalism," pp. 568–570; Shin, "China in Transition," p. 132.

27. Cohen, *Between Tradition and Modernity*, ch. 8; Cohen, "Wang T'ao and Incipient Chinese Nationalism," pp. 565–567; Shin, "China in Transition," pp. 133–134; Hao, *Comprador*, p. 203; Cheng Kuan-ying, "I-yuan" (Parliaments), in *Sheng-shih wei-yen tseng-ting hsin-pien*, I, 49–85.

28. Wang T'ao, *T'ao-yuan ch'ih-tu*, p. 170.

29. Hao, *Comprador*, p. 205.

30. Two exceptions must be noted. Shanghai was not yet a zone of Western penetration at the time of Wang T'ao's birth in 1828 or Ma Liang's in 1840. Moreover, in Wang's case, exposure to Western influence was nil prior to his first visit to Shanghai at age nineteen, which may explain the fact that Wang was in some ways the least acculturated of the "Christian" reformers.

31. Rhoads Murphey, *Shanghai: Key to Modern China* (Cambridge, Harvard University Press, 1953), p. 8.

32. Wang T'ao, *T'ao-yuan ch'ih-tu*, pp. 124–125.

33. Shin, "China in Transition," pp. 49–50. Foreign fear of the growth of Chinese commercial power in Hong Kong was the central theme of one of Wang T'ao's editorials. Wang T'ao, *T'ao-yuan wen-lu wai-pien* 4:1–3. The stagnation of the China trade after 1873 and its growing tendency to pass into native hands were by no means confined to Hong Kong. Nathan A. Pelcovits, *Old China Hands and the Foreign Office* (New York, Institute of Pacific Relations, 1948), pp. 103–104, 111–112, 132.

34. Milton E. Osborne, *The French Presence in Cochinchina and Cambodia: Rule and Response (1859–1905)* (Ithaca, Cornell University Press, 1969), esp. ch. 6.

35. S. Y. Teng and John K. Fairbank, *China's Response to the West* (Cambridge, Harvard University Press, 1954), pp. 115–116; Wang T'ao, *T'ao-yuan ch'ih-tu*, p. 26; Yung Wing, *My Life*, pp. 67–73.

36. Shin, "China in Transition," pp. 132–133.

37. "Li Wen-chung-kung chih Wang T'ao" (Li Hung-chang's appreciation of Wang T'ao), in Hsu K'o, comp., *Ch'ing-pai lei-ch'ao* (A classified compilation of Ch'ing anecdotal material), 92 chüan (Shanghai, 1928) 30:28; Hung Shen, "*Shen-pao* tsung-pien-tsuan 'Ch'ang-mao chuang-yuan' Wang T'ao k'ao-cheng" (An examination of the evidence on Wang T'ao, editor-in-chief of *Shen-pao* and "first-ranking metropolitan graduate of the Taiping rebels"), *Wen-hsueh* (Literature) 2:1034 (June 1934); Shin, "China in Transition," pp. 229–230.

38. Shin, "China in Transition," p. 120.

39. Chang Jo-ku, *Ma Hsiang-po*, pp. 154–161.

40. Shin, "China in Transition," pp. 229–230.

41. For Li's limitations as a reformer, see Kwang-Ching Liu, "The Confucian As Patriot and Pragmatist: Li Hung-chang's Formative Years, 1823–1866," *Harvard Journal of Asiatic Studies* 30:7, 35, 44–45 (1970).

42. Folsom, *Friends*, p. 146.

43. For the Christian influence on the Taiping movement, see Eugene P.

Boardman, *Christian Influence upon the Ideology of the Taiping Rebellion, 1851—1864* (Madison, University of Wisconsin Press, 1952); Joseph Levenson, *Confucian China and Its Modern Fate*, vol. 2: *The Problem of Monarchical Decay* (Berkeley, University of California Press, 1964), chs. 7—8; Vincent Shih, *The Taiping Ideology: Its Sources, Interpretations, and Influences* (Seattle, University of Washington Press, 1967); Jen Yu-wen, *The Taiping Revolutionary Movement*. On Hung Hsiu-ch'üan's career, see Hummel, *Eminent Chinese*, I, 361—367. For Hung's relationship with his American missionary mentor, see Y. C. Teng, "Reverend Issachar Jacox Roberts and the Taiping Rebellion," *Journal of Asian Studies* 23:55—67 (November 1963). For Hung Jen-kan, see Hummel, *Eminent Chinese*, I, 367—369; So and Boardman, "Hung Jen-kan," pp. 262—294; Franz Michael, in collaboration with Chang Chung-li, *The Taiping Rebellion: History and Documents* (Seattle, University of Washington Press, 1966, 1971), I, 134—168; Y. C. Teng, "The Failure of Hung Jen-kan's Foreign Policy," *Journal of Asian Studies* 28:125—138 (November 1968); Jen Yu-wen, *The Taiping Revolutionary Movement*, pp. 351—376 and passim.

44. Schiffrin, *Sun Yat-sen*, pp. 16, 19, 47—48, 52, 66, 89, 172—174; Boorman, *Dictionary*, I, 229—231. Schiffrin, *Sun Yat-sen*, pp. 16, 33, 89, and passim, gives Ou Feng-ch'ih's name as Ch'ü Feng-ch'ih. The character at issue, when used as a surname, is generally read "Ou." Boorman, *Dictionary*, I, 230. Other Chinese Christians active in the early revolutionary movement are listed in Chien Yu-wen, "Kuang-tung wen-hua chih yen-chiu" (The study of Kwangtung culture), in *Kuang-tung wen-wu* (The civilization of Kwangtung), 10 chüan (Hong Kong, Chung-kuo wen-hua hsieh-chin hui, 1941), 8:12.

45. Schiffrin, *Sun Yat-sen*, p. 22.

46. Schiffrin, *Sun Yat-sen*, pp. 89—90, 228—229.

47. Hung's ideas were presented in a pamphlet of 1859 entitled *Tzu-cheng hsin-p'ien* (A new treatise on aids to administration), addressed to Hung Hsiu-ch'üan. For summaries, see So and Boardman, "Hung Jen-kan," pp. 284—291; J. C. Cheng, *Chinese Sources for the Taiping Rebellion, 1850—1864* (Hong Kong, Hong Kong University Press, 1963), pp. 45—60. For a full translation, see Michael and Chang, *The Taiping Rebellion*, III, 748—777.

48. For Yung's relationship with Hung Jen-kan, his visit to the Taiping area, and his proposals to the rebels, see Lo Hsiang-lin, *Hsiang-kang yü Chung-Hsi wen-hua chih chiao-liu*, pp. 80—82; Yung Wing, *My Life*, pp. 107—112. Although Wang T'ao denied ever having presented a proposal to the rebels, the evidence against him is overwhelming. See, e.g., Hsieh Hsing-yao, "Wang T'ao shang-shu T'ai-p'ing t'ien-kuo shih-k'ao" (An inquiry into the matter of Wang T'ao's letter to the Taipings), *Kuo-hsueh chi-k'an* (Journal of Sinological studies) 4:31—49 (March 1934), reprinted with minor changes in the same author's *T'ai-p'ing t'ien-kuo shih-shih lun-ts'ung* (Essays on Taiping history; Shanghai, 1935), pp. 186—211. The evidence on Wang T'ao's relationship to Hung Jen-kan and his visits into Taiping territory is presented in Cohen, *Between Tradition and Modernity*, ch. 2.

49. Schiffrin, *Sun Yat-sen*, pp. 20—38.

50. Tong King-sing died in 1892, Wang T'ao in 1897, and Ma Chien-chung in 1900. It is doubtful whether any of them had affiliations with the young revolutionary movement.

51. Schiffrin, *Sun Yat-sen*, pp. 70—82, 211—212, discusses Ho Kai's role and his limitations as a revolutionary.

52. Schiffrin, *Sun Yat-sen*, 65, 67.

53. Schiffrin, *Sun Yat-sen*, pp. 221, 239, 305; Lo Hsiang-lin, *Hsiang-kang yü Chung-Hsi wen-hua chih chiao-liu*, pp. 106–108.

54. Boorman, *Dictionary*, II, 472–473; III, 455–456.

55. Cohen, "Wang T'ao and Incipient Chinese Nationalism," p. 561.

56. Irwin Scheiner, *Christian Converts and Social Protest in Meiji Japan* (Berkeley, University of California Press, 1970).

57. The original manuscript of Wang's diary, which has no general title (though the separate sections are titled), is in the library of the Institute of History and Philology, Academia Sinica, Taipei. A transcribed copy is in the Harvard-Yenching Library.

58. For the printed version, see Wang T'ao, *T'ao-yuan wen-lu wai-pien* 8:3–5. The manuscript version is reproduced by photo-offset in Lindsay Ride's "Biographical Note," prefacing James Legge, *The Chinese Classics* (Hong Kong, Hong Kong University Press, 1960), I, 16. Although Wang T'ao in his published works never identified himself as a Christian, he occasionally made favorable references to Protestant Christianity and Jesus. See, e.g., his *Ying-juan tsa-chih* (A record of Shanghai miscellany), 6 chüan (1875), 6:11a-b.

59. Several early pieces appear in Fang Hao, *Ma Hsiang-po hsien-sheng wen-chi*, pp. 1–10, but they have to do with Ma Liang's involvement with Korean affairs and the China Merchants Steam Navigation Company.

60. Cohen, "Wang T'ao and Incipient Chinese Nationalism," p. 572.

61. Shin, "China in Transition," pp. 261, 303–305; Boorman, *Dictionary*, III, 455.

62. Hao, *Comprador*, p. 206; Cheng Kuan-ying, *Sheng-shih wei-yen tseng-ting hsin-pien*, I, 335–342. Wang T'ao, Ma Chien-chung, and Yung Wing also ventured criticisms of missionary practices. Jen Chi-yü, "Ma Chien-chung ti ssu-hsiang," p. 68; Wang T'ao, *T'ao-yuan wen-lu wai-pien* 3:2b–6b; Yung Wing, *My Life*, pp. 174–175.

63. Joseph Levenson, *Confucian China and Its Modern Fate*, vol. 1: *The Problem of Intellectual Continuity* (Berkeley, University of California Press, 1958), pp. 120–122.

64. Even Yung Wing, as Westernized as any Chinese in the nineteenth century, had his American citizenship revoked as a result of the exclusion legislation. Worthy, "Yung Wing in America," pp. 283–284.

PHILIP WEST, "CHRISTIANITY AND NATIONALISM: THE CAREER OF WU LEI-CH'UAN AT YENCHING UNIVERSITY"

Note: Administrative Papers and Administrative Correspondence refer to the archives of Yenching University at the United Board for Christian Higher Education in Asia, New York.

1. For this approach, see Dwight Edwards, *Yenching University* (New York, United Board for Christian Higher Education in Asia, 1959); John Leighton Stuart, *Fifty Years in China* (New York, Random House, 1954).

2. Occasionally student publications interpreted Yenching in this manner before 1949, but the view became widespread during the thought reform period of the early 1950s. See, e.g., articles in *Current Background* (Hong Kong,

American Consulate): Lu Chih-wei, "U.S. Imperialist Cultural Aggression As Seen in Yenching University," *Hsin kuan-ch'a* (Peking), Feb. 10, 1951; Su Cho, "Lu Chih-wei and Yenching University," *Hsing-tao wan-pao* (Hong Kong), Feb. 23, 1951; "Ideological Struggle Reaches New High in Yenching," *Chin-pu jih-pao* (Tientsin), Mar. 17, 1952. Also see the complete issue of the *Hsin Yen-ching*, April 14, 1952.

3. The only scholarly study I have found on Wu Lei-ch'uan is Sumiko Yamamoto, "Kirisutokyō to Chūgoku bunka ni mirareru go rai-sen no shisō," *Kindai Chūgoku kenkyū*, July 1960. Yamamoto's study analyzes Wu's *Chi-tu chiao yü Chung-kuo wen-hua* (Shanghai, 1936).

4. John S. Burgess, "Quarterly Report, First Quarter, Apr. 8, 1913," submitted to the International Committee of the YMCA, in miscellaneous papers of Mrs. Stella Burgess; Shirley S. Garrett, *Social Reformers in Urban China: The Chinese YMCA, 1895–1926* (Cambridge, Harvard University Press, 1970).

5. Alice H. Gregg, *China and Educational Autonomy* (Syracuse, Syracuse University Press, 1946), app. A, p. 214.

6. Ch'en Tu-hsiu, "Chi-tu chiao yü Chung-kuo jen," *Hsin ch'ing-nien* 7.3:18 (Feb. 1, 1920).

7. Chao Tzu-ch'en, "Wu Lei-ch'uan hsien-sheng hsiao-chuan," *Chen-li yü sheng-ming* 10.8:483 (January 1937).

8. Wu Lei-ch'uan, "Wo ko-jen ti tsung-chiao ching-yen," *Sheng-ming* 3.8:2 (April 1923).

9. Hu Hsueh-ch'eng, "Hsuan-yen," *Sheng-ming* 1.1:i-ii (Nov. 20, 1919). Among the Western members were John Leighton Stuart, Lucius Porter, John Stuart Burgess, Howard S. Galt, and J. B. Tayler. Among the Chinese figures were Liu T'ing-fang (T. T. Lew), Hsü Pao-ch'ien, Hung Yeh (William Hung), Li Jung-fang, Chao Tzu-ch'en, Cheng Ch'ing-yi, Wu Yao-tsung, and later in Chih-wei.

10. The organization of these intellectually oriented converts into the Life and Truth Fellowships, their quest for an indigenous Christian theology and church structure, and their sensitivity to nationalism bore a striking resemblance to Japanese Protestant converts some fifty years earlier. Irwin Scheiner, *Christian Converts and Social Protest in Meiji Japan* (Berkeley, University of California Press, 1970), chs. 2–4.

11. Grace M. Boynton, "Of Merit in Gardens," n.d. c. 1930, pp. 9–12, in miscellaneous papers of Grace M. Boynton.

12. Wu Lei-ch'uan, "Chi-tu chiao tsai Chung-kuo ti ch'ien-t'u," *Chen-li yü sheng-ming* 1.7:193–4 (August 1926).

13. Wu Chen-ch'un (Wu Lei-ch'uan), *Chen-li chou-k'an* 2.39:2 (Dec. 21, 1924); Wu Lei-ch'uan, "Li-chih yü Chi-tu-chiao," *Sheng-ming* 1.2 (September 1920), and "Sheng-t'ing chieh ti lien-hsiang—Ye-su yü K'ung-tzu," *Sheng-ming* 5.2 (November 1924).

14. Wu Lei-ch'uan, *Chi-tu-chiao yü Chung-kuo wen-hua* (Shanghai, Ch'ing-nien hsieh-hui shu-chü, 1936), pp. 142–44.

15. Wu Lei-ch'uan, "Wo ko-jen ti tsung-chiao ching-yen."

16. Wu Lei-ch'uan, "Wo tui-yü Chi-tu-chiao ti kan-hsiang," *Sheng-ming*, 1.4:4 (Nov. 15, 1920).

17. Wu, *Chi-tu-chiao yü*, p. 10.

18. Wu Lei-ch'uan, "Chung-kuo ch'ing-nien pu tang hsiao-fa Ye-su ma?" *Chen-li yü sheng-mung* 1.1:1 (Apr. 12, 1926).

19. Hsü Pao-ch'ien, "Hsin ssu-ch'ao yü Chi-tu-chiao," *Sheng-ming* 1.2:1 (Sept. 1, 1920); Chao Tzu-ch'en, "The Indigenous Church," *Chinese Recorder* 56.7:502—503 (August 1925).

20. On the Anti Christian Movement, see Tatsuro and Sumiko, Yamamoto, "The Anti-Christian Movement in China, 1922—27," *Far Eastern Quarterly* 12.2:133—148 (February 1953).

21. Wu Lei-ch'uan, "Hu-an yü Chung-kuo Chi-tu chiao ch'ien-t'u," *Sheng-ming* 5.9:17 (June 1925).

22. Wu Lei-ch'uan, *Chi-tu chiao yü chung-kuo wen-hua*, p. 10.

23. Hsü Pao-ch'ien, "Er-shih nien lai hsin-tao ching-yen tzu-shu," *Chen-li yü sheng-ming* 8.4:182 (June 1934).

24. *China Christian Education Association Bulletin Statistics* (Shanghai), 1924—1936, nos. 8, 14, 22, 26, 28, 29, 30, 33, 35, 38.

25. *Pei-p'ing ssu-li Yen-ching ta-hsueh yi-lan* (Peiping, Yenching University, 1931), pp. 319—326; *Pi-yeh t'ung-hsueh lu tsai-pan* (Peiping, Yenching University, 1931), p. 109.

26. Minute, Apr. 10, 1928, Administrative Papers, Minutes of the Board of Trustees.

27. Liu T'ing-fang, "Chi-tu-chiao tsai Chung-kuo tao-ti shih ch'uan she-ma? *Chen-li yü sheng-ming* 6.1:14 (October 1931).

28. Stuart to Trustees, Feb. 25, 1935, Administrative Correspondence of Yenching University, John Leighton Stuart.

29. Wu Lei-ch'uan, "Wo suo hsiang-wang ti hsüeh-hsiao sheng-huo," *Yen-ta chou-k'an* 85:4 (Feb. 5, 1925).

30. Wu, "Wo suo hsiang," p. 5.

31. Wu Lei-ch'uan, "Wei chiao-hui hsüeh-hsiao ti hsüeh-sheng chin i yen," *Chen-li chou-k'an* 3.19:2 (Aug. 9, 1925).

32. Wu Lei-ch'uan, "Chiao-hui hsueh-hsiao yü Chung-kuo chiao-yü ti ch'ien-t'u," *Chen-li chou-k'an* 2.20:2 (Aug. 11, 1924).

33. Wu Lei-ch'uan, "Shuo ch'ing-nien yün-tung," *Chen-li yü sheng-ming* 2.8:207—209 (May 1927).

34. Wu Lei-ch'uan, "Yü hsien-tai ch'ing-nien shang-liang chiu-kuo ti wen-t'i," *Chen-li yü sheng-ming* 1.11:312—313 (Nov. 15, 1926).

35. Wu, "Yü hsien-tai," p. 313.

36. Stuart to North, July 5, 1927, Administrative Correspondence, John Leighton Stuart; Minute, Dec. 9, 1927, Administrative Papers, Minutes of Board of Trustees.

37. Howard S. Galt, "Yenching University, Its Sources and Its History," typescript, 1939, p. 201.

38. "Tung-shih hui chien-chang," *Pei-p'ing ssu-li Yen-ching ta-hsueh yi-lan* (Peiping, Yenching University, 1931), pp. 1—2.

39. Minute, Sept. 23, Oct. 1, 1928, Administrative Papers, Minutes of the Board of Managers.

40. Minute, June 22, 1929, Administrative Papers, Minutes of the Board of Managers.

41. *Pei-p'ing ssu-li Yen-ching ta-hsueh yi-lan* (Peiping, Yenching University, 1931), p. 79.

42. Interview with Mei Yi-pao, July 16, 1968; Galt to Garside, July 1, 1930, Administrative Correspondence, Howard S. Galt.

43. Galt to Stuart, Jan. 10, 1930, Administrative Correspondence, John

Leighton Stuart; President's Report, Administrative Papers to Yenching University, June 11, 1920.

44. Minute, May 15, June 20, 1931, May 1934, Administrative Papers, Minutes of the Board of Managers.

45. Grace M. Boynton, "Red Leather Notebook," A-155.25, p. 137 (Oct. 9, 1948); Stuart to McMullen, July 23, 1948, Mar. 9, 1949, Administrative Correspondence, United Board 1945–1958, John Leighton Stuart.

46. Wu Lei-ch'uan, "Chi-tu chiao ying chu-yi huan-ch'i min-chung," *Chen-li yü sheng-ming* 6.8:1–7 (June 1932).

47. Kiang Wen-han, *The Chinese Student Movement* (New York, King's Crown Press, 1948), pp. 127–128.

48. Wu Lei-ch'uan, "Chi-tu chiao yü ko-ming," *Chen-li yü sheng-ming* 5.4:1–5 (February 1931).

49. Wu, "Chi-tu chiao yü," p. 4.

50. Wu Lei-ch'uan, *Chi-tu chiao yü Chung-kuo wen-hua*, p. 290.

51. Wu, *Chi-tu chiao*, p. 292.

52. Wu, *Chi-tu chiao*, pp. 70–71.

53. Chao Tzu-ch'en, "Ye-su wei Chi-tu, p'ing Wu Lei-ch'uan hsien-sheng chih Chi-tu-chiao yü Chung-kuo wen-hua," *Chen-li yü sheng-ming* 10.7:412–424 (December 1936).

54. Wu Yao-tsung served as editor of the YMCA Press publication series in the 1930s and 1940s and wrote the preface to Wu Lei-ch'uan's book discussed above. In the late 1940s Wu Yao-tsung led the movement to combine Protestant Christianity with the revolutionary program of the Communist Party. See Francis P. Jones, ed., *Documents of the Three Self-Movement* (New York, National Council of Churches, 1963), passim.; and Wu Yao-tsung's writings at the time published by the Ch'ing-nien hsieh-hui shu-chü in Shanghai, *Hei-an yü kuang-ming* (1949) and *Lun wu-wei fa cheng-pien* (1950).

55. Wu Lei-ch'uan, "Chi-tu chiao yü ko-ming," p. 4.

56. Stuart to Members of the Advisory Council of Yenching University, Jan. 26, 1933, Administrative Correspondence, John Leighton Stuart.

57. Galt, "Yenching University," pp. 188–189.

58. For an analysis of articles in Yenching student publications, see Philip West, "Yenching University and American Chinese Relations, 1917–1937" (Ph.D. diss., Harvard University, 1971), pp. 472–492.

59. Kiang Wen-han, "Secularization of Christian Colleges," *Chinese Recorder* 67.5:305 (May 1937).

60. For Yenching's role in the December 9 Movement, see John Israel, *Student Nationalism in China* (Stanford, Stanford University Press, 1966), ch. 5; Jessie Gregory Lutz, *China and the Christian Colleges, 1850–1950* (Ithaca, Cornell University Press, 1971), ch. 9.

STUART CREIGHTON MILLER, "ENDS AND MEANS: MISSIONARY JUSTIFICATION OF FORCE IN NINETEENTH CENTURY CHINA"

1. *San Francisco Call*, May 1, 1899, p. 1. See also Stuart Creighton Miller, *The Unwelcome Immigrant: The American Image of the Chinese, 1785–1882* (Berkeley, University of California Press, 1969), pp. 18, 98, 100–104, 111, 120–129,

133, 137–139. The research for this paper was supported by grants from the Penrose Fund of the American Philosophical Society and the National Science Foundation.

2. *The Chinese Repository* 3:345, 393–405, 425–428 (1835).

3. *The Chinese Repository*, 3:421, 428, 444 (1835).

4. *The Chinese Repository*, 3:352–353 (1835).

5. *The Chinese Repository*, 3:353 (1835).

6. Walter Medhurst, *China: Its State and Prospects* (London, 1838), pp. 370–521.

7. David Abeel, *The Missionary Convention at Jerusalem, or, An Exhibition of the Claims of the World to the Gospel* (New York, 1838), p. 224; Orr to Lowrie, June 1, 1838, "Letters, 1837–1844 (Canton and Macao)," vol. 1, no. 20, microfilm, BFMPC archives, New York.

8. *Missionary Herald* 35:464 (1839); W. E. Griffis, *A Maker of the New Orient* (New York, Fleming H. Revell, 1902), p. 71; *Missionary Herald* 36:115–116 (1840).

9. *Spirit of Missions* 6:366 (1841); McBryde to Lowrie, Sept. 17, 1841, vol. 1, no. 138, BFMPC archives; J. B. Jeter, *A Memoir of Mrs. Henrietta Shuck: The First American Female Missionary to China* (Boston, 1846), p. 38.

10. G. B. Stevens and W. F. Marwick, *The Life, Letters, and Journals of the Rev. and Hon. Peter Parker, M.D.* (Boston, 1896), pp. 172, 174–175; Williams to Anderson, July 1, 1840, ABC 16.3.8, vol. 1a, no. 178. ABCFM archives, Houghton Library, Harvard University.

11. Unsigned printed letter, Jan. 1, 1842, vol. 1a, no. 73, ABCFM archives. A note on it in Bridgman's hand implied that he, Abeel, and Williams had worked on this message.

12. McBryde circular, Jan. 14, 1842, vol. 1, no. 152, BFMPC archives.

13. *Niles' Weekly Register* 60:50–51 (1841); *Sen. Ex. Doc.*, no. 105, 34th Cong., 1st sess. See also Clifton Jackson Phillips, *Protestant America and the Pagan World* (Cambridge, East Asian Research Center, Harvard University, 1969), pp. 190–192.

14. *The Chinese Repository* 9:1–9, 289 (1840); *New York Herald*, Dec. 23, 1842; *Baptist Missionary Magazine* 20:270–275 (1840), 21:91 (1841).

15. *The Chinese Repository* 11:289n (1842); McBryde to Lowrie, Mar. 18, May 12, 1842, vol. 1, nos. 174, 188, BFMPC archives; Stevens and Marwick, *Parker*, p. 168.

16. *Missionary Herald* 35:42–43, 471–472 (1841); *Baptist Missionary Magazine* 21:52 (1841); Williams to Anderson, Jan. 1, 1840, vol. 1a, no. 178, ABCFM archives; Entry in "Journal of John Lewis Shuck," Feb. 19, 1841, Foreign Mission Board, Southern Baptist Convention archives, Richmond, Va.; McBryde to Lowrie, Feb. 12, May 12, 1842, vol. 1, nos. 167, 188, BFMPC archives.

17. In printing these circulars to be sent back to the United States, the missionaries borrowed freely from each other. This statement appears in an unsigned letter, Jan. 1, 1842, vol. 1a, no. 73, ABCFM archives, and in McBryde's printed letter, Jan. 14, 1842, vol. 1, no. 152, BFMPC archives.

18. *The Chinese Repository* 11:628 (1842); Printed circular letter, Jan. 1, 1842, vol. 1a, no. 73, ABCFM archives.

19. Printed letters of J. L. Shuck, July 3, 1841, Aug. 1, 1842, and entry in his "Journal," Feb. 19, 1841, Southern Baptist Convention archives; printed circu-

lar letter, Jan. 1, 1842, vol. 1a, no. 73, ABCFM archives; McBryde to Lowrie, July 27, 1842, vol. 1, no. 228, BFMPC archives.

20. *Spirit of Missions* 7:311 (1842); *Baptist Missionary Magazine* 21:91 (1841), 20:274 (1840).

21. *Spirit of Missions* 8:28–29 (1843); Report of Canton Mission to the Presidential Board, Jan. 1, 1844: unsigned letter, July 1, 1843, vol. 1a, nos. 24, 22, ABCFM archives.

22. *The Friend: A Religious and Literary Journal* 13:360 (1840); *The Christian Examiner* 32:281–319 (1842); *The Southern Literary Messenger* 19:626–627 (1853).

23. See Miller, *Unwelcome Immigrant*, pp. 114–121.

24. For the "lorcha men" and the missionary's disdain for them, see *Missionary Advocate* 8:34ff. (1852–1853).

25. Williams, May 8, 1857, vol. 3, no. 370½; Vrooman, Dec. 9, 1856; both to Anderson, vol. 3, no. 275, ABCFM archives.

26. Bonney to Anderson, Dec. 13, 1856, vol. 3, no. 263, ABCFM archives.

27. Bonney to Anderson, Mar. 14, 1857, vol. 3, no. 264, ABCFM archives.

28. Bonney, June 6, 1857; Vrooman, Jan. 4, 1857, Dec. 9, 1856; all to Anderson, vol. 3, nos. 266, 276, 275, ABCFM archives.

29. Miller, *Unwelcome Immigrant*, pp. 121–122.

30. *Missionary Advocate* 13:51 (1857); Vrooman to Anderson, Dec. 9, 1856, vol. 3, no. 275, ABCFM archives.

31. *Sen. Ex. Doc.*, no. 22, 35th Cong., 2nd sess., 1081–1084; *New York Times*, Oct. 9, 1855.

32. F. W. Williams, *The Life and Letters of Samuel Wells Williams* (New York, 1899), pp. 257, 268; Williams to Anderson, May 8, 1857, vol. 3, no. 370½, ABCFM archives.

33. Macy, Apr. 13, May 8, Jan. 10, 1857 (enclosed was Williams's resignation, Jan. 8, 1857); Vrooman, Jan. 4, 1857; all to Anderson, vol. 3, no. 227; vol. 2, no. 34; vol. 3, nos. 225, 276, ABCFM archives; Preston to Lowrie, Feb. 24, Jan. 26, 1859, vol. 6, nos. 477, 476, BFMPC archives.

34. Kerr, Dec. 4, 1858; Happer, Nov. 13, 1860; both to Lowrie, vol. 6, nos. 471, 522, BFMPC archives; unsigned printed circular, June 22, 1857, vol. 2, no. 267, ABCFM archives (address and note in Bonney's hand); Williams, *Williams*, p. 292.

35. Kenneth Scott Latourette, *A History of Christian Missions in China* (New York, MacMillan, 1929), p. 275–277.

36. *Spirit of Missions* 24:148–151 (1859); *Sen. Ex. Doc.*, no. 30, 36th Cong., 1st sess., 432–434.

37. *San Francisco Call*, Oct. 30, 1900; Feb. 7, 1901.

38. Williams, *Williams*, p. 325.

39. Happer, Preston, and Culbertson, all to Lowrie, Nov. 26, June 16, July 14, 1859, vol. 6, nos. 403, 484, unnumbered BFMPC archives. See also Boone to editor, Jan. 5, 1860, in *Spirit of Missions* 25:146 (1860).

40. Bridgman to Anderson, July 14, 1859, vol. 3, no. 204, ABCFM archives.

41. Preston to Lowrie, June 16, July 28, Aug. 5, 21, 1859, Jan. 27, 1860, vol. 6, nos. 482, 483, 484, 435, 502, BFMPC archives.

42. Happer to Lowrie, Nov. 13, 1860, vol. 6, no. 522, BFMPC archives; *Spirit of Missions* 26:158–159 (1861); Preston to Lowrie, Jan. 27, 1860; Mrs. J. G. Kerr, M.D., to friend, Jan. 10, 1861; vol. 6, nos. 502, 529, BFMPC archives.

43. *Spirit of Missions* 26:62, 266–267 (1861); J. M. Knowlton, "The Opening of China," *Baptist Missionary Magazine* 39:161–168 (1859).

44. Preston to Lowrie, Dec. 14, 1868, vol. 8, no. 244, BFMPC archives; *The Chinese Recorder* 1:107 (1869). The second letter was originally sent to the U.S. Minister, J. Ross Browne, from Ningpo and was signed A.E.M., no doubt the English missionary A. E. Moule, but this American-edited journal gave it their hearty approval.

45. Corbett to Lowrie, Sept. 30, 1868, vol. 8, no. 194 (news release enclosed), BFMPC archives; *The Chinese Recorder* 2:114–115 (1869).

46. Boomerang (pseud.), "The Origins of Missionary Troubles," *The Chinese Recorder* 4:200–205 (1872).

47. Boomerang, "The Revision Controversy, 1867–1868, 1869," *The Chinese Recorder* 4:175–179 (1872).

48. *The Chinese Recorder* 2:109–110 (1869).

49. *New York Herald*, Feb. 11, June 22, Sept. 25, 1869.

50. *New York Herald*, Sept. 1, Nov. 11, Dec. 13, 1868; "Editorial Items," *The Chinese Recorder* 2:114–115 (1869).

51. *The Chinese Recorder* 3:207–212 (1871). See also Baldwin's printed circular ABC 16.3.12, vol. 1, no. 89, ABCFM archives.

52. *New York Times*, July 3, 1871; *The Chinese Recorder* 3:150–153 (1870).

53. See Martin, July 26, 1870; Noyes, Aug. 10, 1870; Dodd, Sept. 15, 1870; Mateer, Oct. 31, 1870; Capp, Nov. 4, 1870; all to Lowrie; vol. 9, nos. 320, 327, 334, 362, 365, BFMPC archives.

54. Mateer to Lowrie, Sept. 5, 1870, vol. 9, no. 336, BFMPC archives.

55. Mrs. Mateer, Oct. 31, 1870; Capp, Nov. 4, 1870; all to Lowrie; vol. 9, nos. 362, 365, BFMPC archives.

56. Happer to Lowrie, Oct. 10, 1870; Jan. 10, 1871; vol. 9, nos. 357, 199, BFMPC archives.

57. *Gospel Message* 4:4 (1895); *Church at Home and Abroad* 17:130–131, 18:208 (1895), 18:200–201 (1895); *Baptist Missionary Magazine* 71:3–4 (1891), 74:435 (1894); *Searchlight* 1:3 (1895); *Assembly Herald* 3:709–712 (1895).

58. Charles Leaman, "The Waking of an Empire," *Church at Home and Abroad* 17:130–131 (1895); Rev. William Ashmore, D.D., "The Missionary Movement in China," *The Chinese Recorder* 29:161–169, 311–320, 373–380 (1898).

59. Mrs. B. F. Witt, "The War Against China," *Woman's Evangel* 18:4–6 (1899); *The Chinese Recorder* 29:311, 318 (1898).

60. William Ashmore, "From the Tientsin Treaties to the Japanese War," *The Chinese Recorder* 29:435 (1898); *Herald of Mission News*, August 1895; *The Missions of the World*, June 1895; *Church at Home and Abroad* 18:209 (1895); Leaman, "The Awakening of an Empire," *Church at Home and Abroad* 17:130; *Baptist Missionary Magazine* 74:435 (1894); *Searchlight* 1:3 (1895).

61. Reprinted from the *Medical Missionary* in *Woman's Evangel* 18:52 (1899).

62. *Woman's Evangel* 18:166–167 (1899); *Church at Home and Abroad* 18:208, 294–295 (1895).

63. *The Chinese Recorder* 29:436 (1899).

64. *Woman's Evangel* 18:166–167 (1899); Henry Blodget, "The Toleration of Christianity," *The Chinese Recorder* 12:1–15 (1881).

65. "Christian Missions: Their Connection with Commerce and Civilization,"

The Chinese Recorder 5:82–90 (1874); *Church at Home and Abroad* 18:471 (1895).

66. *Woman's Evangel* 18:166–167 (1899).

67. *Woman's Evangel* 17:186 (1898); *The Chinese Recorder* 11:374 (1880); *Friend's Missionary Advocate* 16:51 (1900).

68. *New York World*, June 11, 17, 1900.

69. Porter to Smith, Aug. 26, Oct. 10, 1900; Porter to "Dear Friends," Nov. 4, 1900, ABC 16.3.8, vol. 28, nos, 121, 124, 125, 126, ABCFM archives.

70. Sheffield to Smith, Feb. 26, Mar. 26, 1901, vol. 29, nos. 16, 17, ABCFM archives.

71. Marilyn Blatt Young, *The Rhetoric of Empire: American China Policy, 1895–1901* (Cambridge, Harvard University Press, 1968), pp. 187–197.

72. *San Francisco Call*, June 20, 21, Nov. 23, 1900.

73. *San Francisco Call*, Nov. 23, 1900.

74. *New York Sun*, Nov. 18, Dec. 24, 1900.

75. *New York Sun*, Nov. 18, 1900.

76. *Springfield Republican*, Jan. 20, 1901; *New York Sun*, Jan. 20, 1901; *San Francisco Call*, Feb. 10, 1901.

77. *New York Herald*, Feb. 18, 1901; *Nation*, Aug. 15, 1901.

78. Finley Peter Dunne, *Mr. Dooley's Philosophy* (New York, 1900), pp. 120–127; Dunne, *Dissertations by Mr. Dooley* (New York, 1906), pp. 28–29.

79. Mark Twain, "To a Stranger Sitting in Darkness," *North American Review* 172:161–176 (1901); Twain, "To My Missionary Critics," *North American Review* 172:520–534; Judson Smith, "The Missionaries and Their Critics," *North American Review* 172:724–733.

80. *New York Sun*, Mar. 24, 1901.

81. *New York Sun, Mar. 24, 1901.*

82. *San Francisco Call*, Mar. 26, 1901; *New York Journal*, Mar. 25, 1901.

83. Young, *Rhetoric of Empire*, p. 195; *San Francisco Call*, Apr. 26, 1901.

84. Rev. Gilbert Reid, "The Ethics of Loot," *Forum* 31:581–585 (1901).

85. *San Francisco Call*, Apr. 16, 1901.

86. Rev. Gilbert Reid, "The Ethics of the Last War," *Forum* 32:446–455 (1901–1902).

87. *Missionary Herald* 78:114 (1882), 81:405 (1885), 86:317–318 (1890), 96:384 (1900).

88. See Stuart Creighton Miller, "Our Mylai of 1900," *Trans-action* 7:19–28 (1970).

89. *Spirit of Missions* 26:62 (1861).

SHIRLEY STONE GARRETT, "WHY THEY STAYED: AMERICAN CHURCH POLITICS AND CHINESE NATIONALISM IN THE TWENTIES"

NOTE: All Methodist correspondence is in archives of United Methodist Church, 475 Riverside Drive, New York City.

1. *FMCNA*, 1924, p. 201; *ARBFM*.

2. Rev. Charles Stelzle, D.D., "America Demonstrated To Be Strongly Religious," *The Presbyterian Banner*, Feb. 10, 1927, p. 3.

3. H. E. Luccock and Paul Hutchinson, *The Story of Methodism* (New York, Methodist Book Concern, 1926), p. 432.

4. *Foreign Missions Report*, 1924, *ARBFM*, pp. 28–33.

5. Bowen to Gamewell, June 12, 1925.

6. Brown to Edwards, Aug. 1, 1925; Birney to Edwards, June 26, 1925.

7. Memo of the Conference of the East Asia Bishops, Sept. 16, 17, 1925 (Gamewell file).

8. Gamewell to Birney, Nov. 19, 1925.

9. *ARBFM*, 1925.

10. Gamewell to Diffendorfer, June 8, 1926.

11. Romer to Gamewell, Mar. 11, Apr. 1, May 8, 1926.

12. Grose to Edwards, Nov. 11, Dec. 28, 1926; Grose to Gamewell, Sept. 22, 1926.

13. Birney to Gamewell, Nov. 8, 1926.

14. Birney to Gamewell, Dec. 18, 1927.

15. Birney to Gamewell, Jan. 6, 1927; Birney to Gamewell and Edwards, Jan. 21, 1927; Birney to Gamewell, Feb. 14, Mar. 2, 1927.

16. *New York Times*, Dec. 10, 1926, p. 24; Mar. 17, 1927, p. 1.

17. *Christian Century*, Feb. 3, 1927, p. 132; Feb. 17, 1927, pp. 202–204.

18. Birney to Edwards, May 31, 1927; Edwards to Birney, July 12, 1927.

19. Edwards to Birney, July 12, 1927; *Christian Century*, Mar. 24, 1927; *Christian Advocate*, Mar. 10, 1927.

20. Gamewell to Birney, Apr. 25, 1927; *Christian Advocate*, May 26, 1927, p. 644; Edwards to Birney, July 12, 1927.

21. Birney to Gamewell, May 5, 1927; Gamewell to Birney, Apr. 25, 1927; *Christian Advocate*, Apr. 21, 1927, pp. 491–492; *Christian Century*, May 19, 1927, p. 630.

22. *Christian Century*, May 5, 1927, pp. 550–553; Birney to Edwards, May 31, 1927; Grose to Edwards and Gamewell, Apr. 22, 1927.

23. *Christian Advocate*, Apr. 14, 1927, p. 431.

24. Ralph E. Diffendorfer, *The Situation in China* (New York, privately printed, 1927); *Christian Advocate*, May 5, 1927, p. 551; May 26, 1927, p. 643; June 16, 1927, pp. 740–741.

25. Eg., James Franklin in *Christian Century*, July 7, 1927, pp. 825–827; Diffendorfer, *Situation in China*.

26. *New York Times*, Mar. 14, 1927, p. 22.

27. Brown to Gamewell, July 9, 1927; Grose, under a cover letter to Edwards, Dec. 9, 1927.

28. Birney to Edwards, Sept. 23, 1927; Birney to Board, Oct. 20, 1927.

29. Gamewell to Birney, Apr. 6, 25, 1927; Birney to Gamewell, June 3, 1927.

30. Diffendorfer to Birney, Oct. 25, 1927; Gamewell to Grose, Oct. 17, 31, 1927; Edwards to Grose, Oct. 22, 1927; Gamewell to Grose, Oct. 17, 1927.

31. Gamewell to Birney, Nov. 15, 1927.

32. *Presbyterian Banner*, June 2, 1927, p. 6.

33. Stanley High, "China's Christian Nationalists," *Christian Advocate*, May 26, 1927, p. 651.

34. Birney to Edwards, Apr. 22, 1927.

35. *Christian Advocate*, June 16, 1927, p. 749.

36. Diffendorfer to Birney, Oct. 25, 1927; Diffendorfer to Bishops, Dec. 6, 1927; Jan. 6, 1928; Diffendorfer to Grose, Dec. 14, 1928.

37. Edwards to Birney, Apr. 3, 1929.

38. Ernest Tuck to Gamewell, May 14, 1929.

39. Arthur Judson Brown, *One Hundred Years* (New York, Revell, 1936), p. 312; "The Presbyterian Church in the U.S.A.," *Minutes of the General Assembly*, 1927, pt. 1, Journal and Statistics.

40. Lefferts A. Loetscher, *The Broadening Church* (Philadelphia, University of Pennsylvania Press, 1954), esp. p. 25, chs. 11 and 14.

41. *The Presbyterian*, Jan. 6, 1927, p. 1.

42. Eg., R. E. Speer, *The Church and Missions* (London, J. C. Clarke, 1926); *Are Missions Done For?* (Privately printed, 1928).

43. *FMCNA*, 1927, pp. 274, 282.

44. *FMCNA*, p. 285.

45. "Minutes on the China Evaluation Conference," China Correspondence, Presbyterian Historical Society, Philadelphia, Box I, 1927, 2145–2; Rev. Stuart Nye Hutchinson, "Foreign Missions and the Recent General Assembly," *The Presbyterian*, Aug. 4, 1927, p. 8.

46. *The Presbyterian*, Aug. 4, 1927, p. 5.

47. "China Council Letter #116, May 20, 1927," penciled draft, China Correspondence, Presbyterian Historical Society, Philadelphia, Box I, 1927.

48. "Mission Work in China Scarcely Begun," *The Presbyterian Banner*, Mar. 24, 1927, p. 3; Scott to Patton, China Correspondence, Presbyterian Historical Society, Philadelphia, Box I, 1927, 106–11, June 21, 1927.

PAUL A. VARG, "THE MISSIONARY RESPONSE TO THE NATIONALIST REVOLUTION"

1. Earl Ballou, *Letter*, Tientsin Bulletin, no. 8, ABCFM Archives. All letters cited are in the *China Letters* volumes.

2. T. L. Shen, "Christian Movement in a Revolutionary China," *The Chinese Recorder*, August 1928, pp. 475–482.

3. Djang Fang, "The Chinese Church of Tomorrow," *The Chinese Recorder*, November 1928, pp. 679–687.

4. Dizney to Mrs. Lee, July 6, 1927, ABCFM Archives; Leete to William Strong, Feb. 5, 1927, ABCFM Archives.

5. Ballou to "Bob," Jan. 8, 1928, ABCFM Archives.

6. Hubbard to Archibald Black, Apr. 2, 1927, ABCFM Archives.

7. Symposium, "The State of the Chinese Church," *The Chinese Recorder*, April 1929, pp. 209–224.

8. "The Revolution and the Y.M.C.A.," *The Chinese Recorder*, April 1929, p. 268.

9. Birney to Gamewell, December 1927, Methodist Archives.

10. Ballou to "Bob," Jan. 8, 1928, ABCFM Archives.

11. Shepherd to Strong, Mar. 6, 1927, ABCFM Archives; Robert W. McClure to Strong, Oct. 8, 1927, ABCFM Archives; "Midnight Watch," a typed letter prepared at station at Tailau in Shansi, May 1927, ABCFM Archives.

12. Rawlinson to A. L. Warnshuis, Oct. 3, 1927, Rawlinson-Warnshuis Correspondence, Missionary Research Library, Union Theological Seminary, New York City; Summary of a Speech by Henry Hodgkin in the Rawlinson-Warnshuis Correspondence, Missionary Research Library.

13. Birney to Gamewell, Jan. 12, 1928, Methodist Archives.

14. Cartwright to Birney, Oct. 31, 1932, Methodist Archives.
15. Rawlinson to Warnshuis, Nov. 28, 1932, Enclosure "The Chinese Soviet Republic," Missionary Research Library.
16. *Ibid.*
17. Bowen to Friend, Dec. 5, 1928, cites figures gathered by Plummer Mills, Methodist Archives.
18. Bowen to Friend, July 27, 1927, Methodist Archives.
19. Bowen to Gamewell, Oct. 25, 1928, Methodist Archives.
20. Bowen to Friend, Dec. 5, 1928, Methodist Archives.
21. Brown to Gamewell, Feb. 28, 1927, Methodist Archives.
22. Birney to Diffendorfer, Dec. 28, 1927; Birney to Gamewell, Oct. 19, 1928, Methodist Archives.
23. Birney to John R. Edwards, Jan. 9, 1929, Methodist Archives.
24. Birney to Edwards, May 27, 1929; Birney to Cartwright, Dec. 20, 1929, Methodist Archives.
25. Ballou to "Bob," Jan. 8, 1928; Matthews, "Some of Our More Pressing Problems," to ABCFM Nov. 28, 1928, ABCFM Archives.
26. Rawlinson, in editorials in *The Chinese Recorder*, publicized positive achievements but did not publicize his skepticism.
27. Rawlinson to Warnshuis, Oct. 3, 1927, Missionary Research Library.
28. Rawlinson to Warnshuis, Mar. 2, Apr. 9, 1928, Missionary Research Library.
29. Rawlinson to Warnshuis, Jan. 31, 1929, Missionary Research Library.
30. G. W. Sheppard, "The Church of Tomorrow—Its Faith in the Bible," *The Chinese Recorder*, February 1928, p. 97.
31. Warnshuis to Nelson T. Johnson, Apr. 29, 1927, Department of State Archives, File 893.00 Nanking/131.
32. C. C. to Nelson T. Johnson, May 12, 1927, Department of State Archives, File 893.00/8687.
33. Nelson T. Johnson memorandum of interview with William B. Johnson, Sept. 17, 1927, Department of State Archives, File 893.00/9540.
34. *Ibid.*
35. *Ibid.*
36. *Ibid.*
37. Nelson T. Johnson Memorandum, May 24, 1929, "Attitude of Foreign Service Toward Missionary Work," Department of State Archives," File 393.1163/330.
38. Hugh Hubbard to Mrs. Hubbard, Apr. 12, 1927; Rawlinson to Warnshuis, Nov. 1, 1926, Missionary Research Library.
39. F. P. Lockhart, consul-general at Hankow, in a letter to the secretary of state reported that several missionaries had called at his office and approved of the position taken by the United States in the negotiations with China. Missionaries, he wrote, had changed their earlier views. Lockhart to Secretary of State, Sept. 5, 1929, Department of State Archives, File 711.933/153.
40. Hornbeck to Secretary of State, Feb. 2, 1931, Department of State Archives, File 793.003/530-2/20.
41. Perhaps the most illuminating document on the difference between the Chinese and American points of view is the report of J. V. A. MacMurray on his interview with the minister of justice, Wang Chung-hui. According to MacMurray, Wang set forth his views "with excited vehemence and at times with

extreme bitterness." Wang contended that the foreign powers always treated the question as though it were entirely a judicial one, whereas the question was "purely political since foreigners never had been or would be (save in exceptional cases) involved in Chinese judicial matters, desiring only to live comfortably and make money and that in fact it could be shown that in the case of many powers there had been no case affecting their nationals for some years which showed that extraterritoriality really amounted to nothing at all." When Mac-Murray expressed fear that American nationals would not receive fair treatment, Wang replied that this was true, and it was because of the existence of extraterritoriality. MacMurray expressed shock over Wang's admission, which meant that justice "is a matter not of right but of political considerations." Wang then warned that unless the foreign powers came to terms, there would be no system of courts for trying cases involving foreigners. MacMurray was so disturbed that he accused Wang of playing "a shell game." J. V. A. MacMurray to Secretary of State, June 10, 1929, Department of State Archives, File 711.933/63.

42. Memorandum of conversation of Warnshuis and F. E. Jacobs on extraterritoriality, Apr. 30, 1931, Department of State Archives, File 793.003/656.

43. Ballantine to Nelson T. Johnson, Apr. 6, 1931, Department of State Archives, File 393.1163/492.

44. Lockhart to Nelson T. Johnson, Mar. 26, Feb. 19, Mar. 26, 1931, Department of State Archives, File 393.1163/491.

45. Hornbeck, "Notes on Memorandum of Points in Regard to the Problem of Extraterritoriality," Feb. 26, 1931, Department of State Archives, File 793.003/530-15/20.

46. Leete to Strong, Feb. 1, 1927, ABCFM Archives; Adams to the Rev. Herman Klein, June 20, 1932, Department of State Archives, File 393.1163 Property/63.

ARTHUR SCHLESINGER, JR., "THE MISSIONARY ENTERPRISE AND THEORIES OF IMPERIALISM"

1. See Richard Koebner: *Empire* (Cambridge, Cambridge University Press, 1961); Richard Koebner and H. D. Schmidt, *Imperialism: The Story and Significance of a Political Word, 1840–1960* (Cambridge, Cambridge University Press, 1964).

2. J. A. Schumpeter, "The Sociology of Imperialism," in *Imperialism and Social Classes* (New York, A. M. Kelley, 1951), p. 5.

3. Shlomo Avineri, ed., *Karl Marx on Colonialism and Modernization* (Garden City, Doubleday, 1968), pp. 132–133 (dispatch to *New York Tribune*, Aug. 8, 1853), 456 (letter to Engels, June 14, 1853), 94 (dispatch to *Tribune*, June 25, 1853).

4. *Marx on Colonialism*, pp. 94 (dispatch to *Tribune*, June 25, 1853), 138 (Aug. 8, 1853), 86 (June 25, 1853).

5. *Marx on Colonialism*, pp. 133–135 (dispatch to *Tribune*, Aug. 8, 1853), 15 (Engels in *The Northern Star*, Jan. 22, 1848).

6. V. I. Lenin, *Imperialism the Highest Stage of Capitalism* (New York, International Publishers, 1939), p. 93.

7. Hobson in *Contemporary Review*, January 1900, quoted in Koebner and Schmidt, *Imperialism*, pp. 251–252.

8. J. A..Hobson, *Imperialism* (Ann Arbor, Ann Arbor Paperbacks, 1965), pp. 196–197, 203.

9. Lenin, *Imperialism*, p. 84.

10. Excerpt and summary by Ellen Widmer from A. A. Volokhova, *Inostranny Missionery V Kitae, 1901–1920* (Moscow, 1969) Data Paper for Cuernavaca Conference, esp. pp. 1, 2, 48.

11. Schumpeter, "Imperialism," p. 18; Hannah Arendt, *The Origins of Totalitariansim* (New York, Meridian Books, 1958), pp. 151, 189; Joseph Conrad, *Heart of Darkness*, sec. I.

12. Herman Melville, *Typee*, ch. xxvi. Religious outrage forced Melville to delete such remarks from later nineteenth-century editions of *Typee*.

13. Hans Morgenthau, *Politics among Nations*, 3rd ed. (New York, Knopf, 1960), p. 53.

14. J. K. Fairbank, "Assignment for the '70's," *American Historical Review*, February 1969, p. 877.

15. C. M. Cipolla, *European Culture and Overseas Expansion* (London, Pelican Books, 1970), p. 99.

16. Cipolla, *European Culture*, p. 100; J. H. Parry, *The Age of Reconnaissance* (New York, Mentor Books, 1964), pp. 45, 248–250, 325–328; J. R. Levenson, *European Expansion and the Counter-Expansion of Asia, 1300–1600* (Englewood Cliffs, Prentice-Hall, 1967), p. 30.

17. Hobson, *Imperialism*, p. 202; R. J. Bartlett, ed., *The Record of American Diplomacy* (New York, A. A. Knopf, 1968), p. 267; V. G. Kiernan, *The Lords of Human Kind* (Boston, Little, Brown, 1969), pp. 256–258; R. L. Stevenson, *In the South Seas* (1890), pt. 1, ch. 10; C. J. Phillips, *Protestant America and the Pagan World: The First Half Century of the American Board of Commissioners for Foreign Missions, 1810–1860* (Cambridge, East Asian Research Center, Harvard University, 1969), p. 102; Mark Twain, "The Sandwich Islands," in Charles Neider, ed., *The Complete Essays of Mark Twain* (Garden City, Doubleday, 1963), pp. 18–19; F. P. Prucha, *American Indian Policy in the Formative Years* (Lincoln, Neb., Bison Books, 1970), pp. 235–247; S. G. Millin, *Rhodes, A Life* (London, 1933), p. 38.

18. Perry Miller, *The Life of the Mind in America* (New York, Harcourt, Brace and World, 1965), p. 53; J. S. Stone, "The Bearings of Modern Commerce on the Progress of Modern Missions," quoted in J. E. Bodo, *The Protestant Clergy and Public Issues, 1812–1848* (Princeton, Princeton University Press, 1954), p. 248; A. C. Coolidge, *The United States As a World Power* (New York, Macmillan, 1908), p. 328.

19. Commission of Appraisal, William E. Hocking, chairman, *Re-thinking Missions: A Laymen's Inquiry after One Hundred Years* (New York, Harper and Bros., 1932), p. 10.

20. A. K. Weinberg, *Manifest Destiny: A Study of Nationalist Expansionism in American History* (Baltimore, Johns Hopkins Press, 1935), ch. iii.

21. Phillips, *Protestant America*, pp. 261, 262; Josiah Strong, *Our Country*, rev. ed. (New York, 1891), p. 28; T. J. McCormick, *China Market* (Chicago, Quadrangle Books, 1967), p. 66.

22. Phillips, *Protestant America*, pp. 33, 133, 290.

23. *United States Exports*

	1840	1880	1900
(millions of dollars)			
Asia	1	12	68
Australia and Oceania	1	7	41
Africa	—	5	19
Canada	6	29	95
Latin America	24	64	132
Europe	92	719	1040

United States imports			
Asia	10	74	146
Australia and Oceania	—	7	29
Africa	1	4	11
Canada	1	33	39
Latin America	24	179	185
Europe	62	371	441

U.S. Bureau of the Census, *Historical Statistics of the United States, Colonial Times to 1957* (Washington, D.C., Government Printing Office, 1960), pp. 550–553.

24. Alexis de Tocqueville, *Democracy in America*, ed. Phillips Bradley (New York, Knopf, 1945), I, 317.

25. Phillips, *Protestant America*, pp. 33, 243; Perry Miller, *Life of the Mind*, p. 56; Philip Lindsley, "Name of Our Republic," *Works* (Philadelphia, 1866), I, 598, quoted in J. R. Bodo, *Protestant Clergy*, p. 243.

26. Phillips, *Protestant America*, p. 65; Rufus Anderson, "The Theory of Missions to the Heathen, a Sermon on the Ordination of Mr. Edward Webb As a Missionary to the Heathen" (Boston, 1845), in P. D. Curtin, ed., *Imperialism* (New York, Harper & Row, 1971), p. 212.

27. Phillips, *Protestant America*, pp. 105, 119.

28. Bartlett, *American Diplomacy*, p. 267.

29. J. A. Field, Jr., "Near East Notes and Far East Queries," in this volume; J. A. Field, Jr., *America and the Mediterranean World, 1776–1882* (Princeton, Princeton University Press, 1969), esp. pp. 285–297.

30. S. C. Miller, "Ends and Means: Missionary Justifications of Force in Nineteenth Century China," in this volume; P. W. Fay, "The Protestant Mission and the Opium War," *Pacific Historical Review*, May 1971, p. 149; P. A. Varg, *Missionaries, Chinese, and Diplomats: The American Protestant Missionary Movement in China, 1890–1952* (Princeton, Princeton University Press, 1958), pp. 11–13.

31. S. C. Miller, "Ends and Means."

32. Phillips, *Protestant America*, p. 115.

33. Anderson, "Theory of Missions," pp. 211, 212, 221, 219.

34. Phillips, *Protestant America*, pp. 126, 198.

35. Phillips, *Protestant America*, p. 289; Bodo, *Protestant Clergy*, p. 245.

36. Anderson, "Theory of Missions," pp. 215, 216; Phillips, *Protestant America*, p. 261.

37. Phillips, *Protestant America*, pp. 8, 12; Bodo, *Protestant Clergy*, p. 240.

38. H. R. Niebuhr, *The Kingdom of God in America* (New York, Harper, 1937), p. 157.

39. Washington Gladden, *Recollections* (Boston, Houghton Mifflin, 1909), pp. 288–289.

40. Austin Phelps, Introduction to Strong, *Our Country*, p. 14.

41. Josiah Strong, *The New Era or the Coming Kingdom* (New York, 1893), pp. 358, 69; Strong, *Our Country*, pp. 213–214, 225, 219–220.

42. See Bernard Semmel, *Imperialism and Social Reform: English Social-Imperial Thought, 1895–1914* (London, Allen and Unwin, 1960).

43. Hobson, *Imperialism*, p. 216.

44. E. R. May, *Imperial Democracy: The Emergence of America As a Great Power* (New York, Harcourt Brace, 1961), pp. 27–29.

45. J. W. Pratt, *Expansionists of 1898* (Baltimore, Johns Hopkins Press, 1936), pp. 280, 281, 282, 285, 288, 290–291, 293; Varg, *Missionaries*, p. 83; M. B. Young, *The Rhetoric of Empire: American China Policy, 1895–1901* (Cambridge, Harvard University Press, 1968), p. 143; Josiah Strong, *Expansion under New World-Conditions* (New York, Baker and Taylor, 1900), pp. 272, 302.

46. Varg, *Missionaries*, p. 3; Strong, *Expansion*, p. 193; Varg, *Missionaries*, p. 79.

47. Theodore Roosevelt, "The Awakening of China," *Outlook*, Nov. 28, 1908); Strong, *Expansion*, p. 105; Mark Twain, "The United States of Lyncherdom," in Janet Smith, ed., *Mark Twain on the Damned Human Race* (New York, Hill and Wang, 1962), p. 103.

48. Quoted in Mark Twain, "To the Person Sitting in Darkness," *North American Review*, February 1901, in Smith, *Mark Twain*, p. 7; Young, *Rhetoric of Empire*, pp. 188, 196, 214; Gilbert Reid, "The Ethics of Loot," *Forum* 31:582, 584 (1901).

49. Smith, *Mark Twain*, pp. 7, 9; Neider, *Mark Twain*, p. 309; P. S. Foner, *Mark Twain: Social Critic* (New York, International Publishers, 1958), pp. 279, 282; Miller, "Ends and Means."

50. Strong, *New Era*, pp. 80, 355–356.

51. See W. R. Hutchison, "Modernism and Missions: The Liberal Search for an Exportable Christianity, 1870–1930," in this volume.

52. Paul Varg, "The Missionary Response to the Nationalist Revolution," in this volume.

53. *Re-thinking Missions*, pp. 40, 44, 33; C. T. Holman in *Christian Century*, Nov. 20, 1935. For the reception of the Hocking Commission report, see Varg, *Missionaries*, ch. x.

54. *Re-thinking Missions*, p. 11.

55. Parry, *Age of Reconnaissance*, pp. 144–145.

56. William James, *The Varieties of Religious Experience* (New York, Modern Library, n.d.), pp. 361–362.

57. George Santayana, *Dominations and Powers: Reflections on Liberty, Society, and Government* (New York, Scribner, 1951), p. 203.

58. *Re-thinking Missions*, pp. 9–10; Melville, *Typee*, ch. xxvi; Melville, *Omoo* (London, Constable, 1922), pp. 211–212, 216; C. R. Anderson, *Melville in the South Seas*, rev. ed. (New York, Dover, 1966), pp. 253, 256.

59. Phillips, *Protestant America*, p. 270; J. C. Beecher, quoted in Robert McClellan, "Images of Chinese Christian Converts Presented in Selected Missionary Journals, 1807–1839," paper prepared for Cuernavaca Conference, p. 12; *Re-thinking Missions*, p. 31; Conrad, *Heart of Darkness*, sec. III.

60. Richard Faber, *The Vision and the Need: Late Victorian Imperialist Aims* (London, Humanities Press, 1966), p. 48; an 1896 Mark Twain notebook, Foner, *Mark Twain*, p. 279.

61. Coolidge, *United States*, p. 227; Field, *America*, p. 186; Daniel Dorchester, *The Problem of Religious Progress* (New York, 1881), p. 499.

62. S. W. Barnett, "Americans As Humanitarians: Image-Building in China Before the Opium War," paper prepared for the Cuernavaca Conference, pp. 22–25.

63. Strong, *New Era*, pp. 13, 12; Cyrus Hamlin, *Among the Turks* (New York, 1877), pp. 186–192, quoted in Phillips, *Protestant America*, p. 304.

64. Faber, *Vision and Need*, pp. 45, 106-107, 80.

65. Melville, *Typee*, ch. xvii. By the time that he wrote *Mardi*, Melville had discovered ambiguity and evil in the Polynesian paradise. In 1901, Mark Twain in "The United States of Lyncherdom" offered a variant on Melville's *Typee* proposal, suggesting that American missionaries come home and do something about lynching. He pointed out how slow missionary progress was in China: "if we can offer our missionaries as rich a field at home, at lighter expense and quite satisfactory in the matter of danger, why shouldn't they find it fair and right to come back and give us a trial? . . . O kind missionary, O compassionate missionary, leave China! come home and convert these Christians!" Smith, *Mark Twain*, pp. 103, 104.

66. Jean-François Revel, *Without Marx or Jesus* (Garden City, Doubleday, 1971), p. 139.

67. Quoted in Hobson, *Imperialism*, p. 204; Wu Ting Fang, "China's Relation with the West," American Academy of Political and Social Science, *The Foreign Policy of the United States*, Addresses and Discussions at the Annual Meeting (Philadelphia, 1899), pp. 172–173.

68. Gandhi in *Young India*, Apr. 23, 1931, quoted in *Re-thinking Missions*, p. 68; see also p. 40.

69. Frantz Fanon, *A Dying Colonialism* (New York, Grove Press, 1967), pp. 131, 49, 44, 47, 39, 42–43.

70. Frantz Fanon, *The Wretched of the Earth* (London, Penguin, 1967), pp. 52, 32, 36, 62.

71. *The Tempest*, act 5, sc. 1; act 1, sc. 2; act 2, sc. 2; act 4, sc. 1.

72. Ottare Mannoni's *Prospero and Caliban* was first published in Paris in 1950 under the title *Psychologie de la colonisation*. The English translation came out in New York in 1956. Another book drawing its metaphors from *The Tempest* was *Ariel* (1900) by the Uruguayan writer José Enrique Rodó. Invoking Ariel as "the spirituality of civilization" and Caliban as the "symbol of sensuality and stupidity," Rodó wrote a highly influential vindication of Latin American culture against the utilitarianism and materialism of the United States. See the translation by F. J. Stimson (Boston, 1922), p. 4. "Arielism." was for a season a powerful current in Latin American thought. See Jean Franco, *The Modern Culture of Latin America* (London, Penguin, 1970), ch. 2. For still another reading of *The Tempest*, see Leo Marx, *The Machine in the Garden: Technology and the Pastoral Ideal in America* (New York, Oxford University Press, 1964), ch. 2.

73. Mannoni, *Prospero and Caliban* (New York, Praeger, 1964), pp. 85, 40.

74. Frantz Fanon, *Toward the African Revolution* (New York, Grove Press, 1967), pp. 38–39; Fanon, *Wretched of the Earth*, p. 169.

75. Fanon, *Dying Colonialism*, pp. 125, 131; Fanon, *Toward the African Revolution*, p. 102; Albert Memmi, *The Colonizer and the Colonized* (Boston, Beacon Press, 1967), p. 124.

76. Fanon, *Dying Colonialism*, pp. 125, 131; Fanon, *Wretched of the Earth*, pp. 25, 18, 68, 74; Fanon, *Dying Colonialism*, p. 145.

77. Frances FitzGerald, *Fire in the Lake* (Boston, Little, Brown, 1972), pp. 295–298; R. H. Solomon, *Mao's Revolution and the Chinese Political Culture* (Berkeley, University of California Press, 1972), passim.

78. Kiernan, *Lords of Human Kind*, p. 258; Martin Jarrett-Kerr, *Patterns of Christian Acceptance: Individual Response to the Missionary Impact, 1550–1950* (London, Oxford University Press, 1972), pp. 30, 222, 77.

79. André Malraux, *Anti-memoirs* (New York, Bantam Books, 1970), p. 456.

80. Hobson, *Imperialism*, p. 266; Jonathan Spence, *To Change China: Western Advisers in China, 1620–1960* (Boston, Little, Brown, 1969), p. 202.

81. CBS Special News Report, Apr. 19, 1966.

GLOSSARY

ai chi 愛己
Ai-kuang sheng 愛光生
　(see Hsu Wei-ts'an)

chang 長
Chang Ting 張鼎
ch'ang 常
chen-tao 眞道
Ch'en Sung-lu 陳松廬
cheng 正
Cheng Pi-teng 鄭必登
Cheng Yü-jen 鄭雨人
chi fu 積福
chi-ssu 祭祀
chi te 積德
chiang-shu 講書
Chiao-hui hsin-pao 教會新報
chieh 潔
Chieh-yü tzu 劫餘子
chien-i 賤役
Ch'ien Lien-ch'i 錢蓮溪
Chih-fei tzu 知非子 (see Chang Ting)
Chih-tsui tzu 知罪子
Ch'ih-p'ing shou 持平叟
ching-hsu 矜恤
chou-ch'ang 粥廠
Chou Kuo-kuang 周國光
chu chih jen 主之人
Chu Hsing-chou 朱杏舟
Chu Shih-t'ang 朱師堂
Chung-hsi shu-yuan 中西書院
Ch'üan-shan tzu 勸善子

fan ai-chung 汎愛衆

hao-se 好色
heng 恒
heng-ni 橫逆
hsiang-shen 鄉紳
hsiao-tzu 孝子
Hsieh Hsi-en 謝錫恩
hsin-chai 心齋
Hsu Wei-ts'an 許維儔
hsu-wen 虛文

Huai-yuan 懷原 (see Hsu Wei-ts'an)
Huang Mei 黃梅
Huang P'in-san 黃品三
Huang Yun-sun 黃筠孫

i-chi chih li 一己之力
i-hsueh 義學

jen-hsin 人心
jen-jen ai-wu 仁人愛物
jen-li 人力
jen-tao 人道

kang 綱
K'ang-shuang tzu 伉爽子
ko-wu 格物
kuang-ai 廣愛

Liang Chu-ch'en 梁柱臣
Lin Ch'ing-shan 林青山
Lin Lo-chih 林樂知 (Young J. Allen)
Lin Shou-pao 林壽保
Lin Yao-chih (see Lin Lo-chih)
ling-ch'i i kan-hua 靈氣以感化
ling-hun ta-fu 靈魂大父
Long Loh Chi (see Lin Lo-chih)
Lu Ts'ung-chou 路從周
lun-li 倫理

ming te 明德
mu-shih 牧師

nü ch'ing yü nan 女輕於男

pao-pen 報本
pen-ti kung-hui 本地公會
pi hsien ai jen 必先愛人
Pien-cheng tzu 辨正子
P'u-yü t'ang 普育堂

san-chieh 三戒
shan 善
shan-cheng 善政
Shanghai hsin-pao 上海新報

425

shih-shih 實事
shu-fu 庶夫
shuai hsing 率性
Sung Shu-ch'ing 宋書卿

ta-kung wu-ssu 大公無私
Te-chien chai 得見齋
Te-i lu 得一錄
t'ien-tao 天道
T'ien-tao ming-teng 天道明燈
Tong King-sing 唐景星
  (T'ang T'ing-shu 廷樞)
Ts'ao Tzu-yü 曹子漁
T'u Tsung-ying 涂宗瀛
Tun-hsing tzu 頓醒子
Tun-wu tzu 頓悟子

Wan-kuo kung-pao 萬國公報
Wang I-hua 王逸華
  (see Wang Kuang-ch'i)
Wang Kuang-ch'i 王光啓
Wang Yü-shan 王於山
Wei Ts'an-tzu 微粲子
  (see Hsu Wei-ts'an)
wu-ch'ang 五常
wu-yin 無隱

Yen chiao-shih 晏敎師
  (Matthew T. Yates)
Yen Hui 顏回
Ying Pao-shih 應寶時
Yü Chih 余治

426

Index

427

HARVARD STUDIES IN AMERICAN–EAST ASIAN RELATIONS

CONTRIBUTORS

M. SEARLE BATES, sometime Professor of History at the University of Nanking, has had a long experience of mission work in China both as a participant and as an observer. Dr. Bates is retired Professor of Missions, the Union Theological Seminary, and is at work on a history of Christian effort in twentieth century China, a topic on which he has already written extensively.

ADRIAN A. BENNETT, Professor of History at Iowa State University, is the author of *John Fryer: The Introduction of Western Science and Technology into Nineteenth-Century China* (Cambridge, East Asian Research Center, Harvard University, distributed by Harvard University Press, 1969) and various other writings. He is now working on a study of missionary journalism in nineteenth century China.

PAUL A. COHEN, Edith Stix Wasserman Professor of Asian Studies at Wellesley College, is the author of *China and Christianity: The Missionary Movement and the Growth of Chinese Antiforeignism, 1860—1870* (Cambridge, Harvard University Press, 1963) and *Between Tradition and Modernity: Wang T'ao and Reform in Late Ch'ing China* (Cambridge, Harvard University Press, 1974).

JOHN K. FAIRBANK is Francis Lee Higginson Professor of History, Harvard University. He is the author of *The United States and China*, 3rd edition (Cambridge, Harvard University Press, 1971); *China Perceived: Images and Policies in Chinese-American Relations* (New York, Alfred A. Knopf, 1974); and other writings on Chinese history and foreign relations.

JAMES A. FIELD, JR., Isaac H. Clothier Professor of History, Swarthmore College, is the author of *America and the Mediterranean World* (Princeton, Princeton University Press, 1969) and contributes all the more effectively to this volume as an Americanist rather than a China specialist.

SHIRLEY STONE GARRETT is currently a fellow at the Radcliffe Institute. She is the author of *Social Reformers in Urban China: The Chinese YMCA, 1895—1926* (Cambridge, Harvard University Press, 1970). Dr. Garrett is now at work on a study of American relations with Nationalist China.

WILLIAM R. HUTCHISON is Charles Warren Professor of the History of Religion in America, Harvard University, and Master of Winthrop House. He has written extensively on the history of American theology and religious thought. His books are *The Transcendentalist Ministers* (New Haven, Yale University Press, 1959) and *The Modernist Impulse in American Protestantism*, to be published by Harvard University Press.

KWANG-CHING LIU is Professor of History at the University of California, Davis. He is the author of *Anglo-American Steamship Rivalry in China, 1862–1874* (Cambridge, Harvard University Press, 1962), *Americans and Chinese: A Historical Essay and a Bibliography* (Cambridge, Harvard University Press, 1963), and a number of articles on the history of nineteenth century China. He is currently working on a study of the reality of Confucian statecraft, centering on the rise of Li Hung-chang.

STUART CREIGHTON MILLER, Professor of Social Science at San Francisco State University, is the author of *The Unwelcome Immigrant* (Berkeley, University of California Press, 1969; paperback edition, 1974). He is now completing a book, *Benevolent Assimilation: The American Conquest of the Philippines,* to be published by George Braziller, Inc.

CLIFTON J. PHILLIPS is Professor of History at DePauw University and is the author of *Protestant America and the Pagan World: The First Half-Century of the American Board of Commissioners for Foreign Missions, 1810–1860* (Cambridge, East Asian Research Center, Harvard University, distributed by Harvard University Press, 1969). He is now engaged in a study of Anglo-American cooperation in China missions in the nineteenth century.

VALENTIN H. RABE is Associate Professor of History, the State University of New Hork, Geneseo. He is a specialist in the study of institutional growth of American mission boards in the late nineteenth and early twentieth centuries, on which subject he is completing a manuscript for publication.

ARTHUR SCHLESINGER, JR., is Albert Schweitzer Professor of the Humanities at The City University of New York. He is the winner of Pulitzer Prizes in History and Biography. His most recent book is *The Imperial Presidency* (Boston, Houghton Mifflin Co., 1973).

PAUL A. VARG, Professor of History at Michigan State University, East Lansing, is the author of *Missionaries, Chinese, and Diplomats: The American Protestant Missionary Movement in China, 1890–1952* (Princeton, Princeton University Press, 1958), *The Myth of the China Market* (East Lansing, Michigan State University Press, 1968), and *The Closing of the Door: Sino-American Relations, 1936–1946* (East Lansing, Michigan State University Press, 1973).

PHILIP WEST is Assistant Professor of History at Indiana University, Bloomington. He is currently preparing for publication a seminal study of the institutional and intellectual relations of Christianity and nationalism as exemplified at Yenching University in Peking.

DATE DUE

MAY 0 6 1994			